Heath.

800 - 225 - 1388

800 - 428 - 8071

SECONDARY TEACHING METHODS

Kenneth T. Henson

Texas A & M University

SECONDARY TEACHING METHODS

D. C. HEATH AND COMPANY

Lexington, Massachusetts   Toronto

To my friend and colleague, T. M. Stinnett, *who has spent his career upgrading teaching in this country and making it an honorable profession. And to those teachers everywhere who share his ability to see worth in every student. Finally, I dedicate this book to all of you prospective teachers who, through your enthusiasm for your own subjects, will introduce your students to the excitement of learning.*

Foreword

Kenneth Henson's book is an eminently practical guide for the secondary school teacher. Unlike the many general curriculum books heavily larded with content from the foundations of education, Henson's is a book for the secondary teacher. It describes the process of getting to know the secondary school, learning about its students, developing effective classroom organization and discipline, and planning and carrying out instruction. Henson knows the school and knows its problems. He avoids general platitudes about cooperation between teachers and administrators, but discusses the practical ways that they can work together and the kinds of problems that a teacher is likely to encounter. *Secondary Teaching Methods* does not pretend that the world of education is perfect, but it does assert that the world of teenagers and teaching is profoundly exciting. It also blends a well-researched foundation for professional teaching with careful attention to its artistic dimensions.

This is a thorough book, touching all dimensions of the teacher's role. It is also scholarly, based on a thorough culling of the base of knowledge that has been built from research and thoughtful practice. It is realistic, written by someone who *knows* the schools and their problems. Finally, it is optimistic — a practical guide to the creation of exciting teaching careers devoted to the creation of exciting environments for high school students.

BRUCE JOYCE

Preface

Secondary Teaching Methods is designed to prepare prospective junior and senior high school teachers to perform their total roles as educators and to encourage preservice teachers to prepare themselves for the many tasks of classroom teaching.

In addition to the standard topics on lesson planning, classroom management, and evaluation and testing, the book includes coverage of special students, multicultural classrooms, and self-observation techniques.

The practical experiences of teaching are stressed throughout. Each chapter begins with specific learning objectives that focus on the principles presented in the chapter. To emphasize the application of these principles, each chapter contains a set of real classroom experiences, complete with questions and discussion of each experience. The experiences usually center on controversial issues and teacher dilemmas common to secondary education.

Written in a readable and engaging style, the book has a strong, positive tone. For example, the discussions of discipline emphasize that discipline is best achieved through positive relationships between teachers and students. Techniques for helping students feel worthy and capable are also included.

The book is organized into seven major sections. Part One reacquaints the prospective teacher with the nature of adolescence and of American secondary schools. Part Two deals with the discipline problems faced in the classroom and covers the discipline, management, and motivation skills indispensable to today's secondary school teacher.

Since good teaching requires good communication, Part Three covers techniques for improving both verbal and nonverbal communications skills. A special chapter is included on the use of media in improving communications. This section also introduces writing performance objectives and planning the daily lesson.

Part Four discusses long-range planning and how to develop teaching units.

Also introduced are several specific teaching strategies, as well as the advantages and limitations of each.

Some students need special help with their learning; Part Five discusses how to teach unique individuals and unique groups (cultures) of students. Part Six explains the construction, administration, and scoring of tests. The prospective teacher will learn how to use evaluations to promote learning (formative evaluation) and to determine grades (summative evaluation).

Various strategies for observing one's own teaching are discussed in Part Seven. This section also answers a number of the questions frequently asked by prospective teachers.

Recognizing that both men and women occupy roles in the education profession, this text portrays both males and females as administrators, counselors, and teachers. Thus readers should feel comfortable placing themselves in the role of each of these professional positions.

Acknowledgments

I wish to thank George Abbott, Anita Scott, and other personnel at D. C. Heath and Company for their work on this book. I am indebted to David Turney, William Van Til, and my other friends at Indiana State University who have supported and encouraged my writing efforts; to Robert Alfonso, Jerald Firth, Sam Leles, and Adolph Crew, who provided leadership in my own professional preparation; to my teacher-friend Deneese Jones for her help editing and typing this manuscript; and finally, to my wife Sharon and my sons, Randy and Kenny, who make it all worthwhile.

KENNETH T. HENSON

Contents

9   Planning Daily Lessons   171

PART FOUR
IMPROVING INSTRUCTION   189

10   Long-Range Planning   191

11   Teaching Strategies   219

PART FIVE
PROVIDING FOR INDIVIDUAL DIFFERENCES   251

12   Teaching Students with Special Needs   253

SECONDARY TEACHING METHODS

Foundations of Learning
and Teaching

You have decided to pursue an area in which you have much previous knowledge and experience. The purpose of the first section is to help you recall such knowledge and to put it into a framework that will aid you in preparing to teach in secondary schools.

Psychologists often tell us that we are each a product of our experiences and that all that we learn is filtered through our perceptual screens. As you read Chapter 1, you will want to position yourself as much as possible as a student. Try to feel their personal needs, and the pressures placed on them by their teachers, parents, and friends. As you read about the several different learning theories, seek to derive information from each that will help you to better understand how adolescents learn. Finally, try to envision yourself teaching in a junior or senior high school classroom and think about how this knowledge will affect your own teaching.

Chapter 2, "America's Secondary Schools: Past, Present, and Future," is an important chapter in this book. In addition to understanding adolescence, all secondary teachers should understand the nature of the American secondary school. This requires looking at the early schools as they were first developed and seeing how they have changed. Paramount is the understanding of the goals of early schools and the goals of today's schools. If you are to make your mark on education, you will even need to think about some of the goals of future schools. Our schools are changing and we must be aware of these changes if we are to stay tuned to the needs of our society and the needs of our youth.

The Student

OBJECTIVES

Upon completion of this chapter, you should be able to:
1. Name several channels in which the adolescent is growing and discuss the relationships among these growth channels.
2. Interpret the following statement: "The adolescent is facing a dilemma that presents frustration and confusion."
3. Explain what adolescents mean when they say that they want their schools to teach them to communicate.
4. Define these terms: *readiness, self-concept, Gestalt, feedback, cue.*
5. Explain why an eclectic approach toward the psychology of learning is desirable.
6. Make a brief but exact statement about the general trend of the crime rate of adolescents in this country.
7. Design a graph to show the relationship between a particular student's social, emotional, psychological, and physical growth rates.
8. Using your knowledge of Gestalt psychology and connectionism, explain how you would introduce a topic reflecting each school of thought.
9. Apply your knowledge of connectionism to sequence the concepts within that topic.

"Teaching would be a great profession if it weren't for the students." We hear this too often from teachers, even though most of them give "a love for working with young people" as their reason for choosing the profession. Once on the job, most teachers find that they are continuously in situations that make them wish they had a better understanding of adolescents. As a future teacher you need to know what motivates students' behavior and why that behavior is changeable and unpredictable.

Adults cannot view the world as adolescents do, but they can understand the perspective of adolescents better if they are aware of the forces that motivate adolescents either to accept and adjust or to reject and rebel. You will need to know about their value system and how they select those things that they prize most. And especially because of your role in guiding learners, you need to understand how adolescents learn. How do they decide what they will learn? What obstacles delay, limit, or even prevent their learning? How can information be structured and presented so that it is easier to learn? These are a few of the questions that we shall examine in this chapter. As you read, try to remember your own teenage experiences; then picture yourself helping your future students to work out their problems and to appreciate and enjoy your classes.

NEEDS

Adolescents and adults share the same basic needs, but adolescents often feel these needs more intensely. In fact, the teenager often experiences so many needs simultaneously that he is confused, and so strongly that he is frustrated. The teacher who understands the basis for such feelings is more apt to find ways to help the student achieve his desires or to learn to cope without them. Such satisfaction of personal, social, and psychological needs is often necessary before the student can become free to concentrate on lessons.

Two of the most basic needs of all normal human beings include the need to belong to groups of other human beings and the need to learn to value and appreciate one's self. The teacher is in a key position to help students with these needs.

Though all normal human beings feel a need to be accepted by others, some show this need very intensely (socialites), while others appear to experience it in lesser degrees (isolates). Yet all people need other people. Because, in their rapidly changing lives, there are many people that they have to please,

adolescents often find themselves in serious dilemmas; for example, some behavior that will please their friends may alienate their parents.

PEER GROUP PRESSURE

At no other time in life do people experience the closeness of their peers as in adolescence. And because this is a time of rapid development, adolescents look to those who seem best to understand their uncertainties and anxieties — their peers. How often their parents hear them explain their reason for doing certain things as "everybody's doing it." "Everybody," of course, means peers.

Peer pressures on a student's behavior will become obvious to you as a teacher. You will see students look to each other in class for approval. When you ask a question, students may look to others before offering a response; if not, they may hear groans or hisses. Recall your own student days when you may have hesitated to ask a question for fear of appearing stupid. You knew that your response would be judged by the group. Or how many times did you hesitate to purchase a particular shirt or pair of shoes because they weren't "in"? At one high school, students cut the labels out of coats and sweaters, replacing them with a brand name acceptable to their peers. Often students will purposefully work to receive certain grades (either high or low) to please their peers. In some groups an *F* is a disgrace; in others an *A* is an equal disgrace. So the adolescent is forced with trying to conform when often he does not even know the standards. With a combination of unknown standards, ever-changing standards (what's "in" at age fourteen can be totally taboo at age fifteen), and conflicting standards (what my friends expect me to do are often those things that my parents would dread the most), it is no wonder that the adolescent is often confused and anxious. Challenges and failure within the secondary schools can add to this anxiety and hostility.[1]

Another strong need of teenagers is to be very close to a few people. The fortunate ones find this need met in their homes, but millions of youths do not have the kind of home lives that provide them with this needed close relationship. In fact, many home environments are so bad and the relationships between youths and their parents are so poor that two million American youths leave home every year. Young people who do not find warmth at home must look to their classmates and teachers to find warmth, acceptance, and deep mutual respect. The maturing adolescent also begins to look more and more toward members of the opposite sex for close friendship ties.

A recent study by the National Education Association queried ninety-five secondary students as to what they thought might be done to improve their schools and their schooling.[2] They expressed three major concerns. First, they

---

[1] S. Silbergeld, R. W. Manderscheid, and P. H. O'Neill, "Free Association Anxiety and Hostility: View From a Junior High School," *Psychological Reports* 37 (1975): 495–504.
[2] Harold G. Shane, *Curriculum Change Toward the 21st Century* (Washington, D.C.: National Education Association, 1977), pp. 68–69.

wanted schools that would help them learn to *cope* in a world that they find frustrating, distressing, and sometimes frightening. Second, they wanted schools that *cared* about them as people. Since many parents today seem to substitute things rather than giving of themselves, the students looked to their teachers for warmth and personal concern. Finally, they wanted their schools to teach them how to *communicate* their feelings, hopes, and concerns. (While parents may value most the 3*R*'s, students clearly value most the 3*C*'s — coping, caring, and communication.)

In addition to providing students with some needed attention and friendship, teachers are beginning to offer special courses on coping. These courses appear to be working very well; for example, when a junior high school offered four courses in coping with stressful situations, the results were highly satisfactory. Afterward, the students who were in the courses had fewer interactions with classmates, but those discussions were longer, more personal, and had more content.[3] The potential of such programs can be increased by including experiences that help students learn to use their own adaptive assets. In fact, according to one expert, "such programs for improvement of coping skills can be crucial."[4] As a beginning teacher you will want to find out whether your school already offers courses in coping, and, if so, whether you will have the option of recommending some of your students who, you feel, might benefit from such courses. If your school is not currently offering a course in coping, you may wish to discuss with your administrators and colleagues the possibility of developing one.

Independence

In direct conflict with adolescents' needs for acceptance and approval is their need for independence. Since early childhood they have been gradually learning independence, which is natural and necessary for good mental health and even for intellectual growth. Emotional independence from others has been found to correlate highly with the ability to establish relationships with peers, to master intellectual requirements, and to rely on one's own conscience.[5] Of course, learning to rely on one's own conscience is itself a type of independence. Today's teachers and school programs give much attention to helping students of all ages learn to develop and understand their own set of values.

Here, then, is another dilemma of adolescents. They are bound by a need to earn the approval of others and yet by an equally strong need to become independent. Indeed, this is the basis for much of their frustrations, for many situations appear impossible to solve without disappointing either themselves or

[3] S. Silbergeld, and R. W. Manderscheid, "Comparative Assessment of a Coping Model for School Adolescents," *Journal of School Psychology* 14 (Winter 1976): 261–74.

[4] B. A. Hamburg, "Coping in Early Adolescence," *American Handbook of Psychiatry, Vol. 2: Child Adolescent Psychiatry, Sociocultural & Community Psychiatry*, ed. G. Kaplan (New York: Basic Books, 1974), pp. 385–410.

[5] Lee J. Cronbach, *Educational Psychology*, 2d ed. (New York: Harcourt, Brace, and World, 1963), p. 123.

their friends. They need to find alternative ways of responding that meet the approval of their friends, teachers, and parents and yet are acceptable to their own values.

The need for independence increases as adolescents grow older. Often the automobile becomes a means of expanding beyond the physical environment, which they find trying to smother them with demands and expectations. It becomes not only a symbol of freedom and independence but also a way of achieving them.

ADOLESCENT DEVELOPMENT

The awkwardness of adolescence is to a great extent caused by growth patterns. Several characteristics of the growth patterns of adolescence make this a very complex process. First, the adolescent is growing physically, mentally, emotionally, and socially. Second, the rates of growth in the separate areas are different yet are not at all unrelated, since one's growth in one channel can and often does significantly affect growth rate in other channels. For example, the adolescent portrayed in Figure 1.1 is physically more mature than most others in the class. Physical maturity can lead to acceptance and even popularity since it enables the student to compete in sports and may increase favorable attention from members of the opposite sex. The fact that this adolescent's mental growth is slightly below average does not seem to affect his emotional stability. His large physical size and/or coordination probably overcompensates for this lag, leaving him confident about himself.

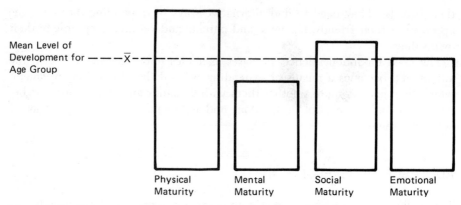

Mean Level of
Development for — — — X̄
Age Group

Physical
Maturity   Mental
Maturity   Social
Maturity   Emotional
Maturity

Figure 1.1 Channels of Adolescent Development — Physical

Physical Growth

Physical maturity is extremely important to teenagers. Size and muscular co-ordination are important, not only for competitive sports but also for everyday situations. The teenage boy who lags in physical development may be ridiculed for his awkwardness or bullied because of his small stature. Girls may experience similar abuse if they become too buxom or too tall. Thus it is not uncommon to see a teenage boy stretch to appear taller and a teenage girl slump to appear shorter. Girls whose physical development rates lag behind those of their classmates may find themselves left out during social events, and boys may be ridiculed if their voices remain at a high pitch longer than usual.

Modern medical science has developed substances which through injection can in many cases increase the growth rate significantly. Much is to be learned about such treatments, but many possible side effects may result that are yet unknown and thus unpredictable.

Mental Maturity

There is more to mental maturity than the accumulation of knowledge or the increasing of one's intelligence quotient. A study of how the mind develops has been made by the Swiss psychologist Jean Piaget, who has described levels of mental maturity in terms of the ability of the mind to perform certain feats. Piaget has found that as mental development progresses, the individual learns to perform increasingly more complex types of operations. His and subsequent studies have found that the mind develops in a definite sequence; the learner cannot bypass one level of performance jumping to a higher level. In other words, the mind develops in a predictable sequence of stages. More information about Piaget's work appears in Chapter 5 on motivation.

The student in Figure 1.2 is smaller than his classmates, but his mental skills are superior. He can think in more abstract terms. At times he may become very frustrated because his mind is able to conceptualize certain things that his

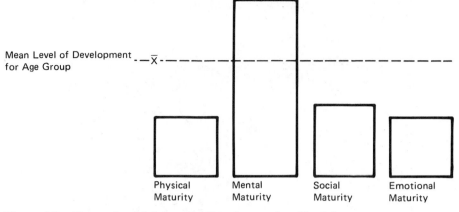

Mean Level of Development for Age Group

Physical Maturity | Mental Maturity | Social Maturity | Emotional Maturity

Figure 1.2   Channels of Adolescent Development — Mental

body cannot do. For example, the ability to play certain sports or to play musical instruments may seem simple, but only when he tries them does he find that he does not have the psychomotor control necessary to succeed. His friends may criticize him and tease him because of his size. This may be hard to accept if he is in other ways more mature than his friends. His mental maturity may win the approval and respect of his classmates or it may even alienate them, depending much on how he uses or misuses his mental superiority. Peer rejection or isolation can lead to feelings of insecurity and eventually may lead to emotional problems.

The student who is capable of performing complex mental operations may even develop a feeling of superiority and exhibit snobbish behavior; thus his social development is curtailed. While the ability of an adolescent to meet those expectations of his family, friends, and teachers is very important, it is no more significant than the ways he chooses to use his abilities.

Social and Emotional Maturity

The teenager's social and emotional growth rates are very closely related. Because the ability to live up to the expectations of others is great, failure to do so over a period of time can lead to emotional problems and social rejection. By ages eleven or twelve, youths develop the ability to conceptualize about their own thoughts. Since peer pressure is great and since at this age they are very egocentric, they fail to differentiate between what others are thinking about and their own mental preoccupations; they assume that other people are as obsessed with their behavior and appearances as they are themselves.[6]

---

[6] David Elkind, "Egocentrism in Children and Adults," Chapter 4 in *Children and Adolescents: Interpretive Essays on Jean Piaget* (New York: Oxford University Press, 1970), pp. 50, 66–67.

Ironically, adolescents' awareness and concern for what others may think of them can become so intense that it can blind them to what those expectations really are. Their preoccupation with themselves can bring a deterioration in their social acceptance. Conversely, the student who relates well to his peers and is well received by them is likely to feel emotionally secure and confident. (See Figure 1.3.)

The ability to adjust socially and the possession of emotional stability requires an adequate, positive view of oneself. The positive view of self comes from an accumulation of success experiences and an attitude toward problems as challenges to a strong self rather than as threats to a restricted self that can-

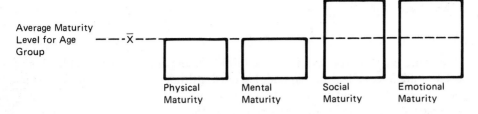

Figure 1.3 Channels of Adolescent Development — Social and Emotional

not be trusted.[7] The teacher's role in providing such experiences essential for systematic social and emotional growth seems clear. Actual techniques for designing of such tasks are found in Chapter 9 on planning.

Adolescent psychologist Erik Erikson has described adolescence as a time of identity crisis. He lists the following seven conflicts that arise during adolescence:

1. Temporal perspective versus time confusion.
2. Self-certainty versus self-consciousness.
3. Role experimentation versus role fixation.
4. Apprenticeship versus work paralysis.
5. Sexual polarization versus bisexual confusion.
6. Leader-and-followership versus authority confusion.
7. Ideological commitment versus confusion values.[8]

Only a brief look at this list gives the reader a feeling for the intense frustration of adolescence. Given the nature of adolescent life, it is not surprising to learn that in this country 43 percent of all serious crimes are committed by young people within the ten–fifteen year age group or that the peak age for committing violent crime is fourteen. By the end of the ninth grade, 20 percent of adolescents will have a drinking problem.[9] While many adolescents vent their frustrations on society, others direct their anger at themselves. Among young people between fifteen and nineteen years of age, suicide is the leading cause of death.[10]

---

[7] Arthur W. Combs, "The Positive View of Self," Chapter 8 in *Perceiving, Behaving, Becoming,* ed. Arthur W. Combs (Washington, D.C.: Association for Supervision and Curriculum Development, 1962), pp. 99–100.

[8] Erik Erikson, *Identity, Youth and Crisis* (New York: W. W. Norton, 1968), p. 336.

[9] Paul Hurd, "Hurd Reports New Data on Adolescence," Washington, D.C.: *ASCD Newsletter* 21 (April 1979).

[10] Richard L. Sartore, "Students and Suicide: An Interpersonal Tragedy," *Theory Into Practice* 15 (December 1976): 337–39.

Phenomenal Theory

As a future teacher, you will find it helpful to know as much as possible about how the adolescent learns. The adolescents' attitudes about themselves, their peers, their school, and their teachers significantly affect their learning. Those psychologists who study the importance of the self-concept (phenomenologists) have made us aware of the importance of how the individual views self, environment, and the relationship of the two. An individual without self-confidence finds it impossible to do the simplest of tasks. Many students perform inadequately throughout their school lives simply because they do not believe themselves capable of doing any better. But research studies show that approximately 90 percent of all students do have the ability to master the tasks assigned in high schools.[11]

Developmental Theory

A second essential element for adolescent learning is that of readiness. There are essentially two fields of thought regarding readiness. Some contend that, when appropriately presented, anything can be learned at any age. Developmental psychologists, however, reject this assertion. They maintain that one has to be mentally mature enough to perform the cognitive operations and cannot be forced or enticed to perform tasks that are at a level beyond the current state of readiness.

Obviously both of these opposing views cannot be totally correct, yet, each group provides some truth. The value of presenting material in patterns that are easy for students to learn is obvious. The advantage of placing that material at an appropriate grade level is equally obvious.

Gestalt vs. Connectionist Theory

There are two major schools of thought on the best way to organize material. The Gestalt (or field) theory maintains that material presented in its entirety has meaning that cannot be found in a sequential pattern. For example, a teacher who wished to communicate the concept of snow might present, in step-by-step sequence, a description of its physical characteristics (coldness, color, weight, and shape). This would not be so helpful as showing the student a field covered with snow. The slogan commonly associated with Gestalt psychology is that "the whole (of a thing) is more than the sum of its individual parts."

In opposition to the Gestalt theory is the connectionist theory, which insists that it is often more effective to introduce lessons step by step. The student can build on previous knowledge, connecting each piece of new knowledge to his

---

[11] J. Carroll, "A Model of School Learning," *Teachers College Record* 64 (1963): 723–33.

already learned concepts. Many schools have spiral curricula designed to meet this goal. Often a unit will begin with the most elementary ideas and progress to the more difficult. In colleges many courses are prerequisites to other courses. These are examples of the connectionist learning theory.

Associationist Theories

Another set of theories for understanding how learning occurs is association. Classical psychologists believe that all human behavior is a series of reactions to stimuli. Thus, if a teacher stimulates the students correctly, they have no choice but to learn. This explanation of learning implies that the teacher needs a variety of audio-visual stimuli. It suggests that models, experiments, and demonstrations be used to stimulate students through their senses of smell and touch.

Other associationists — behavior psychologists — emphasize the use of rewards. Rewards can be applied or delayed to promote learning. The numerous behavior modification studies focusing specifically on learning show that such reward programs promote learning to an astounding degree. The level of achievement of entire classes of high school students has been increased from D to B, along with an increase in attendance from 50 to 80 percent.[12] Giving feedback immediately and frequently is important, as well as the spacing of rewards in unpredictable patterns. Specific information about techniques for rewarding will be found in Chapter 5 on motivation.

Is it possible that the teacher can learn from all of these learning theories, even though they sometimes conflict? Perhaps the subject content or the nature of the teacher and students should dictate the best particular approach for a given situation.

LEARNING CURVES

While no two learners learn exactly alike, learning, nevertheless, often follows a general pattern, which can be shown in graph form. The curve in Figure 1.4 summarizes many features of learning. Notice that this curve has six general stages. The first stage sees no significant progress. Then, once a point of readiness is reached — the individual has had the necessary experiences to pick up needed cues and relate new knowledge to previous experiences, or develops the necessary motor coordination needed to perform a psychomotor skill — then a period of rapid learning occurs. Next, the rate of learning declines as the learner focuses on more minute and specific knowledge and skills. This period of decreasing gains is actually a period of refinement of cognitive and psychomotor skills. For example, a child trying to learn to play a piano may find it impossible until she reaches a certain level of maturation (prereadiness period

---

[12] G. L. Sapp et al., "Classroom Management and Student Involvement," *High School Journal* 56 (March 1973): 274–83.

or period of negligible progress). When this state of readiness is reached, rapid learning may occur (state of increasing gains) until she has mastered some of the common general skills, at which time her learning will experience a decrease in gains as she refines her techniques.

Sooner or later the student's learning will level off to a negligible rate (plateau), where it will remain until a renewed interest occurs. This stimulus may come from many sources, including a change in content being studied, or new insights brought on by associations in the mind, or even by the teacher's change of approach. This renewed interest causes a new learning spurt that may continue until he approaches his possible limit. Of course, there is no way to ascertain this actual limit, if it can ever be reached at all.

The Complexity of Learning

This has been but a brief, cursory introduction to current theories about the very complicated process called "learning." In actuality, our understanding of how an individual learns is at best fragmented and incomplete. (Given the differences and uniqueness among individuals, this comes as no surprise.) Yet it is vitally important that teachers use all the available bits and pieces of knowledge of how learning occurs to plan and coordinate lessons for maximum learning. Therefore, these theories will be discussed in further detail throughout the following chapters. Think about these learning theories and how you can use each to improve learning in your future classes.

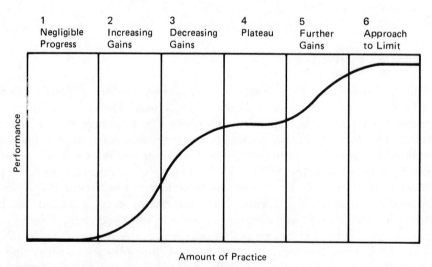

Figure 1.4 A Schematic Learning Curve

Source: Lee J. Cronbach, *Educational Psychology*, 2d ed. (New York: Harcourt, Brace and World, 1963), p. 299.

Adolescents experience the same basic needs that all humans share, including (1) the need for safety, (2) the need to belong, (3) the need for esteem, and (4) the need for self-actualization. Often, though, they may experience these needs much more severely, since they are forever trying to adjust to changing demands. Because it brings a changing environment and inner changes, adolescence is often described as a period of uncertainty, frustration, and even depression. The advent of puberty and a need to display appropriate sexual behavior often accentuates feelings of awkwardness, fear, and depression. The teacher who is aware of these conditions may be able to accept the student along with his or her problems.

Adolescents' strong need for approval leads to many conflicts. The various people from whom they seek approval may expect opposing kinds of behavior from them. Further accentuating the dilemma, at the time in life when they most need approval from others, they are experiencing an increasing need to become independent. When these two needs are in direct conflict, they must try either to please others or themselves. Sometimes the teacher can help them search out a third alternative, which will be acceptable to those that young people wish to please and still let them be true to their own values.

But, as a teacher, your major responsibility regarding adolescents is for their learning; hence you need to understand *how* they learn. Many schools of thought are at work today trying to explain how this process occurs. You will be wise to take an eclectic approach, trying to gain as much understanding as you can from each field.

Understanding the learning process is no simple task; indeed, many theories of learning are in opposition to one another. For example, the connectionist theory says that material is better learned when it is approached step by step, using past learning to build on future learning; whereas the Gestalt theory says that understanding is more complete when the student is introduced to all of the material at the same time. The associationist sees the learner as a subject that can be manipulated by use of rewards and punishment; whereas phenomenal theory, putting the subject (learner) in charge, suggests that after acquiring the necessary self-confidence and desire, the learner will develop the needed motivation internally.

Yet another learning theory sees everything from the development angle. Developmental psychologists tell us that without the necessary prior experience the learner is incapable of mastering the material at hand. We also learn from this theory that the adolescent is developing in at least four channels, and all at once. Furthermore, we see that the rate of development in one channel may surpass or lag behind development in another channel; and that physical, social, mental, and emotional growth rates all affect one another.

We know that learning for any two individuals differs. There are enough general patterns, though, so that pictorial drawings (or general learning curves) can be made to show the steps commonly experienced as the learner matures. Teachers who are aware of these patterns can better understand the learner's behavior; they will plan experiences consistent with the learner's response at different stages of development.

EXPERIENCES

In this chapter we examined several characteristics of adolescents, their needs, and what they find frustrating. Furthermore we focused our attention on what prompts some adolescents to apply themselves to their studies but fails to motivate others.

But for real understanding of adolescents and what makes them tick, we need to see them in action in their complex world. Both of the following accounts are actual experiences representative of those that adolescents are having in today's schools.

Experience 1:   The Weekend Party

Jacki sat up straighter than most of her classmates as she strained to listen to Frank, who was seated directly behind her. As in most older junior high schools, desks were fixed in a straight row and did not rotate. Jacki's face reddened as she heard the faint but clear question from her newly acquired boyfriend. "Will you come over and spend the weekend with me, since my folks will be out of town? Jimmy and Carol are coming."

Jacki was ashamed of herself for getting embarrassed, for she had known that this question was coming sooner or later — but she hadn't prepared herself to answer it. For once she was glad that the old desks were bolted to the floor and she was forced to face away from Frank. She immediately focused her attention toward the teacher and pretended to be interested in the lesson. But then she felt a tap on her shoulder. Frank pushed her for an answer.

"How about it? Will you come?"

"I dunno. I'll think about it."

"I've already promised Jimmy and Carol we'd do it. You've got to let me know now."

Trying to reach the right decision, Jacki considered the pros and cons. Her family would be desolate if she did and they found out. Although she had had some recent arguments with them, she knew how much they loved her and sacrificed for her. But she also knew that she cared a great deal for Frank, who was athletic, cute, and popular. Since she had started dating him, her classmates had begun to see her as someone really worth noticing. But then she thought that what Frank wanted would be morally wrong and she wondered how she would feel afterward. She was afraid that she already knew. And what would her best friend, Carol, think if she declined? Carol might stop being her friend. Jacki really needed more time to think about it.

"How about it? We'll have a real experience."

"I'll let you know later."

▶ *Questions and Discussion*

1. *If you were Jacki's teacher and if she came to you for advice, how would you respond to her?*

   Jacki seems capable of making her own decisions, yet she obviously needs some help with this one. Jacki seems to be weighing out the pluses and minuses of the situation but is focusing her considerations on what would happen now. Perhaps she should be reminded to consider the long-term results that a decision for or against accepting the proposition would have. In other words, what or how would she feel about it in a month or a year? What would her friends think of her in the future? This is one possibility. How would you respond?

2. *If Jacki should ask you to talk to Frank for her, how would you begin your discussion?*

   Frank would probably benefit from setting down the pluses and minuses that are involved for him. You might begin by asking him how he would feel about himself? What problems could arise from such a party? What would his friends think of him? How would Jacki feel toward him if they did decide to go through with it? Can you think of other approaches?

Experience 2: All Adolescents Are Individuals

Bobby Joe and Billy Joe, twins, had been born prematurely and were now the smallest boys in the tenth-grade biology class. Though they looked very much alike, their behavior had little resemblance. Unlike his boisterous brother, Bobby Joe was timid and shy, almost to the point of withdrawal, yet his performance on tests and homework was consistently high. Unfortunately, Billy Joe did not share his brother's love for biology or for any other subject; he was usually at the bottom of the class. Today marked the third time in a week that Billy had been sent to the vice-principal's office to be disciplined.

When Mrs. Wells checked their cumulative records, she was surprised to learn that only during the previous year did Billy's academic performance and behavior take a nose dive. She also noticed that the boys' parents were recently divorced and wondered what implications, if any, that could have had on Billy's behavior.

▶ *Questions and Discussion*

1. *Could Bobby and Billy's size be affecting their behavior?*

   If so, why was the effect different? While size is obviously not the key factor behind Billy's change in behavior, it could be an irritating stimulus that increases the intensity of their behavior. Sometimes it is hard to remember that adolescents are so different — even twins; they react differently to problems and frustrations.

2. *How would you evaluate the emotional welfare of the two boys?
Which seems to be the healthier?*
This question is worth thinking about. But do not worry if you find it
perplexing. Such evaluations as these should be made by a specialist.
Most teachers are not qualified to judge the degree of seriousness of a
student's psychological problems. If it appears that help is needed, the
teacher should speak to the counselor or school psychologist.

3. *How might a phenomenologist approach this problem?*
The phenomenal psychologist would begin by asking, Why does each
boy act as he does? Why did Billy's behavior change so drastically?
Why didn't Bobby also become more aggressive? The phenomenologist
would assume that each boy is behaving in the way that he perceives
most appropriate at the time. Do you accept this explanation? Why?
Why not?

ACTIVITIES

Through these experiences and questions an attempt has been made to involve
you with making decisions. After all, once you begin teaching, the real decisions will belong to you. However, you may feel that you still have some important reactions that you have not had an opportunity to share. The following activities are provided so that you may express special insights and ideas
generated as you read this chapter.

1. Choose one concept that you perceive as important and explain how it relates to one of the experiences.
2. For each experience, write your own question relating to the experience.
3. By this time you must have at least one idea that you want to express, perhaps a question that has been unanswered, an insight about adolescence
that has not been shared, or a point of difference with the author. Express
this idea.
4. List one of your own personal traits that will be an asset to you in working
with adolescents. Explain how you will use this trait to make it as effective
as possible.
5. Now for the tough one. List one of your traits that you believe may inhibit
your relationships with adolescents. Explain how you can change your own
behavior to accommodate this weakness. (Remember that behavioral
changes usually do not come easy or quickly.)

SUGGESTED READINGS

COELHO, G. V.; HAMBURG, D. A.; and ADAMS, J. E., eds. *Coping and Adaptation.* New
York: Basic Books, 1974.
COMBS, ARTHUR W., ed. *Perceiving, Behaving, Becoming.* Washington, D.C.: Asso-
ciation for Supervision and Curriculum Development, 1962.

ERIKSON, ERIK. *Identity, Youth and Crisis.* New York: W. W. Norton, 1968.

FELDHUSEN, JOHN. "Behavior in Secondary Schools." Yearbook, 1978, Part II. Washington, D.C.: National Society for the Study of Education, 1979.

HECHINGER, FRED M. "Growing up in America." *This We Believe.* Washington, D.C.: National Association of Secondary School Principals, 1976.

HENSON, KENNETH T., and HENRY, MARVIN A. *Becoming Involved in Teaching.* Section Two, "Becoming Involved with Students in the Classroom," and Section Three, "Becoming Involved in the Wider Student World." Terre Haute, Ind.: Sycamore Press, 1976.

HURD, PAUL. "Hurd Reports New Data on Adolescence." *ASCD Newsletter* 21 (April 1979).

JACKSON, PHILLIP W. *Life in Classrooms.* New York: Holt, Rinehart and Winston, 1968.

KEYES, RALPH. *Is There Life After High School?* Boston: Little, Brown, 1976.

KOZOL, JONATHAN. *Death at an Early Age.* Boston: Houghton Mifflin, 1967.

SHANE, HAROLD G. *Curriculum Change Toward the 21st Century.* Washington, D.C.: National Education Association, 1977.

SILBERMAN, CHARLES E. *Crisis in the Classroom.* New York: Random House, 1970.

WADSWORTH, BARRY J. *Piaget for the Classroom Teacher.* New York: Longman, 1978.

America's Secondary Schools: Past, Present, and Future

OBJECTIVES

Upon completion of this chapter, you should be able to:
1. Discuss the reason(s) for the Puritans' migration to America.
2. List (with correct dates) and discuss three pieces of legislation that helped shape the American secondary school.
3. Name the Seven Cardinal Principles and write one statement about each, explaining its relevance to today's secondary schools.
4. Explain the nature and impact of the Progressive Education Movement on today's secondary schools.
5. List three goals of today's secondary schools other than the Cardinal Principles.
6. Trace the change of the role of the instructional process in American secondary schools from 1900 until the present.
7. Differentiate between the process and goals of individualized education and personalized teaching.
8. List at least six goals of future schools and explain the importance of each.
9. Describe the curricula in each: Franklin's Academy, the Latin Grammar School, and the Boston English Classical School.

This chapter will survey the beginning of formal schooling in this country and will show how secondary schools came into being and then changed throughout the years. Only by understanding their evolution and metamorphosis can we understand today's schools and what they are trying to do.

You may wonder what all this has to do with teaching methods. For one reason, when you begin teaching (and even during your student teaching internship), each time you select a teaching method, you will want it to be consistent with the purposes of the secondary school. Also, the more you understand about the many services in today's complex secondary schools, the more you will be able to coordinate your efforts with the numerous offices and colleagues at your school. You are all working for one purpose, the benefit of the student.

*Foundations of Learning
and Teaching*

Certainly one of the most colorful characters in history was England's King Henry VIII, noted for his agility, lust for women, temper, and selfishness. When the Roman Catholic Church refused to sanctify his marriage to Anne Boleyn, Henry VIII established his own church, the Church of England, which today remains the dominant denomination in Great Britain. When James I became king in 1603, he made life difficult for the other Protestant churches. The Puritans resisted his pressures, but their resistance brought increased pressure. Finally, after seventeen years under King James, a Protestant group went to Holland to escape religious persecution; but, meeting with great opposition in Holland, they soon left for America. By this time a second group of Protestants had left England for America, and by 1630 both groups arrived in the area that was to be named Massachusetts.

Contrary to popular belief, the Puritans were not seeking religious freedom for all — they were seeking religious freedom for the Puritans! In their strict laws the role of the church was to interpret the will of God, and the role of the state was to enforce it. The church building commonly served as the courthouse where civil laws were made and offenders were tried and sentenced. Since the civil law and the church were inseparable and since obedience to God required a knowledge of His laws, an institution was needed to guarantee that each citizen possessed this required knowledge.

EARLY SCHOOLS

The Latin Grammar School

In 1635 the first Latin Grammar School, forerunner of our modern high school, appeared. Designed after the English schools, Latin Grammar Schools aimed at preparing elite young men for entrance to Harvard, which opened in 1636. They derived their name from their curricula, dominated by the classics, especially Latin and Greek. These schools were never very popular because their classical curricula did not seem relevant to citizens of a rapidly developing country.

Legislative Support

By 1642 every home was required to teach reading, Puritanism, and the laws of the colony, and inspectors went to each house to see that this was being done. This system was, of course, expensive and ineffective; therefore it was soon replaced by the public school. By 1647 Massachusetts towns were required by law to erect and maintain schools. Communities of fifty or more families had to teach reading and writing; those with a hundred or more families had to establish a Latin Grammar School and hire a teacher.

The Academy

Franklin Academy, established in Philadelphia in 1750, was in many ways the very opposite of these schools. It offered such practical subjects as mathematics, astronomy, surveying, bookkeeping, and navigation. By the end of the Revolutionary War, the Franklin Academy had replaced the Latin Grammar School to become the number one secondary school in America.

The Public High School

The Franklin Academy's practical curriculum enabled it to successfully replace the Latin Grammar School; yet, it had one weakness — it was private. Many parents could not afford its tuition. In 1821 the Boston School Committee established the country's first public high school. The Boston English Classical School, later named the Boston English High School, was developed to prepare youth for employment; for many it served as an entry to the university as well. Since these early high schools served these two distinctly different purposes, the curricula in individual schools varied greatly. Most were very pragmatic, but some were highly classical.

By 1860 half of the nation's children were in school. The commitment of the government to education was reconfirmed in 1787 by the Northwest Ordinance, which reserved a parcel of land in every township to be sold to finance public education. Further support came in 1874 in the Kalamazoo case, which gave every town the right to levy taxes to support their secondary schools.

GOALS FOR THE EARLY HIGH SCHOOL

The last quarter of the nineteenth century set some definite trends that are still prevalent in high school education. The once small schools began to grow in enrollments. Teachers and administrators joined to form the first unified coalition of organized educators, the National Education Association. The NEA assumed leadership in determining the goals for the early high schools. In 1892 its Committee of Ten stated that the purpose of the school was to prepare students for life, yet recommended that all students be taught the college preparatory subjects. Three years later the NEA reinforced the college preparatory goal with its Committee on College Entrance Requirements. During this same quarter-century regional associations were formed to inspect and accredit high schools.

The new century brought further clarification of the goals of the high school. In 1918 the NEA's Commission on the Reorganization of Secondary Education listed the following seven principles, formally known as the Seven Cardinal Principles of Secondary Education, as the main goals for secondary (and elementary) schools:

1. Health
2. Command of fundamental processes (development of basic skills)
3. Worthy home membership
4. Vocational efficiency
5. Citizenship
6. Worthy use of leisure time
7. Ethical character

This list of broad goals for high schools is the most important ever set forth for American secondary schools. While it contains only seven entries, each is broad enough to make the list very comprehensive, very inclusive. These goals are also significant for their relevance; they remain so even though society constantly changes with time.

EXPERIMENTAL EDUCATION

From the beginning of public schools in America until 1875 (some 250 years), the school curricula had been largely determined by one type of textbook or another. Initially the main texts were the Bible and the "hornbook." The hornbook was a board that had attached to it a piece of paper with the Lord's Prayer, the alphabet, and some simple syllables. It took its name from the thin sheet of transparent horn that covered and protected its surface.

In the 1690s the first basal reader, called the *New England Primer,* was published. It, too, was a blend of religion and morals. Rhymes called catechisms were used to teach religious doctrine and language skills. "The sin of man, the wrath of God, the judgment of a fiery hell, and the salvation of a resurrected Christ permeated it from cover to cover."[1]

In 1782 Noah Wester's book, known as the *Blue Back Speller,* was published, adding spelling to the curriculum. During the next sixty years, twenty-four million copies were sold. The intentions of the book were to provide moral and nonsectarian religious guidance, to provide valuable knowledge, and to motivate the students' interests.

During these first 250 years, instruction centered around recitation. In other words, the students studied, memorized, and recited their lessons until they were committed to memory; students who failed received corporal punishment. In 1875 this method was openly challenged. Colonel Francis Parker, who, as an eight-year-old orphan was apprenticed to a farmer until age twenty-one, had discovered that life on the farm was very educational. He had found school to be so hateful and unbearable that he attended it only about eight weeks every year. But, instead of turning his back on education itself, Parker wanted to become part of the education process and to improve it. He believed that if education could be acquired so pleasantly in the fields, woodlands, and pastures, it could also be enjoyed in the schools. His dream was to become a great teacher; little did he know that his fulfillment of the dream would result in a revolution of American education.

In 1875 Colonel Parker was selected as superintendent of schools in Quincy, Massachusetts, a suburb of Boston. By establishing teachers' meetings, he gave to his forty teachers, not advice and knowledge, but questions and demonstrations. He did not *tell* them how to teach; he *showed* them. He gave them not only a technique but also a spirit, making them want to put life into their curricula. To build a natural learning environment, Colonel Parker substituted games and puzzles for recitation and rote memorization. In the lower grades he instituted singing, playing, reading, counting objects, writing, and drawing. Above all, he wanted the experiences at his schools to be happy ones. Reversing the traditional teaching process, which began with rules and definitions, he gave students real-life problems that made them seek out the rules or generalizations.

This system, which became known as the Quincy System, gained national attention. In his own words Colonel Parker tells how enthusiastic the community had become over its schools. "Throughout the centuries of Quincy's

---

[1] Benjamin F. Walker, *Curriculum Evaluation as Portrayed Through Old Textbooks* (Terre Haute: Curriculum Research and Development Center, Indiana State University, 1976), p. 6.

history, its people have ever manifested a deep interest in education, and I believe that I am right when I say that at no time in the past has this interest been greater than it is in the first year of the new century [of Independence]." [2]

The Quincy System was the forerunner of other innovative experiments in education. Other notable movements include the Gary Plan, the Dalton Plan, and the Winnetka Plan. The Gary Plan was developed by William A. Wirt, the superintendent of schools in Gary, Indiana, where the elementary and high schools were designed as miniature communities. The system was open and, unlike the other schools that had self-contained classrooms, the students moved freely from one place to another throughout the day in platoons. Like Colonel Parker's system, this system was experimental and student-centered. The Dalton Plan, developed in Dalton, Massachusetts, in 1919, was significant in that it was a highly individualized program. Using contracts, students followed their own progress closely. This program involved students and teachers in the development of curriculum. The Winnetka Plan, developed in the same year by Carleton Washburne, superintendent of schools at Winnetka, Illinois, was also a highly individualized program. Stressing self-expression and creativity, it even used self-instructional materials to teach the fundamentals.

These programs were important in two ways. First, they changed the way that Americans thought about education, which no longer had to be textbook-oriented and dominated by recitation. Students could become the focus or center of the learning experiences, and school could be enjoyed as student activities were not subdued, but encouraged. The belief of seventeenth-century John Locke — that experience is the basis of understanding — was finally being implemented. Second, these programs were important because they led to several national movements in education. Even today, they influence the goals and innovations in our schools.

PROGRESSIVE EDUCATION

The experiment-based movement that Colonel Parker had started in 1875 moved vigorously into the twentieth century. Before his death in 1902, he took a position as head of a normal school in Chicago, which later merged with the University of Chicago, where John Dewey was head of the philosophy and psychology department from 1894 to 1904. Professor Dewey established a school on the university's campus to serve as an experimental laboratory to study education processes. This laboratory school was like any other school except that it was readily available for the professors and students to conduct on-site research on teaching practices. Within a few years almost every state in the nation had at least one university laboratory school. Now, over a half-century later, most of these laboratory schools are still operating. Although

---

[2] Jack K. Campbell, *Colonel Francis Parker: The Children's Crusader* (New York: Columbia University, Teachers College Press, 1967).

some contain nursery school through twelfth grade, the economic recession of the 1970s forced many lab schools to eliminate the junior and/or senior high school grades.

The first quarter of the twentieth century showed true concern for the high school student. This forerunner to the more recent humanistic movement was named the Progressive Education Movement. The term *child-centered*, as opposed to *subject-centered*, became dominant. Though often confused with permissive education, the Progressive Education Movement did not espouse permissiveness. The concept of progressivism is much more akin to pragmatism, for during this era secondary school curricula became much more practical, offering agriculture, home economics, and other vocational subjects. But progressivism meant more than practicality; it also meant that students helped plan the curriculum and sometimes their own individualized learning activities. Arts, sports, and extracurricular activities were also added to the curriculum. Progressive educators' belief in the democratic process led them, furthermore, to involve parents as well as students and teachers.

For fifty years the progressive trend was well accepted by students, who perceived the curriculum as highly relevant. From 1933 to 1941 the Progressive Education Association sponsored the Eight Year Study of the effects of such a general education on learners. Conducted by Harvard University, the study followed students of thirty experimental high schools through high school and college. The graduates of the experimental school equaled their counterparts in the attainment of subject matter, and they outperformed them in attainment of academic honors and grades. Furthermore, these students who had freedom of choice in their curricula proved to be significantly superior in intellectual curiosity, creativity, drive, leadership, and extraclass activities. They also proved to be more objective and more aware of world events.

GOALS FOR TODAY'S HIGH SCHOOL

Cardinal Principles

A brief glance back at the Seven Cardinal Principles will remind us of their relevance in today's schools; in many ways they are needed even more today than when they were written in 1918. Knowing how to use leisure time is especially essential, since the average work load has been reduced to fewer hours per week. A sense of valuing the family is needed more, now that divorce rates are higher than ever before in history. The need for a feeling of patriotism and for doing what is morally right was increased during the 1970s when the Watergate affair did much to destroy the confidence of Americans in the system and in fellow Americans. Certainly the need for good health and vocational skills has not diminished. And what about the remaining cardinal principle, "Command of the fundamental processes"? Much is being heard about our failure to teach the basics or *fundamentals* today. Today's secondary schools do, indeed, need the Seven Cardinal Principles.

Separate Subjects or Interdisciplinary Approach

By the middle of the century, the question of how content should be structured had become a hot issue. The Progressive Movement had blended the various disciplines in the belief that more understanding would result. For example, the "core curriculum" had become very popular: a core of common experiences was believed essential for all students, and some of these experiences were interdisciplinary. But interdisciplinary movements were criticized severely by educators such as Arthur E. Bestor, who believed that these interdisciplinary movements had weakened the curricula. Bestor and others criticized other schools severely for this "anti-intellectualism."

Inquiry or Discovery Learning

In the 1950s, urged on by such critics as California's superintendent of education Max Rafferty and U.S. Navy Admiral Hyman Rickover, the American public reexamined its schools. There was a general attitude of disappointment, climaxed by the Russians' successful launching of the world's first satellite in 1957. Harvard University's president James B. Conant had already been insisting that the secondary school curricula should be more rigorous. He especially urged that stronger minimum requirements be made of all students, even more for the academically gifted.

As a result, a special committee convened in Woods Hole, Massachusetts, in 1959 to design a better system for educating America's youth. The thirty-five leaders in education, government, industry, and science concluded that education should be built around broad theories and concepts. The following year Woods Hole Conference Committee member Jerome S. Bruner reported the general resulting conclusions of the study in his book *The Process of Education*.[3] One of his often quoted statements in that book expresses the emphasis that this committee placed on structuring knowledge so that it can be more easily learned. Said Bruner, "any subject can be taught effectively in some intellectually honest form to any child." [4]

The 1960s saw a deluge of alphabet programs that often integrated two or more disciplines in an attempt to help students learn to inquire and discover relationships. Some of the more popular programs were the SMSG (Science-Mathematics-Study Group), ESCP (Earth Science Curriculum Project), BSCS (Biological Sciences Curriculum Study), PSSC (Physical Science Study Committee), and ISCS (Intermediate Science Curriculum Study). Other contributions were Ned Flanders's Interaction Analysis system for analyzing classroom behavior; and Benjamin Bloom's Taxonomy of Educational Objectives, which enabled teachers to build learning experiences on increasing higher levels of the thought processes. With the development of advanced technical equipment came another reason for structuring learning experiences; students needed to be stimulated to think through processes and to draw relationships themselves, not just to remember facts but to use those facts to solve problems.

Humanizing

A third and important goal of today's schools is that of humanizing the school environment. Our first high schools were typically one-room buildings designed to accommodate at most a few dozen students, but during the early 1950s there was a national trend to consolidate small schools. This resulted in larger and larger schools until today a school of two thousand, three thousand, or four thousand enrollment is common. The advantage was more diversity of subjects, while the disadvantage was the resulting impersonal, dehumanizing environment. Concern for these conditions has resulted in such additions to the curricula as value clarification study.

Multicultural Education

Currently, members of the many different cultures represented in our schools are receiving attention. Researchers are trying to determine the most effective ways to teach in multicultural settings. (These strategies are the focus of Chapter 13.) The area of concern is expanding to include groups that have

---

[3] Jerome S. Bruner, *The Process of Education* (Cambridge: Harvard University Press, 1960).
[4] Ibid., p. 33.

traditionally been ignored even when attention was given to other minority groups.

Individualize or Personalize

The 1960s saw much attention being placed on individualizing the curriculum, and some very good programs have been developed. Individualized Guided Education (IGE), a program developed in Wisconsin, and Individually Prescribed Instruction (IPI) developed at the University of Pittsburg, are two of the most successful. The whole competency-based movement has introduced individualization into American schools at all levels, elementary through university. The competency-based programs have made significant contributions to individualizing education but, ironically and often justifiably, have been labeled "dehumanizing." It is becoming increasingly more obvious that mere individualization is not enough. Our huge secondary schools today with their complicated schedules (many running on double shifts) need more. They need ways of personalizing all aspects of the schooling process.

GOALS FOR TOMORROW'S SCHOOLS

The New Basics

How can anyone know what needs the future will bring and what goals future schools will have? The task is not as impossible as it sounds; in fact, there are some definite goals. Dr. Harold Shane, education futurist at Indiana University, calls them "the new basics" for our secondary schools.[5] These goals include the need to (1) learn how to live with uncertainty, complexity, and change; (2) develop the ability to anticipate; (3) adapt to new structures, new constraints, and new situations without emotional drain and emotional collisions; (4) learn how to learn, that is, learn how to search out contradictions in one's values and understandings; (5) see relationships, sorting and weighing them, (6) understand the facts of life (realities); become aware of alternatives; (7) learn to analyze the consequences of their chosen alternatives; (8) learn how to make choices; and (9) learn how to work together to get things done. For example, youth must learn how to reach compromises and how to accept compromises with honor.

Seven Cardinal Premises

In 1972 the NEA assigned a committee of fifty of the world's most renowned educators, doctors, editors, philanthropists, national leaders of teachers' unions, and scientists to study the validity of the Cardinal Principles. While this was not a research project, the foresight of a committee of this magnitude is worthy

---

[5] Harold Shane, *Curriculum Change Toward the 21st Century* (Washington, D.C.: National Education Association, 1977).

of consideration. The committee reported that we are now moving through a "system's break," that is, we are experiencing total irreversible changes in our universe such as the way that we perceive ecology, our attitudes toward material things, mistrust of institutions, and job alienation. First, the decline of the hydrocarbon age. What does this mean? The federal government estimates that if we should stop importing petroleum we have only enough domestic petroleum to last for twelve years. Second, we must learn to live less extravagantly. Third, we have a psychological problem, an era of entitlements when people feel that the world owes them a living. Fourth, we may have to set a definite growth policy. In 1976 we were importing seven of the thirteen basic ingredients of an industrial society. Before 1990 we are projected to be importing eleven of the thirteen. We are moving toward a more disciplined, more regulated society. If we continue to move toward guaranteed employment, guaranteed minimum wages, guaranteed health care, we must have someone to regulate these programs to prevent freeloading. America is moving toward conservation. We have about twenty years to learn to really use and save wisely. Every fourteen-fifteen days the world grows by almost three million people, the size of the city of Miami or Houston. Every three or four days we add the population of South Dakota or Montana. It took all of human history up until the time of the Civil War to grow to one billion people. The world population is going to expand by this amount in the next nine years. Can the world feed its population tomorrow? Today? No. Each year about one billion people starve. Food production increases 2 percent per year and the population increases by 2 percent. In fact, we can't hold to our current starvation level. Due to spoilage and theft, the net increase of food production is much less than the increase in birth rate.[6]

But how about those Seven Cardinal Principles? This committee predicts that they will be equally relevant as goals for future schools. In the same year as the NEA study, the U.S. Office of Education joined efforts with the National Association of Secondary School Principals to study the same issue.[7] The USOE/NASSP Conference likewise accepted the Seven Cardinal Principles as being important future goals, to which they added consumerism, versatility, flexibility (a vital goal identified by the previous commission), and helping students learn to feel positive about themselves. Special emphasis on cultural pluralism will be needed. The committee further agreed that the schools cannot "do it all." Therefore, they must find new ways to share the responsibility of educating young people in an increasingly complex and often confusing society.[8] As educational critic Lawrence A. Cremin reminds us, the school is only one of the many institutions in our society that are organized to educate our citizens. Others include churches, synagogues, family, libraries, museums,

[6] Shane, *Curriculum Change.*
[7] *New Dimensions for Educating Youth,* HEW Office of Education NASSP, John Chaffee Jr., ed., 1976.
[8] Nan Patton, "Seven Cardinal Principles Revisited," *New Dimensions for Educating Youth* (U.S. Office of Education and National Association of Secondary School Principals, 1977).

Boy Scouts, day care centers, factories, radio stations and television networks.[9]

In the Seventy-fifth Yearbook on the National Society for the Study of Education, the authors caution us repeatedly that even with our awareness of these highly predictable changes, education futurists must remember that no prediction is infallible and that in making predictions of the future, futurists should keep open minds so as to avoid tunnel vision.[10] Shall we begin by keeping our minds open as we read and discuss the following chapters?

SUMMARY

Formal education in America began in the homes, where teaching of reading, Puritanism, and colonial law was required. In 1635 the forerunners of our current high schools appeared; but, designed after the English schools, they were built to prepare the elite for the university. As their curricula were dominated by classical Latin and Greek, they were called Latin Grammar Schools. Because of their impracticality, they soon gave way to very practical types based on the Franklin Academy developed in 1750. But these schools were private and many parents could not afford them. The first public high schools appeared in 1821. Most of these Boston English High Schools were very pragmatic, but some were just the opposite.

In 1918 the NEA appointed a committee to identify the goals of secondary schools. Their findings, called the Seven Cardinal Principles of Secondary Education, are equally applicable today. The twentieth century brought the Progressive Education Movement, emphasizing the practical, child-centered curriculum for fifty years until it gave way to a subject-centered curriculum. This conservative, subject-centered curriculum gave way to a process-centered curriculum following the launching of Sputnik in 1957. The 1970s saw an emphasis on humanizing the high school and on providing for multicultural groups. Future high schools will aim at preparing students to accept change, to learn how to learn, to analyze situations, to understand the facts of life, to make choices and live with them, and to work and live with others.

EXPERIENCES

Some of the aims of American education seem to remain constant from decade to decade; others change as our society changes. Since the realization of these aims will not be reached through the principal's office, but in the classrooms themselves, teachers must stay attuned to them. The

---

[9] Lawrence A. Cremin, *Public Education* (New York: Basic Books, 1976).

[10] Virgil Clift and Harold Shane, "The Future, Social Decisions, and Educational Change in Secondary Schools," *Issues in Secondary Education*, Seventy-fifth Yearbook of the National Society for the Study of Education, Part II, 1976, pp. 295–315.

following experiences illustrate some situations in which teachers have to make some difficult decisions about their exact responsibilities.

Experience 1:   If the World Gives You Lemons . . .

Bob Wallace was enjoying his fourteenth year on the faculty at South Central High. While his colleagues complained daily that teachers were abused by administrators, parents, students, and the legislature, Bob remained positive and happy. He was so frequently labeled an optimist that he collected favorite definitions; for example, he would say that "an optimist is a person who, having fallen from a thirteen-story building, is heard to remark as he passes the second story, 'So far, so good.'" A bright yellow sign running across the top of the blackboard caught the immediate attention of those entering Bob's classroom. The sign read, "If the world gives you lemons, then make lemonade!"

It seemed especially tragic, then, that Bob suddenly became sad and depressed after thirteen years of happy teaching. He had been informed that a lawsuit was being filed against him on behalf of the parents of a new transfer student. Bob had always felt it his responsibility to read a few verses of scriptures weekly to each of his classes. He had chosen the particular ones because he felt that they were rules to live by for all people — even those who were not religiously inclined. They were also chosen because he felt that they could not offend anyone, since they dealt with universally accepted ideals such as honesty, truth, and kindness. The lawsuit made him worry about his own welfare, but he was even more concerned by the state of affairs in a world that seemed so anti-religiously oriented.

▶ *Questions and Discussion*

1. *Since reading the Bible in the classroom has been interpreted as unconstitutional by the Supreme Court, how could Bob achieve his goals in another legal way?*
   One thing is certain: morality cannot be taught by moralizing, if indeed it can be "taught" at all. The teacher can affect the behavior of his students by being honest with them and by setting a good example.

2. *Do teachers have a right or responsibility to teach morality?*
   All teachers have both the right and responsibility to lead students in the development of morals. This duty was reaffirmed in 1918 by the Seven Cardinal Principles of Secondary Education. Teachers in public schools do not have a right to read the Bible in class; such would be a violation of a Supreme Court ruling.

Experience 2:   A Curriculum Outpaces the Community

Weldon Public School was in a farming community of less than a thousand people. When a gradual change in economics forced many small farmers to take up a second job, a new canning factory enabled the community to survive.

About half of the new employees at the factory came from outside the community, many from the closest large city, about ninety miles away. They brought with them many ideas foreign to the Weldonites. One such outsider, Jim Higgins, had recently accepted a teaching position at WPS. He introduced a minicourse entitled "Life in the Year 2000." A number of concerned parents felt it impossible for anyone to know what life in the year 2000 would be like. A few others went so far as to say that the new teacher claimed to possess supernatural powers. The principal, wanting to be fair about the controversy, called a special P.T.A. meeting to give Jim an opportunity to explain this new course to the community skeptics.

▶ *Questions and Discussion*

1. *Is a course that claims to prepare students for the next century feasible?*
   Actually there are a number of courses at all levels (K through university) designed at least in part to prepare students for the distant future. Students who are now in high school will be living most of their lives in the twenty-first century.

2. *What topics might be covered in a future-oriented course?*
   Some definitely needed topics include these:
   How to adapt to change
   Living in a crowded world
   Living with peoples of all cultures
   Strategies for world peace
   Alternative fuel sources
   Can you list others?

ACTIVITIES

The purpose of this chapter was to stimulate you to think about our contemporary schools and to consider how they have emerged to become what they are today. Also, it will be helpful to extend our thinking to include the purposes of our present schools and how their organization and other characteristics relate to their purposes. The following activities should help strengthen your awareness of the purposes of our present schools.

1. Name one goal or aim that you feel is of utmost importance to today's schools. Explain how you, the teacher, can work toward achieving that expectation.

2. List one characteristic of modern classrooms (physical, emotional, psychological, or other) that resulted from the thrust of the Progressive Education Movement.

3. Describe one way that our society is changing and explain how our schools must change accordingly.

SUGGESTED READINGS

CAMPBELL, JACK K. *Colonel Francis Parker: The Children's Crusader.* New York: Columbia University, Teachers College Press, 1967.

CREMIN, LAWRENCE A. *Public Education.* New York: Basic Books, 1976.

CREMIN, LAWRENCE A. *The Transformation of the School: Progressivism in American Education, 1876–1957.* New York: Alfred A. Knopf, 1961.

DAVIS, O. L., JR., ed. *Perspectives on Curriculum Development 1776–1976.* Washington, D.C.: Association for Supervision and Curriculum Development, 1976.

RENNER, JOHN W.; BIBENS, ROBERT F.; and SHEPHERD, GENE D. *Guiding Learning in the Secondary School.* New York: Harper and Row, 1972.

SMITH, FREDERICK R., and COX, C. BENJAMIN. *Secondary Schools in a Changing Society.* New York: Holt, Rinehart and Winston, 1976.

STEEVES, FRANK L., and ENGLISH, FENWICK W. *Secondary Curriculum for a Changing World.* Columbus, Ohio: Charles E. Merrill, 1978.

THAYER, V. T. *Formative Ideas in American Education.* New York: Dodd, Mead, 1965.

WALKER, BENJAMIN F. *Curriculum Evolution as Portrayed Through Old Textbooks.* Terre Haute: Curriculum Research and Development Center, Indiana State University, 1976.

VAN TIL, WILLIAM. *Secondary Education: School and Community.* Boston: Houghton Mifflin, 1978.

Interacting with Students

By this time you are probably wondering when we are going to get to the heart of the matter and discuss the teacher's role in the classroom. After all, such topics as discipline, classroom management, and motivation are the survival skills; without them everything else you might learn about teaching becomes insignificant.

This observation is correct. Without good discipline, management, and motivation skills, today's teacher will have a short career; for these skills are not merely desirable or important but indispensable.

As you read through this section, you are encouraged to think even beyond the survival point. Your interacting with students is essential to their effective instruction. The higher levels of thinking are best achieved through dialectic teaching where the teacher and students share ideas. It is the teacher's responsibility to establish a climate where interaction occurs freely among students and between the teacher and students.

From Discipline to Self-Discipline

OBJECTIVES

When you complete this chapter, you should be able to:
1. Describe the status of discipline in modern secondary schools.
2. Give two reasons why teachers must not rely on power and punishment to discipline their classes.
3. Contrast two different approaches to classroom discipline.
4. Describe the public's attitude toward discipline in today's secondary schools.
5. Define discipline in terms of order and control.
6. Explain the relationship between quietness and discipline.
7. List three rules for conducting a private talk with a student who has misbehaved.
8. Tell what is wrong with the addage "Be tough at first and relax the rules as time passes."

Today some educators seem to be embarrassed by the term *discipline;* indeed, many offer substitutes to dress up the topic, such as classroom management or behavior modification. Yet discipline is one of the most important realities facing today's secondary teachers. The 1979 Gallup Poll again found lack of discipline to be the number one concern of parents.[1] These results have come as no surprise. In fact, discipline has been America's number one educational concern for nine of the last ten years!

A group of teenagers in a small Vermont community sneak over to the home of their assistant principal to loosen the wheels on his car. The next morning he is almost killed while driving down a mountain road. A woman in a southern California high school is accosted by a group of male students who threatened to slash her face if she assigned them a failing grade.[2] A twenty-five-year

---

[1] George Gallup, "The Eleventh Annual Gallup Poll of the Public's Attitudes Toward the Public Schools," *Phi Delta Kappan* 61 (September 1979): 33–45.
[2] Marilyn Whiteside, "School Discipline: The Ongoing Crisis," *The Clearing House* 49 (December 1975): 160–62.

veteran teacher in Oklahoma turns in her chalk and eraser, concluding that "most students have no respect for any person or anything—not even for themselves." [3]

Beginning teachers are concerned about the ability to discipline their future classes, and while many will never experience such dramatic events as the above, their concerns are justified. It will behoove you to learn as much as you can about discipline and proper techniques for establishing and maintaining discipline in your classroom. Unfortunately, most college programs provide little preparation for classroom control.[4]

DISCIPLINE IS YOUR RESPONSIBILITY

Discipline is absolutely essential to the education process.[5] It is imperative that you learn all you can about discipline because discipline is your responsibility. There was a time when it was understood that the school's disciplinarian was the principal, who provided the punishment for misbehavior or delegated the task to the physical education coach. The responsibilities of administrators and coaches have increased from year to year, and they no longer have time to deal with all the discipline problems that develop in the school. Even though many assistant principals are assigned this task, the responsibility for classroom discipline ultimately belongs to the teacher. A second and far more important reason for each teacher controlling discipline is that the traditional approach of administering punishments is now known to be extremely undesirable.

Who's in Charge Here?

A story is told of a mother who could not get her small child to eat. Seeing her in desperation, the father took control. He began by telling the child that he would cook him anything he wanted. The child asked for eggs but took one bite and refused to eat them, ordering pancakes. The father cooked the pancakes, which had similar results. Then the child asked, "Did you say you would cook me *anything* I want?" "Yes, anything." Then, I think I'd like a fried worm." The father, determined to uphold his promise, went to the back yard, dug up a fat earthworm, and, taking a deep breath, prepared and served it. The child paused and demanded that his father cut the worm in half and eat half himself. Still determined to succeed, the father dissected the worm and consumed half of it. Whereupon the child began crying frantically. "What's wrong now?" the father asked with more than a slight note of disgust. The child pointed and cried frantically, "You ate *my* half."

---

[3] Anonymous ex-teacher, "Today's Students Are Impossible!" *Today's Education* 67 (March 1975): 24–28.

[4] Jerry W. Young, "Maintaining Classroom Control," *School and Community* 61 (March 1975): 13.

[5] Ibid.

While secondary teachers don't have to deal with young children, the task is often equally challenging and the relationship is the same. Who's in charge here?" Someone always is. Either the student or the teacher is in control.

All Teachers Have Discipline Problems

If disciplinary actions are divided into two categories, "preventions" and "solutions," we find that the most effective disciplinarian is not the teacher who can immediately resolve a crisis — although this ability is, of course, desirable. The most effective disciplinarian is the teacher who *appears* not to have any discipline problems. The word *appears* is emphasized because actually all teachers experience discipline problems. The teacher who appears immune to discipline problems has learned to plan in advance to avoid problems, and to recognize potential problems early in their development and nip them in the bud. As a teacher, you will better use your time if you exert most of your energy toward the prevention of discipline problems rather than toward their solutions.

Discipline Implies Order and Control

Discipline does not mean punishment, nor does it always mean restraint. In teaching, discipline implies *order* and *control*. Although some may tend to think of a disciplined class as a quiet one, the degree of order and control in the classroom is not necessarily related to the degree of stillness or the noise level. Order simply means that the class is moving toward certain goals along a path mutually clear to both teacher and students. Control means that the teacher can immediately gain the attention of the class. Therefore, a well-disciplined class is one in which students are working toward specific goals under the leadership and with the assistance of the teacher.

Discipline Is Essential for Maximum Learning

The degree of discipline varies from one teacher to another and from one class to another. Some groups of students are much more boisterous and difficult to control than are others. However, if you are to provide the atmosphere for optimum learning, you must have the class well organized. You can begin by helping the students understand what it is that they are trying to accomplish and then helping them to do it. This involves more than telling; it often requires demonstrating the assignment so each student can see how it is to be done. This provides the order, but how about the control?

PLANNING TO AVOID PROBLEMS

Getting Off to a Good Start

Control is best achieved by cooperation between teacher and students; however, it is your responsibility as teacher to control from the first minute — before a cooperative arrangement can be discussed. Begin each year by being especially alert to the needs and desires of students. In this context *needs* refers not so much to present whims, but to serious needs of the present and future. Some of these may be the adolescent's social needs and needs for approval, success, and independence. As the students show that they can handle freedom, you can gradually remove restrictions. Each time you feel that the class has progressed beyond the need for a rule, you can suggest to them that it be removed. This lets them know that you are not being inconsistent with the rules, but that the class has earned the prerogative of canceling the rule if they so wish.

Although it is true that it is easier for the firm teacher to become less strict than for the casual teacher to become more strict, there is danger in beginning the year with too many rules: only essential rules and restrictions should be used.

In the 1950s a university laboratory school principal issued a rule that all boys must wear belts. This was a reaction to the jeans which were worn low on the hips so that the navel would show through the shirt tails, which were often unbuttoned. The boys noticed that the principal did not define "belt." The rule was obeyed. Boys wore short ropes through belt loops, they wore ropes eight feet long (dragging on the floor), they wore string belts, they wore leather belts, but belts they did wear. The principal was also a learner. The rule was rescinded in prompt fashion.

Teachers, like principals, make mistakes. Too many discipline rules, unnecessary rules, and unenforceable rules are among the most common mistakes made by teachers.

Using Enthusiasm

The best single diversion from behavior problems is a well-planned and well-executed lesson that involves all students, especially if the teacher shows enthusiasm for the subject. The lesson will be even more successful if the objectives are clear and if frequent feedback is given to show students how well they are progressing.

Using Names

The teacher who knows a student's name has more influence over that student than he has over unknown students — if he uses the name appropriately. For example, suppose that you are teaching a lesson the first day of the school year and a boy sitting in the back row begins to disrupt the attention of others while you are talking. It would be most awkward to have to stop and count the seats from either side of the room in order to direct your reprimand to the right person. To say, "You in the red and black striped shirt" would provide him with the attention of the entire class and could lead to a repetition of this disruption to regain that attention. To reprimand without designating the individual would be likely to alienate other class members.

Suppose that you knew the boy's name and, as you were presenting the lesson, you dropped his name in the middle of a sentence without even looking toward him and without breaking the pace of the lesson. Such action on your part tells him and the rest of the class that you are very much aware of his attempts to disrupt the class but that the lesson is too imporant to be impeded by anyone's selfish attempt to gain attention.

Helping Students Learn Self-Respect

Students who perceive themselves as troublemakers make trouble. Those who perceive themselves as good students or good guys are obligated to live up to this image. Avoid saying and doing things that tend to downgrade students, and take any opportunity to say and do things that will improve the student's self-image.

Avoiding Threat

Some teachers threaten groups of students and individuals; they do not realize that a threatened person is challenged to misbehave. It is not uncommon for a teacher to remark, "All right, class, I am not going to tell you again to be quiet," implying "I can make you wish you had behaved." Such a statement usually promotes misbehavior. Avoid threats that you never intend to carry out; better yet, avoid threats completely.

Avoiding Public Reprimand

Any serious problem that you have with an individual student should be dealt with privately. To reprimand a student in the presence of his peers is to damage his peer relationships, which are important to people of all ages. It is to force him to either rebut or concede. If he rebuts, his relationship with the teacher is damaged. If he concedes, he loses face with his peers. This unfair technique is also a threat to the rest of the class. Feeling that they could receive the same treatment, they may lose confidence in the teacher.

Avoiding Ridicule

When a student misbehaves, you should try to change his future behavioral patterns. That is all. You should never ridicule a student, whether in public or in private. Ridicule is not aimed at correcting behavior but is directed at the person.

COPING WITH PROBLEMS

Be Prepared to Handle Problems When They Do Develop

Earlier in the chapter we found that the best way to avoid problems in the classroom is to be prepared each day and to have interesting experiences planned for each class. However, even the most effective teachers can experience discipline problems, so let's think about the time when a discipline problem might develop in your class. What will you do?

Always Ask Yourself, Why?

No pupil wants to misbehave. Why, then, do they misbehave? All behavior is caused or purposive.[6] Classical psychologists explain that all behavior is a reaction to a stimulus: that is, everything we do is done in reaction to other people, or other things. Phenomenal psychologists believe that every misbehavior is an expression of a need; therefore, each time a student misbehaves, we should ask ourselves, "What need is he trying to satisfy?"

To ask the misbehaving student what his need is would not help, since he probably does not know. The need may be for more attention, or it may be for the approval of his peers if he does not get adequate reinforcement from his family and his teachers. If a person's behavior is hostile, he may be trying to remove aggressions because of some felt injustice. Sometimes the need is indistinguishable and we are unable to identify the cause of the behavior. The creative teacher is often able to provide acceptable means for students to express themselves.

When a student causes serious disruptions, study his cumulative record and discuss the problem with the school counselor. By learning more about the student, you may get ideas about how to work more effectively with him. Become more tolerant of the student if he attempts to alter his behavior.

---

[6] George H. Thompson, "Discipline and the High School Teacher," *Education Digest* 42 (October 1976): 20–22.

Because misbehavior is often a means of securing attention or of expressing discontent, the person who misbehaves may wish to create a scene. She may seek a confrontation with the person who could draw the most attention to the disruption, the teacher. Sometimes you may be tempted to engage in emotional disputes with students. Remember, though, that the emotional person does not seek reasonable or rational answers; instead, she seeks a way to justify her behavior. Any argument with her will only result in her becoming more defensive. You may be able to help a student realize her misbehavior and provide her with an opportunity to express her opinions, but you can do this only after she has calmed down and become less emotional.

The Private Talk

To avoid a serious confrontation does not mean that you should ignore the student. Ask the student to refrain from the undesirable behavior, otherwise, he and other class members may assume that the teacher does not really care if the rule is broken. The difference between noting a disruption and engaging in a confrontation lies in the manner in which the action is taken, which should be as quietly and uneventfully as possible. If the student responds negatively, she should be ignored. If she continues to disrupt the class, she should be asked to leave the room and wait outside until the end of the period when you are free to arrange for a private talk.

If a circumstance develops in which you must ask a student to leave the

classroom, do not permit him to reenter until you have had a private talk with him. During the private talk you should avoid becoming emotionally involved. You can express disappointment with the student's behavior, but make certain that the student does not interpret this as a dislike for him as a person.

In an extreme case, where the student continues to misbehave after the private talk, you should call for the principal's assistance. Your mission, after all, is to provide a classroom environment conducive to learning, and you cannot afford to allow one student to continue disrupting it.

Firmness and Consistency

All teachers should assert themselves. It is imperative that whatever tactics you choose to maintain discipline be used consistently with all students from one day to another.

The Role of Humor

Firmness does not imply harshness and constant sternness. If you are firm but calm, your students will appreciate it and your health will be better.[7] When the teacher's definition of the situation prevails, it is usually because of his or her good judgment and use of humor.[8]

One educator has identified twelve types of teacher behaviors which he relates to maladjusted personality structure. These include being unfair, rigid, over-reactive, sarcastic, threatening, rejecting, excessively punishing, unfriendly, unsympathetic, dictatorial, irritable, and guilt-inducing.[9] If you choose to teach, try to enjoy each day of it.

MODELS FOR DISCIPLINE

The techniques presented thus far in this chapter should not be used in isolation but should be incorporated into an overall consistent pattern. Several models showing examples of such structured approaches to discipline are available. In her book *Classroom Discipline* Laurel Tanner introduces the following models.

1. Training model
2. Behavior modification model
3. Psychodynamic model

---

[7] Wilburn Elrod, "Don't Get Tangled in Discipline Problems," *Music Educator's Journal* 63 (December 1976): 47–50.

[8] Robert G. Wegmann, "Classroom Discipline: A Negotiable Item," *Today's Education* 651 (Spring 1976): 92–93.

[9] S. Brodbelt, "Teachers' Mental Health: Whose Responsibility?" *Phi Delta Kappan* (December 1973): 268–69.

4. Group dynamics model
5. Personal-social growth model [10]

Training Model

Discipline is always concerned with regulating or changing behavior. This may be achieved either externally or internally. This is to say that the change can be brought on through the use of external stimuli, or it can result from the subject's own purposive behavior. The training model is concerned wholly with the former category, since any training program for classroom behavior is almost certain to result from the teacher's efforts, rather than the students'.

Although the effectiveness of training has been demonstrated by policemen, soldiers, and firemen (to name only a few professions), who must learn to respond immediately and automatically to certain cues, most educators feel that this model is less desirable than the others for use with high school students. Their attitude is understandable, since the purpose of schooling is to prepare students to think for themselves rather than always responding to the desires or demands of others.

Admittedly, even in the high school classroom, some degree of training is helpful. For example, students learn automatically to stop talking when the class is being addressed, to remain seated when they complete an assignment, or to raise their hands when they wish to have the floor. Most of these patterns, though, are holdovers from the earlier grades. High school discipline programs should not overemphasize or overuse the training model.

Behavior Modification Model

Like the training model, behavior modification depends on external stimuli to effect the desired changes in behavior. But, unlike the training model — which requires no thought of its subjects, just automatic responses — behavior modification does depend on the students to change their behavior in order to receive definite rewards.

Neither of these first two models requires students to think through their behavior at a very high level; instead, the subjects are conditioned to behave as the teacher wishes them to behave. Still, there is no denying that behavior modification strategies can and do work at the high school level. As discussed in Chapter 5, behavior modification programs have been known to reduce the amount of inappropriate behavior in secondary classrooms by as much as 75 percent.[11] This method is used extensively with mentally and emotionally handicapped students.

---

[10] Laurel N. Tanner, *Classroom Discipline for Effective Teaching and Learning* (Holt, Rinehart and Winston, 1978), p. 6.

[11] G. L. Sapp et al., "Classroom Management and Student Involvement," *High School Journal* 56 (March 1973): 276–83.

Psychodynamic Model

Unlike the training model and the behavior modification model, the psychodynamic model requires the teacher to know and understand each student. As an outgrowth of Freudian psychology, this model is based on the belief that such knowledge and understanding of the student's behavior will lead to improving that behavior. It is more advanced than the previous models in that it involves a search for the cause of misbehavior. But some educators are critical of this model because it stops at this point without offering suggestions for correcting the behavior.

Group Dynamics Model

This model recognizes the importance of social interactions and social pressures on students. Rather than focusing on an individual student in isolation, it looks at the individual in relation to the total group behavior. The focus is on the teacher, and the goal is to design good working conditions for the total group.

This model differs further from the previously discussed models in that it ties discipline to instruction. To avoid (or in response to) a behavior problem, the teacher would design a learning activity to divert students' attention from the problem toward learning the lesson at hand. The utilization of this model requires an awareness of student behavior to the degree that problems can be "nipped in the bud" as soon as they begin to develop.

Like the psychodynamics model, this model recognizes that learning is a group activity, but it goes one important step further. Whereas the psychodynamics model depends solely on the teacher's understanding the students, this

model requires the teacher to take action; in this sense it is far more practical.

Personal-Social Growth Model

Contemporary educators recognize that merely being able to regulate student behavior and suppress undesirable behavior is not enough. The title of this chapter reflects this concern. Ultimately students must learn to discipline themselves, to manage their own behavior. This requires experience, which means that you, the teacher, must be willing to share your power and responsibility for discipline with your students. Indeed, the students must feel that they are in control. They must also understand the purpose(s) behind desired behavioral patterns. Ideally, they should see the desired goals of the class and choose the ways they are to behave in order to attain these goals.

The order of the models discussed here reflects the chronological pattern of metamorphosis of discipline in American education. At one time the school assumed total authority to define good discipline. As one educator explains, "with evangelic fervor, (in the past) teachers have taught, indoctrinated, and compelled students to who and what they were to comply with and become the ideal model that the school mystically judged as being desirable." [12]

Granted, today good discipline is not considered synonymous with total blind conformity. Students are involved in deciding the type of discipline best for doing the job in their particular setting. Plymouth Junior High School's program for discipline is reflective of many current programs. It strives to (1) put the responsibility on the student whenever possible, (2) be consistent but flexible in enforcing the basic rules, and (3) find alternatives for classroom activities, rewards, and consequences so the student does not force himself into a corner.[13]

A school in Houston, Texas, developed a disciplinary system that reduced the frequency of corporal punishment to 7 percent and suspensions to 20 percent.[14] The program's strategies were to provide an atmosphere of personalness, to assist students with clarifying their values, to provide a crisis intervention center for students with serious problems, and to provide an ever-changing set of clear objectives relating to real-life needs of students.

One reason that schools are turning to less authoritative means for disciplining is because today teachers realize that power does not bring student cooperation; on the contrary, it stimulates more resistance. A second reason (and equally important) is that it would be inconsistent to use force. The end sought by education is to produce students who approach the challenges of life courageously because they are able to relate with others, are resourceful in problem solving, and are responsible in their behavior.[15]

---

[12] J. Merrill Hansen, "Discipline: A Whole New Bag," *The High School Journal* 57 (February 1974): 172–81.

[13] Judy Shook, "Alternatives for Management of Disruptive Classroom Behaviors," *School and Community* 61 (May 1975): 28–29.

[14] Stanley G. Sanders and Janis S. Yarbrough, "Achieving a Learning Environment with Order," *The Clearing House* 50 (November 1976): 100–2.

[15] Don Dinkmeyer and Don Dinkmeyer, Jr., "Logical Consequences: A Key to the Reduction of Disciplinary Problems," *Phi Delta Kappan* 57 (June 1976): 664–66.

SUMMARY

Most beginning teachers approach their careers with considerable concern and reservation because they question their ability to control discipline problems that may arise. A true concern for this responsibility is warranted, since the regulation of student behavior is a part of every teacher's role.

However, once they have taught a few days, most teachers find that they have worried excessively and that, indeed, they are able to cope with most problems, so that major catastrophes are prevented. As a new teacher you should spend your time, not in worrying about handling catastrophes (which rarely develop), but in planning to prevent problems. You should enter the classroom each day with a planned lesson that will involve all students in tasks that have specific, clear-cut goals.

Many of the comments at the beginning of the chapter tend to paint a very bad picture of today's student and a most dismal picture of teaching. Unfortunately, many teachers set themselves up as undesirable models and actually provoke misbehavior, intentionally or otherwise. A Florida teacher, while returning from a field trip, commands two disruptive students to get off the bus in the Everglades twelve miles from the nearest house. A Minnesota teacher sends two boys home for misbehaving in class; hours later they are found frozen on the front porch of one of their homes. Apparently, the teacher did not think of phoning to see if their parents were at home.

Today's students want teachers who are just the opposite of this image. The U.S. Marines' advertisement reads, "We Need a Few Good Men." Today's schools need more good teachers who view their roles positively — teachers who are willing to assert themselves when necessary, yet willing to appreciate the students' perspective.

EXPERIENCES

This chapter has acknowledged the fact that discipline is a problem in our schools and has emphasized teachers' responsibility for disciplining their students. But the ultimate purpose of the chapter is to help you develop your own ability to discipline your future students. The following experiences show some of the real dilemmas in which contemporary teachers often find themselves. As you read each experience, you may wish to imagine yourself in the particular teacher's situation and try to decide how you would handle it.

Experience 1:   A Principal Has Too Many Discipline Problems

Middletown School was divided into a junior and senior high with the lower grades in one building, the upper grades in another, and the principal's office midway between in a breezeway connecting the two buildings. The windows in Jan's classroom faced the breezeway.

She had taught for only a few weeks at Middletown. Each time that a discipline problem developed, she immediately referred the offender to the principal's office. Jan was amused one day to see one of the other teachers leading a student to the principal's office. Later that day she silently chuckled to see a replay of the event. Thereafter Jan began counting the number of teachers who briskly marched offenders to the principal's office. The record for one day was nine trips. The record for one teacher in one day was three trips.

It gradually occurred to Jan that this principal was spending a major part of her time disciplining the students of a few teachers who could not or would not assume this responsibility. She made a resolution to handle all future discipline problems herself, except, of course, in some rare emergency.

▶ *Questions and Discussion*

1. *How are the students' impressions of a teacher affected when she takes a discipline problem to the principal?*
   The first time this occurs, it may go virtually unnoticed by the students. If it is repeated again and again, however, the students will soon realize that this teacher is weak and unable to handle her problems; troubles in this teacher's class will increase.

   Even the best-behaved students may lose respect for this teacher because this obvious weakness may suggest to them that she is weak in other areas, such as her knowledge of the subject that she is teaching.

2. *Does the number of a teacher's discipline problems reflect the quality of her teaching?*
   Yes. The teacher who has planned an interesting lesson involving the students will have fewer discipline problems than the teacher who is dull, boring, and poorly prepared.

Experience 2: A First Phone Call from a Parent

Don Harrader was a quiet, pleasant member of John's ninth-grade science class. In fact, it was hard for John to think of Don as a member of the class because he was very withdrawn. Don was making above-average grades until a unit on simple machines began. He received an *F* at the end of the unit when an exam was administered. When John talked to Don about the grade, he replied that he just did not care for that part of the course.

The next day John was having lunch when the message arrived that Mr. Harrader had called and asked that he call back. He remembered Don's recent decline in grades and suspected this was why his father had called. John left the lunchroom and went directly to a phone.

John's prediction of the purpose of the call was correct: Mr. Harrader immediately asked why Don had made the *F* in John's class. Trying to be objective and honest in his answer, John answered that Don claimed to have no interest in simple machines; and Don's father replied, "I understand, but I want to know if Don has been misbehaving in class." John assured him that the answer was no and the conversation ended.

In the days following the phone call, John thought about Don, his relationship with his father, and his lack of relationships with his peers.

One weekend John had parked by the school tennis courts and was watching some matches when Don walked up. He asked if John played tennis and if he would play a set with him. John agreed, and there was never a happier person. He certainly was not the same boy that John saw each day in science class.

From that day on, John had no trouble stimulating his interest in class. Once, when Don found that his teacher was interested in rocks, he made a collection and brought it to share with the rest of the class. A simple phone call had stimulated his interest in Don. An unplanned tennis match had removed Don's apathy. Together these two events had indirectly resulted in motivating a quiet, shy student.

▶ *Questions and Discussion*

1. *If an angry parent phones, how should the teacher respond?*
   The teacher must try to refrain from showing his emotions, so that the parent can see the teacher's objectivity regarding the student. This is the best method for showing the irate parent that he is the one who is being unreasonable.

   Secondly, the teacher must be honest with the parent. If the student is failing to do satisfactory work, the teacher must say so. Frankness and honesty must prevail before the teacher and parent can begin working together to motivate the pupil, and it is the teacher who must initiate it.

2. *Parental neglect is the cause of many discipline problems at school. How can the teacher provide attention for the neglected child?*
   Undoubtedly you can think of many ways to show interest in a pupil who is neglected at home. Most students have strong interest areas, although they may never reveal them in the classroom. The teacher can often identify a student's interests by observing him outside the classroom during the student's leisure time. Once the teacher shows concern for the student's nonscholastic activities, the student may become inclined to devote more attention to the teacher in class and more attention to the assignments that the teacher gives.

Experience 3:   A Student Conquers Her Parents

School had been in session for only two weeks when we had the first P.T.A. meeting of the year. Mrs. Snyder came by and told me, "Our daughter, Sandy, is in your class. Do what you can with her. Just because we have little control of her certainly doesn't mean that we approve of her misbehavior. Do what you can to discipline her. If it means beating her, that's O.K., too." I shuddered at the thought because I knew that this parent actually meant what she said.

During this most unusual conversation, my mind kept flashing back to the classroom. The only Sandy I could remember was an unusually neat and attractive girl — I remembered looking at her the first day and thinking that she might become one of the top students in the class.

I believe that one of the greatest values of P.T.A. meetings is that they stimulate teachers to become personally interested in their students. This meeting was typical in that respect, for I made a direct attempt to pursue the subject. I found out that Sandy was indeed the neat, attractive, pleasant girl in my eighth-grade class; but it soon became obvious that she was not living up to my hopes for her. She was dating juniors and seniors, staying out until midnight during the week, and never completing her homework assignment if she even attempted it.

I still do not understand how Sandy conquered her parents and took away all their control; but, by admitting to her that they could no longer control her, they made it impossible for her teachers to stimulate her to learn. A person's behavioral patterns do not change much when she walks into a classroom. It is not realistic for parents to expect the teacher to make dramatic progress with a pupil at school when they do not make any progress with her at home. Thankfully, there is always a chance that together parents and teachers can stimulate the student to change her behavioral patterns and direct her energy toward academic achievement — but only if the parents and teacher openly discuss the student's problem.

Although Mrs. Snyder had made the mistake of giving up, she was closer to helping Sandy than she knew because she had admitted to herself that Sandy needed help, rather than pretending that her child was making progress.

I began to watch Sandy each day. When she began to goof off, I was there to offer help. Sandy soon learned that, unlike her parents, I expected quality work from her — in fact, I insisted on it. By my doing so, Sandy became more responsible. By the end of the year she was enjoying her assignments in this class. Her parents soon learned that punishment, which would not help anyway, was not necessary.

► *Questions and Discussion*

1. *Should you defend a student against her parents if they are obviously mistreating her?*
   Recognizing and respecting the close ties between the parent and the student, you must not do anything that will destroy whatever positive feelings an apparently unconcerned parent has for his child. Instead,

try to improve the situation by helping the parent and child learn to respect each other. Avoid downgrading either the student or the parent in the presence of the other.

If the conditions are really serious, you can consult the school counselor for advice and assistance.

2. *What precautions can you take against losing control of an unrestrained student like Sandy?*
Your degree of control over students like Sandy is determined during the first few class periods. Begin by showing a keen interest and a determination to help all students — even those who appear hopelessly unmanageable. Above all, let them know that you expect the highest quality of work that each student can provide, along with constant improvement from day to day.

Experience 4: Poor Management Results in a Near Catastrophe

Of the students in my five sections of eighth-grade science, Tim Walker was among the most easygoing, quiet, and pleasant. Tim was a model student; that is why I was surprised when his accident occurred.

I had stepped outside the room to aid in patrolling the hallway traffic during the changing of periods. Tim and another boy were the first students to enter the classroom. Because they were alone for a minute before the rest of the class arrived, they began playing around. Without their understanding how it happened, Tim tripped. As he fell, he grabbed for a desk, and one of his fingers caught in the corner of the metal desk frame. The finger was almost entirely cut off.

Tim was rushed to a hospital where the finger was sewn back in place. At the end of the school year when I last saw Tim, the doctors had advised him that the finger had apparently been saved and could be rehabilitated. This was a close call for Tim and for me. I was excused because I had been responsible for hall duty at the time of the accident, but for weeks I shuddered when I thought of the many times I had left my room for brief intervals. I am certain that since this accident occurred, I have become less permissive of roughhousing in my classroom.

▶ *Questions and Discussion*

1. *Should you ever leave a student in charge of a class?*
Even if you have placed a student in charge, you are responsible and legally liable for the welfare of every student in your classroom when you go out. Do not leave a student in charge unless you are willing to accept the legal blame and pay the penalty for whatever may happen during your absence.

2. *If a parent comes to your room to talk to you while your class is in session, what should you do?*
Do not leave the room to go elsewhere and talk to him. Do not discuss any subject with him in the classroom that requires some amount

of time or pertains to a student. Tell him you are sorry that you cannot talk now and make an appointment to see him during your next planning period.

3. *What are your legal responsibilities for being in the classroom at specified times?*

As a teacher you are responsible for the safety of students in your classroom at all times that you are scheduled to be there. Exception is made, however, whenever an emergency requires you to leave your room; for example, if the principal calls for you or if you have to take a student to the principal's office for discipline.

Experience 5:   A Real Pro Goes into Action

Randy Graham, a bright and witty student, was especially troublesome in Mr. Hall's junior history class. One day, to show the spirit of a certain age, Mr. Hall read a few verses of poetry, the students following along in their books. At the end of the first verse Randy applauded Mr. Hall. Because Mr. Hall was large, solemn, and stern looking, the other class members were shocked.

Looking directly at Randy, Mr. Hall said very solemnly, "Thank you, Mr. Graham," and continued his reading. Randy never again misbehaved in that class.

▶ *Questions and Discussion*

1. *Should a teacher ever attempt to control misbehavior by applying humor to the event, as did Mr. Hall?*

Humor is always appreciated by adolescents but it must be used judiciously in the classroom. The teacher will find that it can backfire unless he retains a degree of seriousness, even when using humor.

2. *If Randy had caused trouble later during the hour, should Mr. Hall again have used humor?*

One of the greatest dangers of humor in the classroom is its overuse. If Mr. Hall had continued responding humorously, Randy could have started a game that many students might quickly learn to prefer over the studying of history.

Experience 6:   An Experiment with Oral Reprimand

When I accepted my first teaching position, my homeroom consisted of forty-seven seventh graders, who were also my first period math class. There were so many rows that they seemed to merge at the back of the room. From my desk I could see only about two-thirds of the faces at any time. Disruptions were common in the hidden areas of the back rows. I talked with the class about it, but each day seemed a little worse than the day before. I did not want to use derogatory comments, but finally it seemed that I had run out of options.

When two boys in the back row kept jabbing at each other, I asked them to come with me out into the hall. As we left the room, I noticed that the other class members were silent. They could hear the reprimanding remarks I directed to each boy. The boys were embarrassed, and there were no more disturbances for the rest of the week. During the following week when things again appeared to be getting out of hand, I repeated the verbal reprimand. As we left the room this time, the class was not silent, and several giggles could be heard.

During my second month I was reprimanding one student or another almost every day. As I became more and more firm, it was difficult to believe that the corrective measures were having so little effect in curbing the problems. On the contrary, my reprimands seemed to be rapidly promoting more problems. I was baffled.

I vowed to myself to stop using reprimands. Thereafter, each time a problem developed, I merely stopped the lesson, walked over near the troubled area, and silently, without smiling, stared for a moment, then continued with the lesson. The effect was tremendous. I kept verbal reprimands to a minimum because the few positive results were surely outweighed by the trouble that they caused me.

► *Questions and Discussion*

1. *When reprimand or verbal attack is used, what effect does it have on the rest of the class?*
   The use of verbal reprimand almost always has a damaging effect on the teacher's rapport with those students who are not receiving the reprimand. The teacher should remember that a learning environment must be appealing, free from threat and resentment. Verbal reprimand can destroy that kind of atmosphere because it introduces fear and resentment.

2. *Why was verbal reprimand more effective at first than it was later on?*
   A methodology that is directed only toward restraining or penalizing a student rather than toward helping him always becomes less effective as it is repeated. Verbal reprimand can restrain students only so long as it frightens them. At first they were afraid of the reprimand because it was unfamiliar to them; but as they experienced the behavior again and again, they became less afraid of it, and it ceased to be effective.

3. *Can the teacher make verbal reprimand more effective by being increasingly stern?*
   This is very doubtful since any degree of sternness that is familiar to students fails to intimidate them. Also, increasing sternness constitutes a challenge to the student to misbehave even more. In a sense, the teacher is saying that if the previous verbal punishment was not sufficient, the teacher is capable of conquering the students by becoming sterner. Therefore, students are challenged to continue misbehaving to test the teacher's assertion.

According to the Department of Health, Education and Welfare, one student in five exhibits behavior that can be classified as excessive and a cause for concern. You may envision other discipline problems to which this chapter has not attended. The following activities are included to help you further deal with these concerns.

1. From listening to comments of older adults or through the media, you have undoubtedly heard or read statements about school discipline with which you do not agree. Explain one way in which your idea of how students should behave differs with the ideas of your elders.
2. Describe a problem that the schools in your community are currently facing. Explain how you would work to help eliminate that problem if you were teaching in a local school.
3. Develop a discipline strategy using that strength for working with adolescents that you identified in Chapter 1.
4. What would you do if a student became enraged and refused to be quiet? The other students are waiting to see your reaction. How will you handle this situation?

SUGGESTED READINGS

ELROD, WILBURN. "Don't Get Tangled in Discipline Problems." *Music Educator's Journal* 63 (December 1976): 47–50.

GALLUP, GEORGE H. "The Eleventh Annual Gallup Poll of the Public's Attitudes Toward the Public Schools." *Phi Delta Kappan* 61 (September 1979): 33–45.

HANSEN, J. MERRILL. "Discipline: A Whole New Bag." *The High School Journal* 57 (February 1974): 172–81.

HELGE, ERICH E. "Good Discipline: Yours for the Asking." *Lutheran Education* 113 (March–April 1978): 181–85.

HENSON, KENNETH T. "A New Concept of Discipline." *The Clearing House* 41 (October 1977): 89–91.

JESSUP, MICHAEL H., and KILEY, MARGARET A. *Discipline: Positive Attitudes for Learning.* Englewood Cliffs, N.J.: Prentice-Hall, 1971.

MADSEN, CHARLES H., JR., and MADSEN, CLIFFORD K. *Teaching/Discipline.* 2d ed. Boston: Allyn and Bacon, 1974.

THOMPSON, GEORGE H. "Discipline and the High School Teacher." *Education Digest* 42 (October 1976): 20–22.

WEGMANN, ROBERT G. "Classroom Discipline: A Negotiable Item." *Today's Education* 65 (Spring 1976): 92–93.

WHITESIDE, MARILYN. "School Discipline: The Ongoing Crisis." *The Clearing House* 49 (December 1975): 160–62.

WILDE, J. W., and SUMMERS, P. "Teaching Disruptive Adolescents: A Game Worth Winning." *Phi Delta Kappan* 59 (January 1978): 342–43.

YOUNG, JERRY W. "Maintaining Classroom Control." *School and Community* 61 (March 1975): 13.

Classroom Management

OBJECTIVES

When you complete this chapter, you should be able to:
1. Explain the importance of personalizing to the management of students.
2. Name several variables that teachers must manage during each lesson.
3. Describe how student activities should be incorporated into each lesson.
4. Discuss at least two important responsibilities that teachers have in managing equipment.
5. Design a management system that teachers can use to stretch their time.
6. List two techniques for showing students that you are impartial.
7. Compare the role of today's teachers with that of their predecessors.
8. Explain the importance of teacher attitude toward discipline and describe a desirable attitude.

In today's society most professionals find themselves with some responsibility for managing things and people. Teachers, too, are professionals who must manage their operations. They have responsibilities for managing students, lessons, learning activities, equipment, materials, time, and space.

As is shown in Figure 4.1, the teacher's management responsibilities are multifaceted. They can be grouped into two categories: instructional and noninstructional, yet the groups overlap. Remember that good management is indispensable not only to the effectiveness of a good lesson but also when the lesson stops: your management responsibilities continue, since you provide leadership for students' emotional, social, and moral growth as well as their intellectual growth.

TEACHER RESPONSIBILITIES

Students

Too frequently the concept of the teacher as a manager focuses only on student behavior, actually, misbehavior; and (as mentioned in Chapter 3) this leads

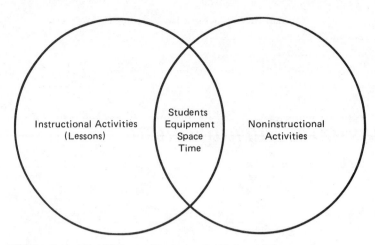

Figure 4.1   Variables in Classroom Management

to the equating of classroom management and discipline. We do not minimize the importance of the teacher's role as disciplinarian when we point out that discipline is only one management responsibility that teachers have. Even there, teachers' roles encompass more than merely trying to see that students behave. It is also their responsibility to see that students cooperate with each other on productive tasks and that they do not abuse or neglect other class-mates.

Lessons

Beginning teachers are the first to recognize the significance of being able to manage their lessons. First, they must learn to plan and deliver the lesson so that it fills the period. If it involves student activities (and all lessons should), these activities should be pursued at the time when they will result in the most learning. If there are laboratory assignments or if the student activities them-selves are time-critical, effective management is even more important. Courses that require special dress — such as physical education, science labs, or dra-matics — require the teacher to manage the lesson within the class period but leaving time for the students to get dressed, clean up, and get things ready for the incoming group.

Equipment

The beginning teacher, often surprised to find teachers so possessive of depart-mental equipment, does not always realize that those teachers may have spent hundreds of hours throughout the years on activities to raise money to pur-chase that equipment.

Recent economic restrictions made upon teachers have made them even more sensitive to their responsibility in seeing that school property is not destroyed. All teachers have some responsibility for protecting their classroom equipment from unnecessary abuse. Those who have some audio-visual items (such as black-out curtains and projection screens, which are easily damaged) know that these will be in jeopardy if the teachers do not assume some responsibility for their protection.

In addition to being responsible for helping protect the school's equipment, the teacher must also be able to utilize the equipment toward productive ends. With limited resources today, it seems shameful for a teacher to have equipment and not know how to use it.

Programs

While we tend to think that teachers' whole work and responsibilities are contained in their classrooms, most secondary teachers are also involved in programs reaching beyond their classrooms, such as the National Education Association or parent-teacher organizations and cocurricular activities. Teacher management responsibilities with such programs may range from very little to almost total responsibility; for example, the teacher who sponsors a club must see that all of the club's activities are acceptable to school policy.

Other programs — less formal but just as real — demand management skills. When planning conferences with students and/or parents, the teacher is re-

sponsible for setting the time, contacting the participants, and coordinating the meetings. These management skills are no different from those required of a business executive, since success with the conferences depends on effective planning, organizing, and coordinating.

In still other ways the teacher's need for management skills is increasing. Many secondary school teachers seek out professionals or experts to speak to their students. Governmental guidelines, too, call for management skills; for example, Public Law 94-142 requires teachers to plan Individualized Education Programs for handicapped students. Each such program requires teacher planning, coordinating, and evaluating. The teacher is responsible for the entire process, from identifying students who need these programs to the evaluation of the program once it gets under way.

Auxiliary Personnel

Since education involves more than mere teaching and learning, today's teachers must work as members of a team that includes other teachers, counselors, administrators, and other educators who assist students in special ways. In fact, without cooperation from teachers the school's auxiliary services could hardly work at all; and it is the teacher who usually initiates the action by referring students to sources of help.

So, we see that teachers are indeed managers and their "classroom management" skills often have far-reaching effects. Any teacher who has faced an irate parent or who has been confronted by a desperate parent or student knows the importance of being able to manage situations.

PERSONALIZING

One effective approach you can take to management is that of personalizing the entire operation. This means that you will take every opportunity to relate to students in ways that show concern for their welfare and exhalts their dignity. If you know those with whom you work personally, you have a better chance of getting their cooperation.

The difference between students who perceive themselves as failures — and then go on to fail — and those who see themselves as successful students is often the same difference between a teacher who expects certain students to fail and one who looks for the best in each student. Research has shown repeatedly that a positive teacher attitude can and does affect student learning.

The instructor walking among students taking a test, whispered comments to different ones:

"Is *that* all you've done so far? Hurry — you're way behind."
"Please be more careful — you're not doing well at all."
"You're doing some very careless things."

In another group, matched by age, ability, and intelligence, the same instructor walked among other students taking the same test and whispered these comments:

"How well you're doing!"
"Look how many questions you've already answered correctly!"
"My, but you're smart!"

How would you estimate the performance of the two groups? Do you think that they ignored the teacher and that one group did as well as the other? Or perhaps those students receiving the negative comments worked harder and scored higher to prove to their teacher that they were more capable than he thought? Think about it for a moment and jot down your prediction before you read the results given in the next paragraph.

As a matter of fact, the behavior of these two groups is highly predictable, for these students responded to the experiment as have other groups when similar experiments were conducted. The difference in their performance was as follows: Although all of the students were equally able, the first students (those receiving the negative comments from their teacher) averaged 55 percent correct, while students receiving the positive comments averaged 85 percent correct.[1] This is just one example of numerous studies showing the effects of the teacher's attitude and behavior upon student behavior. There is concrete evidence that too much teacher disapproval actually increases classroom disruptions.[2] Likewise, there are studies showing that increased use of verbal and nonverbal reinforcement actually reduces problem behaviors.[3,4] When reporting these studies, one author concluded that "teachers who rely primarily on positive strategies are also the teachers who are most effective in managing their classrooms.[5]

For more than a decade our schools have stressed individualizing the educational process. The assumption is that individualized instruction will produce more learning, since individualizing enhances self-responsibility and thus self-motivation. We know for sure that students who are actively involved with the lesson are more likely to achieve than are those who sit passively while the teacher dominates the activities.

But, more recently, educators have become concerned that, though a step in

---

[1] Benjamin Fine, *Underachievers: How They Can Be Helped* (New York: E. P. Dutton, 1966).

[2] C. H. Madsen, Jr.; W. C. Becker; D. R. Thomas; L. Koser; and E. Plazer, "An Analysis of the Reinforcing Function of Sit Down Commands," in *Readings in Educational Psychology*, ed. R. K. Parker (Boston: Allyn and Bacon, 1968).

[3] A. E. Kazdin, and J. Klock, "The Effects of Nonverbal Teacher Approval on Student Attentive Behavior," *Journal of Applied Behavior Analysis* 6 (1973): 643–54.

[4] L. W. McAllister; J. G. Stachowia; D. M. Baer; and L. Conderman, "The Application of Operant Conditioning Techniques in a Secondary School Classroom," *Journal of Applied Behavior Analysis* 2 (1969): 277–85.

[5] James D. Long and Virginia H. Frye, *Making It Till Friday* (Princeton, N.J.: Princeton Book Company, 1977), p. 5.

the right direction, individualizing may not be sufficient. For today's schools are responsible for more than cognitive growth; they emphasize additional goals such as learning to accept change, developing positive self-concepts, learning to live less extravagantly and paying one's own way, and controlling the population growth. These goals will more likely be achieved through interactions with other people than by working alone; and the teacher has a major responsibility for arranging and supervising these interactions. But before teachers can expect to achieve open, clear communications among students, they must establish a climate in which each pupil will feel free to interact with the teacher. The attainment of the goals of much of the rest of this text such as discipline, motivation, and lesson planning depend upon good rapport. This chapter is devoted to examining techniques that the teacher can use to establish a positive personal rapport with each student.

TECHNIQUES FOR PERSONALIZING

Teacher Attitude

Basic to the more conspicuous, observable techniques for personalizing your teaching is your attitude toward yourself, your students, and your role as teacher. A recent study shows that school district superintendents consider the teacher's personality the single most important factor in successful teaching, more so than grade point average or academic background.[6] But how should you, a teacher, feel about yourself? The most important attitude you can have about yourself is one of self-confidence without feeling superior. Above all, a teacher cannot afford to act omniscient. All teachers err occasionally in matters of judgment and in the recall of facts, dates, and concepts. No teacher is a walking computer with the facts and answers to all possible questions. Students are not impressed with teachers who pretend to have no limitations; but, on the other hand, they will tire of hearing "I don't know" all day, every day. It will be best received when it is followed by "I'll find out," but *only* when the teacher does make a habit of reporting the correct answer at the next class. With a few very rare exceptions, you will be able to find the answers to student questions. The main requirement is effort. In the coming months and years, as your own library expands with professional books, journals, and newspaper articles relating to your subject, you will find answers quicker and easier. Do not turn questions into homework assignments; in the future, students will squelch their curiosity.

Of equal or more importance is your attitude toward your students. Today's students are rich with knowledge, much of which comes from outside the classroom. They are more widely traveled, see more public media, and assume more self-responsibility than yesterday's pupils. We must learn to respect them

---

[6] Frank S. Endicott, "Who Gets a Teaching Position in the Public School?" ASCUS (Madison, Wisc.: Webrafters, 1975), pp. 6–8.

for their knowledge and their more mature attitudes. We will be far ahead once we learn to *use* their knowledge and opinions, and their ability to retrieve information and to draw conclusions. They should not be perceived as a threat to the teacher, whose role is becoming less and less that of dispenser of knowledge and more and more a guide in the learning process. Mastery of the skills discussed later in this book will lift you out of defensive attitudes.

Finally, teachers must have correct attitudes toward their role and their profession. Granted, salary is important and teachers should work to improve salaries, but teachers who work only for financial rewards are likely to feel seriously underrewarded. But once you learn to enjoy interacting with and helping young people, you will find teaching to be highly rewarding. It can and should be fun. It is a challenge. Every day brings the unexpected. But, fortunately, young people enjoy themselves and they will make your classes enjoyable once you learn to plan, organize, relax, and yes, even smile.

Time for Students

A recent survey showed that the single teacher quality that secondary school students desire most is concern and time for their students.[7] Unfortunately, today's schedule is very demanding, and most teachers cannot find that extra

---

[7] Kenneth T. Henson, *Secondary Teaching: A Personal Approach* (Itasca, Ill.: F. E. Peacock, 1974), pp. 3–4.

time they wish they had for their students — especially if they have two hundred or more to accommodate each day. Budgeting your time to make it more efficient is one solution; for example, plan a few minutes into each lesson for students' questions. Always take time to answer a question, assuming, of course, that it is a serious one. Since some students are reluctant to raise questions in front of their peers, you should plan time in each day for students to come to you with any question or problem. Just a few minutes each afternoon will usually meet this need.

Most students want you to show interest in their nonacademic lives, too. One effective approach is a visit to the sports arena to watch students as they prepare for a game or match. Play a game of table tennis with a student who did not make the basketball team. Sit in on a jam session of the school band or a small group pop band and attend as many school activities as possible, including sports events, science fairs, and bake sales. Sponsor an interest group (extracurricular) club. You'll probably find yourself enjoying these activities more and more.

Finally, by keeping alert, you will come across many students outside the school in supermarkets, theaters, churches, restaurants, and almost anywhere you go. If you don't recall their names, don't worry; speak anyway. You'll most likely be introduced to family, date, or friends and will be remembered in a special way from that day on. Students enjoy seeing their teachers outside of school. Your image can probably improve from these informal associations.

Fairness

The same survey shows that running a close second to interest in the students is whether or not the teacher's reputation is one of a "fair" or "unfair." [8] Most teachers perceive themselves as fair, but students often pick up vibrations conflicting with this idea. Surely no teacher would purposely show favoritism to students; yet, without realizing, they often behave in ways suggesting that they have pets. For example, almost any classroom has a few highly capable students who volunteer answers to all questions. In the same room are a number of students who refuse to answer questions when called on, let alone ever volunteer an answer. Ironically, they will often feel that you are showing favorites if you let the first group answer too many questions, go to the board to work problems, or receive any type of constant attention. Therefore, it will behoove you to find ways of enticing the would-be-quiet, reserved students and the noisy students — who get involved in everything except the lesson — to share their ideas and opinions.

Success with each of these endeavors will come more readily once you really do become interested in each student as a student, an athlete, and a person.

---

[8] Ibid., p. 3.

All teachers should be aware of some of the advantages of grouping and the techniques needed for realizing these advantages. Some teachers use grouping to curb misbehavior, while others isolate students as a form of punishment for misbehaving. Such groupings are usually instantaneous, on-the-spot reactions that are done without much (if any) advanced planning or follow-up study. Its effects are apt to be equally moderate and temporary.

Teachers need to be able to use grouping in ways that will achieve certain desired goals. For the high school teacher, the most important goals are the improvement of the learning process and the socialization of students. Educators at the University of Chicago have reported that grouping students into small groups (2 or 3 peer groups) and presenting each group with appropriate instruction is the most effective means of increasing learning in the classroom. When done correctly, 95 percent of the students in high school today have been found capable of learning the expected knowledge and achieving the teacher's objectives. The power of groups to influence the development of social skills and attitudes seems obvious.

Before a teacher decides to use grouping, the purpose(s) or intended outcome(s) should be clearly understood to ensure worthwhile results.

A second area of understanding is essential prior to effective grouping. This involves the student. Effective grouping — grouping that achieves optimal results — requires matching the students with the learning processes. Of course this necessitates having knowledge about the students including their abilities, interests, needs, and relationships with their classmates. Such knowledge can be attained through numerous activities, such as examining the students' cumulative folders, talking to the students or their parents about their interests, and administering exams to measure their attitudes, interests, and abilities. According to one educator, "The purpose of the group should determine the group size" and "Groups should be business-like and organized but not rigid."[9]

Who Will Lead Each Group

Obviously the teacher cannot guide every group. Unfortunately teachers seldom (if ever) have enough aides to assign one to each group. Some groups will be able to direct and control themselves without a great deal of attention of the teacher. If students lead, the leadership may be designated or emergent. When groups operate without direct leadership from the teacher, it is essential that the teacher knows what is happening in each group and the rate of progress of its members. As indicated earlier, although the teacher may wish to lead one of the groups, the most effective group leaders have been found to

---

[9] Elizabeth Stimson, "Groping or Grouping: How to Reach the Individual," *Kappa Delta Pi Record* (December 1979): 51–53.

be someone other than the teacher.[10] Why? Because a different leader is bound to approach the topic from a different perspective. Small groups can further improve the instructional program by providing the teacher more time to observe student behavior and thus become better able to provide the types of stimuli that better fit the needs, interests, and abilities of the particular students.

Because the techniques for grouping to achieve social goals are discussed elsewhere in this book, they will be mentioned only briefly. Ideally such groups should be larger than the groups of two or three students established to facilitate instruction, and the members should be of similar characteristics. For example, by grouping the more assertive students together, they are forced by their fellow group members to give others a chance to talk and lead. By grouping the more reserved students together, they will be forced to assume leadership responsibilities. Similar benefits from grouping gifted students together and slower students together are obvious.

When you begin assigning groups, remember to keep the purpose of the group foremost in your mind. All decisions affecting each group should be based on its purpose. Will you make mistakes? Of course you will. Don't worry, though. Just remain alert to the behavior and needs within each group, and remain flexible enough to change the group's membership and activities. Good grouping requires close supervision at all times. This is no time to grade papers or fill out reports. When using groups the teacher must be able to orchestrate the behavior of all groups and see that continuous progress is being made toward the individual and group objectives. The most difficult job may be the sharing of leadership responsibility.

SUMMARY

Teaching requires a very complex set of management activities. Teachers must simultaneously manage lessons, learning activities, equipment, materials, time, space, and students. Each management responsibility can be placed into one of two groups: instructional or noninstructional. Teachers are responsible for student behavior *and* student learning. While students may behave without learning, optimal learning requires appropriate behavior.

An important influence on student behavior is the teacher's attitude. Classroom management requires a teacher who (1) relies primarily on positive strategies and (2) plans an effective lesson and directs student attention, not toward misbehavior, but toward the lesson.

Students want most from their teachers concern and understanding. Those teachers who are willing to admit their own limitations are respected more than those who try to appear omniscient. This, however, does not minimize the im-

---

[10] Benjamin Bloom et al., *Formative and Summative Evaluation* (New York: McGraw-Hill, 1970), pp. 48–49.

portance of planning good lessons and involving students in the planning of the
lessons and in the attainment of the objectives of the lesson.

69

Classroom Management

EXPERIENCES

This chapter on classroom management showed techniques for managing
students, equipment, time, space, and learning activities in order to improve the quality of learning. The following activities are included to
illustrate the complexity of the teacher's role in management and to provide you with an opportunity to strengthen your own management skills.

Experience 1:   Are the Expectations Realistic?

Jeff was an English honors student whose almost *A* average led to his
graduating magna cum laude. He approached his first teaching assignment with much self-assurance, worrying only that his students might not
have the capacity to benefit from all that he had to offer.

It's no wonder that Jeff was surprised and disappointed to learn that
some of his students were not capable of keeping up with their reading
assignments, and even more appalling was that many more did not care
whether they fell behind or not.

Jeff carefully analyzed the situation. His instruction had been well
planned, and the course objectives for each class were clear. His only
conclusion was that his students were dumb and lazy. Since his basic
educational psychology had taught him that it is nearly impossible to
raise one's I.Q. significantly, Jeff concluded that his only alternative was
to wake up the lazy students. Increasing the amount of material covered
in class, he simultaneously increased the length of the daily homework
assignments. To his further disappointment and bewilderment, neither of
these changes increased the quality or quantity of work by his students.

▶ *Question and Discussion*

1. *Why did Jeff's strategy fail?*
   Jeff's solutions were based on the assumption that his students were at
   fault. When additional demands are made in a positive, challenging
   manner, they may stimulate learning; but when the same demands are
   made in a threatening or punitive manner, they may have the exact
   opposite results. By making his students appear even more lazy and
   stupid, Jeff made himself look like a pitifully incompetent teacher.

Experience 2:   No Smiles until after Christmas

To say the least, Joni was very enthusiastic about her future career. She
was eager to meet her directing teacher and her new students. But this
eagerness was soon to be shattered by what Mrs. Grey called "the real

world." If Mrs. Grey had ever had one iota of enthusiasm toward teaching, which was hard to imagine, she had long since lost it. In fact it was rather obvious that she was "put out" by Joni's zeal. To her, teaching like any job was just that — no more, no less. Like any other job, teaching was a way of keeping the wolf from the door.

Joni was disappointed when Mrs. Grey informed her of the unwritten policy in her classes. She stated very frankly that she did not want any laughing in her classes until after Christmas. The rationale was that teachers who remain stern until after Christmas can afford to let up a little in January. "But," Mrs. Grey explained, "to relax the rules before Christmas would be suicide, for this is a downtown school, you know." Joni wondered, had she really been so naive? Had college filled her with a host of unrealistic expectations? Was she silly to think that teaching could actually be enjoyable?

▶ *Questions and Discussion*

1. *Should an urban teacher set forth such policy as the "No smiles until after Christmas"?*
   Certainly you will agree that this rule is, to say the least, "poor." If we only put ourselves in the roles of Mrs. Grey's students and try to understand how they might feel, surely we can see the fault with this rule.

2. *Is it unrealistic to expect teaching to be enjoyable?*
   If a teacher is going to teach, she should take responsibility for finding ways of making her classes enjoyable — even in urban schools. If she sets forth clear, daily objectives and plans participative lessons within the ability range of her students, Mrs. Grey can afford an occasional smile.

Experience 3:   There's No Time to Teach

Like most schools with enrollments exceeding two thousand, Dolphin High had a busy schedule. Operating on the quinmester plan, using a split program (two shifts daily), and offering numerous minicourses all added to the already hectic pace. The common daily expression in the teachers' lounge was "If I only had time to teach. . . ." And a beginning teacher could understand that complaint. Besides all the interruptions over the intercom system and student messengers, there were the many nonacademic clerical tasks assigned to each teacher.

▶ *Questions and Discussion*

1. *How should a beginning teacher at Dolphin High respond to the comment "If we only had time to teach"?*
   Actually, the best teachers — those who are the most committed to doing a superior job — are those who would seem most bothered by con-

tinuous interruptions and noninstructional tasks. But Dolphin High is not unique. Most contemporary secondary schools are so large and so complex that their operation requires making many interruptions and the assigning of clerical tasks to teachers.

Teachers at Dolphin High could approach this problem by analyzing their own behavior. They would design and apply their own observation systems to see where time was being wasted. Once they saw how much time they wasted, they would more likely increase the time spent on instruction.

2. *Why do teachers need time at school beyond their teaching hours?*
Given the hectic pace and pressures placed on today's teachers, you would probably agree that all teachers need at least one planning period each day — time to plan lessons and prepare materials such as transparencies, mimeographs, and equipment for demonstrations and experiments. Also, there should be time when students who have special problems can go to the teacher in private. Many students would never discuss a personal problem in the presence of their peers.

Experience 4: A New Teacher Meets New Standards

In his teacher education program Sterling Austin had heard of the new state-adopted minimum standards for graduation, but he had not really given them much thought. He was too busy taking care of his course work and, of course, his social life, to dwell on a remote topic. Had he only known about his coming involvement with these exams, he surely would have exerted more effort to learn all that he could about their origin and purposes and especially their implications for teachers.

Sterling was only a few weeks into his first teaching position when results of the first statewide administering of the minimum competency exams were returned. A major newspaper carried a two-page report headed, "State Eleventh Graders Fail New State Requirements." Besides stating that 38 percent of all eleventh graders in the state had failed these exams, the paper disclosed the average scores for eleventh graders in each school throughout the city. This brought the roof down on Sterling and his fellow teachers at Terreville High.

An emergency faculty meeting was called for that afternoon to discuss the "poor showing of Terreville High." Though the paper had been out only a few hours, rumors were already spreading throughout the school. Sterling heard in the lounge that all teachers whose classes scored below the national mean would have their tenure reviewed; and that those who did not hold a tenured position would not be retained for even another year unless remarkable improvement was shown in a second testing six months later. As the last bell rang, Sterling walked slowly toward the meeting area wondering if these rumors were really true and if teaching would be this "temporary" anywhere that he might go.

► *Questions and Discussion*

1. *Was this teacher's concern warranted?*

    It would be unrealistic to expect a teacher not to feel anxiety when confronted with such circumstances. Since none of the rumors had been confirmed, however, Sterling's degree of worry may have been unnecessary. Teachers usually have enough problems without adding on new ones before they have to. Schools are usually hotbeds for rumors, and teachers should learn to get the facts before worrying needlessly.

    Teachers should accept the fact that the state minimum competency exams are quickly becoming realities in most states. Every opportunity to learn about their direction, purposes, and administration should be seized.

2. *Should he try to defend himself and his students?*

    Certainly not. At least, not at this time. Rather than worry and make up excuses, this teacher should get together with his department chairperson to see how his class scores compared to other classes in the department. He might ask the chairperson for suggestions to improve the future performance of his students.

ACTIVITIES

As we have seen in the preceding pages, each teacher has important management responsibilities. Classroom management should be used not just to suppress negative behaviors but also to enhance learning. This chapter has suggested a systematic, positive approach to management. But the author realizes that each teacher's system will (and should) be different from those of fellow teachers. It is essential that you be given an opportunity to begin selecting and designing your own strategies for managing the many variables in your classrooms. These activities are suggested to help you begin this task.

1. Make a list of useful management strategies that go beyond the suppression of negative behavior and contribute to the effectiveness of the planned instruction. Try to include ways of managing time, space, materials, and student activities.

2. You have observed others who have management responsibilities (cooks, secretaries, restaurant managers, service station attendants). Select one of these occupations (or another one) and describe one or more management techniques used by these managers that can be used by teachers. Explain how you could best utilize this technique to enhance the instruction in your classroom.

ANDREW, MICHAEL D. *Teachers Should Be Human Too*. Washington, D.C.: Association of Teacher Educators, 1972.

BAUGHMAN, M. DALE. *Baughman's Handbook of Humor in Education*. New York: Parker Publishing Company, 1974.

DIAL, D. "Heightening the Student's Self-Image." *School and Community* 42 (October 1976): 23.

COMBS, ARTHUR W.; POPHAM, W. J.; and HOSFORD, P. L. "Behaviorism and Humanism." *Educational Leadership* 35 (October 1972): 19–24.

HENSON, KENNETH T. "Humanizing the Classroom." *The High School Journal* 59 (December 1975): 144–47.

JONES, V. F. "Humanistic Behaviorism: A Tool for Creating Healthy Learning Environments." *Journal of School Psychology* 15 (Winter 1977): 320–28.

NEILL, A. S. *Summerhill*. New York: Hart Publishing Company, 1960.

RUBIN, LOUIS J., ed. *Facts and Feelings in the Classroom*. New York: The Viking Press, 1973.

SHANE, HAROLD G. *Curriculum Change Toward the 21st Century*. Washington, D.C.: National Education Association, 1977.

TRAVERS, ROBERT M. W., and DILLON, JACQUELINE. *The Making of a Teacher*. New York: Macmillan, 1975.

WEIL, MARSHA; JOYCE, BRUCE; and KLUWIN, BRIDGET. *Personal Models of Teaching*. Englewood Cliffs, N.J.: Prentice-Hall, 1978.

WILSON, CHARLES H. *A Teacher Is a Person*. New York: Holt, Rinehart and Winston, 1956.

Motivating via the Student's Point of View

OBJECTIVES

When you have finished this chapter, you should be able to:
1. List ten techniques for stimulating pupil interest.
2. Explain the role of competition in motivating the student.
3. Name two ways in which a teacher can solicit the cooperation of parents.
4. Explain Piaget's concept of "equilibrium."
5. Draw a chart to show Piaget's explanation of readiness.
6. Role-play a teacher being confronted with an angry parent.
7. State the relationship between self-concept and motivation.
8. Describe the teacher's main responsibility in the self-concept development of students.
9. Explain the teacher's role in the use of humor in the classroom.
10. Give three guidelines for using student contracts.
11. List five guidelines for using reinforcement in the classroom.

IMPORTANCE OF RESPONSIBILITY

Our busy world is full of people competing for attention. Individuals try every means imaginable to gain our attention so that they can sell us material goods and ideals. Institutions have organized strategies to capture our attention. Industries launch continuous advertising campaigns, using psychologically proven techniques. All types of media are used, including the television, radio, newspapers, magazines, and even the telephone, to enter our homes and infiltrate our minds.

Everyone is wanting to sell something. Whether we need it does not seem to matter so long as we buy it. After we fall victim a few times (and we all do), we become skeptical and are forced to protect ourselves. We do this in several ways. A friend of mine, who is a professional artist, keeps a few paintings in his home to use to defend himself against salespeople. When asked at his front door if he wishes to purchase a $300 set of encyclopedias, he cordially invites the person inside to see a $300 painting that he offers to trade for the encyclopedias. He insists that the technique is effective and that everyone should keep some type of goods in his home to sell to door-to-door salespeople.

Others of us defend ourselves by becoming aggressive and forcing the salesperson to leave. But most of us are too polite for that. Not having a stock of $300 items to trade, we have learned to stand or sit patiently, pretending to hear while our minds completely tune the words out. And, furthermore, we become quite skilled in pretending to listen. But, as a college student, you don't have to be told that.

So it is with students, who are constantly being forced to hear sales pitches by teachers who are overloaded with knowledge of questionable value. Like the ill-tempered adult, some youths speak out and tell us what they think about our product. (I believe the word they use is *irrelevant*.) But, like most adults, many adolescents are too polite to do this; so, for their own defense they shut us out and pretend to listen. Like any disinterested client or customer, they do a good job of faking their interest. They learn to watch others for cues that tell them when to laugh and when not to. Some fake it even further by asking questions and then do not even listen to the answers.

Daily the teacher faces (not all, but many) disinterested students who, skeptical of the teacher's goods, feel that their time and energy could be spent more wisely elsewhere. The teacher is largely responsible for their changing these attitudes.

Having spent four years studying a particular subject, you, like other enthusiastic young teachers, may assume that others share at least some of this interest. But to *assume* is dangerous. Instead, you will be wise to analyze your students to find out exactly what interests do exist about your subject, if, indeed any at all. Then you may kindle even a small spark of interest into a more serious commitment.

"But," you may respond, "can I really make all the students like my subject and be interested in the lessons?" This is an excellent question, to which the answer is no. You can no more make students interested against their will than you can force students to learn. Your best strategy is to entice students; but before you can do this successfully, your students must have an appropriate mind-set for the subject, toward themselves, and toward you, the teacher.

Student Attitude Toward the Subject

While many students are turned off by studying, others are equally "into" learning. If members from both groups described their school subjects, their chosen adjectives would certainly differ drastically. And this is true for every subject; some students actually love it, while others hate it. Most who hate it find it either boring or difficult, or both. Let's first examine those students who find your subject boring, and then learn what you can do about it.

As was mentioned earlier, students are concerned with relevance. They are

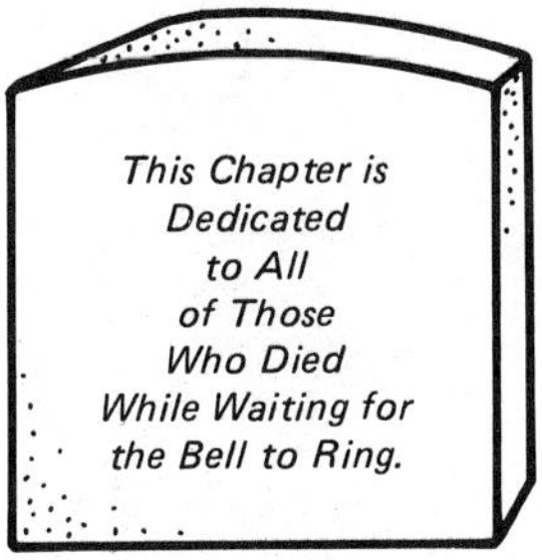

This Chapter is
Dedicated
to All
of Those
Who Died
While Waiting for
the Bell to Ring.

Figure 5.1 An Epitaph for Student Victims

confronted with so much knowledge that they must be highly selective, choosing that which can be useful to them. Thus, you need to show students how to apply the materials to solve practical problems, preferably in their own lives. For example, math ratios may be very boring to some students until they learn to use ratios to determine the power and economy of their automobiles. One major make of a full-size station wagon retained the same size engine and relatively the same carburetor from 1971 to 1973; however, the manufacturer's changing the ratio in the transmission resulted in a loss of more than 33 percent of gas mileage. Other students may think ratios useless until they realize that they use them in cooking.

The wise beginning teacher prepares a response to the age-old question "Why do we have to study this stuff?" After all, it does seem unfair to force students to come to school to listen to something that they perceive as useless. It is impossible for a textbook to provide this answer. It must come from you. You might begin by analyzing your own reasons for enjoying your subject(s). (Take a moment now to list a few reasons why you chose it for a major.)

Now examine your list of reasons to see what potential each has for convincing a disinterested student that your subject is worthwhile. If your explanations seem ineffective, consider some other ways that you might convince students of the worth of your subject. Try to recall the successful efforts of your teachers. Perhaps they used demonstrations, anecdotes, or even personal examples to awaken your interest. Can you think of a few such techniques to stimulate your students? Imagine that you are introducing a new unit of study. How might you use each of the following approaches to gain everyone's attention?

Demonstration

Problem

Personal experience

Group assignment

Questioning session

Debate

Joke

Discussion

Remember that students always perceive in terms of *their* prior experiences, not yours. Can you alter each of your ideas to fit your class's age group?

Since we know that learning flourishes when students are involved vigorously, see if you can discover ways of increasing that involvement within each approach. For example, you may have students assist with the demonstration. Remember, though, that involvement is a better motivator when it is meaningful. More than helping with the equipment, students should also be allowed to participate in the demonstration itself. With the problems approach, you might introduce a puzzle for all to work on. When you use personal experiences, ask for volunteers to share their experiences. Were you able to think of ways to increase student involvement in the other areas? If not, give it another try. Once you begin to think of a classroom where students are *always* active, it becomes much easier to plan meaningful experiences.

Student Attitudes Toward Themselves

Motivation depends on self-perception. Each student comes to your room with a definite self-portrait — as a person and as a student. If either image is negative, it will act as a strong learning barrier. Your job is to recognize these attitudes so that you can help the student change a negative self-concept. While the task may seem monumental — and perhaps it is — one of the greatest rewards of teaching is knowing that for some students you will be the person who helps them to find themselves, and to discover their own potentials. Unfortunately, not all students ever make this discovery; some drop out of school before that discovery is made. Others seem just to putter along, somehow managing to get through high school or to complete a high school equivalency program. Some of those who get into college wake up to the realization that they are infinitely more capable than even they ever realized.

You may hear some teacher respond, "It's not my fault if they bring these attitudes to my class." That may be true. The fault may belong to their previous teachers, parents, friends, or to themselves. But that is not the point. What teachers should realize is that they themselves can become powerful negative motivators simply by the way that they relate to students. Avoid negative comments *to* the student or *about* the student such as "You know him. He's a hopeless case"; or, "Her entire family is that way, dumb." Another commonly heard comment among teachers is, "You can't make a sculpture out of mud." But we should remember that on first appearance, all clay looks a great deal like mud!

It is true that not all individuals can become Einsteins, and we cannot always mold people into the patterns that we design; but we are not asked to do either of these. The teacher's role is to provide a climate in which students can see their own strengths, believe in themselves, and become what *they* want to become.[1] The students must perceive at least the possibility of success before they will even attempt it. Once they experience success again and again, they will eventually become successful in whatever the field of endeavor, school or otherwise. Although it has already been said, it bears repeating. Students who perceive themselves as good students will work hard to protect that image, just as athletes who have good reputations are willing to give their very best.

The cliché "success breeds success" is very true, but it may stop short of helping the teacher to become a good motivator, because it does not explain how the teacher is to provide success for students who normally are not successful. Actually, no teacher can *provide* success for anyone. All that you can do is to create a climate conducive to learning, experimenting, and even failing. Since some failure is inevitable, it must be expected. The failure itself isn't important, rather it is how your students perceive and respond to it. If they see it as defeat, it can be devastating, but if you teach them to view it as stumbling blocks for growth they can learn and grow from their mistakes.

Student Attitudes Toward the Teacher

Chapter 4 reported on a survey taken to identify the qualities that students perceive as most significant for teachers. We shall return with the results of that survey, but, first, we will identify teacher qualities that are important to you. Close your eyes for a moment and think of the best teacher you ever had. List five most important qualities that made you like that teacher.

Getting back to that survey, you can now compare your list with those of other students. In your list did you include a statement that tells how the

---

[1] Arthur W. Combs, "A Perceptual View of the Adequate Personality," in *Perceiving, Behaving, Becoming,* ed. Arthur W. Combs (Washington, D.C.: Association for Supervision and Curriculum Development, 1962).

teacher felt about you? The students in the survey did. In fact, the most frequently mentioned quality was that the favorite teacher was concerned with the student, and in a very special way. The ideal teacher was determined to see that the student achieve in the subject and took whatever time necessary, in class or out, to explain the subject. An expert in the subject, this teacher knew how to "get it across" and was even willing to help students in areas outside the academic arena.

So we have now begun to build a profile of a good teacher. And this profile extends beyond knowledge and teaching skills to include how the teacher actually *feels* about the subject and the students. Few students will get excited over any subject about which the teacher appears bored. A teacher who shows an intense excitement or a serious love for the subject entices students to learn the reason for that enthusiasm.

Another teacher quality rating high in the survey was humor. Educators are just beginning to learn about the role that humor plays in motivation. For the prospective teacher many questions quickly come to mind: "How can I use humor when I can't even tell a joke? How much humor should I allow? And by encouraging humor, am I not inviting discipline problems?"

In his book *Baughman's Handbook of Humor in Education*,[2] Baughman answers our questions about the teacher's responsibility for using humor. Not always planned, humor is better described as an attitude or philosophy. In other words, the role of the teacher is merely to be accepting of humor. The students themselves will provide creativity and the delivery skills if you will provide a climate for its development.

The other questions are good questions, too, for you do not want your classroom to turn into a circus, as could easily happen. You can control the humor in your classroom through an understanding that it must be kept clean in content and vocabulary and that rudeness is not permitted. Short disruptions in a serious lesson may bring needed relaxation, for humor is psychologically relaxing; yet those disruptions must be kept short, and this is the teacher's responsibility.

It is easy to return to the lesson if the lesson itself is interesting and well structured. For this reason, a good lesson plan with clear objectives and an ample amount of student involvement is indispensable to classroom motivation. The pace should remain crisp, and students should remain challenged.

TECHNIQUES FOR STIMULATING INTEREST

A Need for Structure and Informality

An informal atmosphere can be more conducive to learning than an overly formal climate. Research studies have found that a classroom characterized by friendly, integrative affiliative nurturant behavior is important in public school

---

[2] M. Dale Baughman, *Baughman's Handbook of Humor in Education* (New York: Parker Publishing Company, 1974), p. 50.

teaching.[3,4] These same studies also found that friendly teachers inspire more student-initiated work than do reserved teachers. But for learning to occur in an informal setting, you must have a well-structured lesson planned. How informal should a class be? A good rule of thumb is that you should make your class as informal as possible, retaining only enough structure to move through the lesson systematically as it has been planned. When the class becomes especially interested in a part of the lesson, allow time for them to discuss that part, but always return to the lesson plan.

Enthusiasm

As was previously mentioned, talk at length about how important a subject is or that certain information is an essential base for future learning, but unless you yourself appear interested in a lesson, your words will probably go unheard. On the other hand, if each day you appear excited about the lesson, students will often become spellbound, anxious to find out what it is that so interests you.

To behave enthusiastically does not mean becoming hysterical or overly emotional, yet you cannot afford to be nonchalant or just mildly interested in the

[3] M. L. Cogan, "The Behavior of Teachers and the Productive Behavior of their Pupils: II, Trait Analysis," *Journal of Experimental Education* 27 (1958): 107–24.

[4] D. G. Ryans, *Characteristics of Teachers* (Washington, D.C.: American Council on Education, 1960).

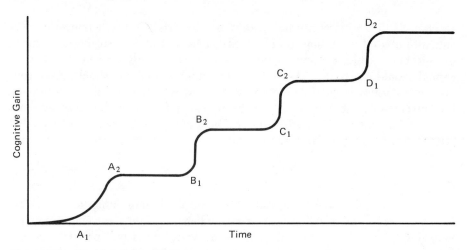

Figure 5.2 The Learning Pattern

lesson. You need not compete with the entertainment world, for what you have to offer — useful knowledge — is better than mere entertainment. When you explain why the lesson is being pursued and how it can be applied, you want to be taken seriously. How can you appear both serious and excited about your lessons? Think for a moment of your current college courses and select a class that you really enjoy. How would you describe the teacher? Does she speak in a monotone? Does she read a lecture to the class each day? Is she afraid to let the class laugh a little when a humorous incident occurs? Does she always sit behind her desk and require you always to sit at your desk? Probably not. Most teachers whom we enjoy are neither foolishly funny nor extremely strait-laced, and probably are intensely interested in their subject.

Keeping Students Challenged

The most important type of motivator is the one that comes from within, especially after having experienced success. According to Jean Piaget, each individual strives to achieve and maintain a state of equilibrium. In other words, when a student sees an inconsistency in what he knows, he is internally motivated to remove that inconsistency. Figure 5.2 shows how a child's learning progresses in steps or plateaus. The distance from A_1 to A_2 represents a quest for learning as it is being satisfied. When satisfaction is reached at A_2, the pupil is in a state of equilibrium and remains there until another contradiction arises at B_1.[5]

Compare this diagram to Figure 1.4 on page 14. It is interesting that two models so similar as these represent the work of different psychologists who have never worked together and who are of different nationalities.

---

[5] Richard I. Evans, *Jean Piaget: The Man and His Ideas* (New York: E. P. Dutton, 1973), p. 141.

Each time he satisfies the reason for an apparent inconsistency in his knowledge, the pupil has gained a higher plateau and reaches a state of equilibrium in his thinking. The teacher should not allow the student to become idle when he levels off, but should always be prepared to present the student with further contradictions to his knowledge. Does this suggest that the teacher's role is to introduce problems or contradictions purposefully to *puzzle* students instead of helping students to find answers? To this Piaget would answer yes. A contradiction, in simple terms, occurs when a student discovers that he holds understandings that contradict or appear to contradict each other. The teacher, in one way or another, guides him to realize his lack of knowledge and then provides one or more learning experiences that will help him gain this needed understanding. There is no "force feeding" from the teacher, for he must internally feel the need to erase this contradiction. Once learning has taken place, the student is at peace, resting on a plateau. It is then that the teacher must make him aware of another contradiction, and the whole process begins again. This is motivation by keeping the student challenged. This is the author's interpretation of Piaget's theory of learning.

It should be noted that presenting too many contradictions at one time can be a nonmotivating move on the teacher's part; for, when faced with what he considers to be an impossible task, the student will tend to give up, feeling that success is out of his reach. But it is equally important to realize that student interest can be increased dramatically simply by increasing the academic demands in the classroom. As one educator explains, "Today, students want to be challenged more. Most teachers don't realize it, but many students are bored because teachers are not adequately challenging them." [6] A recent Gallup Poll adds credibility to this claim. Approximately half of the teenagers contacted throughout the nation said that students do not have to work hard enough in school or on homework. [7] Even the learning materials in most schools are not interesting. According to Frymier, 70 to 90 percent of the curriculum materials are low in their ability to motivate, stimulate creativity, and challenge the intellect of students. [8] Therefore, if students are to be challenged, it will probably be left up to the teacher to initiate the challenge by introducing more rigorous and yet relevant knowledge and activities.

Clarifying Goals and Procedures

Students will work more intently when they know where they are headed and how to get there. When they lose sight of their goals, they often lose interest. When they find that they do not understand the procedures for working on assigned tasks, they become frustrated and discouraged. Both instances usually result in poor work. Each task should begin with a clarification of the

---

[6] Jack Frymier, Address to Southwest Educational Research Association, Second Annual Meeting, Houston, February 3, 1979.

[7] Stanley M. Elam, "Gallup Finds Teenagers Generally Like Their Schools," reports on a Gallup Poll of teenagers taken in November 1978, *Phi Delta Kappan* 60 (June 1979): 700.

[8] Frymier, Address.

unforeseen outcome. In other words, show your students how to recognize the answer (or a concept or principle) when they find it.

To be sure that your students understand the proper procedures, you might begin each assignment by working a sample problem and then having the students work another problem collectively. Encourage questions and have students assist each other with the sample problem. Once the actual assignment is given, however, your job is far from over. Some pupils will still have questions concerning the goals and procedures. Now you can help by circulating among the students and answering individual questions as they arise. Knowing that the teacher is available and therefore concerned with their learning, students who need help will be motivated to ask questions.

Considering and Using the Opinions of Students

Make a special effort to seek the opinions of students, letting them know that you value their suggestions, their likes and their dislikes, and above all, their judgment. Providing them an opportunity to express their ideas can help identify any misconceptions on the part of students or the teacher. Until an individual has had an opportunity to express his opinions, he is not free to consider the opinions of others. In addition, just knowing that their questions and opinions are valued is great motivation. Consider one or more teachers you have had who appeared to be intolerant of your questions or concerns. You soon lost the desire to ask about anything, didn't you? You probably lost some respect for yourself and for those teachers, also.

Student Contracts

While competition among students often has many serious side effects — such as making the less capable feel down on themselves, alienating students from their peers, and encouraging snobbishness in high achievers — competition can be a strong motivator. Americans are, indeed, a competitive people, and the competitive attitude has been largely responsible for America's rapid development. One way to retain the motivation without the undesirable side effects is to encourage students to compete with themselves. It is an accepted fact that many of the best athletes compete with themselves rather than with other athletes. In fact, once golfers or bowlers get too interested in the performance of others, their performance often fails. Like bowling and golf, learning is a somewhat individual activity in which learners compete with themselves. They are always challenged, yet they find that success is possible.

You can use student contracts to encourage students to compete with themselves. Unlike most teacher-made tests, which are norm-referenced and set the individual against his entire class, student contracts are criterion-referenced and set the student only against the tasks at hand. Most contracts run for the duration of a grading term. Figure 5.3 is an example of a contract on a unit on art history.

CONTRACT

Art History

Grade **Requirements**

A   Meet the requirements for the grade of *B* plus visit a local art gallery. Sketch an example of a gothic painting. Visit a carpenter gothic style house and sketch the house. Show at least three similarities in the two products.

B   Meet the requirements for the grade of *C* plus name and draw an example of each of the major classes of columns used in buildings.

C   Meet the requirements for the grade of *D* plus submit a notebook record of the major developments in art since 1900, naming at least six major painting styles and two authors of each style.

D   Attend class regularly and participate in all classroom activities.

I _____ agree to work for the grade of _____
      (student's name)   (specify grade)
as described in this contract.

To encourage students to be realistic in their expectations, you may stipulate that the student can at any time lower his expectations, but the contract may contain a built-in penalty for any alterations. Most contracts do not permit the student to raise his grade expectation, but in designing yours, try to fit them to the needs of your particular classes. The major disadvantage of using contracts is that you will need extra time to design, complete, and keep up with a large number of contracts.

Grades and Tests

Many teachers believe that pop tests and threats of assigning low grades can be effective motivators. The research, however, does not support these conjectures. When tests and threats are used in the traditional manner, the downgraded students continue to fail. Low test scores can also be discouraging, especially if the teacher does nothing to help the student attain the missed knowledge and skills. Unfortunately, teachers and students usually spend very little effort on reviewing and building the skills that have not been learned.[9] Another study found that anxiety produced by grades actually lowered the grades

---

[9] Normal M. Chansky, "The X-ray of the School Mark," *The Educational Forum* 12 (March 1962): 347–52.

of middle-ability students.[10] So it appears that, while tests themselves can be sources for learning when time is spent going over the material covered on them, the use of tests or grades (or threats of either) to motivate is a serious misuse of them and does not increase the motivational level significantly.

Term Projects

When correctly used, individual or group projects can be a highly motivating device in secondary schools. First of all, they must be truly term projects, meaning that they last for the duration of the term. This gives students time to select and research their chosen area of study. A list of topics provided by you can be very helpful in suggesting ideas and boundaries, but it is important to let students be free to choose their particular project.

To increase the motivation for student projects, you should find ways of displaying the projects. A science fair, art exhibit, or similar event is an excellent means of achieving the necessary exposure. Occasional attention given to these projects during the term by parents and relatives can spur on the investigators and whet their enthusiasm for their projects.

Assignments for Extra Credit

Assignments for extra credit are common in many classrooms, yet, their power to stimulate interest is very limited. In fact, they often produce the opposite effect. If they are to motivate positively, the task must be meaningful and must be selected far in advance of the end of the term, preferably at the beginning of a term or study unit. To give a student an opportunity to copy down a ten thousand-word report from an encyclopedia at the end of a semester is likely to produce a negative attitude toward learning rather than increasing the student's motivation.

Reward and Reinforcement

The use of rewards by teachers can be an important motivator or stimulator of student interest. Some students work to please their teachers; others watch their teachers closely for feedback that reassures them that they are achieving at an acceptable rate. Your use of rewards (or lack of it) can bring reinforcement to both types of student. Two writers on motivation give the following suggestions to help teachers improve their skills using rewards.

1. Reward new behavior every time it occurs.
2. Once a student becomes established, gradually reduce the frequency of reinforcement until the reinforcement comes at occasional and haphazard intervals.
3. At first, reward the behavior as soon as it occurs. Then, as students become more confident, delay the reward somewhat.

---

[10] Beeman Phillips, "Sex, Social Class, and Anxiety as Sources of Variation in School Activity," *Journal of Educational Psychology* 53 (1962): 361–62.

4. Select rewards which are suitable for the individual pupils.
5. With recalcitrant or resistive pupils, begin by giving small rewards.
6. Use contingency contracts.[11]

Behavior Modification

As used in education, behavior modification, like a contingency contract, is an agreement. But instead of earning grades, the student earns certain stated rewards for displaying certain types of behavior (or certain tasks). Behavior modification is especially popular in elementary schools; it is much more difficult to find adequate reinforcers for high school students.[12] One reinforcer that has proved effective for secondary classes is free time earned by the student through certain specified performance. For example, in one English grammar class a 75 percent level of bad behavior was reduced to 15 percent by a contract that rewarded proper behavior by giving free time.[13]

In a predominantly black inner-city class of underachievers, a program that provided the opportunity to earn free time, listen to records, read comic books, play games, receive candy bars and bubble gum, and participate in planning class activities, the average student grades rose from *D* to *B* level. The class attendance rose from 50 percent to 80 percent.[14] While one would not expect always to produce such dramatic effects as these, such results do give much encouragement for the use of behavior modification programs in secondary schools.

MOTIVATION STRATEGIES LIST

Since any one technique for motivation is apt to produce different results with each application and with each group of students, you will probably profit more from concentrating less on specific techniques and more on the general strategies that have already been discussed, to motivate your students. Here is a summary of those strategies:

1. *Be honest with students.* Don't pretend to know everything. It is far more important that a teacher remains approachable than impeccable.
2. *Use the subject to motivate.* Emphasize those areas of knowledge that have special appeal to the particular age group of each class.
3. *Be pragmatic.* Show the students how they can use the knowledge in their daily lives.

---

[11] Leonard H. Clark and Irving S. Starr, *Secondary School Teaching Methods,* 3d ed. (New York: Macmillan, 1976), pp. 69–70.

[12] Mimi Warshaw, "Behavior Modification in Secondary Schools," *Educational Technology* (August 1975): 21–25.

[13] G. L. Sapp et al., "Classroom Management and Student Involvement," *High School Journal* 56 (March 1973): 276–83.

[14] Ibid.

4. *Use a variety of approaches.* For each topic of study, select the approach(es) that you believe will best stimulate student interest.
5. *Involve all students.* All students should be actively involved in each lesson. Remember that in a sense all individuals are motivated. The teacher's challenge is to provide meaningful activities for students to pursue, that is, activities that lead to the discovery of knowledge and relationships pertinent to the lesson.
6. *Be positive.* Students work harder and achieve more when they feel competent in what they are doing. Serious use of reinforcement by teachers can lead to improving the self-confidence of students.
7. *Be personal.* Don't be afraid to relate to students on a personal basis. Those teachers who remain formal at all times build barriers between themselves and their students.
8. *Use humor.* Don't be afraid to enjoy your students. There's no time when student attention is more completely captured than when humor is occurring. Relax occasionally and let it happen.
9. *Be enthusiastic.* Plan events into the lesson that you will enjoy. Enthusiasm is highly contagious.
10. *Challenge your students.* Nothing is more boring than a lesson that fails to challenge the learners. Try to keep the pace brisk yet within reach of the students.

SUMMARY

The worth of any lesson depends on, and is limited by, the degree to which it captures and holds the students' interest. Teachers are becoming more aware of their responsibility for making each lesson interesting. They are also becoming more capable in doing so.

To provide a maximum level of interest, the teacher should be informal and yet retain structure in each lesson. Rather than doing all the talking, the instructor should create a dialogue constantly involving students; in a setting where they feel that they have some input, they will want to learn.

As a teacher you can show that you feel your subject is important by planning a lesson that you yourself find stimulating and enjoyable. Yet, you must also show that you feel that your students are important. Each lesson should be made as personal as possible. Not only should you *permit* time for student questions but also *encourage* them by asking for student opinions, concerns, and judgments.

Each lesson should have planned into it ways of involving all students. Whenever possible, involve them physically as well as mentally. To make that involvement meaningful, be sure that the goals and procedures are clear.

Effective teaching requires the students to be motivated, and the teacher is the one who is primarily responsible for this. You must try to provide an atmosphere in which the students have an inner desire to learn, for self-motivation is more powerful than any stimulus from the outside.

EXPERIENCES

This chapter has emphasized the need for motivation in all classrooms and that the teacher must include motivation strategies in each daily lesson plan. As you read the following experiences, you may wish to begin making a list of strategies that you will use throughout the year to elevate your own level of enthusiasm as well as that of your students.

Experience 1:   A Student Is Labeled a Failure

Mike Creswell was a quiet boy, although a bit mischievous at times. He often blushed and bowed his head whenever Jane, his teacher, mentioned his name in the classroom. Jane's heart really poured out to Mike. He reminded her of a kicked-around animal that never knew when, or from whom, more punishment was forthcoming. Mike appeared not to trust anyone, and this probably explains why he had no close friends.

Meeting Mike's parents at a social affair, Jane noticed that the father avoided mentioning that Mike was in her room. Once she became convinced that he was not going to mention Mike, Jane simply stated that she was pleased to have him in her class. Mr. Creswell immediately apologized for his son's inadequacies and quickly changed the conversation to a discussion of another of his sons who was more academically inclined. Jane could see that Mr. Creswell was actually ashamed of Mike and didn't really like the boy.

Through talking with other teachers, Jane learned that the father constantly yelled at Mike at home and sometimes had even actually beaten him for failing to live up to his father's expectations. Jane guessed that Mike preferred the beatings to the verbal downgrading because the pain of physical punishment is temporary, but the pain of being told that you are unable to measure up never ends.

Some students never get over the damage their parents and teachers do by measuring them against a brother or sister who performed better in school. Most youths do not have the insight to see that what they can do and achieve is important, regardless of how much more or less someone else achieves. Unfortunately, many adults tend to lead students to thinking this way.

Jane began encouraging Mike and verbally rewarding him for each successful task that he performed. By the end of the year she could see some improvement in the quality of Mike's work, and he had begun to relate better to her and to some of his classmates.

▶ *Questions and Discussion*

1. *If you see that a parent of one of your students is ashamed of his child, how should you react to him?*

    Though the parent who is ashamed of his son or daughter will probably try to avoid discussing the student, you may feel obligated to do so at every opportunity without being overly obvious about it. The parent who reacts to an apparent weakness by ignoring his child is not behaving in an acceptable way. You can encourage the parent to discuss the student's weakness; and, if the weakness does exist, you can always seek to aid the parent in helping the student correct it. You may be able to think of other approaches that suit your particular personality.

2. *How could Jane make Mr. Creswell feel proud of his son?*
She could tell him about Mike's strengths, academic or otherwise. She could also check Mike's cumulative records, his standardized examination scores, and his previous grades, and talk with other teachers to identify Mike's strong areas. This would provide topics for discussion with Mr. Creswell.

3. *How can you encourage other students to associate with a lonely child?*
By assigning the student tasks of which he is capable, the teacher can allow him some success, and his peers may begin to take notice of him. Also, you can assign group projects, making sure that the particular student's group has a task to which he is capable of contributing.

4. *How could Jane convince the parent that he should not compare one sibling with another?*
She could emphasize that each individual excels in different areas. Furthermore, she might remind Mr. Creswell that Mike's failure to achieve might not indicate that he is not capable, but rather could be indicative of a failure of both teacher and parents to motivate him.

Experience 2: A Student Teacher Uses Threats to Motivate

Bob Wright was really eager to begin student teaching. On the first day that Ms. Lee, his supervisor, visited, Bob was presenting a well-organized lesson. Though he had a beautiful outline on the board and was talking about some interesting things, the students seemed complacent and unconcerned. The supervisor did not mention this to Bob, and he was unaware of the pupils' lack of response.

During later observations it was obvious that Bob had noticed something wrong and was becoming very upset with his students because they appeared so disinterested. Throughout the period he would remark, "You had better pay attention because this will be on our next test." Some of the few who initially were interested began to lose interest.

Ms. Lee suggested to Bob that, instead of threatening to give a test, he try actually giving the test, that each time he caught himself on the verge of saying "you had better ... or else," he should go ahead and administer the "or else."

By the end of the semester Bob found healthy discussion in each class. The students began listening to him and interacting with him.

► *Questions and Discussion*

1. *Is the teacher justified in giving a pop quiz when his class fails to complete their assignments?*

   Probably not, unless he is certain that the failure is due to laziness and he truly feels the quiz will do some good. His energy would be better spent on improving his teaching. Using pop quizzes can even be a way of punishing students for the teacher's inadequacy. Perhaps an announced quiz set at a specific time each week would be a stronger motivator than would an unannounced "pop" quiz, and Bob did announce the tests. How do you feel about the use of pop quizzes to motivate?

2. *How was the idea of a test used by Bob?*

   Even though Bob had favorable results, he should not have used a test as a threat. Students can be led to see tests as a valuable learning aid. Tests as weapons against pupil misbehavior are negative. As was mentioned in an earlier chapter, threatening pupils in any way is really poor teaching practice.

Experience 3: A Parent Learns How to Motivate Her Son

Bobby Tyson, a pleasant, well-adjusted boy, seemed interested in classwork but was never prepared. Bobby's mother, a leader in the community, was vitally concerned with his success in school. Each morning she brought him to school in a shiny Cadillac, and when the last bell rang in the afternoon, she was always waiting for him. One afternoon she asked Bobby's seventh-grade teacher, "What can I do to get Bobby to become more interested in school? His father and I have done everything we know to do and nothing seems to work." Having learned that Bobby had plenty of time to study, the teacher asked if he had a satisfactory place, quiet and well lighted. He realized that his question was misinterpreted when Mrs. Tyson replied, "Yes, we have provided a very comfortable study room for Bobby, and just last month we had a color television installed. He spends four or five hours in his room each evening, but he still doesn't seem interested in his school work."

Mrs. Tyson failed to understand that a comfortable place for study meant a place free from interruptions. She didn't realize that television would be particularly distracting to someone who enjoys it more than he enjoys his lessons — and many students (and some teachers) do. Still she was seriously trying to help her son and was absolutely sincere in her efforts.

Because of her closeness to Bobby, Mrs. Tyson was not aware that she was providing a hindrance rather than a motivation. The teacher casually remarked that perhaps the television could be distracting Bobby from his lessons and suggested she try removing it from his study room. Mrs. Tyson took the advice. Bobby began turning in completed assignments.

► *Questions and Discussion*

1. *How can the teacher secure the aid of those parents who are not as
   interested in their children as Mrs. Tyson was?*
   The teacher should alert parents to activities that provide opportunities
   for talking about the student and should not hesitate to ask them to
   come in for a conference. Often, telling the parent "I need you help"
   will motivate the parent to get interested in the student.

2. *Why is it necessary that parents see their children more objectively?*
   If parents are not objective, they will likely make excuses for their children and avoid recognizing their weaknesses. Until parents can admit
   to themselves that all youths need help from time to time, they will not
   be able to help their children. Some parents can look objectively at
   their children, but the ones who cannot cause the teacher numerous
   problems. Motivating them to look at both sides of the issue is the
   teacher's responsibility.

Experience 4: A Teacher Learns How to Clarify Assignments

Beginning his teaching career with an abundance of optimism, Mr. Kirk's
energy and attitude were a real boost to the faculty. Although he did not
appear overly extroverted with his colleagues, the students soon spread
the word: Mr. Kirk was a very ambitious teacher whose well-planned
activities made his classes enjoyable and his students enthusiastic. Here
was a teacher who was well liked by all students, who made the school
subjects come to life each day, and who appeared to enjoy the process.

Had you known Mr. Kirk, you would have been as surprised as the
faculty was to hear that, after only a few years, he was having health
problems because of what he interpreted as a lack of success with his
classes. His doctors warned him that he was developing ulcers from the
work that had once been so enjoyable.

Wanting to remain in teaching, Mr. Kirk analyzed his problem. He
realized that his worries centered around his students' problems with
their assigned homework. Each day he asked students if they understood
their assignments; each day they assured him that they did. The homework they handed him, however, always informed him that they did not
understand the assignment as well as they had indicated. What could
he do?

After failing in a variety of attempts to clarify the assignments, he decided to provide class time for the students to work their assignments and
to ask a few questions. As a result, the related assignment was done pretty
much correctly by most students. Thereafter, Mr. Kirk always allowed
class time for students to finish their work.

► *Questions and Discussion*

1. *Why didn't Mr. Kirk's students voluntarily admit that they did not
   understand their homework assignments?*

At first, they probably did not realize their lack of understanding. Perhaps they understood the assignments when received but forgot the processes involved when they actually began working. Have you ever begun a homework assignment only to find that, even though you felt certain you knew how, you realize that you have a problem once you try?

Once Mr. Kirk began providing class time for homework, any questions could immediately be answered and misunderstandings could be corrected before the students forgot the processes involved in solving the problems.

2. *When you provide class time for problem solving, what is your role?* You should make yourself available for questions. Because some bewildered students are reserved, circulate among them throughout the problem-solving session. Your proximity will encourage them to ask questions.

Usually you cannot afford to spend much time with any single student. Rather, pause momentarily to see that each student is on the right track, then move on to another. For those students who have questions requiring more than a couple of minutes to answer, you could assign another student who understands the assignment to assist, or you can draw a small group together for some additional instruction.

Experience 5:   Mrs. King Runs Out of Material

The day had finally arrived for Mrs. King to begin teaching her own classes. It was exciting just to hear her describe the experience in the teacher's lounge later that morning. All had not gone well, however, and some teachers recalled a similar experience early in their own careers.

It seems that Mrs. King's first class started well. She had before her a well-structured lesson that immediately captured attention. When after a few moments she realized that the students were more interested in the lesson than in her, she felt very relieved, and the first half of the hour went very well. Time passed quickly but so did the lesson; suddenly the material was all used up, a good fifteen minutes before the bell. What could she do?

Though Mrs. King lacked experience, she did not lack creativity. She immediately thought of reviewing the lesson. When the review of the lesson took only five minutes, she was again at the point of panic. Then a student asked a question. From Mrs. King's report it was certain that the question was thoroughly answered, since all ten remaining minutes were utilized in answering that one question. It was not an experience that Mrs. King wished to repeat. She began thinking of ways to avoid the task of stalling and ad-libbing to kill time.

► *Questions and Discussion*

1. *What can you, as a new teacher, do to prevent running out of planned lesson material?*

Always come to school with at least two days' plans in hand. Then, if you finish with the first sooner than you expect to, you can begin another. Can you think of other such planned ways to cope with this emergency?

Lesson plans that surprise a teacher and are completed sooner than expected are usually those plans that do not involve the students. As this book has stressed, you should plan student involvement into every lesson. Often student involvement will increase a one-day lesson to more than a single class period, but this should be cause for celebration rather than concern.

Both you and the students should ask questions throughout the period. (Teachers who feel that they do not have time for questions are probably the same teachers who find themselves with a completed lesson in fifteen minutes.)

It should be pointed out that at the end of the planned lesson you should feel free to engage the students in a variety of activities. Not so long ago in many school systems each teacher was required to have the daily schedule posted on the classroom door, and that schedule was supposed to be followed precisely. Except for a few very rare cases, today's teacher is given more freedom than that.

2. *If a question is not posed, how can you fill the remainder of a class period?*

Most teachers find this an opportune time for student involvement. If the students have been somewhat passive during most of the class period, they will be physically and psychologically ready for some action. To ease this "tension," you might try changing the routine, such as having the students come to the board to work problems, or dividing the class into small groups to formulate questions for discussion. The important thing is that you enable each student to become active in working with the lesson. (Does this suggest another answer to the preceding question?)

ACTIVITIES

It goes without saying that you do not want to become another boring teacher. (Heaven knows that is just what the profession doesn't need.) Granted, no teacher wishes to be boring, but some are extremely so. Think now how you will prevent boredom in your future classrooms. The following activities are suggested to help you as you begin to plan for a more stimulating climate.

1. Examine your own personal traits. For each adjective that you would use to describe yourself, describe at least one way that you can use this trait to make your class environments more interesting.
2. A degree of informality seems essential for maximum motivation in the classroom. Student teachers often ask, "How informal can I/should I be

with my students without their taking advantage of my friendship?" Make a list of ways that you can behave to show your concern for your students. For each of these, explain how you can prepare to prevent their taking unfair advantage. It may be helpful if you decide at this time exactly where you will "draw the line."

SUGGESTED READINGS

BAUGHMAN, M. DALE. *Baughman's Handbook of Humor in Education.* New York: Parker Publishing Company, 1974.

CLARK, LEONARD H., and STARR, IRVING S. *Secondary School Teaching Methods,* 3d ed. New York: Macmillan, 1976.

COMBS, ARTHUR W., ed. *Perceiving, Behaving, Becoming.* Washington, D.C.: Association for Supervision and Curriculum Development, 1962.

GUFFEY, L. "Bored Students." *School and Community* 64 (March 1978): 29.

HOOVER, KENNETH A. *The Professional Teacher's Handbook: A Guide for Improving Instruction in Today's Secondary Schools,* 2d ed. Boston: Allyn and Bacon, 1976.

KELLER, FRED S. *Learning Reinforcement Theory.* New York: Random House, 1968.

SYMONDS, PERCIVAL M. *What Education Has to Learn from Psychology,* 3d ed. Columbia University, Teachers College Press, 1968.

Communications

Without communications teaching could not occur. Communications expert Marshall McLuhan has said that "the medium is the message." In the classroom there are (should be) many media including the teacher, audio-visual materials, and students. Not all of these communications are audible. Teachers often communicate by the way they stand or by the way they look at students. For example, a well-timed stare can curb undesirable behavior. A smile can convey approval, or a mysterious, puzzled look can arouse curiosity and enthusiasm.

This section will help you become familiar with the use of various types of audio-visual materials. It will also provide assistance in locating commercially made materials and in helping you learn how to make your own materials. As you read, think about the subjects and students that you will teach; be on the alert for discovering effective ways to utilize these materials.

Communications

OBJECTIVES

Upon completion of this chapter you should be able to:
1. List three voice qualities important to teaching and explain how each can be improved.
2. Give one suggestion for helping a teacher improve the quality of classroom questions.
3. Define "cognitive set" and name two techniques for establishing cognitive set in the classroom.
4. Name and describe at least five verbal teaching skills.
5. Give two rules for using examples in teaching.
6. List and describe two correct uses of feedback.
7. Name two nonverbal mistakes common to novice teachers.
8. Describe two conditions under which a teacher should strive for silence in the classroom.

As we have already seen, teaching is, to say the least, a complex set of activities. Teachers are expected, more and more to perform many roles, but their primary responsibility is to ensure that learning occurs. This role — regardless of the teaching techniques, methods, or strategies used — requires communicating. The many other roles of today's teachers also require communicating.

Your ability to produce changes in student behavior, learning or otherwise, will depend on your ability to communicate. So often the difference between stimulating and exciting teachers — who cause their students to think, learn, and feel — and dull teachers — who bore students with the subject — is the difference in their ability to communicate.

Students are slow to arrive at Ms. Simms's history class. As the tardy bell rings, there are usually a few still coming in and casually walking over to their desks. Equally predictable is the way Ms. Simms will present the lesson. She always begins by mumbling a few words about yesterday's lesson, even while the latecomers are ambling over to their chairs. Early in the year these students got the impression that Ms. Simms did not really care whether they learned the subject or not. They still do not know whether her knowledge of history is inadequate or whether she is merely unable to communicate.

This scene is not to be compared in any way to the climate in Miss Armstrong's class, where students arrive quickly, find their seats, and open their books and note pads. Miss Armstrong's expertise in the subject is obvious; as her Texas students have remarked, she comes to class with her pistols loaded. She begins each lesson promptly and assertively. The concepts that she presents are many, but they are clear; it is obvious that she cares whether her students understand. Furthermore, she seems to know when even one student is confused. Right away she gives an example that perfectly fits the problem. By the end of the period she has, like an artist, painted a clear picture of the era in history; and the personalities have come to life.

Why are some teachers, like Ms. Simms, confusing and boring, while others, like Miss Armstrong, are clear and interesting? The difference may not be so much in the teachers' understanding of their subjects but in their communicating of this knowledge. The teacher who communicates well makes the subject interesting and easy to learn, while the poor communicator makes her lessons boring and confusing. This chapter on communications skills is included to help you focus on your own abilities to communicate. Before you go any further, take a few minutes to list your strengths in communicating, along with your limitations that may need some attention. Consider such things as your voice, vocabulary, repertoire of examples and jokes, ability to ask questions, and ability to listen to students or to use expressions and movements to show others how you feel. Your lists should contain verbal and nonverbal skills, for both are necessary to effective communication. We shall first discuss the verbal skills and in the last part of the chapter attend to nonverbal skills.

While initially we may tend to think of classroom communications as a line extending between the teacher and student, this is, of course, a gross oversimplification of what actually happens in the classroom. The actual process more closely resembles the pattern shown in Figure 6.1.

While Figure 6.1 may seem to depict the teacher's role as impossibly complex, it is actually a pretty accurate representation of the communications aspect of teaching. Effective teachers seem to develop a sixth sense that picks up and responds to the many student comments which at times seem to come in continuous batteries. The process can perhaps be more accurately described as an acute alertness to students. Teachers also learn to respond in ways that serve a number of expressed concerns (and even unexpressed ones) simultaneously. Besides using verbal transmission and responses, teachers often learn to communicate in many nonverbal ways. As you continue through this chapter, see how many new verbal and nonverbal communications skills you can add to your initial list.

Voice Control

Some of us are gifted with stronger voices than others, but many qualities besides volume are important to a teacher's voice; these, as well as voice volume, can be improved by every teacher. Some teachers have such weak voices that they cannot be heard by most class members, so their valuable planning is largely wasted. How can you assure yourself that your voice will be heard by everyone? The seemingly obvious answer is to speak louder, but saying this and making the correction are two different things.

One way to increase your volume is by looking at individuals in the back of the room and talking to them during the lesson. Even when you are answering a question posed by a student in the front row, you should let members in the back row know that they are not being ignored. Just because a student in the front row asked the question, don't feel that others in the class already know the answer. The chances are good that others also need to hear your response.

The volume of your voice becomes even more crucial if you are teaching in

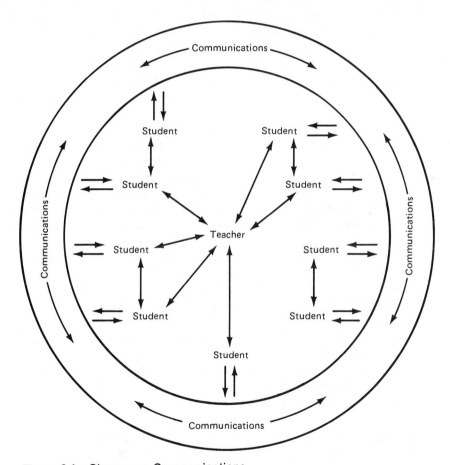

Figure 6.1 Classroom Communications

an open-concept situation. Many school buildings designed for this include carpeting and sound-absorbing ceiling tile, which make it somewhat difficult for students to hear you from any distance.

An equally common voice problem is lack of clarity, which is almost always caused by speaking too fast. The teacher should remember to speak slowly enough to give students time to absorb her message. Almost all beginning teachers talk too fast, leaving behind confused and discouraged students.

At times you should pause momentarily to give students time to think. When you introduce an important idea, stop for a moment, then continue. Also, when directing a question, give the pupil time to collect and organize an answer. Research shows that the most productive time lapse following a question is three seconds; however, on the average, teachers are uncomfortable with silence and rush on after pausing only one second.[1] Finally, if a student directs a question to you, your answer will be much better if you pause for an instant to think about the question before answering. A poor answer blurted out immediately is still a poor answer; a good answer is worth a moment's waiting.

Another way to help yourself to be heard is to reduce sound interference; for example, you could close the windows and doors to keep out distracting sounds. However, if your school lacks air conditioning (and many schools do not possess this luxury), you will sometimes have to keep windows and doors open for cross-ventilation. Traffic noises and the sounds of students in your class will therefore require you to increase your volume even more.

Once you have achieved adequate volume, examine your voice to see if it is monotonous. As you talk, listen to yourself. When you do, you will feel obligated to speak louder, more clearly, and more interestingly. If you have the facilities, have one of your lessons video-taped. If not, make an audio tape of your classes. The advantage of the video tape is that you can also begin improving your eye contact (a nonverbal skill) by seeing yourself on video tape.

Even now, in your education courses, you may wish to tape a short lesson given to a class of your peers. If so, try to have a minimum of ten or twelve students spaced throughout the room. Don't be ashamed to let others help in critiquing your lesson. You might ask one group to observe your voice while another observes your eye contact.

Each of us has experienced the boredom of sitting through a speech or lecture where the one who was supposedly imparting great wisdom was speaking in a monotone. Once he was finished, we could say only, "I'm glad he's through." In trying to reconstruct what he said, we found ourselves to be at a loss; for instead of listening, our minds were on something else.

As teachers, we must be aware of how we come across to students. If we speak in an uninteresting way, we cannot possibly expect much learning to occur. Taking the time and making the effort to improve voice inflection is a responsibility we cannot set aside.

---

[1] Mary Budd Rowe, "Wait, Wait, Wait," *School Science and Mathematics* 78 (March 1978): 207–16.

Set

A major difference between the beginning teacher and the experienced teacher's classes is often the amount of attention that prevails at the beginning of the period. The experienced teacher may refuse to begin a lesson until he has the undivided attention of every student. Getting students quiet is necessary because the teacher generally begins a lesson with an explanation of some kind. This could include a description of what he has planned, or it might be directions for something that he wants the students to do. In either case, the teacher would prefer to say what he has to say only once. Until the students are ready to listen (have a cognitive set), the teacher should refrain from beginning.

Suppose you remember each day to postpone the lesson until you have the attention of everyone. You reach the front of the room and still do not have the attention of the total class. What can you do? There are several alternatives.

One of the most effective is to do nothing at all but simply to stand facing the class, looking at those whose attention you must capture. If you begin talking before the others are quiet, they will usually get louder. Once things are quiet, you might feel the need to say, "It took us a little while to get started. Is there a topic that needs to be discussed before we begin?" Frequently there is, and a few minutes discussing it will be a good investment.

Another method for getting total class attention is to begin the lesson with a subject that is vitally interesting to the group. It may or may not be closely related to the day's lesson or even to the subject. If you listen to the class conversation, you can find out what the students are already interested in and begin the lesson with a discussion of that topic. You need not feel obligated to lead the discussion. Just remark, "Tom, you seem awfully interested in something. How about letting the rest of us in on it?"

Teachers tend to develop little tricks for getting the class as a whole to develop cognitive set. For instance, some teachers will begin the period by talking very low; they raise their voices to normal when students get quiet. Students know that it is a signal and, surprisingly, it tends to be effective all year long.

A few days of experience will help you to become alert to and recognize times when catching class attention will be very difficult. For example, a drastic change in the weather from hot to cold or rainy to fair, or vice versa, is an indicator of forthcoming boisterousness among students. An important school event will often have this effect, also. Keeping up with the local news, school news, and the weather will be to your advantage. You can then plan an appropriate entry in the day's lesson, such as "Who attended the basketball game last evening?" or "Did you hear this on the local news . . . ?" Once you let someone express her opinions about the topic that holds her interest, she will become free to concentrate on other topics, and then you can introduce the day's planned lesson.

Another effective method for establishing set is to use suspense. Begin the class by letting students guess what a diagram on the board represents, or begin by introducing a hypothetical case that will lead into the lesson. Perhaps you have a model that you can place so that it will be visible to all, or you may present a demonstration to the class; you will find such practices effective in capturing attention. If you can use a few students in the demonstration, or perhaps the entire class, you will quickly capture attention.

Using Examples

You will need to use examples to clarify the lesson and to make it a personal experience for each student. To improve the clarity of the lesson, select and use examples that relate to the principles being taught. If the example is to help the students, they must see its relation to the lesson. To assure yourself that the selected example will be understood and the communication will be made, you could begin with simple examples, moving to the more complex ones until the desired degree of sophistication of understanding has been achieved.

Students enjoy most lessons that involve the teacher's previous experiences or their own out-of-school experiences. Each lesson should contain examples from activities most interesting to the specific grade level addressed.

Students, too, should give examples from time to time. When you ask them to give examples of the principle just introduced, you can determine how clearly they understand the lesson. Too many teachers follow the introduction of information with the question "Does everyone understand?" But students who tell you that they do not understand admit a weakness for which they might be embarrassed. If you ask for an example from an average achiever, you can gauge how clearly you have presented or structured the lesson.

Students admire and respect the teacher who takes enough time and has enough patience to help those who have difficulty understanding what is being discussed. This frequently requires repetition. When and what should you repeat? One time when repetition is always needed is when students request it. Never refuse a request to repeat as long as the pupil is seriously trying to understand; however, do not make the repetition verbatim. Explain the concept in a different way, since saying the same thing, word for word, may only elicit the student statement "I still don't get it."

Frames of Reference

Repetition is not only for the student who appears to be misunderstanding. Few of us are capable of full comprehension of certain concepts upon hearing about them one time only. Do not assume that only one student has failed to understand what you have said; a wiser assumption is that the student is one of many who should hear it again, but in a different way.

Your degree in teaching will not guarantee that you can explain everything well. In fact, there will likely be students in your class who, if asked to repeat what you have said, can do so in such a way that the others will learn better than if you were doing all the talking.

Bear in mind that because some students who have uncertainties often refuse to admit them, you might overlook the need for repetition. On the other hand, to repeat everything would be boring to everyone. Therefore, you should practice repeating the most important ideas in the lesson. If you do not take adequate time for repetition and the lesson goes unlearned, even your best planning has been for naught.

Variety

Variety may or may not be the spice of life, but it certainly is the key to good teaching. Every class session should hold several different experiences for each student. Activities such as lecturing (teacher talk) or reading to pupils should not last for more than ten or fifteen minutes, and immediately afterward the class should be invited to contribute.

varying stimuli

Variety is also needed from day to day. If most of today's lesson involves lecturing (heaven forbid), tomorrow's lesson should be built around group work, a field trip, a film, assignments at the chalkboard, or another totally different activity. Usually a film or a group discussion should not be used for two consecutive days. The activities should be varied daily or, better yet, they should vary within the period.

Using Questions

As was just hinted, students often become bored with lessons that tend to be more teacher talk than student-involved learning experiences. Much of the information pertinent to any lesson is of a general nature and already known to the students. To prevent monotony, intersperse questions with your talking.

questioning strategies

The questions asked of students should not always be simple and basic, for

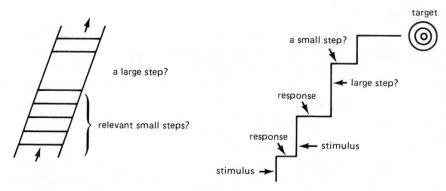

Figure 6.2 Using Questions to Guide Learning

This figure reminds the teacher that it is essential to remain alert to the size of the cognitive steps that are being dealt with. The size of the step determines the pace of the progress. Large steps may require large reinforcements with long intervals, whereas smaller steps may require reinforcements of less magnitude.

Source: Muska Mosston, *Teaching: From Command to Discovery* (Belmont, Calif.: Wadsworth, 1972), p. 124.

questions can be used to make students think. Good questions do not ask students to state a rule or to quote a definition; instead, they ask to have the rule applied to something. A good classroom question prompts students to use ideas rather than just to remember them. Using this type of question is a simple operation. You need only remember to ask the student for more information: "Why?" "How do you know that?" "How do you feel about that?"

You will find it helpful to direct such questions to an individual; otherwise, they may go unanswered, or the same few members in the class may answer all the questions. Suppose you direct a question to a student who is unable to provide the correct answer: Is it fair to her if you embarrass her with direct questions? Once you direct a question to an individual, you are obligated to help that student find an acceptable answer. This will not be difficult if you remember to (1) pause, giving time for organization of thoughts, (2) modify the answer until it is acceptable, and (3) provide hints for getting started. When used in this manner, questioning becomes a form of guided discovery. One former teacher recognizes that at times student answers will be incorrect or at best tangential, and that in either case the teacher is obligated to protect the integrity of the students. He gives the following example of how the teacher can effectively respond to an incorrect or tangential answer, "My question was not clear. Let me try this one . . ." [2]

Mosston, an expert on guided discovery, used diagrams (in Figure 6.2) to show how a series of carefully selected questions can guide students to discover relationships. Notice that the size of the steps (of progress) are not

---

[2] Muska Mosston, *Teaching: From Command to Discovery* (Belmont, Calif.: Wadsworth Publishing Company, 1972), p. 124.

always equal; neither are the sizes or frequencies of the reinforcements. To some extent these variables are affected by the nature of the subject being discussed, the abilities of the learners to follow a line of pursuit, and especially by the skill of the teacher to guide and reinforce them until they reach the goal being sought. Mosston reminds us that in guided discovery the teacher, never the student, is always the cause of failure.

CLASSIFYING QUESTIONS

By this time you are probably beginning to wonder why a taxonomy of questions rank-ordered into higher and lower levels is not provided. But ranking questions from good to poor is difficult, since teachers use questions to achieve very different types of objectives. In his book *Strategic Questioning*, Ronald Hyman classifies questions according to cognitive process and to other considerations.[3]

Cognitive Processes

The basic purpose for categorizing questions is to make them understandable. No researcher could design a system for improving the use of questions in the classroom by trying to study every imaginable question. The thousands of questions that arise in classrooms every day would be overwhelming even to the most capable investigator. Therefore, it becomes necessary to reduce the number of elements under study by establishing categories of questions. But because the number of possible categories is also staggering, a system is required to limit the number of categories. For example, classroom questions could be categorized according to the number of words per question or the number of words required to answer the question. But, of course, such a categorizing system would be pointless and, indeed, a waste of time. A more effective approach would be to group the questions according to the mental processes involved. The most commonly used system for categorizing questions has been of this type, that is, grouping according to cognitive processes.

There are three main types of cognitive process questions that are used regularly in classrooms. These three types are definitional, empirical, and evaluative. No one of these types is necessarily of a higher order than the others, that is, no hierarchy is implied. Now let's look more closely at each of these types of cognitive questions.

Definitional Questions

Obviously, definitional questions require students (or teachers) to define a word, term, or phrase. The following are examples of definitional questions:

1. What is a tornado?

---

[3] Ronald T. Hyman, *Strategic Questioning* (Englewood Cliffs, N.J.: Prentice-Hall, 1979).

2. Give an example of a verse of iambic pentameter.
3. What does it mean to play "piano"?

Notice that definitional questions search for exact or "true" answers. They leave no room for the respondents to express their feelings. In other words, you either know the correct answers or you do not.

Empirical Questions

Unlike definitional questions that ask for a definite, specific answer, empirical questions give the respondents an opportunity to express their perception of the world. These questions may ask for facts, generalizations, comparisons, explanations, conclusions, or inferences. For example:

1. Who wrote *Strategic Questioning*? (*fact*)
2. What generalization can you make about the lifestyle in Great Britain? (*generalization*)
3. How are American football and European football similar? Different? (*comparison*)
4. What did Tennyson mean by the lines, "Oh, what tangled webs we weave when first we practice to deceive"? (*explanation*)
5. What conclusion do you draw from the fact that the number of lives lost in traffic accidents decreased by fifty percent following the 55 mph national speed limit law? (*conclusion*)
6. It has been said that on any day of the year, the number of drownings in the state of New York correlates significantly with the total sales of ice cream in the state. What do you infer from this data? (*inference*)

Each of these empirical questions forces us to use our senses to observe the world around us.

Evaluative Questions

We have learned that definitional questions seek definite, specific answers and empirical questions seek answers that, sooner or later, can be verified. Evaluative questions ask students to express their opinions or values. They either ask the respondent to express an opinion or to justify one. For example,

1. Who is the greatest living fiction writer? (*opinion*)
2. Why do you say that the Rolls Royce is the best car ever made? (*justification of opinion*)

Now that the three major types of cognitive process questions have been introduced, consider the categorization of the following questions according to the expanded set of five categories:

1. Definitional   1. Definitions
2. Empirical   2. Facts
                   3. Relations between facts (generalizations, comparisons, explanations, conclusions, or inferences)

3. Evaluative   4. Opinions
              5. Justification of opinions

Using these five categories, write your categorizing number by the left of each question.

1. Which is worse, a tornado or hurricane? (*4, opinion*)
2. What is a sonnet? (*1, definition*)
3. You said that the Edsel was actually a very good car. How do you know this? (*5, justification of opinion*)
4. In what year did the Revolutionary War end? (*2, fact*)
5. What do you think is the major difference between the Democratic and the Republican parties? (*3, comparison*)
6. Who is the greatest U.S. president of this century? (*4, opinion*)
7. How fast does light travel? (*2, fact*)
8. What did Patrick Henry mean by "Give me Liberty or give me Death!"? (*3, explanation*)
9. What is a decibel? (*1, definition*)
10. When did the stock market first crash? (*2, fact*)

OTHER WAYS OF ANALYZING AND GROUPING QUESTIONS

As we have seen, questions used in the classroom should be selected, analyzed, and grouped according to the cognitive processes that the questions provoke. But there are other considerations determining the use of questions in teaching. For example, what demands does the question place on the respondents? Does it require them to reproduce information given in class or does it demand that they assemble information to produce their own answer? Another consideration might be, What kind of mental activity or process does the question require? With the exception of rhetorical questions, which do not intend to solicit a response, all questions must tell the respondents what type of behavior is expected of them. A third possible consideration of questions is, What type of cue, if any, does the question give the respondent to help clarify what type of answer is expected? Now let's examine each of these considerations.

Production Type

Production type indicates either a question asking students to produce their own information (productive question) or asking them to reproduce an answer given earlier by another source, such as the textbook or teacher (reproductive question). The context of the question will determine whether it is a productive or reproductive-type question. For example, "Why did the issue of Russian military forces in Cuba resurface in 1979?" If this had been discussed in class or if reference is made to a certain cause given by specific media, the question is of the reproductive type; however, if the issue has not been previously discussed, no reference is being made to a particular source, and the students are being asked to create their own explanation, then the question is of the productive type.

Information-Process Activity

A second consideration which should be given to questions is the information-process activity that you want the respondent to perform. There are three general ways in which you may expect students to perform: yes/no, selection, and construction. An example of a yes/no question would be: In the 1976 Presidential election, did Jimmy Carter carry the state of New York? Selection questions require the respondent to select from two or more given alternatives. For example, is *lonely* an adjective or adverb? Construction questions require students to construct their own response, such as: Explain your position on abortion.

Response Clue

Response-clue questions, giving clues as to the type of response desired, are of five types: wh-words, parallel terms, cited terms, excluded terms, and questions that lead the respondent. Wh-words such as *when, why, what, who* and *how* may clue the student to answer in terms of time, reasons, people and number.

Parallel terms ask the student to provide more information about the same topic: "Can you give another reason?" "And then what happened?" "Who else was involved?"

Cited Terms

Questions with cited terms offer a framework for the response. For example, "Who is the best college football team this year, *in terms of cooperative teamwork?*" "What were the major causes of the American Revolution, including social, economic and political?"

Excluded Terms

These questions tell the respondent what not to include in answering; for example, "Other than its cost, why is electricity an undesirable source for heating homes?" Or, "Besides earning good grades, why do you believe it necessary to learn all you can?"

Leading the Respondent

These questions lead the respondent to a *yes* or *no* response. (The British make extensive use of these questions). For example, "Don't you agree?" "It's rather humid today, isn't it?" "Most American cars aren't sub-compacts, are they?"

You have been introduced rather quickly to several types of questions. Now, let's review them:

1. Production type
   a. Productive
   b. Reproductive
2. Information-process activity
   a. Yes/no
   b. Selection
   c. Construction
3. Response clues
   a. Wh-words
   b. Parallel terms
   c. Cited terms
   d. Excluded terms
   e. Leading the respondent

Questioning Grid

The questioning grid shown in Figure 6.3 can be used as an observation instrument in the classroom to record and classify questions as they are asked. For this purpose you may wish to record a *T* in the appropriate boxes for all questions asked by the teacher and an *S* in the appropriate boxes for each question asked by students. By each question, list its appropriate type. Consider the following example questions and their classification.

Practice Question	Question Type
1. To convert from centimeters to millimeters, do you divide?	Yes/no; reproductive
2. What is the symbol for silver — Ag or Si?	Selection; wh-productive
3. What is the best gas to burn in a lawnmower — regular or hi-test?	Selection; wh-reproductive
4. Is Athens the capital of Greece?	Construction; reproductive
5. If we exhaust our petroleum, will we turn to using coal?	Yes/no; productive
6. What are the basic differences between the Democratic and Republican parties?	Construction; wh-productive
7. If the electric engine proves effective, will it become popular?	Yes/no; productive
8. If you overeat and go swimming, what will happen — besides getting indigestion?	Construction; reproductive
9. Why do you prefer football over basketball?	Construction; productive
10. Why else do you prefer football over basketball?	Construction; parallel terms; wh-productive

The teacher can elicit desired pupil behavior by using reinforcement. All students want to feel that they are capable of answering questions and performing assigned classroom tasks. Not only do they wish to feel adequate, but they also want to believe that the teacher looks upon them favorably.

Some students do not believe they can benefit from school because they feel themselves incapable of "fitting" in the school. Such special cases will be dealt with in a later chapter, but first let's analyze how a teacher can affect the student's self-attitude through reinforcement.

Too often the teacher responds to a student with, "You're right, but that's not the answer I wanted." This leaves the student with a feeling of failure and some confusion. Couldn't the teacher reverse this response, make the correction, and leave the student feeling that he is correct? For example, "Your response is not what I was seeking, but you are absolutely correct," or "That is interesting. I was expecting you to say . . . but you didn't. You gave an answer that I had not even thought about."

To be effective, reinforcement must be sincere. When it is sincere, each statement will address specific achievements. Too often teachers get into a rut, using the same reinforcement for every student. For example, a teacher may overuse such general expressions such as "good" and "okay." When this happens, the reward becomes routine and ineffective. On the other hand, some teachers overemphasize or overdramatize reward. When this occurs, the students sense the insincerity and become very skeptical of the teacher. How can you judge how much emphasis to place on rewarding? Perhaps the best guide to follow is to avoid using any rewards when you feel that the person has not earned the reward. And, before automatically responding "good," or "okay," it will be effective if you remember to pause momentarily to think about what

	Production Type		Information-Process Activity				Response Clue			
	Productive	Repro-ductive	Yes/No	Selection	Construc-tion	Wh- Inter-rogative Words	Parallel Terms	Cited Terms	Excluded Terms	Leading the Respondent
Short Set — Expanded Set										
Definitional — Definitions										
Empirical — Facts										
Empirical — Relations Between Facts										
Evaluative — Opinions										
Evaluative — Justifica-tions										

Figure 6.3 The Questioning Grid

Source: Ronald Hyman, *Strategic Questioning* (Englewood Cliffs, N.J.: Prentice-Hall, 1979), p. 29.

you are rewarding and never give more or less reward than you feel has been earned.

The key is to allow each student to feel successful at least one time every day; unfortunately, you will really have to concentrate to make this a reality with some students. With experience, however, you will create opportunities for these students to experience success.

REVIEW

Twice within each lesson you should review: at the beginning of the lesson and at the end. During the time that lapses between your contact with the students in a particular subject (generally one day), many things intervene to distort the student's memory of the previous lesson. It is for this reason that you should begin each lesson with a brief review of the previous day's high points. It serves to tune students back into the topic that they are currently studying. You need another review at the end of the period to reemphasize the major points covered during the lesson. This clarifies the lesson, removes some misconceptions, and gives the student more of a feeling of accomplishment.

When reviewing, never try to cover every fact and detail mentioned during the whole lesson. Rather, the review is a sorting out and clarification of the major concepts developed during the hour. The students should be encouraged to ask questions if they do not understand any part of the review.

NONVERBAL COMMUNICATION

Many teachers rely upon words and verbalisms to convey meaning during instruction. They believe that teaching is telling. They readily accept the notion that to be instructive is to be verbal or that to be verbal is to be instructive. They view words as the very miracles of learning. "How many times will I have to explain this?" "Haven't I explained that a hundred times already?" "Were you listening when I told you that?" "All right, everybody pay attention, I am only going to say this one more time." Although these statements by teachers do not characterize teaching, they do portray a reliance on the power of words.[4]

The preceding are the words of Charles M. Galloway, professor of education at Ohio State University. Since the beginning of the 1960s, he has researched nonverbal communication in teaching. As Galloway says, teachers are often inclined to think that their sole communication with pupils is through words. In reality, students are taking in much more. They are turned on less frequently by *what* you say than they are by *how* you say it; they constantly

[4] Charles M. Galloway, "Nonverbal Communication in Teaching," in *Teaching: Vantage Points for Study,* 2d ed., ed. Ronald T. Hyman (Philadelphia: J. B. Lippincott, 1974), p. 395.

watch for excitement or enthusiasm in your expression. Even when you are not instructing verbally, students are continually gaining information about how you feel. Your attitudes, likes, dislikes, approval, and disapproval are all communicated through facial expressions and other body language.

For example, some teachers, with or without realizing it, use their desks as walls for protection from their students or as a symbol of authority. Besides being a protective device, the desk is actually a psychological barrier to good teacher-student communication. Until the teacher moves from behind it, true communication will be next to impossible. Some teachers sit at their desks while reading to, lecturing at, or discussing with their students. On the surface, it might appear that things are fine, but, deep down, both sides can feel something lacking.

Other teachers move freely throughout the class as if to say, "We're all here for the same purpose; let's work together." There is no success unless the students succeed, for ultimately the teacher and students are seeking the same goals. Those goals are reached when the teacher-learning situation reaches the optimal level. This optimal level is hypothetical, because it is impossible to reach; still, the teacher and students should strive for it constantly.

The next time that you are a classroom observer, take notes on the teacher's nonverbal communications. See how many different ways you notice. If, before you graduate, you have an opportunity to peer-teach a lesson or to teach a lesson to public school students, near the end of the lesson you might ask your students about the different ways that they felt you communicated nonverbally with them. Ask them how they felt about what you did and how you did it. Today's students tend to be honest and say what they feel, so you should be able to learn much from them.

Feedback

While the students are receiving nonverbal communications from the teacher, the teacher can simultaneously receive feedback. An experienced teacher, watching and listening to the students, is aware of their emotions. Good teachers do not stop there; they will always use this knowledge about the students to adjust their teaching methods. For example, suppose, while you are teaching, that several students begin yawning. You might open a window or lower the room thermostat. If the drowsiness continues, you might change your teaching approach to include more student activity. You may also need to change your verbal teaching style to include more inflection in your voice. By and large, unless you are dealing with students who came from very poor home situations — and thus have poor nutrition and inadequate sleeping facilities — the yawning can probably be attributed to something you are or are not doing. Again, be aware of any clues that the students give you regarding a communication breakdown.

One fairly new method for obtaining feedback is that of devising some type of bulletin board that allows students to express their impressions of the teacher. For example, at the end of each lesson or at the end of each day, students might be given a positive *thumbs-up*-tab or a negative *purple shaft-*

tab to attach to the board to show how the teacher left them feeling on that particular day. For best results, the students should be able to place the symbols on the board anonymously; if not, some may respond in the manner that they feel you want them to respond. It is important that you use this information in attempting to change your teaching behavior.

Eye Contact

One of the most important teaching skills that you will ever develop is eye contact, for you should do more than talk to (or with) the class. Teaching should be a multichanneled dialogue. Because beginning teachers are sometimes uncertain and insecure, they avoid looking directly toward the students and look instead at their notes or toward the windows. At best, many beginning teachers look toward the class but see only one large audience.

To prevent looking too much at your notes, you might try using fewer notes. You may find that just a list of the major ideas — or at most a broad outline — of the lesson will work better than a lesson plan that has everything spelled out. To avoid looking at one general audience, try to focus on a few individuals in each conversation. Public school teaching is not lecturing but is a multicommunicative process between teacher and student or among students themselves.

We all know people who, when talking to us, look over our shoulder, above our head, anywhere but directly at us. We become so engrossed with this annoying behavior that what they are saying becomes secondary to what they are doing. It's no different in the classroom. Without eye contact you will experience a communication breakdown, and the teaching-learning situation will be far from that hypothetical optimum mentioned earlier.

Suppose that, when you begin teaching, you sit behind the desk. There will be no way for you to have eye contact with every member of your class. Very likely you will be unable to see *any* part of some students on the far side of the room, let alone their eyes. This lack of eye contact would in itself be a barrier to good classroom control.

Other Nonverbal Teacher Behaviors

Much of what a teacher does can be characterized as a combination of verbal and nonverbal behaviors. When you ask a student to settle down, you are verbally communicating; however, at the same time, you may be gesturing with your hands or "giving a look" that is actually more effective in getting your point across. Let us take a few examples depicting these combinations of verbal and nonverbal communications but address most of our concern to the nonverbal. For instance:

1. You have asked a question to which the student has responded incorrectly. Smiling, you indicate, in a nice way, that you were looking for a different answer. Your smile alone says, "That's all right. Don't be afraid to raise your hand to volunteer an answer to any other question I might ask."

2. A student is poking his pencil at a classmate during a time when the teacher is reading a story to the class. Seeing this, you pause and, tilting your head downward, look over the top of your glasses. The "foolishness" stops immediately.

3. While giving a test, you see a girl looking on another's paper in hopes of increasing her own performance. (This is a kind way of saying that the girl is cheating.) You walk over to the girl and inconspicuously shake your head. At the same time, you firmly but gently grasp the girl's shoulder, indicating that there are no hard feelings, and the issue is closed.

These three examples show only a small fraction of the times when your nonverbal behavior can play an extremely important role in student-teacher relationships. With verbal reprimands only, these relationships would tend to weaken.

Body Movement

The time when the teacher hides behind a desk is, we hope, long since gone. As mentioned earlier, you need to circulate among your students. By doing so, you can communicate with each individual. Since talking to individuals will often be disturbing to others, much of this communication must be done nonverbally. Walking throughout the room, pausing momentarily to place a hand lightly on a student's shoulder, or giving a smile and a nod of the head, you can capture the confidence that students should have in their teacher. (Older students prefer nods, winks, and hand signals over excessive touching.) Even more importantly, this type of recognition can help build self-confidence.[5] Students who know that a teacher is pleased with them will feel good about themselves.

Using Silence

An almost universal problem that teachers have is talking when they should be listening. Too much teacher talk leaves little opportunity for pupil participation. Learning to remain quiet requires a great deal of self-discipline and, for one reason or another, teachers do not exercise this enough.

When advised by her supervisor that she talked too much, a first-year teacher made tapes of her classes and kept a daily log of her experiences. Over a period of time she was able to analyze, record, and evaluate her progress; however, she also did one additional thing to discipline herself. On her desk, where she could easily see it, she placed a sign that read in Swedish, "Shut Up."

The girl explained that her tendency was to answer her own questions before the students had an opportunity to do so. She then noted, "The uncomfortable

---

[5] Charles M. Galloway, *Silent Language in the Classroom* (Bloomington, Ind.: Phi Delta Kappa Educational Foundation, Fastback No. 86, 1976), pp. 22–23.

quiet can actually be a time for thinking . . . and if the teacher outwaits the students, one of the latter will begin speaking." [6]

As you observe yourself in various settings, begin asking yourself how much silence you can tolerate. See how much *you* can refrain from talking instead of being concerned with the students' talking too much. Rather than feeling obligated to respond to the comments made by students, can you encourage other students to enter into the discussion? Instead of picturing yourself as one who *dominates* discussions, try to develop the ability to *lead* those discussions.

One of the most difficult times to do this is when you are asked to share your opinion on a controversial or debatable subject. For instance, during presidential election years, students will ask about your views of each candidate. If ever there was a time to refer to that message written in Swedish, this surely must be it, especially if you have a definite bias for or against one of the candidates. We have already suggested some body language that lends itself to effective nonverbal behavior. Let's consider some additional ones.

The question put to you is, "Is it true that so-and-so will take all the money from the rich and dole it out to people on welfare?" Rather than saying, "I didn't know Robin Hood was a candidate," merely extend both arms out to your side, palms of your hands up. This implies, "I don't know" or "Your guess is as good as mine." At the same time, ask others what they have heard. Is this a cop-out? Maybe, but it serves a good purpose in that pupil talk is increased. And, unless you know for sure what so-and-so will do, any response that you make is pure conjecture and thereby adds nothing of real value to the discussion.

As one additional point, consider the fact that numerous questions are going to be asked of you to which you really do not know the answer. To attempt bluffing your way out of this is pure folly. For you can give incorrect information that will either give students false learning or show you to be less honest if they later determine what you actually should have said. Too often, teachers feel that they are expected to have all the answers. Admitting that you do not know an answer will not be showing a weakness but will rather make you appear human after all.

Detecting Boredom

One final group of nonverbal signals whose recognition is indispensable to teachers are those that signal boredom. The popular trade book *How to Read a Person Like a Book* includes in this group: resting one's head in his hands, giving a blank stare, and doodling.[7] There are also others, such as yawning and

---

[6] Karen Drury Norris, "Getting the Teacher to Shut Up," in *Teaching Strategies and Classroom Realities,* ed. Mildred G. McClosky (Englewood Cliffs, N.J.: Prentice-Hall, 1971), pp. 35–36.

[7] Gerald I. Nierenberg and Henry H. Calero, *How to Read a Person Like a Book* (New York: Pocket Books, 1971), pp. 122–24.

squirming. The most obvious indicators of boredom are squirming (because it involves movement of the entire body as one shifts weight from hip to hip while simultaneously repositioning arms, legs, feet, and hands) and yawning, which adds the dimension of sound. Squirming might carry other messages, such as a need to use the restroom, and yawning may indicate a physical need for sleep; but what they probably mean is that communications are breaking down. Students are also frequently seen resting their heads in their hands. They may or may not be aware that this gesture also symbolizes boredom. By the time that they reach high school, most students know that most of these movements are considered impolite and have begun substituting more subtle expressions such as giving a blank, glassy stare or silently doodling. Granted, a few highly creative individuals express their creativity through doodling, and a few great thinkers appear glassy-eyed when they engage in deep thought; however, these are a very small minority and their wisdom can be detected by examining their drawings and by pursuing their thoughts with questions. Sometimes students may offer fake, hollow stares to trick the teacher, but most students today are quite open, both verbally and nonverbally.

You must be a good communicator before you can be an effective teacher. Besides being aware of your voice quality — including volume, tempo, and clarity — you should take care to see that your eye contact is good. Both skills can be improved by a personalized approach to teaching, which includes talking to individual students and calling them by name.

You should also master nonverbal communications. Both technical and nonverbal teaching skills can be improved through peer teaching, in which your colleagues provide objective critiques about your strengths and weaknesses. Audio and video tape recorders, allowing you to observe yourself in the teaching role, are another effective means of improvement.

EXPERIENCES

Chapter 4 portrayed the teacher as a manager of students, equipment, space, and activities. That list purposefully omitted communications because an entire chapter was needed to show the teacher's role in managing the complex communications in the classroom. The following experiences are provided to give you practical examples of the importance of good communications to instruction.

Experience 1: Teach Students, Not Subjects

When Sue began teaching in high school, her students were amazed at her obvious brilliance. Though she seemed to have the facts, names, and dates all memorized and could give from memory every detail of any war, she never tried to show off her ability. Sue was, in fact, a borderline introvert. When the beginning bell rang for each period, Sue seemed to lack the courage necessary to start the lesson. After calling the roll, she would then mumble about the homework assignment without actually looking up from her book for several minutes. A typical lesson was as follows.

(Looking downward at her text): All right, class, what did we learn yesterday? What did we say was the cause of World War II? What did we learn about Germany's economic status at the time? Why did the United States stay out of the war for so long? etc., etc.

▶ *Questions and Discussion*

1. *Why do you think Sue talked to her book instead of talking to her students?*
   Like all beginning teachers, Sue was a little nervous. Lacking the courage necessary to face her students, she resorted to looking at her book whenever she began talking.

2. *How could Sue improve her questioning?*
She could begin by directing each comment to a particular student. She could further improve her questioning by avoiding such general questions and making each question specific. The questions "What about Germany's economic status?" And, "Why did the United States stay out of the war for so long?" could have many answers. Exactly what points about each topic were discussed in class? Each question should be designed to solicit each of these important concepts.

Experience 2:   A Need for Tact in Questioning

Jack Cobb was a good biology teacher who planned thoroughly. Each day's lesson was highly content-oriented, but he did allow for student participation and thus could claim to be somewhat student-centered in his approach. He was not, however, very patient during his questioning.

One particular class period stands out, for in less than forty minutes he had damaged, to some degree, the self-concepts of three students, all of them already considered by their classmates to be slow learners. In each case he had asked a question to which the student responded incorrectly. His reaction was, "That's wrong. Who knows the answer?"

► *Questions and Discussion*

1. *How can students be made to feel successful when they respond incorrectly to a question?*
Earlier in this chapter we implied that the teacher has both the opportunity and the responsibility for making a student feel successful. Regardless of how incorrect the response might be, a resourceful teacher will be able to guide the student out of despair and/or embarrassment. Some techniques have been discussed, but here is another possibility.

It is apparent that Jack Cobb did not realize, or did not care, that his remark "That's wrong. Who knows the answer?" was a negative type of reinforcement. He could have said, "I don't believe you're fully correct. Would you like some help?" The student would surely have responded affirmatively. Then he could ask for volunteers. When the correct answer was given, Jack could go back to the original student and say, "Do you think that's right?"

Please notice how the first student (let's call her Jill) will feel if Jack does this. Jill will know that she was incorrect, but she will not be excluded from the rest of the group, for she makes the decision to seek assistance. Jill will again be involved when Jack comes back to her for verification of the correct response.

Your working with students humanely will be noticed by the entire class. Even though many will "see through" your actions, they will admire your motives and will most certainly respect you a great deal for it.

2. *Should "slow" learners be asked questions in class?*

All students should have an opportunity to respond to questions or to originate questions of their own. The teacher's job is to be selective as to which questions are asked of which students.

Teachers' questions range from the most superficial to the fairly detailed and abstract. Unfortunately, too many require short, crisp answers of yes or no, but these may be the best types to ask when dealing with the pupil of low achievement. Although such shallow questions and responses result in a small amount of additional knowledge, they do give the student a chance at being successful.

There is an exception to directing only low-level questions to the slow student. When a student who normally would not be expected to respond shows that she wants to answer a question, no matter how detailed, let her have a go at it. If she is correct, she will be pleased, and so will you. It might just give her the encouragement she needs to attempt learning some other things.

ACTIVITIES

As we have seen in the preceding pages, good teaching requires good communication, and good communication does not always happen automatically. Some teachers depend mostly on verbal communications; others, less verbose, use more nonverbal strategies to communicate. Every teacher should combine verbal and nonverbal strategies to improve two-way communications in the classroom. The following activities may challenge you to relate these strategies to your own behavior style.

1. How much do you talk? When you are in a one-to-one conversation with a colleague, who dominates the discussion? Think about it. Do you tend to talk too much? too little? Devise a plan for helping yourself reach a more even balance.
2. Now that you are aware of a number of effective nonverbal strategies for communicating, it is now time to relate this knowledge to teaching. Considering your own unique attributes, explain how you can use nonverbal communication techniques in your classroom.
3. From your own previous experiences as a student, can you list any techniques not included in this book that could be effective for classroom application?

SUGGESTED READINGS

GALLOWAY, CHARLES M., ed. *Theory Into Practice* 91 (June 1977). This entire issue is on nonverbal communications.

HANNAM, CHARLES; SMYTH, PAT; and STEPHENSON, NORMAN. *Young Teachers and Reluctant Learners.* Baltimore: Penguin Books, 1971.

HYMAN, RONALD T. *Strategic Questioning.* Englewood Cliffs, N.J.: Prentice-Hall, 1979.

JOHNSTON, WILLIAM. *Monday Morning Father.* New York: Grosset & Dunlap, 1970.

MOLDSTAD, J. A., ed. "Role of Technology in Improvement of Instruction: Symposium." *Viewpoints* 51 (Spring 1975): 1–77.

MOSSTON, MUSKA. *Teaching: From Command to Discovery.* Chapter 4. Belmont, Calif.: Wadsworth Publishing Company, 1972.

PEACOCK, F., and PATRICK, J. "Making Media Fit." *Industrial Education* 66 (May 1977): 19–20.

RUBIN, LOUIS J., ed. *Facts and Feelings in the Classroom.* New York: The Viking Press, 1973.

WEIL, MARSHA, and JOYCE, BRUCE. *Social Models of Teaching.* Englewood Cliffs, N.J.: Prentice-Hall, 1978.

WILLIAMS, S. S. "Observational System for Analysis of Classroom Communication." *Clearing House* 51 (March 1978): 346–48.

Using Media

OBJECTIVES

When you have completed reading this chapter, you should be able to:
1. Name two widely used forms of media in secondary schools.
2. Give two rules for using the bulletin board.
3. Give one guideline for introducing any audio or visual production and two helpful guidelines for concluding its use.
4. Name two types of teacher- or pupil-made media.
5. Name two newer types of media and explain an advantage of each over its predecessors.
6. Name and explain a common misuse of media.

Recent technological advancements in this country have been numerous and diverse. So common are they that we Americans tend to take for granted, underappreciate, and underuse these developments in many fields, including education. The purpose of this chapter is to alert you to many current media uses in the classroom and to challenge you to discover new ways of employing media as you develop your own teaching style. You may even be stimulated to begin a personal repertoire of media aids to use in your student teaching and beyond.

THE MEDIA IN YOUR OWN SCHOOL

When you go to student teaching and then on to your first teaching job, you will find that most teachers have access to numerous teaching aids, such as projectors, films, posters, and records. If the school is fairly large, it may have its own media center, possibly in conjunction with the school library. If not, media will be housed in one central location within the school district and will be available to each teacher on a one- or two-day notice. The teacher who avoids using media is possibly short-changing students, omitting an additional learning experience that could reach some students better than any other strategy could.

As we examine some of the media available, you may decide what will be worthwhile to you and your future students.

The 16 mm Projector

To the carefree student, viewing a film is synonymous with seeing a movie — if the film is entertaining. From a teacher's viewpoint a film should be both entertaining and educational; above all, it should assist the students in attaining some definite course objectives. The teacher can help by introducing the film before showing it, giving pupils a few specifics to look for. Upon completion, the film may be reviewed by involving pupils in a discussion of those key points. Whether or not note taking is required should be the decision of the teacher, depending, of course, on how quickly material is introduced, the purpose of the film, and whether there is adequate light in the room for writing. Such instructions require that the teacher previews the film before showing it in class.

Some teachers wish to show a film to fill in time, such as a Friday afternoon before a lengthy vacation. This practice is highly questionable, since it could encourage students to think of films purely as entertainment items. It cannot be stressed too much that films should be selected for their ability to promote learning. They should be planned into the instructional program and coordinated with the rest of the unit.

A good film can be an excellent means of introducing a topic and of creating enthusiasm. Teachers also find films very useful for reviewing a topic or unit because films have the capacity to summarize much information quickly. Some films are technical in nature and are therefore excellent for teaching highly technical processes. (For example, a physical education teacher may use films on bowling, golfing, swimming, and other sports to show the skills and techniques.) Whatever the purpose for using a film, the teacher should always select the film for that purpose and communicate that purpose to students.

Before graduation you will probably take a class that includes working with various equipment found in a media center. Apply yourself in this setting, since you will likely be the one to operate the equipment in your own classroom. If you are unable to thread a projector, you will cause unnecessary confusion in your classroom, to say nothing about student disappointment if the scheduled film is not shown.

The Filmstrip and Film Loop Projectors

Like the 16 mm film, a good filmstrip or film loop (a miniature motion film that runs for only a few minutes, and then repeats itself) is an excellent addition to a unit of study. These, too, should be previewed and planned into the lesson. The teacher's role is to alert the students to topics to look for and — to see that this is achieved — to hold a discussion or question-answer session at the end of the filmstrip. The advantage of the filmstrip over the 16 mm film is that it allows for discussion, and possibly for more understanding, during the showing.

The Overhead Projector

Aside from the chalkboard, the most commonly used audio or visual medium in the classroom is the overhead projector. It offers two distinct advantages over most other types of audio-visual machinery: it is available and versatile. You can make transparencies easily with a few sheets of inexpensive clear acetate and a grease pencil. Or you can use colored felt pens made for writing on acetate; and the color will add interest to the lesson.

The major advantage of the overhead projector is that you can face the class at all times, seeing hands as they are raised and retaining good control. The chalkboard, of course, does not always provide this opportunity.

Success with the overhead projector depends on good, appropriate materials and correct usage of the machine. Since both a knowledge of securing good materials and effective use of the machine are indispensable, let's examine each of these in their respective order.

SECURING MATERIALS

The general quality of overhead projectors in this country is very high. Most machines have a standard size surface and produce an image of somewhat

equal clarity. The success of contemporary overhead projectors can be attributed to their 500-watt intensity, which is capable of producing a clear image on a screen without the use of blackout curtains or even without turning off the ceiling lights. With no abuse these machines are durable and seldom require maintenance. The teacher's main concern, then, should be in getting good materials to use on the projector. Their acquisition involves one of two approaches: teachers can either purchase the materials or produce their own materials.

Purchasing Materials

The most commonly purchased material for the overhead projector is the simple transparency. Commercial publishers offer a wide range of transparencies in all subjects for use at different grade levels. Most of the transparencies sold today are multicolored and are designed to capture students' attention and to communicate concepts simply and clearly.

You will want to check with your own department head and with your school's learning center and/or media center to see what supplies you have available. You will also find catalogs for ordering these and other audiovisual materials. When you order transparencies, be sure to check the age group (or range of ages) for which the transparencies are designed. Following is a list of sources of transparencies.

Audio Visual Communications, Inc., 159 Verdi Street, Farmingdale, New York 01135.

AeVac Educational Publishers, 1604 Park Avenue, South Plainfield, New Jersey 07018.

Encyclopaedia Britannica Film, Inc., 425 Michigan Avenue, Chicago, Illinois 60611.

ESSCO Educational Supply Co., Inc., 2825 East Gage Avenue, Huntington Park, California 90255.

Johnson Plastic, Inc., 526 Pine Street, Elizabeth, New Jersey 07206.

Miliken Publishing Company, 611 Olive Street, St. Louis, Missouri 63101.

Scott Reprographs Division, Holyoke, Massachusetts 01040.

The Lansford Publishing Company, 2516 Lansford Avenue, San Jose, California 95125.

Valiant Industries, 172 Walker Lane, Englewood, New Jersey 07631.

PRODUCING MATERIALS

Transparencies

For reasons of economy, convenience, and suitability to lesson plans, many teachers make their own overhead transparencies. There are several processes for this; but, since some are rather elaborate and require machinery not available to most teachers, we shall examine only the easiest and fastest methods.

If your school has a thermal copying machine (and most schools do), you can merely place a sheet of special transparency film over the sheet that you wish to copy and run it through the machine. This method, which takes about ten seconds, can be used to copy pictures or print with a carbon base. Since most printed materials do use carbon, they can be quickly reproduced. Even pencil drawings and theme papers, problems, and the like usually work well. Copyright laws forbid the reproduction of copyrighted material for profit. In the past, teachers were permitted to copy materials for use in their classes; however, because of abuse and because copyright laws are changing, you should check with your administrators to see that your projects do not violate the law.

A second method of producing transparencies is equally inexpensive, easy, and fast. Just get a sheet of frosted (matte) acetate and run it through the spirit duplicator as you would a piece of paper. The image will be printed on the sheet. For further detail on the production of transparencies see this chapter's Suggested Readings, especially the entries for Kemp and for Haney and Ullmer.

The Overhead Projector

As was mentioned earlier, effective results with this machine depend on good materials and good utilization. The following list provides a good guideline for using the overhead projector.

1. Use good transparency pencil or transparency pen (not ordinary felt pen).
2. Check the best position in the classroom for projection, so that all students can see the projection clearly.
3. Face students when speaking to them (you don't have to turn around every time as you would do when using chalkboard).
4. Any transparent models or objects such as plastic ruler, protractor, ripple tanks, and test tubes can be projected vividly.
5. Tracing charts or drawings on construction paper or on chalkboard can be easily done by simply projecting the original transparency.
6. When you do not want to show the entire transparency, cover up the portion of the contents with paper (masking technique).
7. When you want to add or correlate the contents simultaneously, simply add on another transparency (overlay technique).[1]

Once you have acquired the materials, concentrate on the next important step, the actual positioning and focusing of the machine. Before attempting to focus it, determine the distance from the screen that the machine should be positioned. This is easy: direct the light onto the screen and move the pro-

---

[1] Eugene C. Kim and Richard D. Kellough, *A Resource Guide for Secondary School Teaching*, 2d ed. (New York: Macmillan, 1978), p. 139.

jector away from the screen until the light fits just immediately within the boundaries of the screen. Then the image can be brought into focus simply by changing the distance between the lens and the machine's surface. Most machines have a knob that can be turned to achieve focus.

There is one more matter to consider when you use the overhead projector. You have the option of preparing the transparency in advance or of writing, sketching, or drawing on a clear sheet of acetate paper during the lesson. Bringing the transparency to class already prepared offers an advantage over using the chalkboard. The teacher does not have to take time from the lesson and attention from the students to write the paragraphs, make the lists, or draw the diagrams. But there is also an advantage to developing the visual material during the lesson, stopping to involve students at strategic points.

Overlays

Because transparencies are clear, they can be stacked on top of one another to add dimensions or details to the image. Since such superimposure requires accuracy in placing each one exactly over the one below, you will find it helpful to make a cardboard frame for the first transparency; then tape one side of the second transparency to the left side of the frame. If yet another superimposure is desired, tape the top of the next transparency to the top of the frame. Continuing to tape one side of each transparency at a 90-degree angle to the previous one, you can stack up as many transparencies as you wish.

During your education courses (as you teach peer lessons) and your student teaching internship, you will have opportunities to experiment with making your own transparencies, with using some prepared materials, and with preparing some during the lesson.

The Opaque Projector

Before the availability of the thermal copy machines and the overhead projector, the opaque projector was frequently used in classroom instruction, and it does have some advantages. It can project an image on a screen directly from the book, saving the time and expense of making a permanent copy of the material; also there is no question of infringement of copyright laws.

With these advantages, you may be wondering why the opaque projector is almost moribund (although there are a few moth-eaten specimens left). Its greatest problem is its bulky size, blocking the image from many of the students. It also forms a major barrier between the teacher and many of the students. A second design problem is in the weakness of the image. A good image often requires total darkness in the room, leaving students unable to take notes or work problems, but free to engage in other less academic pursuits of their own choosing.

The opaque projector has even other disadvantages. It is noisy; and its opening, although adjustable, prevents the use of very thick books. If a book is left too long on the projector, the intense heat will damage the page. With so many disadvantages, you may never wish to use this machine in teaching a lesson; yet you or your students may find it very useful in projecting very large images on the wall for the purpose of tracing.

The Slide Projector

Like the overhead projector, the slide projector produces an image so intense that it can be closely seen in most lighted classrooms. One advantage of slides is their capture of real scenery, people, and events that are relevant to the class's subject. Just think how much more interesting a Spanish class can be if the teacher shows a collection of slides that she took on her vacation to Mexico last year. Or the social studies teacher can intensify the interest in his class with slides he took of people at work in different countries. The biology teacher can produce a similar effect with slides taken of plants and animals as he visited the deserts, mountains, plains, and seashores.

Although the 110 mm instamatics produce a slide that is too small to be seen clearly in most classrooms, the common 126 mm instamatic cameras work well. The 35 mm cameras (which are more expensive) produce even better slides.

The main thing to remember when you take pictures for slides is to take more than one of each promising subject. This, of course, increases the likelihood of getting quality results. If people are being photographed at a close range, be sure to get their permission. Students should also be encouraged to take slides to share with the class. Field trips should always have follow-up discussions — good slides will enhance such follow-ups.

The Record Player

Even though you associate music and dancing with the record player, you should not limit its use to these alone. A story or poem read by Orson Welles or a ballad sung by Burl Ives communicates in very special ways. As with other media, the purpose should be made clear from the beginning and re-emphasized at the end, and the students should be assigned tasks that will involve them with the content portrayed through the media.

An area where the record player can have good application is in the language arts, most specifically in developing listening skills. Good questions before the record help guide the students toward better listening. Equally good questions during the discussion following the record are a means of positively reinforcing those pupils who did listen attentively.

Television

No discussion of the role of media in education would be complete without including the television. The effect of TV on today's youth is reflected in one survey that found the most admired female to be a TV actress and the most admired man a TV actor.[2] Americans spend an enormous amount of time

---

[2] Mary Susan Miller, "The Farrah Factor," *Ladies Home Journal*, June 1977, p. 34.

watching TV. The average range is from twenty-three hours a week (for children under five) to forty-four hours for adults. The American student spends more time watching TV than he spends in school! To be sure, much of the results are negative. Experts tell us that television promotes violence (at the present rate, by age eighteen today's youth will have seen 18,000 murders), passiveness, and sex bias while discouraging creativity.[3] But this is not to deny that some excellent programs are being produced, like the Abraham Lincoln series, the Ben Franklin series, and the culturally rich programs of the Public Broadcasting System (PBS).

Surely the future will see television playing an important role in the education of school-age youth. You can help by bringing discussions of quality programs into your classrooms. Your associations and unions can lobby for the production of more quality programs and programs designed for adolescents at each age level. And, of course, you can support the educational networks and encourage others to do likewise.

The Bulletin Board

Good media are not always bought; they can be made by the teacher or by students. When properly used, the bulletin board (or cork board or felt board) is an excellent means for stimulating thinking. This board should never be

---

[3] Harry F. Waters, "What TV Does to Kids" *Newsweek*, February 21, 1977, pp. 62–66.

allowed to become dated, and the contents should revolve around a central theme.

You can use a bulletin board to help make your subjects come alive. Posters and pictures depicting an aspect of a unit being studied give all students a similar opportunity to learn, regardless of their home backgrounds. Consider, for example, that you are starting to teach a unit on Africa: on the bulletin board you could place a map of Africa with a photo of the leader of each country pasted in the respective country. During discussions of leaders, countries, and events, each student can identify the leaders and locate the events. Without this visual aid, those students who do not watch the news regularly and who undoubtedly have never visited Africa would be at a disadvantage. Although a picture cannot replace direct personal experience, it does narrow the gap between the students who have some awareness of the country and those who do not.

You can use the bulletin boards in other positive ways. Try placing a "Problem of the Week" in one corner of the board and encourage students to attempt solution at any time that their work is completed. In a week's time every student will have had the opportunity to solve it, and they will be eager to compare their answers with what the teacher feels is correct. Such a practice builds enthusiasm.

One teacher uses her bulletin board to a make a time line when studying social studies. Each day a few students are given the responsibility for "bringing it up to date," based on the material they have learned that day.

Many teachers place less importance on how a bulletin board looks than on what it says or does. The students are solely responsible for it, thus everything on it represents their efforts. Throughout the year, the board is constantly changing, because the world is ever-changing. A few teachers place a chart or a graph on the bulletin board, indicating the progress that each student is making. As the year progresses and the range of achievement increases, some pupils "stick out like sore thumbs." The able students' lines on the progress graph go quite far from the left to the right, whereas a few students are lagging far behind, as evidenced by the same graph. Teachers will defend this action on the grounds that it increases motivation, but this is not true for all the students. The more capable will tend to compete with one other when the graph tells them who is "ahead," but students who are unable to keep up suffer embarrassment and some lack of self-respect. Even though they are trying, they cannot expect to compete with those who are much more capable; therefore, many will tend to do even less well. Competition is fine as long as all competitors are on somewhat of a par.

And then there are the teachers who feel an attractive bulletin board is a mark of a good teacher. They spend hours cutting out letters and making an eye-catching display, especially before an open house or parent-teacher meeting, most assuredly during American Education Week. Never mind that the bulletin board lacks function, that is, students learn nothing from it — it looks good and a few visitors will be impressed. Unfortunately, some principals like to see this neatness and thereby encourage teachers in this direction.

The Chalkboard

The chalkboard has value beyond its common uses. The students' attention should focus on it automatically, without a request from the teacher. Some teachers achieve this by placing a thought for the day at the top of the board and leaving it there all day. Graffiti can also be used to get pupils' attention. For example, imagine students entering a room to see the following message staring at them:

!EREH KCAB DEPPART M'I !EM PLEH ESAELP

Colored chalks can be stimulating, but before you use any, check with the custodian. He may discourage you because colored chalk is often difficult to remove, even with soap and water. In some cases chalkboards have even been damaged through using white or yellow chalk that was nonstandard.

Some Newer Types of Media

In recent years audio-visual equipment has been altered, making it more attractive and effective. The dimension of sound has been added to both the filmstrip projector and the slide projector. Some schools even afford the facilities for teachers to make their own sound slides. This could be an interesting project for you and your class, regardless of subject content. As a beginning teacher, check out the audio-visual facilities and possibilities offered in your school.

The Video Tape Recorder

This chapter will end with a discussion of the video tape recorder, not because it is still considered a new medium but because it has vast potentials for use in the secondary classroom.

Obviously the VTR is unique in that it makes possible the viewing of television programs aired at times other than class time. A program can be duplicated simply by taking a close-up picture of the television receiver as it is being shown, but always secure permission from the network showing the program. This should provide little problem if the request is made on the school's letterhead and cosigned by an administrator. Wait for the permission to be granted. A lawsuit was filed by a network against a university using its newscasts regularly without having ever received permission from the network.

Another important application of the VTR is capturing students' behavior as they perform psychomotor skills (as a student bowling, or a drama class acting), permitting students to study their techniques. The VTR enables them to see their mistakes either in isolation (by freezing the picture) or in connection with a whole process.

Media combinations can enhance almost any lesson. For example, prior to showing a film, filmstrip, or video tape, you could outline the purposes of the media on the chalkboard or overhead projector. (These may be used again for review at the end of the period). Or, as a tape recorder or record player plays a new dance, you could outline the steps on the overhead projector.

Some teachers become very sophisticated with their development and use of audio-visual equipment. Others use media only in simple ways, which can still be very effective.

SUMMARY

A secondary school teacher, though primarily concerned with teaching only one or two content areas, is still responsible for helping students improve in all areas. Since no one is designated to help students develop socially, and no one is appointed to help students learn cooperation, responsibility, and self-respect, each teacher must share this role. When used properly, media can help achieve these objectives.

There are more media than films and filmstrips. Also included are the chalkboard, bulletin boards, television, the overhead projector, and the video tape recorder. Because students learn best through a variety of sensory experiences, you will be wise to provide as many of these experiences as you can. What comes easily for one student through reading a text may be learned by another only when seeing it on film, television, or the bulletin board.

We live in a technological society, so we can expect that much hardware and software will be found in the school. Taking the time to familiarize yourself with what is available to you as a teacher will be time well spent.

To utilize media correctly, you must select or develop appropriate media and coordinate it with the lesson. You will need to preview films and listen to records before using them in class. Always tell your students the major concepts to look or listen for. After the media use, students can summarize these major ideas. Students can and should participate in the planning.

EXPERIENCES

This chapter has discussed how several types of media can be used to improve instruction. The following experiences portray several mistakes that teachers make when using media. For each misuse you may wish to make your own mental corrections to reverse the effects of these media on students.

Experience 1:   Much Research Is Conducted in the Teachers' Lounge — Too Much

Mark found his first two weeks of teaching to be a variety of everything but teaching. He called rolls, made seating charts, began filling out a state attendance record, and distributed textbooks (although he wasn't sure why, since there seemed to be no time to use them). By the beginning of his third week he accidentally overheard a couple of colleagues expressing his very sentiments in the teachers' lounge.

MR. MILLER: Mary, I don't know how you do it. You seem to have your classes running so smoothly and yet you are acting chairperson of the Social Studies Department and sponsor of the United Teachers of Social Studies Club. What is your secret?

MRS. JENKINS: Tom, you're too flattering. I'm sure your classes are well organized, too.

MR. MILLER: No. Wait now. I'm dead serious. I seem to work harder and get farther behind. You know the old adage: The faster I work, etc., etc.; I just barely seem to place one foot ahead of the next. I mean, having to lecture for five hours daily with only one planning period is more than a full-time job in itself; then we have all the clerical tasks and the ball games to work. I really mean it, I'd like to know how you manage everything.

MRS. JENKINS: Well, I may not know what I do, but I know one thing I don't do and that's to lecture all day. I use a number of good films that I order during the summer and have them coming in all during the year.

With this information at hand, Mark walked silently out of the lounge and to the resource center. Within the next twenty minutes he had found dozens of films that seemed appropriate for his classes. He chose only those that ran for one or two full periods and only those that could be used in both his history and his government classes. With this accomplished, he felt that he could relax a little, at least emotionally.

Indeed, the coming weeks saw a new Mark with a fresh new style. With films on Tuesday and Thursday, he could relax and plan only every other day. This was much less demanding than the old style of planning new lessons for every day. The kids welcomed it, too. The first few films provided great entertainment. Mark's classes soon earned the reputation as Mark's Cinema. He enjoyed the humor and laughed when a fellow teacher would kiddingly accuse him of serving popcorn and soft drinks. But all good things must come to an end and this magic system was no different. As strange as it sounds, the students were the first to tire of the abundance of films. When the class turned into chaos, Mark was astounded and perplexed. How could such a neat system turn so sour?

▶ *Questions and Discussion*

1. *Was Mark wrong in selecting his films several months in advance of when they would actually be used?*
No. Actually, this is a very practical system for utilizing films, for it ensures the availability of popular films and enables the teacher to coordinate the films with the lessons. Good films can complement even the most interesting lessons. A good film is also often an excellent means of introducing a new study unit because of the vast amount of material that a film can cover in a short period of time.

2. *Why did Mark's students come to dislike the new system?*
Because of the incorrect way that Mark used the films, all that they actually offered to his students was a change from his old lecture routine. Soon the films became an old routine and then an old rut, boring the students as much as the lectures had.

3. *What was wrong with Mark's system?*
Mark chose films that ran the full length of each period. This did not leave him time to introduce or follow up each film. Second, Mark tried to substitute the films for lessons instead of using them to enrich each lesson. Finally, Mark used each film in both his history classes and his government classes. It is highly unlikely that even one film was appropriate for both subjects. Mark apparently did not even bother to preview any of the films; and whenever possible, the teacher should always see the film before showing it in class.

Experience 2: A Bulletin Board Is Misused

During her second full week of student teaching in ninth-grade English, Carla Cromwell was assigned to take over composition writing. Carla was quite aware that students who do good work need to be positively reinforced, so she included in her plans a way of giving those students a feeling of success.

On Friday, after giving a special writing assignment, she posted the six best papers from the group of twenty-three. The caption at the top of the bulletin board, in large colorful letters, read, "We Have Some Good Writers."

In that same class, six other students had papers with *A* grades, and only three had made below a *C*.

▶ *Questions and Discussion*

1. *Should a teacher post papers of students on the bulletin board?*
   The answer to this is both yes and no, for different situations call for handling this matter in far different ways. In general, putting the "good" papers on the bulletin board will, in fact, positively reinforce the owners of those papers, but the teacher needs to consider the effect on the other pupils.

   It is possible that other papers should have been posted, especially the six with grades of *A*. The way it was, only a virtually perfect paper was recognized as being good; therefore, the others must have been less than good.

   More often than not, a student whose paper is displayed for reasons of its quality is the student who already has high self-esteem. It is the student who seldom does good work who needs to be reinforced in a positive way but will likely never see his paper among the good ones.

   There are, moreover, talents other than academic. The teacher who looks for promptness, cooperation, creativity, decision-making ability, communication skills, or other desirable traits will be able to recognize *every* student for being good at something. This is the time to make it known to all by placing the actual work, or a note describing it, on the bulletin board. The following list is only a sample of what could be displayed.

   a. Paula was the first to complete the term project.
   b. Did you see the paintings that Carol and Susan entered in the school exhibit?
   c. John and Dave really make a smooth team in tennis doubles.

   The point is, when only good work in a single subject is posted, some students will surely become discouraged. They will feel that they have no chance to be recognized. On the other hand, *never* giving reinforcement in this way can be detrimental to motivation of the higher-achieving pupils. Therefore, it is a good idea to mix up the routine, making sure that each student is positively recognized from time to time.

2. *How could Carla have been more humanistic in dealing with the compositions?*

Here, again, the alternatives are so numerous that it would take a long time to mention them all, but there are a few that stand out.

First of all, why post them at all? Rather, write words of encouragement such as, "Good work," or "Way to go!" Carla could talk individually with the few who did poorly and encourage them to improve their work.

Another possible approach would be to establish certain standards for each student to meet on the assignment. For instance, Jack, a very poor speller, has fewer spelling errors on a new paper than on his previous paper. That should be considered progress, indeed even success, regardless of the exact number of errors in the new paper. Carla can enter into a contract with him to get a score commensurate with his abilities. She would do the same for each of Jack's classmates. Each pupil who fulfills his contract would get his name on the bulletin board under the heading "Writers for the Week."

Experience 3: Television Is Used for Instruction

Jerry Baxter, a seventh-grade teacher, was asked to teach some summer classes for his school. The summer program was expected to differ from regular schooling; that is, teachers were encouraged to "stray" from the normal curricular offerings for the purpose of enriching those students who attended. Summer school was voluntary for students and lasted but half a day for only five weeks.

Jerry had decided to spend some time each day dealing with current events. Where, normally, newspapers would most often be used for this, Jerry felt that he would receive better results if television were the instructional medium. Furthermore, two of the major networks had news programs airing for an hour at about the same time that the school day began.

During the first two weeks Jerry felt that his idea was working successfully. In fact, an interesting facet to his original objectives had been added. Not only were the students learning and discussing national and world events, but at the students' urging, a mini-unit concerning the field of advertising had been started. Primarily, interest was focused on the television commercials themselves, with discussion centering on the visual stimulation and the verbal emphasis that advertisers placed on key words and phrases to increase the sales of their product.

Beginning the third week a new sponsor began to cause Jerry problems. On each day, about halfway through the program, a well-known maker of women's lingerie displayed one or more of these wares (or would it be "wears"), and some of the students would begin to giggle. By the third consecutive day of this, Jerry felt it best to make some changes. He walked to the front of the room, switched off the television, and let the students know how disappointed he was in them: Furthermore, he told them that newspapers would replace the television for the remainder of the school term.

► *Questions and Discussion*

1. *Did Jerry have any reasonable alternatives to turning off the television set?*

   Jerry's concern was in the reaction the students had to seeing the various articles of women's foundations. We can state, without reservation, that he overreacted. It was as if he felt guilty for introducing the class to some pornographic film. Although the alternatives are many, let us discuss two of them.

   First of all, ignore the giggles, for this is a common reaction from students of this age. It isn't as though they are realizing for the first time that females wear something other than outer clothing. Jerry's reaction only reinforced their feelings that a bra or a pair of panties is something to snicker about. By just ignoring their behavior, Jerry would soon see it diminish and eventually disappear. It would, however, have been difficult to carry on a normal discussion of the strategies of advertising using that particular commercial.

   Another alternative would be to say, "Look, we all wear underclothing. It's just a natural thing, so there's no need to be shocked or feel funny when we see it advertised on television." To alter the behavior of the class, such a statement will usually suffice.

2. *Should current events be a regular part of the ongoing school program during the academic year?*

   While this decision is generally left to the teacher's discretion, many teachers evidently feel it should, because they do include it. English, math, science, and the social sciences are not entities in themselves. *Not* to discuss what is happening in the world is unrealistic, for students arrive at school talking of things they have heard about from friends, family, or the media. These topics must be aired before students' minds are free to concentrate on the lessons. Since school is a reflection of society, it seems right only that students learn what they can about society at large; and a regular discussion of those things currently happening is a means of reaching this goal.

Experience 4: A Teacher Has Problems with a Film

Sharon Croft was in her first month of teaching in a twelfth-grade Spanish class. In the film catalog she located a twelve-minute color film with a description appropriate for her class. She ordered it from the school system's central media library, but instead of receiving it on the day she requested, she received it on the day planned to show it.

Having taken a course in college dealing with utilization of multimedia, Sharon felt confident in threading and operating the projector. Getting ready to use the film proved to be no problem; during the actual showing, however, Sharon noticed something wrong.

For some unknown reason, the take-up reel was spilling film onto the floor, and by the time Sharon realized it, much of the footage lay in disarray next to the projector stand. Although alarmed, Sharon decided to finish the film rather than to turn off the machine.

► *Questions and Discussion*

1. *Was Sharon's decision a good one?*
   Yes, Sharon probably did what was best. If she had noticed the spillage as soon as it began, she would have needed only a little time to turn off the machine and correct the problem. However, since so much film was on the floor in this case, any real benefit of the film's showing would have been lost by stopping it and rewinding. Any action Sharon would take, other than what she did, would be disruptive to the class.

   Remember that the film Sharon was showing was not a lengthy one. If the class had been viewing a thirty-minute film, Sharon's decision to continue would not have been so practical.

2. *What harm can be done to film when it spills onto the floor?*
   The major harm, and not always a result, is scratching from furniture or dirt on the floor. If the teacher is careful when rewinding, the film may not suffer to any noticeable degree.

   Another possible problem — and this will be during the rewinding process — is breaking or "crimping" of the film itself. Again, care should be taken.

Experience 5:   Dated Material Decorates the Room

Ms. Jefferson's room in Public School No. 128 had a bulletin board running the complete length of the wall, from the front of the room to the back, ending at the doorway. Having taught in this one room for more years than she cared to admit, Ms. Jefferson was constantly faced with the problem of having the bulletin board used for something.

Out of frustration she had decided to caption it WHAT'S HAPPENING NOW and had taken pains to gather materials from newspapers and magazines about developments in the Spanish-speaking countries of the world. When completed, it actually was a colorful collage, a real "mixed bag" of names, places, faces, and events. All visitors to her classroom noticed it immediately; upon closer inspection, however, they realized that the material was outdated. Nothing more recent than the previous year was included.

► *Questions and Discussion*

1. *What psychological effect might the display of "old news" have on students?*

Either consciously or unconsciously, students may view the teacher as an outdated person. Since Ms. Jefferson was known to have been teaching for a long time, it is safe to assume that she was "getting up there in years." As teachers get older, they do not necessarily become outdated. (In fact, most retain a youthful exuberance, probably the result of continuing to deal with younger people.)

Although students notice age in people (they often guess a new teacher's age as being somewhere between eighteen and fifty), the particular age is not really important. What does affect their feelings is the manner in which the teacher operates. In Ms. Jefferson's classroom she was about a year behind.

2. *How can the problem of bulletin board obsolescence be avoided?*
Whatever the alternatives, they should all involve the students themselves. With as much bulletin board space as existed in Ms. Jefferson's classroom, it is no wonder that she had difficulty keeping up with it. Having students keep it up is not wrong at all, for people tend to learn best when they are actively involved.

Committees could be chosen for the purpose of changing the display every two weeks or so. Students who participated would have the opportunity to add some of "life's skills" to "school learning." They would be given responsibility for doing a good job and might even be held accountable by their peers. They would further develop their abilities to work effectively with others.

The "prettiest" bulletin boards tend to be those made by teachers; the "best" ones are likely the results of student efforts.

ACTIVITIES

Since you have grown up with media, you probably have many ideas for applying them to instruction — ideas not covered in this chapter. The following activities give you a chance to relate the material in this chapter and your previous knowledge about media to improve the teaching of your own subject(s).

1. Make a list of anecdotes that you can use throughout the year with your students. Explain the media that you will use for each.
2. Select an important theme (concept) in your field and devise several ways of introducing it, using different media with each introduction.
3. Devise one good multimedia presentation to introduce a topic in your major field. If you have skills in photography, art, music, or drama, consider using these in your presentation.

SUGGESTED READINGS

ADAMS, RAYMOND S., and BIDDLE, BRUCE J. *Realities of Teaching with Video Tape.* New York: Holt, Rinehart and Winston, 1970.

CLARK, LEONARD H., and STARR, IRVING S. *Secondary School Teaching Methods.* Chapter 14. New York: Macmillan, 1976.

ERICKSON, CARLTON W. H., and CURL, DAVID H. *Fundamentals of Teaching with Audio Visual Technology,* 2d ed. New York: Macmillan, 1972.

GLEAVES, K. S. "School Media Center: The Changing Scene." *Peabody Journal of Education* 55 (April 1978): 169–204.

HANEY, JOHN B., and ULLMER, ELDON J. *Educational Communications and Technology.* 2d ed. Dubuque, Iowa: William C. Brown, 1975.

HOOVER, KENNETH H. *The Professional Teacher's Handbook.* 2d ed. Chapter 18. Boston: Allyn and Bacon, 1976.

KEMP, JERROLD E. *Planning and Producing Audio-Visual Materials.* 4th ed. New York: Thomas Y. Crowell, 1980.

KLEIN, GEORGE, and SWINTON, GARY. *Television Teaching Techniques.* Sidney, Australia: Angus and Robertson Publishers, 1972.

TRAVERS, ROBERT M. W., and DILLON, JACQUELINE. *The Making of a Teacher.* New York: Macmillan, 1974.

WEGNER, H. *Teaching with Film.* Phi Delta Kappa Fastbacks, No. 103:5–42. Bloomington, Ind.: Phi Delta Kappan, 1978.

An Introduction to Planning

OBJECTIVES

Upon completing this chapter you should be able to:
1. Explain at least three advantages of using objectives in daily planning.
2. Differentiate between educational aims, goals, and objectives.
3. Name and discuss the three divisions (domains) of educational objectives.
4. List three criteria essential to all performance objectives.
5. List and define all levels in each of the three domains.
6. Explain how performance objectives and daily lessons fit into the total curriculum.
7. Give an example of a well-known educational aim and explain why aims are needed.
8. Write one goal that would be appropriate for the subject and grade level that you plan to teach.
9. Write an affective objective at each of the five respective levels.
10. Write a cognitive objective at each of the six respective levels.
11. Write a psychomotor objective for each of three different levels.
12. Describe a desirable use of textbooks in curriculum planning.
13. List at least three ways of involving students in curriculum planning.
14. Give three guidelines for using homework.

Once you accept a teaching position, one of your first decisions will be about the content that you will cover within each subject. Some school systems regulate the content to be covered in each class so closely that they virtually dictate what you will teach. Through providing externally designed curriculum plans, guides, and syllabi, these school systems may, in some cases, even go so far as to specify the content to be covered on each day of the year. Curriculum directors, supervisors, assistant superintendents, and assistant principals in charge of curricula may periodically visit each teacher's classes to make sure that, indeed, each class is studying the prescribed lessons. Yet, even within such dictatorial systems, you may find much flexibility in determining *how* you teach these lessons.

At the opposite extreme are the many school systems that do no more than

provide general guidelines. As a matter of fact, some teachers are not given anything more than a textbook from which they are to design their own curricula. Fortunately, most school systems operate somewhere between these two extremes. They realize that teachers need not only suggestions and guidelines but also freedom to select content and to plan their curricula according to the needs and interests of their students and the community.

THE CURRICULUM

The word *curriculum* has its derivation in a Latin word meaning "racecourse." [1] (Undoubtedly, many of our students would feel the definition very appropriate to describe their schools.) Actually the concept of curriculum has changed considerably ever since the American school emerged. At first, *curriculum* meant program of studies — the curriculum, then, was the same as a list of the courses being offered — later the word changed to mean the content within these courses. But today many educators define curriculum in terms of learning experiences. One such contemporary definition is as follows: Curriculum means "the formal and informal content and process by which learners gain knowledge and understanding, develop skills and alter attitudes, appreciations, and values under the auspices of the school." [2] In other words, most contemporary educators view the curriculum as the content and experiences planned

---

[1] Robert S. Zais, *Curriculum: Principles and Foundations* (New York: Thomas Y. Crowell, 1976), p. 6.
[2] Ronald C. Doll, *Curriculum Improvement: Decision Making and Process,* 4th ed. (Boston: Allyn and Bacon, 1978), p. 6.

by the schools for students. It can mean either the plan (document) itself or the actual functioning curriculum.[3] For our purposes in this text, we should think of curriculum in this more recent context. The curriculum is the purposefully planned content and activities selected to help students achieve the goals and objectives of the school.

DEFINITION OF TERMS

To some degree you will be responsible for developing the curriculum for your classes. Since the resulting curriculum should be consistent with what you, the school, and the community want to achieve, you should examine these expectations at various levels. Educational expectations are categorized according to their degrees of immediacy and specificity. The following discussion begins with the broadest and most general and progresses toward the most immediate and most specific.

AIMS. Educational aims are the most distant and most general expectations of all, so much so, in fact, that they can never be fully achieved. A good example of educational aims is the list of the Seven Cardinal Principles for Secondary Education. Once again, let's look at that list:

1. Health
2. Command of the fundamental processes
3. Worthy home membership
4. Vocational efficiency
5. Citizenship
6. Worthy use of leisure time
7. Ethical character

Obviously each of these expectations cannot ever be completely fulfilled or attained (for example, one should work a lifetime to preserve his health, develop his morality, or to be a good citizen). This is true of all educational aims; they are essential for providing long-term direction, yet they can never be completely fulfilled or attained.

GOALS. Educational goals are those expectations that take weeks, months, or even years to attain. A particular high school may have for one of its goals that all its students will become literate by the time of their graduation. For sure, this goal may not be realized for every single student; yet some (probably most) will achieve this goal.

But a goal need not take six or twelve years to reach. For example, a biology teacher may set a goal for all students to appreciate all forms of life by the end of the school year (a year-long goal). Or that same teacher whose students

---

[3] George A. Beauchamp, *Curriculum Theory*, 3d ed. (Wilmette, Ill.: The Kagg Press, 1975), p. 7.

spend six weeks studying endocrines may set as a student goal the under-standing of different processes of reproduction, transportation, and respiration. Clearly, then, an educational goal can be reached (although many students may not actually reach it), and its attainment requires from several days to several years. The length of a goal is usually set to correspond with a certain program such as a high school program, a semester, a six-weeks' grading period, or any other grading period.

OBJECTIVES. So that educational objectives will not be confused with other types of educational expectations, this book will use the term precisely to re-fer to the daily expectations of students. We might think of these as per-formance objectives, for each refers to the ability of students to perform se-lected tasks in certain specific ways. Since performance objectives are the most specific of all expressions of educational expectations, they must be written in highly specified ways. The following section is an introduction to the tech-niques of writing performance objectives.

WRITING PERFORMANCE OBJECTIVES

Depending on his own use of the objectives and the content involved, each college instructor of education courses teaches students how to write objectives in his (the professor's) own unique, preferred way. Yet, most authorities seem to agree that at least three criteria are essential for all objectives. They must:

1. Be stated in terms of expected student behavior (not the teacher's);
2. Specify the conditions under which the students are expected to perform;
3. Specify the minimum acceptable level of performance.

The learning unit or unit plan is not only an outline of the subject material to be explored within a certain topic; it is this and much more. Although there are many variations, most units contain the following parts: a statement of philosophy, a list of general objectives or purposes, a list or outline of content, a description of activities for students to engage in, and an evaluation system. (See Figure 8.1.) The significance of involving students in planning is ex-pressed by Doll, "despite the imperfections and general functioning one can find in instances of teacher-pupil planning, the dividends that such cooperative planning pays in pupil interest and achievement have resulted in its acceptance as a valid instructional process." [4]

Figure 8.1 Anatomy of a Learning Unit

Philosophy ⟶ Purposes ⟶ Content ⟶ Activities ⟶ Evaluation

[4] Ronald C. Doll, *Curriculum Improvement: Decision Making and Process,* 4th ed. (Boston: Allyn and Bacon, 1978), p. 393.

The philosophy is merely a statement of the teacher's beliefs about the purposes of the school, the nature of adolescence, how adolescents learn, and the purposes of life, in general. This is the most neglected part of learning units because teachers spend too little time reflecting on their beliefs about these all-important issues. Yet the first question that they hear at the beginning of a new unit is often "Why do we have to study this stuff?" Only by thinking these broad issues through can you prepare to answer this question intelligently.

The statement of purposes is a list of general expectations that you wish the unit to achieve. For example, a tenth-grade unit in government may include such general expectations as these: to understand how a bill is introduced; to become more tolerant of the opinions of others; or to appreciate democracy as a type of government. Unlike the performance objectives of daily planning, which are stated in very specific, observable, and measurable terms, the statement of purposes in a unit should be more general.

Your selection of content for any unit should be based on three broad considerations: (1) the *significance* of the content in attaining the purposes of the particular unit (in other words, content that must be learned in order to reach the general objectives); (2) the importance of the content to society; and (3) the needs and interests of the learners.

Choose the activities on the same bases: select experiences that will enable students to learn the content. Do not feel obligated to select one activity for each objective, for some of the best activities serve multiple purposes and lead to the attainment of several objectives. For example, one activity for a senior English class might be to write a composition contrasting Shelley's poetry with that of Lord Byron. Such an activity would undoubtedly provide opportunities for both attaining writing skills and for sharpening concepts of an author's style by contrasting it with the other author's. Some teachers feel that they cannot afford the time for multiple objectives in their classes; but they should realize that several objectives can be fulfilled simultaneously. Clearly the specification of multiple objectives activities does not necessarily promote inefficiency.[5] Each learning unit should contain two types of student performance, including a variety of types of measurement — written tests, oral tests, debates, term projects, homework assignments, classwork, and perhaps performance in class or group discussions. This type of evaluation which examines the quality of a product is called product evaluation.

Another type of evaluation that should be applied to each learning unit is called process evaluation. This is merely a description of the effectiveness of the teaching or the unit. Process evaluation analyzes the various parts of the unit in isolation to see if it needs improvement. It also looks at all parts together to see how they relate to one another. Ask yourself such questions as: Is my philosophy sound? Does it convince these students that the unit is important? Are the purposes important ones? Am I being realistic in expecting

---

[5] Robert S. Zais, *Curriculum Principles and Foundations* (New York: Harper and Row, 1976), p. 357.

these students to achieve them in this length of time? Is the content in this unit that which is needed to achieve the unit's stated purposes? Are these activities helpful in attaining these objectives? Is the evaluation fair to everyone? Does it discriminate between those who have met the objectives and those who have not achieved the objectives?

Learning units should also include certain practical information. Besides the title, subject, and grade level, they should contain a list of necessary resources, consultants, equipment, facilities, and supplies needed to teach the unit, especially audio-visual aids. They should include a list of references or bibliography that supports the unit and that can be used to pursue the topic further. Finally, each unit should contain performance objectives that (1) are stated in terms of student behavior, (2) specify the minimum acceptable level of performance, and (3) describe the conditions.

Now quickly reexamine the three criteria for writing objectives. Stating objectives in terms of expected student behavior is important because all teaching is directed toward the students. Any success will depend on what happens to the students. More exactly, the school exists to change the behavior of students: mentally, physically, socially, emotionally, and even morally. When you state all objectives in terms of desired student performance and use specific verbs that are observable and measurable, you and your students will better understand what things are expected and to what degree they are being accomplished. The following lists of terms will help you become accustomed to the types of verbs that are specific, observable, and measurable (YES column) and those which are too general and vague to be accurately observed and measured (NO column).

NO	YES
Appreciate	Build
Consider	Classify
Desire	Contrast
Feel	Demonstrate
Find interesting	Distinguish
Have insight into	Evaluate
Know	Identify
Learn	Interpret
Like to	Label
Love to	List
Really like to	Match
Recognize	Measure
Remember	Name
See that	Remove
Think	Select
Understand	State
Want to	Write

Since the students can grasp only a limited number of major ideas within a period of forty-five or fifty minutes, the daily lesson plan should contain only four or five major ideas. Suppose that you are an English teacher who wishes to teach composition writing: you could select four or five of the most important ideas about capturing and holding the reader's attention. These will become the content for the first day's lesson in the unit "Composition Writing." You may find that there are five ideas essential to capturing the reader's attention and four ideas essential to holding it, once captured. If so, you could plan one lesson on "how to capture the reader's attention" and a subsequent lesson "how to hold the reader's attention."

Your objectives should be written in terms of desired student behavior. The emphasis should not be on "Today I'll teach" but "As a result of the lesson, each student will be able to. . . ." Second, you should state the conditions under which the students are expected to perform ("When given a list containing vertebrates and invertebrates, . . ."). Third, state the expected level of performance ("with 80 percent accuracy or without error"). Finally, avoid using verbs that cannot be observed or measured, such as *learn, know,* and *understand.* Instead, your plan should contain such explicit action-oriented verbs as *identify, list, explain, name, describe,* and *compare.*

VARYING LEVELS OF OBJECTIVES

But obviously some of the aims and goals of education deal with thinking; others involve physical skills; and still others focus on attitudes. Examples of each would be, respectively, command of the fundamental processes, physical education, and development of moral character. It is essential that you establish performance objectives in each of these domains (cognitive, psychomotor, and affective) for each of your classes. Fortunately much work has been done to assist you in writing objectives at varying levels of difficulty in each domain. We shall now examine each domain.

THE COGNITIVE DOMAIN

The first real systematic approach to assist teachers in writing objectives at specified levels came in 1956 when Benjamin S. Bloom led a group of students at the University of Chicago in the development of a taxonomy of objectives. The resulting taxonomy of educational objectives in the cognitive domain included the following six levels:

Level 1. Knowledge
Level 2. Comprehension
Level 3. Application
Level 4. Analysis
Level 5. Synthesis
Level 6. Evaluation[6]

---

[6] From *Taxonomy of Educational Objectives: The Classification of Educational Goals: Handbook I: Cognitive Domain* by Benjamin S. Bloom et al. Copyright © 1956 by Longman, Inc., New York. Reprinted with permission of Longman, Inc., New York.

If your classes are to involve students with tasks that require them to operate at these different levels, then you must be able to write objectives at each specific level. Therefore, let's examine each level and see how objectives can be written at each.

Level 1: Knowledge

Obviously the simplest and least demanding objectives are those that require only the memorization of facts. Before students can move on to more advanced levels of tasks, they must first know certain basic facts. For example, most secondary mathematics problems require students to multiply. The learning of the multiplication (or times) tables can probably best be done by simple rote memorization. Unfortunately, many secondary classes fail to go beyond this most elementary (knowledge) level. In essence, there is nothing at all dishonorable about introducing assignments or tasks at the knowledge level, so long as such assignments are intentional and purposeful and so long as they do not dominate the curriculum.

An example of an objective at this level would be as follows:

> When given a list of ten elements and a list of atomic weights, the student will be able to correctly match eight of the ten elements with their correct atomic weights.

Another example of a knowledge level objective would be:

> When given a list containing ten vertebrates and ten invertebrates, the student will correctly identify eight of the ten invertebrates.

Notice that both objectives begin by stating the conditions under which the students are expected to perform the task (*When given . . .*). Both objectives are written in terms of desired student performance (*the student will . . .*). Both objectives contain action-oriented verbs that can be observed and measured (*match, list*). Both objectives end with a statement of minimum acceptable level of performance (*eight of the ten*). (See Table 8.1.)

Table 8.1 Anatomy of a Performance Objective

Objective: When given a list containing ten vertebrates, the student will correctly identify eight out of ten invertebrates.

Criterion 1:	Statement of conditions under which the student is to perform	*When given a list containing ten vertebrates and ten invertebrates,*
Criterion 2:	Stated in terms of student behavior	*the student will correctly identify*
Criterion 3:	Minimum acceptable of performance	*eight out of ten invertebrates.*

Objectives written at the comprehension level require more of students than mere rote memorizing. Objectives written at this level require students to translate, to interpret, or to predict a continuation of trends.[7] For example, an English teacher who wishes students to know the differences in phrases and clauses may set the following objective: When given a paragraph containing two clauses and three phrases, the student will correctly underscore the phrases, using a single line, and the clauses, using double lines.

Can you tell what the minimum acceptable level of performance is for this objective? Actually, since there is no specific mention of an acceptable level, it must be assumed that the students will be expected to perform with 100 percent accuracy.

Now see if you can write one objective in your teaching field at the comprehension level that requires the students to translate, an objective that requires them to interpret, and one that requires them to predict. (Hint: You may wish to use charts, maps, graphs, or tables.)

Level 3: Application

Objectives written at the application level require students to use principles or generalizations to solve a concrete problem. For example, a mathematics teacher might write the following objective for geometry students.

> Given the lengths of both legs of a right triangle, the student will use the Pythagorean theorem to solve the length of the hypotenuse.

An English teacher might use the following objective:

> Given the beats and measures in an iambic pentameter, the student will write a five-stanza poem and set it into iambic pentameter without missing more than one beat per stanza.

Level 4: Analysis

Like the application level objectives, analysis level objectives require students to work with principles, concepts, and broad generalizations, but the students must work on the principles themselves. In essence, students are required to break down the concepts and principles so as to better understand them. Thus, they must understand not only the content but also its structural form.

For example, a government teacher might assign the following objective to a class who is studying how a bill becomes a law:

> Given a particular law, students will trace its development from the time it was first introduced as a bill, listing each of the major steps without missing any of them.

---

[7] Ibid., p. 149.

A teacher of auto mechanics may write the following objective for a group of students who have been studying the electrical system in an automobile:

> Starting with the positive battery terminal, the student will trace the current throughout the automobile until it returns to the negative battery terminal, discussing what happens in the coil, generator, distributor, and condenser without getting more than one of these steps out of sequence.

A biology teacher might ask students to trace the circulatory system in a similar manner. Suppose you are teaching the circulatory system to a biology class. See if you can write an objective that will enable students to understand the sequence in which the blood travels throughout the body. (Hint: You may wish to designate one of the heart's chambers as a beginning point.)

Now check your objective to see if it includes the three designated criteria. First of all, is it written in terms of expected student performance? If so, underscore that part of the objective identifying both the performer and the performance. Is the verb you used one that expresses action? Can it be observed? measured?

Then see if your statement of conditions is clear. Circle this statement. Does it accurately describe those conditions under which you expect the student to perform? Did you begin the objective with such a statement as "Given ..." or "When given ..."? This is an easy way to make sure that you include a statement of conditions in all of your objectives. Is your statement very general, such as "When given a test," or "Following a lesson"? If so, can you make it more specific? Can you think of a way to alter the task, making it easier to perform simply by changing the conditions?

Finally, examine your objective to see if it includes a statement of minimum acceptable level of performance. Draw a box around this statement. Does it tell the student exactly how accurately this task must be performed before it will be acceptable? Does it contain a percentage or fraction, such as "with 80 percent accuracy"? or "four out of five times"? Can you think of other ways to express your concept of minimum acceptable level of performance without using percentages or fractions?

Now you probably would like to start over and rewrite your original objective, improving each part.

Level 5: Synthesis

In a way the synthesis level objective is the opposite of the analysis objective, for it requires the student to take several parts and put them together. But the synthesis level objective is more demanding because it requires students to form a *new* whole. Unlike the analysis level objectives, synthesis level objectives require students to use divergent thinking and creativity.

Of special importance at the synthesis level is the student's attitude. Synthesis requires experimentation, investigating the new. Furthermore the student must understand that the teacher does not have a definite solution or a preconceived notion in mind for the student to reach.

For example, a history teacher who wishes students to understand the problems faced by the first settlers of this country might preface the unit with an assignment involving the following objective:

> Suppose you are a member of a team of explorers who are going to another inhabited planet to start a new colony. List at least ten guidelines you would propose to guide the behavior of the new nationals, making sure that at least five of these rules will serve to protect the interests of all the native inhabitants.

Because of their divergent and creative nature, synthesis level objectives are difficult to write. You may need much practice before you feel comfortable and competent in writing objectives at this level.

Suppose you are an art teacher. Your class has studied such concepts as cubism (using cubes to form objects) and pointism (using pencil points to form objects). Can you write an objective at the synthesis level? (Hint: You might begin by identifying a particular effect that you would like your students to achieve through the use of cubism and pointism. This might be a specific feeling or mood.)

One example of such an objective might be as follows:

> While looking at a couple of examples of cubism in Picasso's paintings and at a couple of Renoir's paintings that reflect the use of pointism, the student will combine these two techniques, along with a new technique, to create at least three of the five feelings: happiness, surprise, sadness, anger, and love.

One final suggestion may help you in the writing of synthesis level questions. You must provide enough structure to make the assignment meaningful and yet allow enough freedom for students to put themselves into the work.

Level 6: Evaluation

The highest level in Bloom's cognitive domain is the evaluation level. Here the student is required to make judgments. More than mere biased opinions, these judgments must be based on definite criteria. Evaluation level objectives contain various mixtures of elements in the first five levels.

A speech teacher might use the following objective with students who are studying diplomatic and persuasive techniques:

> When viewing a video recording of the President's two most recent addresses to the people, each student will rate the speeches in terms of their use of tact and persuasion, pinpointing at least three areas of strength and three areas of weakness in each address.

Or a physical education teacher who is teaching bowling may wish to write an objective that involves the starting position, delivery, and follow-through. Can you help this teacher by writing an objective at the evaluation level? If you do not bowl, you may substitute another activity, such as golf or diving, that also involves these three steps.

Now examine your evaluation level objective. Does it require the student to make a judgment? Does it require that this judgment be based on supportive data or on either internal or external standards?

Your ability to write objectives at each cognitive level is crucial, since this is the only way you can be sure that your students will learn to develop their intellectual skills at each level. This is perhaps the most important work a teacher does, since the first and foremost function of the teacher is to effect learning. And this requires clarity. You may wish to ask a classmate to read a few of your objectives to see if, indeed, they do communicate clearly.

THE AFFECTIVE DOMAIN

In recent years educators have become increasingly more concerned with the effect of schooling on students' attitudes. This concern has in part been stimulated by the students' own acknowledgment in the differences between their attitudes and values and those of the "system." Such differences began to show up in the 1950s with the beatnik generation, who rebelled against the material wealth syndrome that swept the country during that decade. Everyone seemed determined to get ahead of the Joneses by building a larger house and by owning a larger car or boat. Then the youth of the 1960s expressed their dissent toward our involvement in Vietnam by burning their draft cards and holding moratoriums and demonstrations. Further dissent was expressed with civil rights marches.

In recent years the community at large has blamed the schools for such social ills as pollution of the environment, exhaustion of our natural resources, and economic recession; but by far the greatest accusation aimed at the schools was their failure to teach students to perform basic skills (cognitive domain) and, of even greater concern, to discipline today's youth (affective domain).

It seems safe to say that our schools will never completely rid society of all its ills, yet it seems equally clear that they will affect the ways that students feel about such important issues as the equality of all people, world peace, honesty, integrity, and the value of life itself.

"But," you may ask, "exactly what is the role of the school or the teacher in governing the values of students?" You may even question the right of teachers purposefully to influence the value systems of their students. But, try as you may to avoid it, it is impossible for you not to affect the values of your students. Moreover, you, as well as all teachers, should try to perpetuate such values as honesty, fairness, and citizenship. On the other hand, you surely should not attempt to persuade your students to accept your own religious, political, and cultural or ethnic values.

Another important role of the school and teacher in the realm of values is to help students become aware of their own values; to question these values; and to discover the basis of these values, whether they be factual and logical or prejudiced and illogical.

In 1964 David R. Krathwohl led the development of a system to categorize values. The outcome was a hierarchy of objectives in the affective domain. These are as follows:

Level 1. Receiving
Level 2. Responding
Level 3. Valuing
Level 4. Organization
Level 5. Characterization by a value or value complex[8]

Level 1: Receiving

Receiving refers to the students' being aware or alert to things. Students receive information in varying degrees. In a single class, some may not receive the information at all, while others attend or receive at a low level of awareness. Still others may be very selective in their attention, attending only to those things that hold the most meaning for them. Students can, of course, be encouraged and taught to develop their attention skills.

All teachers want their students to listen carefully to their lessons and to be aware of the feelings of their peers. Can you write an objective that would enable you to measure the student's degree of attention to a lesson?

Now examine your objective. Does it include a statement of conditions under which you wish the students to perform? Does it specify a minimum acceptable level of performance? Is it observable and measurable? An example might be as follows:

> When participating in a group discussion, the student will ask every other student at least one question.

Could you write an objective at the receiving level for a ninth-grade art class that is taking a field trip to a local museum?

Level 2: Responding

At this level the student reacts to the phenomenon that has gained her attention. This requires physical, active behavior. Some of these responses may be overt or purposeful behaviors as contrasted to the simple automatic responses. A student who becomes involved at the responding level might, at the teacher's instructions or even voluntarily, go to the library for researching the issue further. Or she may obey the rules set forth in the class.

Can you write an objective at the responding level? Try a responding objective for a homework assignment. You choose the subject and grade level.

Examine your objective to see if it involves active student participation. Does it reflect the student's attitude(s)? It should. Specifically, the performance of this objective should show a commitment to the homework assignment that a student who does not complete the objective might not have.

---

[8] From *Taxonomy of Educational Objectives: The Classification of Educational Goals: Handbook II: Affective Domain* by David R. Krathwohl et al. Copyright © 1964 by Longman, Inc., New York. Reprinted with permission of Longman, Inc., New York.

Level 3: Valuing

A value is demonstrated when someone prizes or cherishes a behavior enough to be willing to perform it even in the face of alternatives. A value is not necessarily reflected when one reacts on a spur of the moment without having had time to think about it or about the consequences. In other words, a person who really values a behavior will likely perform it regardless of the known results, and will do so repeatedly.[9]

For example, a mathematics teacher whose students are learning to use simulation games might write the following valuing question:

> When given free time at the end of each period next week to read, play simulation math games, talk to friends, or sleep, each student will voluntarily choose to play simulation games at least two out of the five days.

Note that the objective requires the student to choose of his own free will and to repeat that choice. Also notice that he has other alternatives from which to choose.

Level 4: Organization

This level of behavior requires individuals to bring together different values to build a value system. Whenever conflict exists between two or more of their values, they must resolve the conflict. For example, secondary school students are constantly involved with conflicting expectations held by their friends and those held by their parents. Hopefully as students mature, they will not always react according to the expectations of their company of the moment, but will learn to combine the two sets of values with their own existing beliefs and their knowledge about themselves. They will respond to the orderly composite of the combined values, developing their own value system. At this level students may change their behavior or defend it.

For example, a teacher might assign students to defend opposing positions on a controversial issue. By defending both sides, each student will, in effect, compare the two points of view and may even learn to compromise between the two extremes.

A teacher of U.S. government might introduce a hypothetical bill and have students form two teams, those who favor the bill and those who oppose it. The objective might read like this:

> After having had the opportunity to support the bill and also the opportunity to try to defeat it, each student will combine all information and write a statement expressing his feelings for and against the bill. Given the opportunity, he will choose to modify the bill to make it better fit with his own value system.

---

[9] Sidney B. Simon; Leland W. Howe; and Howard Kirschenbaum, *Values Clarification* (New York: Hart Publishing Company, 1972).

At this level the student has already developed her own value system. She so consistently behaves the same general way in all situations that she can be stereotyped accordingly. Also at this level the student must demonstrate a degree of individuality and self-reliance.

An example of a Level 5 objective is as follows:

> Each student will bring one newspaper article or news report to class and explain at least two ways in which the article has caused her to change or alter her position on a controversial issue.

Does this objective prove that the student has really changed her values? What if she just says that she has changed? At the moment she may believe this, but what about a week from now or a year from now? Can you rewrite this objective so that this doubt will be removed or reduced?

THE PSYCHOMOTOR DOMAIN

The psychomotor domain involves development of physical skills that require coordination of the mind and body. It is especially relevant to such courses as physical education, art, drama, music, and vocational courses, but all subjects provide many opportunities for the development of psychomotor skills.

Although this domain was the last to have a taxonomy developed for it, at this time at least two such scales have been developed. The following is based on one that was developed in 1972 by E. J. Simpson. It has the following seven steps.

1. Perception
2. Set
3. Guided response
4. Mechanism
5. Complex overt response
6. Adaptation
7. Origination[10]

Level 1: Perception

Purposeful motor activity begins in the brain, where phenomena received act as guides to motor activity. The performer must first become aware of a stimulus, pick up on cues for action, and then act upon these cues. For example, a writer discovers that she is separating her subjects and verbs, thus diluting the impact of her themes. Or a baseball batter notices that he is flinching and

---

[10] E. J. Simpson, "The Classification of Educational Objectives in the Psychomotor Domain," *The Psychomotor Domain,* Vol. 3 (Washington, D.C.: Gryphon House, 1972).

taking short steps away from the plate when he strikes. This is causing him to miss the ball. Or a piano student learns that he is failing to reduce the interval between double notes. A sample objective is the following:

> Following a demonstration, a geometry student who has been confusing x and y axes in plotting graphs will notice that the x axis always runs horizontally and the y axis always runs vertically.

Level 2: Set

In the psychomotor domain, set refers to an individual's readiness to act. It includes mental readiness and also physical and emotional readiness. For example, a highdiver is always seen pausing before a dive to get a psychological, emotional, and physical set. Emotionally she must feel confident of her ability to make a safe and accurate dive. Psychologically, although she may have performed the exact dive hundreds of times, before each dive she takes this time to think through the sequence of steps. Physically she must ready her muscles to respond quickly and accurately. On a less dramatic scale, a student preparing to take notes or to perform a writing assignment may be seen flexing his fingers, rubbing his eyes, and in short getting set to perform at his best.

An example of a psychomotor objective at this level is as follows:

> Upon the signal "ready," each student will assume proper posture and place the fingers in correct keyboard position.

Is there a minimum level of performance specified? Can you write one that improves the task? Taking a moment to think about this objective, list two ways that you could establish minimum levels of performance.

Does either of your objectives explain what is meant by "correct" posture? or "correct keyboard position"? Do both of your suggested changes help make the act measurable?

Level 3: Guided Response

Once students see the need to act and ready themselves to act, they may find that, whenever the act involves complex skills, they will need guidance through their first few responses. For example, students in the photography club may need oral guidance as they process their first negatives. An example of an objective to enhance the development of these skills is as follows:

> When given step-by-step directions in the dark room, each student will open the film cylinder, remove the film, and, without touching the surface of the film, wind it on a spool so that the surface of each round does not touch previous rounds.

Level 4: Mechanism

This level involves performing an act somewhat automatically without having to pause to think through each separate step. For example, the above photography teacher might want the students eventually to be able to perform the entire sequence of development operations while simultaneously counting the number of seconds required to wait between each step. Or a chemistry teacher might write the following objective at the mechanism level:

> Given a series of compounds to analyze, the student will operate the electron microscope without having to pause even once to think about the sequence involved in mounting the slides, focusing the projector, and changing the lens size.

Level 5: Complex Overt Response

This level is an extension of the previous level but involves more complicated tasks. For example, a driver education teacher may write an objective at this level such as the following:

> When given the unexpected and abrupt command "stop," the student will immediately respond by applying the correct amount of pressure to the brakes, giving the correct signal, and gradually pulling off the road.

Level 6: Adaptation

At this level the student is required to adjust performance as different situations dictate. For example, the driver would adjust her brake pressure and swerve to allow for an icy surface. Or the cook would adjust his timing as he goes from an electric to a gas-operated stove. A boxer would alter his style to adjust for a left-handed opponent.

An example of a psychomotor-objective at the adaptation level is as follows:

> When planning a budget vacation, the student (without being reminded of the gas supply shortage and cost increase) will eliminate unnecessary automobile travel and substitute gas-saving strategies.

Level 7: Origination

At this, the highest level of the psychomotor domain, the student creates new movement patterns to fit the particular situation. For example, the cook adds his own touch of genius, and the piano student alters her style or the music itself.

An art teacher might write an objective as follows:

> Given a mixture of powders and compounds of varying textures, the student will use these to further accentuate the feeling he is trying to communicate in an oil painting.

OTHER PLANNING STRATEGIES

Besides varying your lesson plans, you will also need to use a variety of types of learning such as textbooks, discussions, field trips, oral reports, term projects, and homework. Now we shall examine each of these strategies and your role in using each.

Textbooks

In Chapter 2 we saw that throughout the history of American secondary schools one sort of textbook or another dominated the curriculum. At first it was the textbook that determined the content to be studied. There were virtually no other experiences than rote memorizing and recitation, which often resulted in a boring, irrelevant curriculum. The twentieth century challenged the textbook's role as sole determinant of content, but this does not mean that the textbook has no role in today's planning. Let's examine some effective uses of the textbook.

One common use of a textbook is to build the curriculum around it. Although the textbook may be the center of the curriculum, it is not the total curriculum but is supplemented by other textbooks, journals, magazines, and newspapers. This approach is probably a good choice in communities or school systems that press for traditional education and in schools with very limited resources. But it is much more likely to succeed if the teacher includes some contemporary problems and helps students apply the acquired knowledge toward solving them.

Another approach is to use the textbook along with other materials. Instead of letting the textbook lead the teacher (and students) in the selection of content and experiences, the teacher (and students) may take the lead in designing the curriculum. For example, the teacher would determine the sequence of topics, rather than following the textbook organization from Chapter 1 to Chapter 2, and may decide that some chapters are not worthy of inclusion. As teachers have become increasingly competent in curriculum development in recent years, more and more are insisting on the freedom to shape their curricula as they see fit.

But not all school systems provide teachers with complete freedom to develop their own curricula. Concern that students may not "cover" all content needed for the following year or for college is always present. Of course, such concern is very legitimate. School administrators know that they may be held accountable to see that their total school curricula do not have major content gaps. Many of the larger secondary schools hire a curriculum director, curriculum supervisor, or assistant principal who is responsible for that. Teachers should work with this curriculum person and/or with their fellow teachers to avoid curriculum redundancy and curriculum gaps.

Still other teachers make even less use of the textbook, almost totally avoiding the use of it. Instead, they substitute current problems, learning-activity packages, or their own self-developed learning units. Of course these teachers happen to teach in school systems that permit an unusual degree of teacher freedom. Such systems are not typical.

Whatever freedom your system permits you in using the textbook, there are several things you should remember about utilizing it. The obvious, of course, is that you should not spend most of the class period reading the text or requiring students to read it. It would be much better to assign a chapter the evening before and to use the class time to discuss it. The suggestions below will help you design and direct such discussions.

Discussions

Today's students want to be involved. They feel that their own opinions and judgments are worthwhile, and they want to share them. For this reason the discussion has increased in popularity throughout recent years. A good discussion, then, involves all participants; all have an opportunity to relate the topic to their own experiences. This sharing of various perspectives also enriches the knowledge and understanding of individual participants.

But to avoid having discussions that are no more than meaningless and rambling gossip sessions or sharing of ignorance, you should plan discussions carefully. First, group students according to their interest in the topic to encourage total participation. This can be achieved by letting students choose discussion topics. Second, avoid assigning very passive students and aggressive students to the same groups. When you place the reserved students together, you will force out some leadership; and when you place aggressive students in the same group, some are forced to learn to yield the floor to others. By assigning roles such as discussion moderator and recorder, and then varying these roles, you will prompt all members to participate even further.

Select topics that have answers, although there may be multiple answers depending upon individual perspective. By letting students know that a definite outcome is to be reached, you will give them a sense of purpose and responsibility.

If the moderator fails to keep the group discussion progressing and on target, you may feel that you must intervene; but too much interference leads to the group's becoming dependent on your leadership. Take care, also, to assure that the group moderator does not dominate the discussion. The discussion must be bound to the belief that all serious comments are worth being heard, regardless how inaccurate or insignificant that others may think they are.

A free-flowing discussion is a valuable opportunity to develop social skills, in itself an important goal for secondary students. It also helps students identify with their peers. Remember, from Chapter 1, that all adolescents need to belong, and all need positive recognition and approval from their peers. Group discussions should help fulfill these needs.

The participants should know that each has a definite role in every discussion. First, they are obligated to read the assignment so that the discussion will begin from a common base. Second, they are responsible for contributing additional information. Their opinions are prized only when they can present evidence or knowledge to support them. Third, each participant is responsible for listening to others and, when possible, referring to specific comments of others. This assures all that their comments are being considered.

You, the teacher, are responsible for seeing that the environment remains informal, pleasant, and nonthreatening for everyone. You are also a facilitator who helps students to locate adequate resources and to plan their discussion. When the discussion is over, you should aid them in evaluating their discussion techniques and redesigning their strategies for future discussions.

Field Trips

Like the Edsel, Studebaker, Hudson, Cord, and dozens of other fine inventions in this country, the field trip has become almost prematurely moribund, while it still has many unique advantages to offer. The reason for its loss of popularity is multidimensional. First, there has been a growing tendency for individuals to bring lawsuits against schools, and the courts have begun to find more and more schools liable as charged. Since administrators and teachers can also be found liable, many of them are reluctant to encourage field trips, which they perceive as unnecessary risks.

This is unfortunate, for field trips still have all the unique potentials that they ever had. Obviously, there is no better way for a social studies class to study the habits of an ethnic group than to go visit a local community. A group of students interested in aerodynamics could find nothing more meaningful than a visit to a wind tunnel. An agricultural class may benefit tremendously from a visit to an agricultural education agency, experimental station, or local farm.

Before you arrange a field trip, your first step is to check the school policy, for many schools forbid field trips of any type. But, even if you should find yourself teaching at such a school, you might try to bring the "field" to the school. For example an earth science teacher might arrange for truckloads of several types of soil and rocks to be dumped on the school grounds so that students can take an on-campus field trip.

If your school does permit field trips, you might find it advantageous to let

your students suggest the need for one, assuming that they are mature enough and self-disciplined enough to be trusted. Some groups are simply too risky, and a teacher would be foolish to pursue a trip with such students. If the idea belongs to the students, they may be willing to work harder and organize better. Next, you must see that the trip is indeed necessary and purposeful. Each student should be assigned (or should assume) definite responsibilities for the gathering of specific data. They may also share the responsibility for organizing the trip, clearing it with the principal's office, arranging the visits, filling out the necessary insurance forms, and securing the necessary permissions and finances.

Upon completing the trip, you should hold a follow-up lesson in which students report their data and discuss implications. As with all other instructional approaches, you should plan an evaluation of each trip to improve the quality of future trips. This should be done immediately after each field trip while you and the students still remember the particulars.

Oral Reports

For several decades oral reporting has been popular in secondary schools. Its success, however, is very much dependent upon its use. The following suggestions are provided to help you plan and use oral reports.

When you consider using oral reports, first decide on their purpose. Too often, teachers have made assignments without really thinking through the purpose for the reports. Students are left wondering exactly what they are supposed to report on, what to emphasize most, and how to deliver the report.

The teacher cannot answer these questions until having decided the purpose of the report.

Several purposes may be considered important goals of oral reporting. For example, you might assign a report to an advanced student who is delving into one aspect of a topic. The report would provide that student with an opportunity to share his or her expertise while simultaneously enabling the rest of the class to benefit from the study. Or a teacher might assign a report to a group of students to provide them an opportunity to learn to work together cooperatively. Still another teacher might assign reports to provide students experience in public speaking.

Each of these purposes can be legitimate and worthwhile so long as the teacher communicates the main purpose(s) of the report to the students. However, the assigning of a report to punish misbehavior or to substitute for teacher planning would not be wise. Students would quickly connect the report with these purposes and would likely fail to expect any significant learning to result from the experience. Such is the case when reports are used at the end of a grading period to provide students opportunity to improve their grades.

Whatever your reason for assigning oral reports, you must communicate to the reporter(s) the primary purposes for the report. Other members of the class should be informed of their roles during the report. Should they take notes? ask questions? take issue with the speaker? Should they ask for clarification when they do not understand? Should they interrupt the speaker to add comments, or should they wait until the end of the presentation? Will they be held accountable on the next test for the information presented orally by their peers? By answering these questions before the presentation is made, you can draw each student into the oral presentations made by their peers. Surely you will want to stimulate as much interest and involvement as possible.

EVALUATION. As a precaution against students' taking reports too lightly, you might consider a policy of always assigning credit for oral reports and perhaps to the rest of the students for their responses. You can do this without presenting a threat to the students. Consider a positive reward system that would enable students to earn credit for their participation in the discussion without penalizing those whose contributions are minimal.

SCHEDULING. The timing of oral reports can be critical and should be given careful attention. Avoid scheduling too many reports in succession. The student who is giving the twelfth consecutive report in class is at a definite disadvantage. To avoid such repetition and the boredom that students experience when too many reports are given, spread the reporting out so that no more than two are given in any week.

Students need ample time to prepare for their reports. Depending on the level of sophistication of the subject, a minimum of one week to several weeks lead time will be needed. Since many secondary school students hold down part-time jobs and since extracurricular activities consume much out-of-class time, you might allot some class time for preparing oral presentations. This is especially needed when students are planning group presentations.

One final precaution is in order. Perhaps the most destructive thing that can happen to oral presentations is for teachers to make assignments without giving opportunity for presenting the results. Of course, teachers would not intentionally be so callous as to make assignments without providing students opportunities to share their findings with their classmates. Yet, sometimes they forget to save enough time in the term for the reports. To avoid this mistake, remember to schedule the reporting date at the time of making the assignment. Thus, students will not be disappointed, and they will perceive oral presentations as valuable.

Projects

Whatever subject you teach, you will find that assigning projects is valuable. Types that you can choose from include these: long-term projects (which may last for a grading period or even a semester), short-term projects, group projects, and individual projects. You probably have considered several types of projects as assignments for oral presentations, but not all projects must end in oral presentations. Some may conclude with written reports or the presentation of concrete products that have resulted from the assignment. But, regardless of the type of product that the project produces, students should be given an opportunity to show their creations. For example, a science teacher may wish to arrange a local science fair to display the students' insect collections, or a music teacher may wish to provide a student recital.

Teachers who offer projects as options (not required of all students) may use a very liberal grading system to evaluate them. One great advantage of projects is that they permit those students who — for one reason or another — do not benefit from didactic forms of instruction to become totally involved. Many teachers take advantage of the opportunity to grade these activities in such a way as to reward student effort. Surprisingly, many students who appear to be total failures on tests produce excellent projects. Perhaps that is because they *want* to do the projects or because they feel more competent with working with their hands; it may be a combination of the two. Many teachers, therefore, view projects as an opportunity to provide successful experiences for everyone. You might wish to experiment assigning all A's and B's or all A's to the projects for one term. Of course, you are free to let it count as much or as little of the total term grade as you prefer.

Homework

During the so-called "educational reform" of the 1960s and 1970s, homework for the public school student lost much of its prestige; but by the end of the 1970s it had regained a fairly positive reputation. As was mentioned in Chapter 5, half of the secondary students themselves said that they were not getting to work hard enough on homework.[11] Obviously such a statement from stu-

---

[11] Stanley M. Elam, "Gallup Finds Teen-Agers Generally Like Their Schools," reports on a Gallup Poll of teenagers taken in November 1978, *Phi Delta Kappan* 60 (June 1979): 700.

dents is evidence that, when properly assigned and utilized, homework can be meaningful. The following suggestions are provided to help you design and implement a system for assigning homework that will work well for you.

CLARIFY THE ASSIGNMENT. Homework assignments must be made clear. If they involve problem solving, you may want to give students an opportunity to work at least one problem of each type in class before being asked to work them at home. Using verbal instructions and explanation often is not enough. Perhaps you can remember when as a student you thought you understood how to complete an assignment perfectly clearly as the teacher was explaining it. Then, when you got home, you found that you could not even start the problem because you didn't know how to begin. If you had had an opportunity to work just one problem in class, you would have then raised questions about any of your uncertainties.

INDIVIDUALIZE HOMEWORK ASSIGNMENTS. Obviously those students who cannot understand how to do their classwork with the help of the teacher will benefit little from an assignment of more of the same sort of work. Consider the abilities and needs of each student. Certain homework assignments for the slower students will help them catch up with the rest of the class, while the more advanced students can explore in depth areas of special interest to them. This individualistic approach to homework assignments can help relieve the ever-present dilemma in which teachers find themselves — trying to challenge the brightest students without surpassing the slower students.

MAKE HOMEWORK CREATIVE. Today teachers realize that the old practice of assigning students to "read the next chapter and work the problems at the end of the chapter" is often far from challenging or stimulating. Homework assignments are more interesting when they contain variety. Students may be asked to respond to something that is on the evening news, in the daily newspaper, or on an educational television program. Many multisensory activities can be used to replace pencil and paper assignments. True, creativity cannot be forced; however, you can establish a climate that stimulates and nourishes creativity: let your students utilize all their senses and manipulate objects; have them investigate problems that have no single fixed answers.

BE REASONABLE. Avoid making too many demands on students' time at home. Many students come from homes without books or any room or space that is well lighted or quiet enough for studying. Continuous disruptions from brothers and sisters may make homework very difficult for many students. Then, too, many secondary school students hold down part-time jobs, on which their families are dependent for some daily essentials. For these students homework assignments that require a few hours each evening are impossible. Secondary teachers must also remember that students take several other courses and may be receiving homework assignments in all of them.

When you evaluate homework, take into account the conditions under which students are forced to perform. As with classroom or term projects, your grading of homework should be lenient enough so that those students who are faced with the most adverse environments will not be discouraged.

Follow-Up.   Nothing can be more discouraging to a student than to spend time and energy on an assignment only to have the teacher forget about it or push it aside for more critical matters. If you schedule a follow-up time at the time of the assignment, you can prevent these annoying situations.

The following steps for assigning homework can be used as a summary of this discussion and as a guideline for making homework assignments.[12,13]

1. As an alternative, plan for assignments to be completed at some time during the school day in a supervised area.
2. Be sure the purpose of every homework assignment is clear in your mind and that you have made it clear to the students.
3. Try to match assignments with students, making sure each student is treated fairly and equally.
4. Be sure every student knows exactly what is required.
5. Check the assignment when it is due.
6. Don't expect homework to teach a student who is not learning properly in the classroom.
7. Remember that assignments that use a multisensory approach are most effective in teaching.

These seven steps were actually designed for elementary school teachers. Do you think that any (or all) of them are adequate guidelines for the secondary teacher?

We have now discussed the uses of textbooks, discussions, field trips, oral reports, term projects, and homework. Perhaps the most important question a teacher can ask when making any of these assignments is, What will this special assignment permit students to do that they cannot do in class? And, how can I (we) design the assignment to benefit the student and perhaps the rest of the class?

SUMMARY

Now that you have learned the objectives at each of the levels of all three existing domains, think about what they will really mean to you when you begin teaching. Obviously you cannot even dream of including all levels of objectives in every lesson plan, not even in one lesson plan, but you can try to include objectives from all levels in each long-term unit. Even then, you may find it impossible to think of meaningful objectives at some levels. When this is the case, do not force students to comply to objectives that are illogical or impractical. In essence, teachers should use their own judgment in deciding what

---

[12] Lillie Pope, "A New Look at Homework," *Teacher* 96 (October 1978): 94–95.
[13] Kathryn Berry, "Homework: Is It for Elementary Kids?" *Instructor* 86 (February 1977): 52.

levels to include in each lesson, trying to include some objectives from all domains but basing their final choices on the nature of the subject and the needs of their students.

Lesson planning is complete only when it includes such strategies as homework, discussions, field trips, oral reports, and projects. Though frequently overused, the textbook is a valuable teaching tool, especially when it is one of several sources of content. Discussions and field trips should be selected for their special ability to motivate and provide first-hand experience. Both should be carefully planned. Oral reports and projects can provide added depth to the topics being studied, but should be assigned with specific purposes in mind, and never to simply provide students with a means of improving their grades.

EXPERIENCE

This chapter discussed techniques for writing behavioral objectives. Although most contemporary teachers realize the significance of objectives to teaching, you will undoubtedly hear many complaints about objectives among your future colleagues. The following experience shows some of the reasons for negative feelings about behavioral objectives. As you read it, you may wish to consider your own degree of application of objectives in your future lesson planning.

Experience 1:   A Principal Misuses Objectives

Lincoln High School had a reputation of being one of the most innovative, experimental, and advanced schools in the district. The large number of oil wells in the area made financing problems one of the principal's least worries. When Sondra Bell assumed this office last year, she promised the board of trustees that with their support she would lead the school to even greater heights.

As she planned her annual report to the board, she realized that they had delivered their part of the bargain. She wondered if they felt as positive about her. The annual report contained two parts: "In Retrospect" and "In Prospect." Since she felt that the first part looked a little weak, Sondra decided to make up for it by planning an impressive "In Prospect" section.

She began spelling out her objectives for the coming year. Could she impress the school board by planning everything for the coming year around those performance objectives that she would set for her students? It seemed logical enough, so Sondra got an idea of what she felt she must do. From the notes in her methods course, she pulled out a taxonomy of educational objectives. For each daily lesson, she wrote an objective at each level of the cognitive domain. But when she began writing objectives for all levels of the affective domain, her task became substantially more difficult. Although she had initially planned to write objectives representing all levels of all three domains, Sondra gave up in despair long before the task was completed.

Rather than to admit failure, Sondra appointed a committee consisting of the department heads and one or two members in each department. She assigned them exactly the same task: to write sample objectives at all levels in all domains for each subject in the entire school curriculum. To say the least, the faculty was not happy with this new turn in events. Most of them were already using objectives in planning their lessons, but they felt that this was going too far.

► *Questions and Discussion*

1. *Was this principal wrong in requiring her faculty to use objectives in their planning?*

   Actually, the mistake this principal made was more in the degree of this requirement than in the decision to require the use of objectives. Won't you agree that all teachers should use objectives to help clarify their expectations of students and to better organize their lessons? Yet, when taken to this extreme, the objectives could become a nightmare to the teachers and to the students.

2. *Why did Sondra have trouble writing objectives at all levels in all domains?*

   For any one person to try to force herself to write so many objectives in all levels for all the subject is absurd, if not literally impossible. The goal itself is admirable, since sample objectives can be very helpful to those teachers who do not have extensive experience writing objectives. Teachers should remember how difficult this is, so that they will know better how to respond to such demands.

3. *If you were a teacher at Lincoln High, how would you respond to this requirement?*

   So long as you are not forced to write too many objectives for each lesson, you will probably find that having objectives in the affective and psychomotor domains can really add meaningfulness and stimulation to your classes. Hopefully you will never be required to write an absurd number of objectives. Even if you are, don't turn against the whole concept of writing objectives for your classes.

ACTIVITIES

For various reasons contemporary teachers view the need for objectives differently, but most recognize that they will not reach their broader goals unless they use carefully written, specific behavioral objectives.

1. Each teacher has different aspirations for students. Consider your subject and write one broad goal that you feel is absolutely essential for students to understand. Write several specific behavioral objectives to help your students reach this goal.

2. Think about the problems plaguing our modern society. Write a general attitudinal goal toward eliminating or minimizing one of these problems. Now write a few specific behavioral objectives to help students attain this goal.

3. Have you any opinion(s) about objectives that you are willing to share with your classmates? If so, write these down and get one or two fellow students to listen to your opinion(s). Of course, you will then listen to theirs.

4. Choose a topic for class discussion. Write five objectives for the discussion and select a reading for all members. Now identify at least one or two related sources that give information not contained in the student assignment.

5. Plan a field trip for a learning unit in your major field. Start by listing five objectives. Now construct a short questionnaire to evaluate the degree of success of the trip.

SUGGESTED READINGS

BEAUCHAMP, GEORGE A. *Curriculum Theory.* 3d ed. Wilmette, Ill.: The Kagg Press, 1975.

BLOOM, BENJAMIN S. *Taxonomy of Educational Objectives: The Classification of Educational Goals: Handbook 1: Cognitive Domain.* New York: David McKay, 1956.

BLOOM, BENJAMIN S.; HASTINGS J. THOMAS; and MADAUS, GEORGE F. *Handbook on Formative and Summative Evaluation of Student Learning.* New York: McGraw-Hill, 1971.

DOLL, RONALD C. *Curriculum Improvement: Decision Making and Process.* 4th ed. Boston: Allyn and Bacon, 1978.

FIRTH, GERALD R., and KIMPSTON, RICHARD D. *The Curriculum Continuum in Perspective.* Itasca, Ill.: F. E. Peacock, 1973.

GIROD, GERALD R. *Writing and Assessing Attitudinal Objectives.* Columbus, Ohio: Charles E. Merrill, 1973.

GRONLAND, NORMAN E. *Stating Objectives for Classroom Instruction.* 2d ed. New York: Macmillan, 1978.

KRATHWOHL, D. R.; BLOOM, B. S.; and MASIA, B. B. *Taxonomy of Educational Objectives: The Classification of Educational Goals: Handbook 2: Affective Domain.* New York: David McKay, 1964.

MAGER, ROBERT F. *Preparing Instructional Objectives.* Palo Alto, Calif.: Fearon Publishers, 1962.

SANDERS, NORRIS M. *Classroom Questions: What Kinds?* New York: Harper and Row, 1966.

SIMON, SIDNEY B.; HOWE, LELAND W.; and KIRSCHENBAUM, HOWARD. *Values Clarification.* New York: Hart Publishing Company, 1972.

TRUMP, J. LLOYD, and MILLER, DELMAS F. *Secondary School Curriculum Improvement: Meeting Challenges of the Times.* 3d ed. Boston: Allyn and Bacon, 1979.

ZAIS, ROBERT S. *Curriculum: Principles and Foundations.* New York: Thomas Y. Crowell, 1976.

Planning Daily Lessons

OBJECTIVES

Upon completion of this chapter, you will be able to:
1. Define *daily lesson plan* and *unit plan,* and differentiate between the two.
2. Write five behavioral objectives that include the four essential parts of any behavioral objective.
3. List in order six pertinent parts of a daily lesson plan.
4. Write a plan for each of two daily lessons, including the six parts that you have identified as essential.
5. Describe two very different activities that can be used to achieve the same objective.

In Chapter 8 you saw how important planning is to teaching. You learned to begin each year by identifying the broad areas of content to be covered during the year and to identify goals that you hope to achieve periodically. Finally you learned how to design learning units through which you could achieve these goals.

But, as essential as they are, by themselves, goals remain no more than glittering generalities. To make them attainable, the teacher must design daily lesson plans that include these general expectations (goals) but that translate into more specific terms. Each daily lesson plan should be developed to achieve a particular part of the unit; in fact, most units contain a series of daily lesson plans. This chapter examines the process used to develop daily lesson plans.

SIGNIFICANCE

Since the teaching unit is usually content-oriented and does not specify the experiences needed for learning each day's lesson, you will need to develop a daily strategy for helping students move nearer to the unit goals. This is the daily lesson plan. For a teacher to attempt to teach a class without the aid of a lesson plan is analogous to a pilot's taking off to a new destination without a map. Like the map, the lesson plan provides direction toward the objectives. If the lesson begins to stray, the lesson plan enables you to steer it back to the main course.

Lesson plans come in many sizes and varieties. To be sure, some are much better than others, but this is not because of the length or style of the plan. A good lesson plan can be a very comprehensive outline formally worded and neatly typed on bond paper enclosed in a neat plastic binder, or it can be a very brief outline written in pencil on 3″ x 5″ cards. The styles of good lesson plans vary as much as their length. A good lesson plan contains enough material to challenge students throughout the hour and includes activities to involve every student. The format will be such that you can follow the plan with only brief glances and never have to stop the lesson to read it.

To argue about which type of lesson plan is best would be a waste of time. The lesson plan should be thought of as a tool and, like any tool, will be no more effective than the person using it. At the same time, the worker who has good machinery has an advantage over the worker who has faulty equipment. The important point, then, is that you develop and correctly utilize a lesson plan that works for *you*.

SETTING OBJECTIVES

As in planning a unit, the planning of a daily lesson always begins with the answer to these questions: In what ways do I want this lesson to change my students? or, What will they be able to do as a consequence of the lesson? If you state these proposed behavioral changes at the outset, your daily activities will have direction. Since the actual technique for writing performance objectives was explained in Chapter 8, it will not be repeated in this discussion.

ORGANIZING MATERIALS

Having decided what material to include in the lesson, you must next decide on the sequence in which the material is to be presented. Sometimes the nature of the subject dictates the order of presentation; thus, you should check the major ideas that you wish to cover to see if there is a natural sequence. For example, a physical education teacher who wants his students to learn to drive a golf ball, will ask himself, What few ideas are most important to understanding this process? He answers, "Addressing the ball, the backswing, the downswing, and the follow-through." When he asks, What sequence should I follow?, the answer is obvious because a natural process is involved.

A home economics teacher is planning a lesson: "How to bake a chiffon cake." Again the process dictates the sequence of the content. A history teacher would prepare many lessons in which the sequences of the content would follow in chronological order.

If the four or five objectives of the day's lesson have no natural order, you can determine whether a particular sequence would make the lesson more easily understood. The chemistry teacher probably would not teach formulas of compounds until the students had learned to recognize the symbols of the elements contained in the compound.

SELECTING EXPERIENCES

Our definition of curriculum selected earlier includes those planned experiences that the student is provided by the school. Generally, more emphasis is placed on experiences than on content, because today's American educators recognize that the experiences students have are the major means through which they learn. For this reason a lesson plan must describe the experiences through which the teacher expects to teach the content. And, as students often criticize their courses for lacking relevance, educators tell us that we must provide *meaningful* experiences. How can you make experiences meaningful so that, in turn, your courses will become relevant? And, since students should not engage in an activity without knowing what they are trying to accomplish, how will you plan their involvement?

Now review the partially completed lesson plan. You began by stating how you wanted the lesson to change the students, that is, the objectives of the lesson. Next, you selected and then organized a few major ideas that you wished to develop. Now you are ready to plan involvement by assigning a task that will require the student to *use* each of the major ideas in the lesson. The English teacher who is planning a lesson on "how to capture the reader's attention" would assign tasks that demand a student's use of the content learned. Presented with several compositions, the students are asked to identify the principles of capturing the reader's attention each time that they appear. Later in the hour each student will write the leading paragraph of a composition employing the five techniques of capturing the reader's attention introduced earlier in the hour.

The physical education teacher who wishes to teach the correct process for driving a golf ball may demonstrate each of the steps, asking students to identify mistakes that the teacher deliberately makes in each phase. Eventually the students follow through the processes themselves while other students criticize. The vocational shop teacher would follow a similar process.

Notice that each of these experiences is an assigned task. Each requires students to do things that they could not perform correctly unless they understand the content taught in the earlier part of the lesson.

SUMMARIZING THE DAILY LESSON

End your lesson plan with a review of the *main ideas* covered in the lesson. The summary should not attempt to review every detail covered in the lesson, nor should it merely list the main parts of the lesson. A statement of each main idea should be followed by a brief summary of the development of the idea during the lesson. Finally, the relationships among the major ideas should be shown in the review, thus tying together the parts of the lesson.

For example, the physical education teacher who is planning a lesson on "how to drive the golf ball" would include in the review each of the major ideas — the address, the backswing, the downswing, and the follow-through. As each of these main ideas is introduced, he would review the main points related to each. He would begin the review with the first idea — how to address the golf ball. This would include the major points involved in the proper address as they were mentioned in the lesson. The English lesson on "how to capture the reader's attention" would include each point and its development.

SAMPLE DAILY LESSON PLANS

Following are some sample daily lesson plans. Notice that they differ in style but that each contains a few major ideas, arranged in a sequence to facilitate learning. Notice also that each major idea is followed by an assigned task requiring students to use the idea. Finally, you will notice that each sample lesson ends with a review tying together the major ideas in the lesson.

Examine these daily plans. The parts vary from plan to plan. Make a list of all of the parts that you find in these plans; place an asterisk by those parts that you believe will be helpful to you when you teach. You can use the results as an outline to make a lesson plan in your subject area.

LESSON PLAN 1

Physical Education: Grade 9

Purpose:	To develop the ability to score a complete bowling game.
Materials:	Score sheet and a lead pencil with an eraser for each student
Equipment:	Overhead projector
Main Ideas:	How to score and add an open frame
	How to score and add a spare
	How to score and add a strike
	How to score and add the last frame
Procedure:	Five-minute explanation of each concept
	Demonstration of scoring a game
Assignment:	Each student is to score and add the following game at his desk:

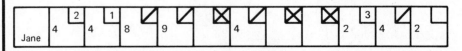

Summary:	The teacher will show a transparency of the game on the overhead screen and will use questions to lead the class in filling out each step in the game.

Do you like this first lesson plan? Is it clear? Among its strongest assets are its initial statement of purpose telling immediately what the lesson should do for the student, its clear statement of the ideas being taught, and its summary. The task is also clearly stated. Notice that the teacher selected for use as an example a game that started with the simplest ideas and moved to progressively more complex ideas until everything one needs to know to score a bowling game was covered. Note also that because this game contained all the essential ideas of scoring, it provided a satisfactory review of the whole lesson.

How could this plan be improved? Notice the procedures. Wouldn't it be easier to follow if the time limits were stated alongside the activities? Can you think of other ways to improve it?

LESSON PLAN 2

Mr. Hulsey

Date: December 2   Class: Tenth-Grade Business

1. Descriptive Title: "How to Prepare a Balance Sheet"
2. Concepts in Logical Sequence:
   a. The balance sheet tells what is owned, what is owed, and what the owner is worth on a specific date.
   b. Assets and liabilities determine owner's equity.
   c. Assets are entered in the left column, and liabilities and owner's equity are entered in the right column.
   d. The total of both columns must equal. If they do not balance, an error has been made.
3. Presentation: Discussion is the method to be used in presenting the concepts while working through a sample balance sheet on the board.
4. Assign Task: Each student will prepare a balance sheet to determine what he owns, what he owes, and what he is worth.
5. Summary: Go back over the four concepts, having students check to be sure that they have followed these concepts in preparing their balance sheet.

Discussion of Lesson Plan 2

Compare the format of this plan with Lesson Plan 1. Which is the easier to follow? Notice that this plan has no time indicated for any part of the lesson. Is that good, or would you need time limits to determine how long you should spend on each part of the lesson?

LESSON PLAN 3

Mr. Alfred Harding   Class: Speech, Grade 12

1. Title: "How to use TIME when reading with expression." Establish set by reading a poem ("Richard Cory") aloud as monotonously and ineffectively as possible, no pauses, no variance in speed.

2. The essential concepts of time: pause, rate, duration. Introduce these concepts (pause, rate, and duration) in that order because we go from time where no words are involved to time that involves several words, down to time that involves just one word.

3. a. Pause — the pregnant space of time when no sound is uttered; the dramatic pause after a heavy statement — give an example; the anticipating pause — slight hesitation before key word, often used both in dramatic and comedy punch line — give an example.
   b. Duration — the amount of time spent on just one word. Used for emphasis and imagery. Show how one can stretch out a single word and how it highlights the meaning of a passage.

4. Assignment: Go around room and have each one say, "Give me liberty, or give me death," using the three concepts of time for more expression.

5. Summary: Read same poem ("Richard Cory") as in beginning, only read it well and with expression. Then ask class if they've heard it before. They probably won't recognize it as the same poem. Tell and then show how important the proper use of those three concepts is for effective communication. Demonstrate how those three concepts worked in the second reading.

Discussion of Lesson Plan 3

What is your major criticism of this plan? Do you find the format complicated and involved? This lesson plan has some definite assets. Can you recognize them? The introduction would be effective in almost any class. The lesson content is divided into three clear categories so the class would not be overwhelmed with too much content. The summary is very good because it allows a comparison so the student can actually see the value in the main ideas developed — pause, rate and duration. Can you think of any ways to improve it?

LESSON PLAN 4

Class: Mr. Robert Pabst, Sociology, Grades 11 and 12

Topic: The Social Problem of Population

Objectives: To give the students a new awareness and knowledge of the population problem from various viewpoints, relating causal factors and discussing possible solutions. This lesson and the unit as a whole should provide the students with practical knowledge that will be helpful to them in doing their part to help control or solve the population problem.

Content:

I. The Population Problem	Introductory remarks by teacher.
A. Decline in Death Rate	Question-answer discussion about benefits of concepts to be gained by this unit. Check of student opinion and responses to this subject.
1. Man's expanded knowledge of himself and his environment has enabled him to exert some control over the death rate of our population.	Distribute handout study guide for this lesson.
a. Industrialism	Brief lecture by teacher on major concepts of population.
b. Scientific advances	

B. Problems in the United States	
1. Rapid growth — WW II birth boom	Discussion by class on feasibility of solutions.
2. Food production — Factors of economics and technology	Distribute booklet "This Crowded World."
3. Attitudes and socioeconomic factors	Show filmstrip "A Matter of Life and Death."
C. Possible Solutions	Summarize and review major points.
1. Family size	

2. Birth control
     a. Role of religion
     b. Role of government
	Give a ten-point quiz on population lesson for task and evaluation.

Assignment:
Read booklet distributed in class and make a brief outline of major points (written in longhand, about one page) to be turned in. Read at least the first ten pages of chapter "Population" in the text (pp. 30–40). Make notes on major points and topics you found interesting. These notes should be written neatly in the semester notebook to be turned in later.

Discussion of Lesson Plan 4

Hopefully, when you examined this lesson plan, you noticed that it includes a statement of the lesson's objectives. Are these objectives too general? (How could you test the class to see if these objectives were attained?) They could be improved by stating them in more specific terms; for example, the expression "various viewpoints" could be spelled out.

This lesson plan is longer than the previous ones. Is it too long? Do you like having the activities listed in a vertical column corresponding to the content? Notice that it enables the teacher to see at a glance what activity will be used to teach each unit of content. Is there anything missing in this plan?

LESSON PLAN 5

Mr. Robert Bullen   Equipment: None

Class: Business   Facilities: None

Grade: 12   No. in Class: 30

Date: June 30

1. Title of Lesson: How to read and analyze a newspaper's financial page effectively.

2. Reason for Lesson: To show how a person is allowed, through a stock exchange, to put his capital to work whenever and in whatever way he chooses.

3. Points to be reviewed:
   a. Just what Common Stock is
   b. What Common Stock means to an issuing corporation
   c. What Common Stock ownership means to the investor
   d. Advantages and disadvantages of Common Stock

4. Content:

Content:	Activity:
A breakdown of the different headings contained in the stock quotes.	Each student will be asked in advance of my explanation as to their meanings.
The prices will be analyzed as to what they actually mean.	Different prices will be put on the board with students giving the answer in dollars and cents.
Actual examples from a newspaper will be analyzed as to their meanings in relation to other stock quotes.	Each student will recite the quotes from a newspaper handout and will tell what they mean to him.

Summarizing the above concepts:

5. Evaluation: A simple quiz will be given consisting of the material just covered and the review work. A simulated paper quote will be provided so that I can test whether or not they understand all the aspects of the heading and the prices contained in the quote.

6. Assignment: They will be given a project of keeping the daily price quotes of a particular stock, which will be turned in at the end of the week and evaluated. Each student will be assigned a different stock.

Discussion of Lesson Plan 5

Did you notice anything in this plan that was not part of the other plans? Notice the section titled "Reason for Lesson." What advantage is there in having this as part of the actual lesson? Do you believe that students want to know why they are studying certain content? They do; and unless you can give them a meaningful reason, they may be very casual or even bored throughout the lesson.

This plan has a means for evaluating the lesson. It could be improved by stating the objectives in terms of expected student behavior and gearing the evaluation to measure the degree to which the student has met the originally stated objectives.

LESSON PLAN 6

Mrs. Grace Rockharts

Class: English, Grade 9

Concepts: The student should understand the importance of using proper grammar.

Teach students to identify nouns and know their classes.

(5 min.)   I. Introduce subject — Grammar
      a. Give a brief outline of the plan of study.
      b. Announce the noun as the first part of speech you will study.

(10 min.)   II. Present the idea that proper use of grammar is important.
      a. Give one example.
      b. Ask students for other examples.

(15 min.)   III. Give the definition of nouns and explain classes.
      a. common
      b. proper
      c. abstract
      d. concrete
      Give an example of each on the board.
      Ask students to give other examples and add to list.

(15 min.)   IV. Have each student make a list of fifteen nouns naming objects seen in the classroom. *(3 min.)*
      a. List the four classes on the board.
      b. Call on students for nouns and have them designate the proper list of each case.

(5 min.)   V. Summary
      a. Conduct a brief questioning period reviewing the definition and classes of nouns.
      b. Evaluate the effectiveness of the lesson by the response of the students. Did they understand the various classes? Could they easily choose the appropriate list for each noun?

Discussion of Lesson Plan 6

What is your reaction to the time indicators in this plan? Would they help you teach this lesson, or would they make you uncomfortable? Perhaps they are too restrictive.

The teacher's activities and the students' activities are listed in steps. Do you like this? Notice the objectives stated in the beginning. How could these be improved? There is no evaluation at the end. Wouldn't it be difficult to evaluate the accomplishment of the stated objective, "to understand the importance of using proper grammar"? Can you rewrite this objective, stating it in performance terms?

LESSON PLAN 7

Mr. Redlhammer

United States History — U.S. Civil War 1863–65

Grade 11

Aim: Discuss some major battles and what effect they had on the outcome of the war.

Points covered: Battle of Gettysburg
                 Battle of Vicksburg
                 Appomattox

1. Confederates were the farthest north that they had ever been.

2. Union and Confederate forces happen to meet and clash at a little town called Gettysburg.

3. Battle itself wasn't one big battle, but a series of small skirmishes.

4. Union took a position on Cemetery Ridge and Confederates on Seminary Ridge.

5. First day of battle ended with no headway.

6. July 2 started with intense fighting, and by evening the South was winning.

7. July 3: North shifted position and occupied both Seminary and Cemetery Ridges.

8. Confederates led the famous Pickett's Charge and were massacred.

9. Ask why this battle was important and list reasons on board.

10. July 4: Vicksburg fell, another Union victory.

11. Vicksburg was a key and strategic position that the South held on the Mississippi River.

12. Vicksburg located on high cliffs. Why did the city's location make it a key point?

13. Grant tried attacking from the river, but was defeated.

14. Grant planned to go twenty miles down river and come back to attack by land.

15. Grant encircled the city, cutting off all food supplies, and starved the city to surrender. Do you think that Grant was fair in using this tactic?

16. What do you think was the significance of this battle?

17. Last brave struggle of the South was at Appomattox.

18. South forced to surrender because of dwindling forces. What do you think caused this reduction in their army? Could this reduction have been prevented?

19. Grant and Lee met at Appomattox to discuss peace terms.

20. Terms of surrender were lenient.

21. South may have lost the fighting, but not their pride. Discuss this last statement.

22. Summarize important points.

Activities: Get in discussion groups and discuss this statement: "If the South had won the war."

Assignment: From the ideas discussed, write a short report on what the South would be like if it had remained split from the U.S.

Discussion of Lesson Plan 7

What is your reaction to the length of this lesson plan? It was used by a prospective teacher to teach a lesson in a secondary education methods class. The lesson was very interesting and well organized, but it was too long for one period; this discussion should have continued for the next several lessons.

The group discussions were the climax of the lesson. Following the group discussions, a representative from each group gave a brief capsule report of the conclusions of his group. This oral report is not included in "Activities." Should it be?

SUMMARY

Begin each daily lesson by asking yourself, "What changes do I want this lesson to make in my students?" The four or five most desirable changes should form the skeleton of the day's lesson. During the lesson each student should be assigned tasks that require a correct understanding of the ideas covered in class.

Each daily lesson plan should end with a summary. Instead of repeating everything covered during the hour, it should present the four or five major ideas along with some important points about each of them. A good summary will point out the relationships among the major ideas in the lesson.

EXPERIENCES

The importance of planning cannot be overstressed. No teacher can be successful without adequate planning. The following experiences portray the importance of planning. Poor planning, overstructuring, and planning lessons that are too short or too long leads to serious problems. The following experiences show some problems that teachers have experienced through inadequate planning.

Experience 1: A Teacher Attempts to Be Democratic in His Planning

It was a year to remember — 1976 — the nation's bicentennial birthday. Mr. Henry, a first-year teacher, was dedicated to establishing a completely democratic classroom atmosphere. Although he was young and inexperienced, he was determined to develop a feeling of freedom within each student so that everyone could better understand the true meaning of democracy.

Mr. Henry's approach to creating this atmosphere was quite sensible. From the first day he incorporated democratic machinery into his tenth-grade democracy classes. Every controversial idea was put to a vote. The opinion of the majority always determined the class's direction and behavior. To say that the students enjoyed his classes is an understatement — at least throughout the first term.

The students decided to determine subject content on a completely individual basis. Some of the more studious quickly identified their area of interest and immediately began their projects. Some of the slower students did not reach definite decisions for several days; yet it was clear that they did not worry about it. Mr. Henry was patient and gave his assistance when asked to do so.

All was well and everyone was happy as the term got well under way. Many students were thrilled with this fresh new approach and the complete freedom it provided — something that they had not experienced in previous classes. The first students to become concerned, and later doubtful about whether the approach was "right for them," were the high-performing students. Since most members of this group were planning to attend college and would take courses in American Democracy, they began to wonder if they were getting the foundations that they would need when they reached their college democracy classes. Mr. Henry assured them that they should not worry because they would probably be even more adequately prepared than their fellow students in future democracy classes. He brought to his classes some research studies showing that several nondirective and open-ended mathematics and science classes had prepared students so well that they outscored their counterparts in traditional classes on standardized college entrance examinations. This pacified some of the students, but it failed to erase their doubts completely.

As the end of the first grading period approached, the previously concerned students began worrying again. When they asked how their grades would be determined, Mr. Henry replied, "How do you wish your grade to be determined?" They soon realized that the competitive exams to which they were accustomed were not adequate to test the content in this class. When Mr. Henry proposed that each student provide evidence of his academic progress and let fellow class members determine the appropriate grade, the students rejected this proposal hands down.

The class appeared to be in trouble; so did the teacher. This approach had not produced the uniformity of content that is found in traditional classes. Mr. Henry wondered how he could have democratic classes and yet avoid these problems.

► *Questions and Discussion*

1. *How much freedom should a secondary school class have in selecting content?*

    The idea of providing complete freedom for any group of people (youth or adults) is a misguided one. People who have guidelines are the freest of all — far more so than persons who have no rules to follow. The person who has no regulations finds himself wandering aimlessly without purpose and without direction. Therefore, the teacher who attempts to provide his class with absolute freedom of choice and freedom of behavior usually finds that his students do not appreciate his completely nonstructured approach.

    Every teacher has gained knowledge through professional education courses and through practical experiences. From them he can identify certain information that his students need to prepare for the future. By sharing essential experiences, which is the teacher's right *and* responsibility, the teacher can then assist the students in the selection of other content and experiences.

2. *Should Mr. Henry discontinue using democratic procedures in the classroom and teach the principles of democracy as content rather than practice?*

    Definitely not. Democracy should be practiced in all classes. Teaching the rules of democracy is essential, but the best method of doing this is by having the students practice them. Aristotle once said, "We learn virtue by being virtuous." Democracy is a way of treating others as you would have them treat you. This cannot be achieved through learning rules, principles, and definitions.

3. *How could Mr. Henry retain structure in the class and yet involve students in the planning of his classes?*
   The teacher's role is to guide the students in selecting content appropriate to the class. One method would be first to discuss with the students the objectives that he expects the class to achieve, showing them why each objective is needed. Then he could let the students decide how they wish to achieve these objectives.

   Actually, the matter of content to be covered is less important than the development of understanding. If Mr. Henry is more concerned with the ultimate goals of the class — and he should be — he will not worry so much about content but will concentrate on objectives and the planned experiences that will keep the students working toward these goals. You can probably think of other ways to let students share the planning responsibility.

4. *What can you say about when the evaluation system was determined?*
   Mr. Henry waited too late to decide how the grades would be determined. Students should have this knowledge from the beginning to direct their activities and to help them to prepare for evaluations.

Experience 2:   A Teacher Uses Note Cards for Planning

Every student in school liked Mr. Little, the teacher who supervised my student teaching experience. Mr. Little's classes were both entertaining and successful. Learning seemed to occur automatically in his classes. During the three months I spent in this teacher's classes, I never once saw a detailed lesson plan.

During class, Mr. Little, who incidentally was small in stature, always sat in front of the room, perched on a high stool. As he talked, joked, and laughed with his students, he continually shuffled a few 3″ x 5″ note cards, glancing at them while carrying on a dialogue with his students. After his introductory lesson on rocks and minerals, I examined Mr. Little's note cards (see Figure 9.1).

Although the cards were not at all detailed or impressive, they did provide structure to the lesson. Each item was mentioned very briefly. Key words and phrases were used rather than complete sentences. This style enabled Mr. Little to glance at his notes without taking his attention away from the students and, I felt, contributed significantly to his unusually effective teaching.

▶ *Questions and Discussion*

1. *What are some advantages of brevity in lesson plans?*
   a. The teacher is less inclined to "read" the lesson to the class.
   b. Flexibility is provided. The teacher has time to let the class pursue

```
ROCKS & MINERALS    #1
1. Why study rocks
2. Joke
3. Basic types of rocks
   a. Sedimentary
   b. Igneous
   c. Metamorphic
4. Rock collecting
```

Figure 9.1   3" x 5" Cards Used for Planning

the planned topics and related topics and materials that interest them.

c. A brief lesson plan leaves time for students to become involved.

2. *What are some dangers in plans being too brief?*

a. The teacher may run short of material and find that there is time left in the hour with nothing planned.

b. The brief lesson may be "shallow." It may not challenge students to think.

3. *Can a lesson be too highly structured?*

Yes, if this means too detailed. When the lesson is too detailed, the teacher is likely to dominate the class, leaving the students no opportunity to question and comment about the lesson. If you interpreted the question literally and answer no, I would have to agree with you. The more structure a lesson has, the more likely the students will be to reach the set goals. Although we often stress the value of pupil-centered, discovery approaches, we should realize that this type of method cannot succeed unless there is much planning and hidden structure. Although pupil-centered classes may seem to have little structure, the successful ones are usually more highly structured in terms of objectives and activities than are traditional classes.

Experience 3:   A Teacher Fails to Use Objectives

At college our biology teacher had a style of her own. Each hour Mrs. Woods promptly opened her notebook and began the lesson. She wrote everything she said on the board in perfect outline. Her speaking speed was equaled only by her writing speed; not a moment during the hour was wasted.

Students were amazed by the neatness, formality, and professional approach in every lesson that Mrs. Woods taught. She always kept to the objectives for the day. Once when she was absent, her husband, who was also a biology teacher, took over for the day. Having specified no objectives, he kept students wondering when he was going to get into the lesson. They complained, saying that his remarks had nothing to do with the topic being studied. Mr. Woods understood biology; yet his lecture seemed to confuse students.

Some of the best students in school received their lowest marks in Mrs. Woods's classes; furthermore, they said they had learned very little about biology. Students were dazed at having benefited so little in the class of a teacher who was not only brilliant in her subject but extremely well prepared for every lesson.

► *Questions and Discussion*

1. *Did Mrs. Woods's lessons lack structure?*

   By no means: every minute of Mrs. Woods's classes was thoroughly planned in advance. Her classes lacked variety, student involvement, and student interaction, but they did not lack structure.

2. *Why did these students feel so lost in Mr. Woods's class?*

   Mr. Woods made the fatal mistake of trying to teach without first identifying lesson objectives. Even when teachers do not share the list of objectives with their students, the objectives often become apparent because they cause the teacher to structure the lesson systematically.

Experience 4: A Teacher Gets Lost in His Own Lessons

Each day when my students returned from their music, they inevitably complained to me about their homework assignments. I heard such complaints as "This assignment has nothing to do with what we studied in class today," "I don't see the value in this," and "Why does he make us do this?"

Each day I reminded them that they were not to direct their criticisms of another teacher toward me, that for me to discuss this issue with them would be most unprofessional and unethical. Each day I refused to make a comment about Mr. Marshall; yet each day I heard similar complaints: "Mr. Marshall rambles," "He skips around with the material so much that it doesn't make sense." Finally, the news reached the administrators, who asked to speak with Mr. Marshall about the issue. I never knew what was said during the meeting, but apparently it did produce a change in Mr. Marshall's teaching because the complaints became fewer and fewer. I always wondered how Mr. Marshall managed to change so quickly and to improve his teaching so effectively.

► *Questions and Discussion*

1. *Often teachers of special subjects such as music, art, and physical education are assigned to teach several sections of the same class. This often contributes to the teacher's forgetting just what he has covered*

with each group (as Mr. Marshall apparently did). What would you do should you ever find yourself forgetting where you ended the previous class and exactly what content you covered in it?

This problem is a common one, and you should not be surprised if someday you experience it. Since it can be very frustrating to you and to your students, you should give it some previous thought. One precaution is to be practical. Do not try to impress the students with your ability to remember everything about the previous lesson. One simple yet effective solution is to draw an arrow with the class hour on the lesson plan, indicating where yesterday's lesson stopped. Second, you might develop a habit of beginning each lesson with a review of the main ideas covered in the preceding lesson. Encourage students to comment if and when you cover material in the review that was not in a previous lesson.

2. *When teaching multiple sections of the same class, should you make separate lesson plans for each section?*

This would depend on the difference in ability of the classes. If the difference is large, it will probably be impossible to use the same plans for both sections; however, if the difference is small, you may find it much more manageable to use the same plan for multiple sections.

3. *Are there times when the teacher should stray from the planned lesson?*

Yes. Often a class will become very interested and enthusiastic over a particular part of the lesson. When this happens, you should be willing to deviate from your plan, letting the class explore their chosen areas of interest. On the other hand, when the planned lesson seems very boring to a particular class, change your approach drastically.

The lesson plan should never be considered an end in itself; rather, it is a means to an end — the objectives of the lesson. If you see that another means of reaching these objectives may be more effective than your previous strategy, do not hesitate to lay aside the lesson plan and continue pursuing the desired objectives.

4. *Does a teacher's ability to plan improve as a consequence of experience?*

This is not necessarily so. With experience you can assess the speed with which a class can grasp material, and hence your ability to judge the appropriate length of a lesson. However, experience alone will not necessarily make your lessons clearer and more interesting. These qualities come only when you study your approach and deliberately adjust your lessons to make them so.

Experience 5: A Senior Teacher Uses Repetition

Mr. Myers had been teaching English at Clapham High longer than any other teacher. Through the years he had not lost interest in young people but had become more and more concerned for them. Since most Clapham High students went on to attend a highly respected university, Mr. Myers felt responsible for preparing them for the demands he knew they would face at the university.

Taking every precaution to avoid having the students miss important content, Mr. Myers began each lesson with a review of the previous lesson. As he introduced new material, he did so very slowly. He constantly repeated the important ideas to make certain that they were not forgotten. When a student was absent from the previous day's lesson, Mr. Myers repeated every part of the lesson.

The complaints about Mr. Myers were just the opposite of those directed toward Mr. Marshall: his students were bored. They remarked that they wished he would move on to new material, that they were tired of hearing the same old thing again and again.

How do teachers achieve the correct balance that lets them cover the subject fast enough to avoid boring the students and yet slowly enough so that everyone can understand the lesson?

► *Questions and Discussion*

1. *How can the teacher tell when the lesson plan contains too much material for a lesson?*
   Actually, the teacher should have no fear of planning a lesson that is too long, for there is no obligation to cover a whole lesson plan in one period. It is much better to present the material at a reasonable pace, dividing the lesson into two parts, than to rush to complete the lesson in one hour. A teacher realizing that the planned lesson is too lengthy should, instead of speeding up, continue at the same pace until a few minutes before the period ends, then review the material covered during the period. The students will never know that the original plan was to go beyond that point.

2. *How much material is too much for a lesson?*
   Ideally, the lesson should be long enough to keep the class challenged, yet short enough that the class will not be overwhelmed with information, resulting in confusion. Lessons that confuse students discourage them, but lessons that are too shallow bore students; when this happens, the students learn to find other ways of entertainment.

ACTIVITIES

In this chapter you have seen several examples of daily lesson plans. Now develop a daily plan in your major teaching field. Specify the subject and grade level and include performance objectives, content generalizations, activities for students to experience for attaining the objectives, and a summary of the most significant ideas in the lesson.

Communications

BLOOM, BENJAMIN S.; HASTINGS, J. THOMAS; and MADAUS, GEORGE F. *Handbook on Formative and Summative Evaluation of Student Learning.* New York: McGraw-Hill, 1971.

BLOOM, BENJAMIN S. *Taxonomy of Educational Objectives: The Classification of Educational Goals: Handbook 1: Cognitive Domain.* New York: David McKay, 1956.

CLARK, LEONARD H., and STARR, IRVING S. *Secondary School Teachings.* 3d ed. New York: Macmillan, 1976.

HAGER, HERBERT K. *First Steps in Secondary Teaching.* Columbus, Ohio: Charles E. Merrill, 1973.

HOOVER, KENNETH H. *The Professional Teacher's Handbook.* 2d ed. Chapter 3. Boston: Allyn and Bacon, 1976.

KIM, EUGENE C., and KELLOUGH, RICHARD D. *A Resource Guide for Secondary School Teaching.* 2d ed. New York: Macmillan, 1974.

KRATHWOHL, DAVID R.; BLOOM, BENJAMIN S.; and MASIA, BERTRAM B. *Taxonomy of Educational Objectives: Handbook 2: Affective Domain.* New York: David McKay, 1964.

MAGER, ROBERT F. *Preparing Instructional Objectives.* Palo Alto, Calif.: Fearon Publishers, 1962.

MOSSTON, MUSKA. *Teaching: From Command to Discovery.* Belmont, Calif.: Wadsworth Publishing Company, 1972.

OLIVA, PETER F. *The Secondary School Today.* 2d ed. San Francisco: Intext Educational Publishers, 1972.

RENNER, JOHN W.; BIBENS, ROBERT F.; and SHEPHERD, GENE D. *Guiding Learning in the Secondary School.* New York: Harper and Row, 1972.

TYSON, JAMES C., and CARROLL, MARY ANN. *Conceptual Tools for Teaching in Secondary Schools.* Boston: Houghton Mifflin, 1970.

Improving Instruction

PART FOUR

Many teachers would quickly agree that continuous improvement in their instruction is likely to come not from a series of sudden insights or unrelated impulses. Continuous improvement is far more likely to result from good, systematic planning that is later transferred into good instruction.

A chapter on long-range planning is included to help you learn how to select broad goals and then to plan learning units to achieve them. Finally, the section ends with a discussion of a number of teaching strategies, along with the advantages and limitations of each.

Long-Range Planning

OBJECTIVES

Upon completing this chapter, you will be able to:
1. List at least four or five sources for determining curriculum content.
2. Describe in detail an effective approach to using textbooks to identify curriculum content.
3. Give three reasons why teachers should plan their own curricula.
4. Explain the student's role in curriculum development.
5. Describe the role of the teacher's philosophy in curriculum planning.
6. Differentiate between goals and objectives.
7. Explain the relationship between curriculum objectives and curriculum content.
8. Explain the relationship between curriculum content and student activities.
9. Discuss in detail Taba's Inverted Curriculum Model and list at least three of its unique characteristics.
10. Develop a learning/teaching unit for the subject and grade level that you plan to teach.

Have you ever wondered who decides the nature of each class: What content will be covered? What will the general goals of the course be? What experiences will be contained in the course? Will there be field trips, guest speakers, or other special events? Or who determines whether there will be one or two units of composition in an English class, or whether the geometry class will spend six weeks or six months studying solid geometry as opposed to plane geometry.

Is the decision made from the number of chapters devoted to each topic in the textbook? If so, who chooses the textbook? Surely it is not the principal or superintendent. As you have undoubtedly surmised from reading the previous chapter, the teacher plays a significant role in the making of these all significant decisions. This means that the quality of the education of each of your future students throughout your teaching career (these may number in the thousands) will depend on your success in long-term planning.

Some teachers, of course, are willing to follow their textbooks, chapter by chapter, and bring no supplementary material to their classes. Letting the authors of the textbooks be the major curriculum determinants is unfortunate, since the authors know nothing about the uniqueness of your students, their aspirations, and their strengths and weaknesses. Furthermore, the authors know nothing about the resources of your community. Are there facilities for good field trips? Are there resource people in town who could give excellent talks? Is there a good zoo, museum, park, or industry that would offer valuable learning experiences? And does the textbook content correspond with your background so that you can use your expertise? Or perhaps you have omissions in your preparation and thus cannot teach others the content you yourself do not understand.

Because of textbook limitations, most teachers insist in becoming as involved as possible in the long-term planning of their courses. Although most teachers do not have the freedom to make all of these decisions alone, they can have considerable influence in all of them. Through experience, teachers learn how to increase their influence in the total planning of their courses.

THE QUESTION OF CONTENT

At the beginning of each school year one of your first and greatest decisions will be what content to cover. Like all teachers, you will feel some obligation to cover the content that students will need as background for their courses during the following year. But an even greater concern is that they possess the *understandings* and *skills* that will be needed the following year and throughout their lives.

Perhaps by this time you are wondering how teachers determine what a student should learn in each class. Take a moment to make a list of at least ten ways a teacher can find information about what instruction students will need in a particular class. You might head it "Ways to Identify Content." Surely no two teachers' lists will be identical.

One logical place to begin this search is the state curriculum guides. Each state produces its own guides. Such guides are important, for they consider a course's content in relation to the previous and following years. In other words, the developers of state curriculum guides consider the total content needed by students throughout their total school program through grade twelve. A second important feature of state curriculum guides is their focal points. They begin with broad goals and identify general understandings that students are expected to develop at each grade level.

A second source of information is the syllabi that local teachers of the next grade up from yours use to teach your subject. By paying special attention to the beginning of each unit of study, you can quickly grasp what the students are expected to know as they leave your class.

One of the most popular sources of information about what should be covered each year is textbooks. While you should not let a single textbook dictate your total curriculum, looking at several will remind you to incorporate important content from each. Start by examining several current texts at your particular grade level and make a content comparison chart. This way you can compensate for any deficiencies of your own particular text. Table 10.1 is an example of a chapter comparison of general secondary methods texts. Although such an examination of chapter comparisons is a very broad and therefore a rather crude assessment of content in textbooks, you will probably agree that it is a step in the right direction.

Table 10.1 Content Comparison

Chapter Topics	Book A	Book B	Book C	Book D	Book E	Book F	Book G	Book H
Adolescence & Learning	X	X	X	X	X			X
Planning	X	X	X	X	X	X	X	X
Classroom Management	X	X	X	X	X	X	X	X
Evaluation	X	X	X	X	X	X	X	X
Teaching Styles	X	X	X	X	X			X
Motivation	X	X						X
Multicultures or Disadvantaged		X		X	X			X
History & Aims		X						X
Audio-Visuals		X	X					X
Teaching Special Pupils		X	X					X
Communications			X					X
The Professional Teacher/ Getting a Job		X	X					
Student Teaching		X	X					
Teacher & Community			X					
Observing Yourself							X	
Questions Prospective Students Ask							X	

But if you have time to examine the texts in your field more closely, you can check the major concepts or principles found in each content area. For example, a junior high earth science textbook should cover the following major fields of study: astronomy, geology, meteorology, oceanography, and physical geography. Figure 10.1, which compares four popular texts, may startle you when you note the small percentage of pertinent principles represented in each of these four books. Such poor coverage is not at all uncommon; in fact, the actual coverage in these texts ranges from about 8 percent to about 33 percent. (See Figure 10.2.) It is this failure of textbooks to cover all of the important principles and concepts that makes any text (or even a combination of them) an incomplete source for determining what should be included in a course. Ideally, textbooks should be one of *many* curriculum determinants. A further common weakness of textbooks is their sparcity of content at the higher levels of the cognitive domains. In fact most textbook content is written at the bottom level of the cognitive domain; studies by O. L. Davis and Francis P. Hunkins have found that over eighty-five percent of the content of textbooks is written at the recall level (Orlich, 1980).

Another important source of information for determining course content is the students themselves. From the very beginning of the year, involve your students in curriculum planning. A way to do this was developed in the 1950s by Hilda Taba. In contrast to the other curriculum models, which are developed outside the school, Taba's is developed by teachers and their students. This model is so different — in that it starts at the bottom (in the classroom)

Figure 10.1   Variance in Representation of Principles Among Four
Basic Science Textbooks (A, B, C, and D)

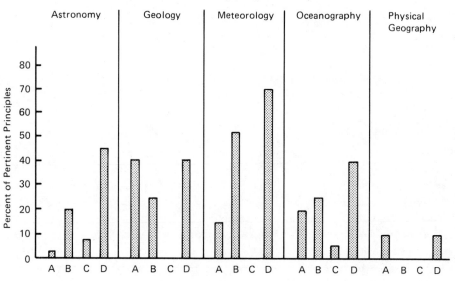

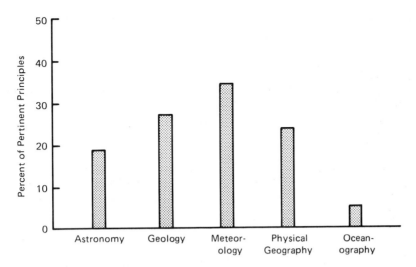

Figure 10.2 Mean Representation of Pertinent Principles for Each
Science Subject

and moves upward — that it has come to be known as Taba's Inverted Model.
Obviously it has the advantages of including the desires and abilities of your
students; also, since it is developed by you, the teacher, you will be more likely
to use it and to do so more effectively than if you were using a unit developed
externally.

Another unique feature of Taba's model is that it connects curriculum with
instruction. She achieved this by making the learning unit the center of her
model. In other words, you and your students together will choose major topics
of study (such as astronomy, geology, etc.) Then you, by yourself, will develop,
for each topic, a unit lasting from a few weeks to several weeks. For convenience they are usually the same length as the grading period in the school
system. Since most school systems report grades every six weeks, most units
are six weeks long; however, there is nothing wrong with having two three-
week units or three two-week units in a grading period.

THE UNIT

For each major objective you hope to accomplish during the year, you should
have a specific plan of attack — the unit plan. For example, a teacher of junior
high earth science would probably wish each student to acquire some understanding of astronomy, ecology, geology, meteorology, oceanography, paleontol-
ogy, mineralogy, and physical geography. For each of these areas the teacher
may wish to plan a unit of study, each lasting from a few days to a few weeks
and containing the topics that the teacher believes essential to a general understanding of earth science.

Planning the Unit

Once you have selected your unit topics, you will be ready to begin planning each unit. The planning can be a joint effort by you and your students. This does not mean, however, that you should have the same role in the planning as the students do. Before you approach the class with the project of planning a unit of study, you may wish to determine your exact role and theirs.

Your extensive study of the subject gives you insights into what the student should know about the unit — insights that the student does not have. Therefore, a major part of your role is to specify some of the important ideas or concepts that will be developed in the unit and explain why this material is important. The class may attempt to have some ideas or sections of the unit deleted solely on the basis of dislike for the material. Of course, if you feel these concepts are essential, you will not allow the class to dictate the unit material.

A second function of your role in planning a unit is to give students an opportunity to include areas within the unit that they think should be studied. Although you may think these topics less pertinent than some others that are not being included, you should remember that the mere fact that the students find a topic interesting makes it relevant and meaningful to them.

A third part of your role in planning a unit is to guide the class in selecting the activities necessary for developing understanding of the unit. Again, this does not mean that the teacher selects some of the activities and the students independently select the rest of them. When you present the problem of selecting activities, have on hand a list of suggested activities for the class to choose from. This provides a start in the desired direction; however, if the students wish to add other activities that seem feasible, why not let them? You might ask yourself about each proposed activity, Is it contrary to school policy? Is it dangerous or harmful to me, the class, or others? Is it something that I should first check with the principal? Is it worthwhile? and, finally, Is it something we could try? If so, because the students are interested in that particular activity, it may prove worthwhile.

Parts of the Unit Plan

The learning unit or unit plan is much more than an outline of the subject material to be explored within a certain topic. Although there are many variations, most units contain the following parts: a title; a statement of philosophy; goals; objectives; a listing of the daily lessons to be studied within the unit (an outline); and a method for evaluating the degree of understanding developed while studying the unit. It may also include a list of resource people (consultants) and resource materials (bibliography). The following unit plans are provided for your analysis. Notice that the title describes the unit; the statement of purpose or objectives describes a desired change in the students; and the evaluation is made in terms of the objectives stated at the beginning of the unit.

SAMPLE UNIT PLAN

Title: *What Meteorology Means to You*

Purpose:
1. Knowledge: to understand:
   a. The different types of weather
   b. The principles of weather formation
   c. The role of the weatherman
   d. The names and principles of commonly used weather instruments
   e. Weather vocabulary

2. Attitudes: to appreciate:
   a. The damage weather can do
   b. The advantage of good weather
   c. How weather affects our daily behavior
   d. The rate of accuracy of weather predictions
   e. The precision use of weather instruments
   f. The fallacies of superstitions about the weather

3. Skills: to develop the ability to:
   a. Read and interpret weather instruments
   b. Read and interpret weather maps
   c. Predict future weather

Outline of Daily Lessons:
1. Definition of weather

2. Precipitation
   a. The different types of precipitation
   b. How each type of precipitation is formed

3. Reading the weather map

4. Reading the weather instruments

5. Predicting weather

6. Effects of geographic location on weather

7. Effects of the earth's rotation on weather

8. Effects of the earth's tilting on weather

9. How to change the weather that can hurt you

Materials:
1. Weather reports from newspapers

2. Weather maps

3. Equipment for making fog: air pump, water, and jar

4. Barometer, thermometer, anemometer, and wind vane

5. Graph paper for each student

Evaluation: Tests for each section of this unit: approximately one test per week's study of topic.

Discussion of Unit Plan

The above plan was chosen for its brevity and its simplicity. By no means do these features make it a superior plan, yet such brief units are often used. Do you think that this unit is too skimpy? The other units chosen for inclusion in this chapter are much more detailed. What do you think about this format?

Is the outline adequate? Figure 10.3 shows the parts commonly found in a unit. What parts are missing in this sample unit?

Did you notice that this unit has neither a statement of philosophy or rationale to show the significance of the unit? Many educators feel that you need a statement of philosophy to clarify in your own mind your broad beliefs about life, school, and adolescents and how they learn. Surely the unit's goals and objectives should be consistent with and reflect your basic beliefs. Other educators prefer a statement of rationale to a statement of philosophy: when you state a rationale, you justify the unit to yourself. You, in turn, use it to convince the students that the unit is worth their time and energy.

This unit has no sections entitled "Teacher Activities" and "Student Activities." That is unfortunate, since the teacher should at this time make certain decisions, such as whether to take the students to a weather station and whether to show a film or two on weather. The weather station may need advance notice. Also the students will need to know in advance what they should be looking for during the visit. Films must be scheduled (and ordered) well in advance if they are to be available when you need them, and you also need to preview them. You have probably identified several other weaknesses in this unit plan.

Now examine the following, more comprehensive plan. It should have fewer weaknesses (but you will be the judge of that). It was chosen because it does seem to have most of the pertinent parts, those that many educators feel essential to any unit; however, this unit has room for improvement. As you exam-

Figure 10.3 Diagram of a Learning/Teaching Unit

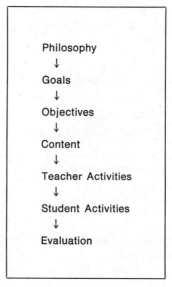

Philosophy
↓
Goals
↓
Objectives
↓
Content
↓
Teacher Activities
↓
Student Activities
↓
Evaluation

ine it, you may wish to make notes (written or mental) on its strengths and weaknesses. Pay particular attention to the overall structure and organization of the unit. Can you improve it?

Following is a sample chemistry unit that has been designed for use in an eleventh-grade class.

Statement of Purpose
for the Unit:
The Organization of Chemistry*

The chapters covered in this unit are designed to introduce the beginning chemistry student to the basic background and structural knowledge needed for further development of chemistry. Topics to be covered include Atomic Structure and the Periodic Table.

Let's Talk *A statement of general purpose, aims, goals, or rationale is helpful to orientate the teacher to the unit. It can also be used to introduce the unit to the students. The overall purpose of the chapter can also include general changes in student behavior. But since the reason for teaching is to change students' behavior, a much more specific list of performance objectives is used to explain precisely those capabilities the teacher expects the students to be able to perform from having studied the unit. This unit is built around two chapters; therefore, the following list of objectives will be for both chapters.*

Performance Objectives
for the Unit:
The Organization of Chemistry

Chapter 1 Atomic Theory

The eleventh-grade general chemistry student will be able to:

Lesson 1:
1. Define an atom correctly when asked to on a closed book test.
2. Give the size of an atom when asked to on the unit post-test.
3. Identify the parts of an atom by name and describe the parts of the atom, given an unlabeled diagram of the atom. Four of five parts must be correctly labeled and described.
4. Match the mass of the parts of the atom to the correct path, given a list of masses.

Lesson 2:
5. Define the atomic number of an atom.
6. Define the mass number of an atom when asked to on a closed book test.
7. Utilize the concept of isotopes by correctly grouping given atoms into isotopic groups.
8. Apply the concept of energy level shells by designating the number of electrons in each shell, given an atomic number.

Lesson 3:
9. Correctly define atomic mass when asked to on a closed book test.
10. Define Avogadro's number when asked to on a closed book test.
11. Apply the concept of a mole by the amount of a substance in a mole of a given substance.
12. Define the atomic weight of an atom on a closed book test.
13. Apply the concepts of atomic number, Avogadro's number, mole, and gram atomic weight in solving simple stoichiometric problems. Given the problem and required information, the student must solve

* Appreciation is given to Mr. Stephen R. Burks for his counsel and expertise in the development of this unit.

for the asked for information, correctly answering 80% of the problems to receive credit. (Partial credit given for correct set-ups.)

Let's Talk   *Each performance objective should contain four parts. You may
wish to check these objectives against these criteria. It is as simple as A, B, C, D.*
Audience: *The student should be the subject of each objective.*
Behavior: *The student's behavior should be the verb of each objective.*
Conditions: *The objective should describe the conditions under which the
student is expected to perform.*
Degree: *The degree or level of performance required of the students
should be specified.*

Chapter 2   Periodic Table

The eleventh-grade general chemistry student will be able to:

Lesson 1:   1. List at least three of the four basic elements.
             2. Identify the common elements by symbol. This will be shown by
                correctly giving the elements or symbol asked for in 15 of 18 questions on two in-class quizzes.

Lesson 2:   3. Obtain atomic numbers of elements from the periodic table with an
                accuracy level of 80%.
             4. Obtain the mass number of elements from the periodic table with an
                accuracy level of 80%.
             5. Obtain a given element's electron configuration from the periodic
                table.

Lesson 3:   6. Define periodic law.
             7. Define a "group of elements."
             8. Define "period of elements."
             9. Distinguish the characteristics of families of elements by matching
                the correct family with the given characteristic with a minimum
                accuracy level of 80%.
            10. With 80% or above accuracy, match the correct family with the given
                element.

Attitudinal Objective for Unit

The eleventh-grade general chemistry student will be able to participate in class
discussions. This objective will be met when 80% of the class answers general questions, directed to the class as a whole, during the course of the discussion.

Let's Talk   *Following are two lists: a list of concepts and a list of content
generalizations. A check to see if students know these terms can help the teacher
begin at the appropriate level. But the second list — content generalizations —
is even more important. These are the major understandings that should come
from this unit. Notice that they are essential for the attainment of the preceding
objectives.*

**Concepts and Generalizations
for the Unit:**
The Organization of Chemistry

Topic 1   Atomic Structure

Concepts:

1. atomic theory
2. atom*
3. proton*
4. neutron*
5. electron*
6. nucleus*
7. element
8. mole
9. Avogadro's number
10. angstrom, A
11. gram-atomic weight
12. atomic weight
13. energy level
14. mass number
15. nuclide
16. atomic mass
17. particle
18. configuration
19. isotope
20. naturally occurring atoms

Generalizations:

1. Atomic theory has been developed to support observations.

2. Each subparticle composing the atom (electron, neutron, proton) has certain characteristics and is unique.
   in energy levels or shells.

3. Each atom has its electrons arranged

* students should already be familiar with these concepts

Topic 2   Arrangement of Electrons in Atoms

Concepts:

1. orbitals
2. orbital notation
3. electron configuration notation
4. electron dot notation

Generalizations:

1. Quantum numbers describe the orientation of an electron in an atom in terms of: (1) distance from the nucleus; (2) shape; (3) position in space with respect to the three axes (x, y, z); and (4) direction of spin.

Topic 3   Periodic Table

Concepts:

1. periodic table
2. series (period)
3. group (family)
4. noble gas family
5. sodium family
6. calcium family
7. nitrogen family
8. oxygen family
9. halogen family
10. transition elements
11. rare earth elements
12. ionization energy
13. electron affinity

Generalizations:

1. The periodic table organizes the elements; properties can be predicted from the elements' positions.

2. Elements with similar arrangements of outer-shell electrons have similar properties.

Let's Talk   *Now that we have identified a general purpose for the unit, set down the precise objectives for the lesson, and selected the major concepts and content generalizations that will be needed to achieve these objectives, it is now time to plan the daily activities. These should include the teacher's activities and the activities in which the students will be involved.*

The following daily lesson plans tell us what will be happening throughout the hour. Can you think of more meaningful ways to involve the students?

DAILY LESSON PLANS

Subject: Atomic Structure   (*5 periods*)

General Purpose: The set of lessons is designed to introduce the student to the basic structure of chemistry, its subparticles and arrangements.

Major Lesson Objectives: 1. Each student will be able to define an atom and to identify the parts of the atom.
2. Each student will be able to formulate electron shell configurations for a given atom.
3. Each student will be able to calculate the mass in grams of a given number of moles of any atom.

Sequence of Teacher Activities

Lesson 1 (*2 periods*)

Roll call, seating chart (*10 min.*)

1. a. Atom — ask class who can define, lead discussion   5 min.
   b. Particles of matter idea   5 min.

2. Atomic theory
   a. Dalton's
      1) law of definite composition
      2) way/proportions in which substances react with one another
   b. Today's
      1) structure and properties of atoms
      2) kinds of cpds. atoms form   10 min.
      3) properties of cpds. that atoms form
      4) mass, volume, and energy relationships of rxn between atoms
   c. Review lecture points   5 min.

3. a. Atom (definition) — is smallest unit of an element that can exist
                          either alone or in combination with other   5 min.
                          atoms like it or different from it
   b. Never directly observed — have you ever observed atom?;   10 min.
      use black box experiment

Roll call (*5 min.*)

   c. Review atom's definition   2 min.

4. Scientist's conclusions
   a. All matter is composed of very small particles called atoms   4 min.

b. Atoms same element *chemically* alike; atoms different elements chemically different

c. Atoms of an element have a def. avg. mass that is char. of the element

d. Atoms of diff. naturally occurring elements have diff. avg. masses

e. Atoms are not subdivided in *chemical* reactions (are in nuclear rxns — atomic bomb)

(avg. mass defined later)

5. Structure of atom

a. size — total = 1–5 Å (angstrom) diameter
$Å = 10^{-8}$ cm $\rightarrow 10^{-12}$ cm $= 10^{-4}$ Å (0.0001 diameter of the atom)

b. nucleus = positively charged central part of the atom; discovered by Rutherford who bombarded a thin sheet of gold with speed positively charged particles — many passed through which meant nucleus very small

15 min.

1) protons — positively charged particles in nucleus

2) neutrons — neutral particles found in the nucleus

c. mass of atom — most found in nucleus, but most of atom total space distribution (size) lies outside nucleus

masses:

proton 1.673×10^{-24} g
neutron 1.675×10^{-24} g
electron 9.110×10^{-28} g

1) electrons — negatively charged particles found outside the nucleus (all electrons are identical but nuclei differ with each element)

6. Illustration of atom (to be used with lecture notes)

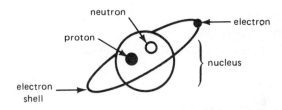

7. "A is for Atom" film

16 min.

8. Discuss film and review lesson

8 min.

Lesson 2 (*1 period*)

Roll call (*5 min.*)

1. Atomic # = # protons in nucleus of atom

2. Mass # = sum of protons/neutrons in nucleus

3. Isotopes = atoms of the same element (same atomic #) which have different masses (mass #)

Use drawings on board for sample

4. History of the concept of the atom — early Greeks, planetary model, etc.

5. The electrons are arranged in energy levels or shells around the atom:

1st energy level (K-shell) has 2 electrons

2nd energy level (L-shell) has 8 electrons
3rd energy level (M-shell) has 8 electrons   15 min.
Electrons fill shells in order unless in the excited state where have
enough energy to jump to an empty outer shell

6. Worksheet (individual) done in class,   20 min.
   with discussion of answers, upon completion   10 min.

Lesson 3 (*2 periods*)

Roll call (*5 min.*)

1. atomic mass = mass of an atom expressed relative to the
   "Carbon 12 = exactly 12" scale
   mass # is also whole # closest to the atomic mass

2. Avogadro number = # of atoms in the atomic mass
   = 6.022169×10^{23} 15 min.

3. mole = amt. of substance containing the Avogadro # of any
   kind of chemical unit
       12 g of carbon-12
       1.007825 of hydrogen-1
       12 eggs in a carton

4. gram-atom weight = mass in grams of one mole of naturally occurring atoms of an element
   atomic weight = numerical portion of gram-atomic weight

5. Sample problems employing concepts:
   What is mass in grams of 3.50 moles of copper atoms?
   a. find gram-atomic weight from back of book = 63.546 g   10 min.
   b. set up equation

   $$3.50 \text{ moles} \times \underbrace{\frac{63.546 \text{ g Cu}}{\text{mole}}}_{\substack{\text{def. of gram-} \\ \text{atomic weight}}} = 222 \text{ g Cu}$$

6. Troubleshoot student problems. Assign questions from end of
   chapter (2,4,5,9,11,12,14,16,20,21) to be worked on in class and
   finished at home   ~20 min.

Roll call (*5 min.*)

7. Take up assignment

8. Discuss questions & review for quiz tomorrow (use answer sheet &
   past notes)

9. Use black-box demonstration experiment (small object in closed
   box — ask students what's in it/how to find out); correlation to   1 period
   evolution of atomic theory where atom is too small to be seen

10. Give quiz next class period   20 min.

Sequence of Student Activities

1. Participate in review discussions
2. Watch film
3. Worksheet
4. Homework set
5. Quiz

Materials Needed

1. Text: *Modern Chemistry,* by Metcalfe, Williams & Castka
2. Film: "A is for Atom"
3. Black box and small objects

Evaluation Procedures

Daily: Discussions, worksheets, or homework (written assignments graded and discussed).

Final: On unit post-test, each student will be able to:

1. Label and define parts of the atom, giving sizes and total mass of the atom.

2. Formulate a shell configuration, given an atomic number.

3. Calculate the mass in grams of an atom, the number of moles, or the portion of Avogadro numbers present.

Let's Talk *Now that you have examined these several daily lesson plans, surely you can think of many ways that you would improve them. You might wish to add several classroom activities for the students and/or a good field trip. Or you may wish to add a few teacher demonstrations. You may even prefer to change the format of these plans. As the teacher, you have this prerogative. Your lesson plans are only good if they work for you.*

Since teachers are required to give tests and grades, the following tests are provided for these lessons. Examine the questions. Do they measure through the levels of the cognitive domain? Do they measure for achievement in the affective and psychomotor domains?

Chapter 1 Quiz

Atomic Structure

Objective 3

Correctly identify the parts of the atom, numbered on the diagram, and give a brief definition of each. (Credit for Objective 1 = 4 of 5 parts correctly labeled and defined.)

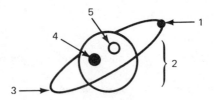

1. _____

2. _____

3. _____

4. _____

5. _____

Objective 8

Designate the electrons in energy level shells for each atom given. (Credit for Objective 8 = 4 of 5 problems correctly predicted.)

1. Chlorine (Cl), atomic number 17
2. Oxygen (O), atomic number 8
3. Magnesium (Mg), atomic number 12
4. Lithium (Li), atomic number 3
5. Boron (B), atomic number 5

Objective 13

Showing set-ups, complete following problems. (Credit for Objective 13 = 4 of 5 problems correct.)

1. What is the mass in grams of 4.0 moles of oxygen atoms?

2. How many moles are present in 6.3 g of hydrogen?

3. The mass of 6.23 moles of lead is _____.

4. How many moles of atoms are present in 0.333 g of aluminum?

5. The mass in grams of 9.09 moles of nitrogen is _____.

Let's Talk *The following lesson plans cover the second half of this unit — The Periodic Table. Compare them and their tests with the previous ones. Can you improve them?*

How do you feel about a lesson plan format which lists the time that will be spent on each activity? Some teachers find this necessary to help them pace the lesson so they don't run out of time or material. Other teachers are made uncomfortable by this since they feel it is too restricting. What is your preference?

Chapter 2:

Periodic Table (*6 periods*)

General Purpose:	This set of lessons is designed to help students understand the organization of the periodic table and the characteristics or particular groupings within the table.
Major Lesson Objectives:	1. Each student will be able to identify the common elements by symbols.
	2. Each student will be able to obtain information, such as mass #, atomic #, electron configuration, from the periodic table.
	3. Each student will be able to separate the elements by Groups and Periods and list the elements contained in and the characteristics of each division.

Sequence of Teacher Activities

Lesson 1 (*1 period*)

Roll call/return quizzes with discussion (*10 min.*)

    1. Introduction of the Periodic Table   20 min.
      a. explanation of terms

   b. 104 research paper/text: history of assembly
      1) *500 B.C.* Empedocles — 4 basic elements — earth, air, fire, water
      2) *Middle Age* Alchemists — combinations of 3 principles (elements) — sulfur (burning), salt (earthiness) mercury (perfect metalness)
      3) *1789* Lavoisier — 23 chemical elements (H,O,N,C,S,P, & 17 metals)
      4) *1869* Mendeleev — periodic chart with similar properties

2. Explanation of symbol "abbreviations"   10 min.
   a. Latin names for older elements: e.g., Au, Fe, Hg, Sn

antimony	(stibium)	Sb
copper	(cuprum)	Cu
gold	(aurum)	Au
iron	(ferrum)	Fe
lead	(plumbum)	Pb
mercury	(hydrargyrum)	Hg
potassium	(kalium)	K
silver	(argentum)	Ag
sodium	(natrium)	Na
tin	(stannum)	Sn

3. Learn symbols for common elements (*use samples*)   5 min.
   a. flashcard method
   b. list in front of text
(Give quizzes beginning class, while checking roll)

4. Assignment — memorize 1st column for tomorrow, 2nd column for the next day   5 min.

Lesson 2 (*1 period*)

4b. Play Tom Lehrer tape "The Elements" — tell students this is a quiz!   2-min. tape

4c. give real quiz   8-min. quiz

5. Explain the numbers contained in each box of the periodic table   15 min.
   a. atomic no.
   b. atomic mass
   c. electron config.
      1) octet = stable

[0.000]	∘
El	
0	∘ ∘

Use symbols for elements; should know-give element (symbol) for other half

6. Have the students complete worksheets dealing with locating elements on table and retrieving the asked for data from the table (in-class ind. assignment).   20 min.

7. Retrieve worksheets and discuss problems   5 min.

Lesson 3 (*4 periods*)

4d. Quiz 2 on symbols   8 min.

8. Define Periodic Law = The physical properties of elements is periodic fxn. of atomic #
   a. prop. elements → pattern of change
   b. elim. w/sim. prop. occur at certain intervals

*Use Halogen transparency — on screen as explained; use
Family overlay transparency*

9. Introduce Group/Period
   a. Group = vertical column ($\simeq$ Family)
   b. Period = horizontal row ($\simeq$ Series)   25 min.
   c. Series char. = increase atomic radium → ,
      reference to noble gas preceding for giving
      orbitals Li = (He) 2s↑
   d. Group char.
      1. reactivity
      2. outer shell arrangement
      3. metal, metalloid, ?
      4. atomic size
      5. ionization energy

10. Show movies on important Chemical Groups   15 min.

11. Explain rare earth and transition elements   5 min.

12. Data Retrieval Chart on Group char. — divide class
    groups 4–5, complete data chart, have debriefing and   20 min. in group
    tally session   10 min. in tally

D R Chart
Chemical Group Characteristics

Group	Family Name	Elements in Group	Char. (at least 3/group)
I			
.			
.			
.			
VIII	Noble Gases		

Roll call (*5 min.*)

13. Review lessons 1 & 2
    a. flash card game w/symbols   10 min.
    b. Use lg. periodic chart, ask students questions
       (objective 2)   5 min.

14. Give pop quiz over chapter   15 min.

15. Review unit questions for unit post-test   10 min.

Roll call/return quiz w/discussion (*10 min.*)

16. Give unit post-test   30 min.

17. Take up test/discuss questions   10 min.

Sequence of Student Activities

1. Overnight memorization of symbols assigned, using flashcard
   method.

2. In-class completion of worksheet.

3. In-class data retrieval of group characteristics.

Materials Needed

1. Text: *Modern Chemistry* by Metcalfe, Williams & Castka
2. 104 research paper on elements
3. Flashcards of symbols/elements
4. Tom Lehrer tape: "The Elements"
5. Worksheet on elements/Periodic Table
6. Data Retrieval Charts
7. Halogen family/family overlay transparencies

Evaluation Procedures

Daily: Quiz and/or worksheet graded and returned (70% →
credit) Discussion as needed or noted on plan.

Final: On unit post-test, each student will be able to:
1. give names/symbols of elements
2. define group/period
3. From Data Retrieval Chart, list the characteristics of a
given element

Chapter 2 Quiz

The Periodic Table

Objective 2

Place either the correct name or symbol to the left of each name or symbol given.
(Credit for $1/2$ of objective 2 = 15 of 18 correct.)

Quiz A	Quiz B
1. Au	1. Sn
2. Pb	2. O
3. Bi	3. Ag
4. As	4. Mg
5. Fe	5. Sr
6. Al	6. Ni
7. Ca	7. Si
8. Cr	8. Pt
9. H	9. Ti
10. iodine	10. zinc
11. barium	11. nitrogen
12. antimony	12. potassium
13. carbon	13. sulfur
14. cobalt	14. phosphorus
15. bromine	15. sodium
16. fluorine	16. mercury
17. chlorine	17. manganese
18. copper	18. tungsten

Chapter 3 Quiz

Periodic Law

Objectives 3–5

Write the correct answers in the spaces provided at the right.
(Credit for objectives = 8 of 10 questions correctly answered.)

1. The mass number for phosphorus is _____.	30.9738
2. The number of outer shell electrons in iodine is _____.	7
3. Zinc's atomic number is _____.	30
4. Tungsten has how many electrons?	74
5. Copper has a mass of _____.	63.546
6. In its M-shell, arsenic has _____ electron(s).	18
7. Antimony has _____ proton(s).	51
8. The name of the element having 17 electrons is _____.	chlorine
9. The atomic weight of manganese is _____.	54.9380
10. Sodium's L-shell contains _____ electron(s).	8

Objectives 9–10

Match the correct family with its characteristics or elements.
(Credit for objectives = 8 of 10 correctly matched.)

A. Sodium family
B. Calcium family
C. Nitrogen family
D. Oxygen family
E. Halogen family
F. Noble gas family

B	1. two electrons in outermost shell
F	2. outer shell octets
A	3. very active metallic elements
E	4. fluorine
C	5. some members exhibit both metallic and nonmetallic properties
A	6. one electron in outermost shell
D	7. sulfur
B	8. radium
F	9. neon
D	10. six electrons in outer shell

Discussion of Unit

This unit may seem lengthy, but most educators would agree that most of its parts are desirable and, in fact, essential. Does it need a philosophy? Some students and teachers may question the value of including a philosophy statement in each unit plan. Others feel that without it any unit is incomplete. (The author of this book would like to think of himself as fitting somewhere near the middle of these two extremes.) Surely many teachers never write out their philosophies; yet clearly many teachers could improve their teaching through sharpening their own understanding of the purpose of each unit and then teaching accordingly.

How about the statement of goals for this unit: Does it seem clear? Is it descriptive enough? Could you improve it? It is significantly weakened by focusing on content to the extent of ignoring skills and activities. It might be improved if it were altered to read: "The purpose of this unit is to enable students to grasp an understanding of some of the basic principles of the structure of atoms *and* to become skillful in using the periodic table to find atomic weights and molecular weights to determine atomic structures."

Very early in the unit is found a list of concepts and generalizations for the unit. These are the conceptual schemes and content generalizations that help show the interrelatedness of the various facts. Notice that these precede the unit objectives. Should they? In other words, should you say, "O.K., I know what I should cover in this class; now let me next decide the course objectives." Probably not. It seems more logical that you first ask yourself What are the basic purposes of schools? How should schools change students? Then examine the nature of this class to see which of these changes this class can promote. Finally, you must identify the content essential to the students' achievement of these objectives.

What did you think about the diagnostic instrument? Some units use diagnostic instruments to determine the placement level of each student in the class. Most teachers feel a need for this to get everyone started off at an even keel. What do you think?

How about the activities sections in this sample unit? More attention seems to be placed on teacher activities than on student activities. This is unfortunate, since lessons should always involve students as much as possible. Could you construct an instrument to evaluate this unit?

SUMMARY

As a teacher you will have a role in planning the overall curriculum for your students for the entire school year. Whether they will exit your course prepared to take on the challenges of the following course next year will depend heavily on your expertise in long-term planning. Most teachers feel obligated to "cover the material" that is generally covered in each particular course; some feel a commitment to take up topics that their students find the most interesting.

As a contemporary teacher, you realize that just covering the material is not enough. As you introduce your students to the most important principles and concepts in the course, you must include activities or tasks that require them to use these major content generalizations. You can identify necessary principles and concepts in state curriculum guides, local teaching units, and a combination of textbooks. Also consider the resources in the community; your own expertise; and the needs, aspirations, and abilities of your students.

Good long-term planning is always systematic. One of the most widely accepted systems for curriculum planning is Taba's Inverted Model, which begins in the classroom as the teacher develops a teaching/learning unit. Though you let students help select broad topics for the year, the ultimate planning responsibility is always yours. You must include some topics that the students feel are important, but you must also include other topics that you know through your own experience to be essential for the particular course. Finally, you must select goals and objectives and then lead students in the selection of activities for achieving them.

In reality no two teachers' learning units are the same, yet all good units have several common features. Most contemporary educators believe that a unit should begin either with a statement of your general philosophy or a statement of rationale that clarifies in your own mind the importance of this unit to the students. Both the general unit expectations (goals) and the daily expectations (objectives) must be stated in the unit. It should also specify the knowledge and skills to be attained and the activities of the teacher and students. Finally, the system used to evaluate student success must be included.

When a unit is completed, check each part to see if it is consistent with your statement of philosophy. The activities should indeed be those that enable students to attain the objectives. The evaluation should assess their attainment of the major concepts, principles, and skills as stated in the objectives.

EXPERIENCES

This chapter, which focused on the teacher's role in long-term planning, suggested general guidelines to help you as you begin planning learning units for periods that may range from a few days to a few weeks. But it has purposefully avoided blanket statements that dictate step-by-step planning. With these general guidelines and some experience, you will develop your own comfortable system, which will enable you to provide the type of learning experiences that your students need.

This is not to suggest that there will be no problems or struggles. The following experiences are provided to show some of the dilemmas that teachers encounter as they plan their teaching units.

Experience 1: Should Lesson Planning Be Sequential?

Bongo Nagatah was realizing his dream of attending an American University, where he would learn to become a master teacher; then he would return to his country for a lifetime of service. Throughout his program Bongo applied himself totally. He had indeed mastered his chosen teaching field, mathematics, which he enjoyed for its exactness and structure. He had done equally well in his professional education courses; but this is not to suggest that he had no problems. On the contrary, and though it may seem ironical, much of his frustration resulted from his love for structure.

When his methods course began developing learning units, Bongo began searching for guidelines or rules that would help him as he developed a required learning unit. He began by writing a brief philosophy statement for the unit, but then he was not sure what to do next. His professor had instructed him to follow by stating some general goals for the unit. Bongo felt as though he were leaving out some important content and that perhaps he should first make a content outline and then identify the goals. Later, when he began identifying content and activities, the same dilemma emerged. If he selected the activities first, how could he assure adequate coverage of content? On the other hand, if he selected the content first, how could he take advantage of several opportunities that he wanted to offer his students, such as field trips, speakers, and civic activities. For example, he especially wanted to encourage his students to enter projects in the regional science and mathematics fair.

► *Questions and Discussion*

1. *Is there a definite planning sequence that should be followed when you develop a unit?*

   In a general sense there is. Your philosophy statement should be written first. The goals should precede the behavioral objectives, and the behavioral objectives should precede the selection of content and activities. But while most teachers feel that this procedure is helpful, many feel that following it "to a tee" in all situations is restrictive and would, in fact, damage their units.

2. *How can you ensure complete content coverage and also take advantage of opportunities to involve students in valuable learning experiences?*

   As was previously stated, many teachers feel that a general sequence of design can be helpful but that an iron-clad sequence of procedures can be damaging to the unit. Therefore, you may prefer to follow the accepted development sequence until you see a specific need for jumping from one step to another. Oscillating from one step to another seems to help many teachers.

Experience 2: A Principal Requires Six Months' Advance Planning

Upon moving from rural school teaching to my first urban school, I learned the true meaning of planning. In the smaller rural school I had never heard lesson planning mentioned; yet during my first faculty meeting at the urban school each teacher was handed a 300-page spiral book and instructed to enter in this book his lesson plans for the following six months. Since I had never planned for more than a week or two in advance, I was overwhelmed by this order. I looked around at my new fellow faculty members to see if there were any reactions. There were none: the principal's demands were accepted.

Following the meeting I asked if the principal actually checked the plans to see if they were filled out so far in advance. I was told that a surprise check would probably occur once or twice during the year. In addition I was assured that should I be absent and require a substitute teacher, I would be asked to leave my lesson plan book in the office where it would be examined by one of the administrators.

The other teachers assured me that there was no required length to each lesson and suggested that I list only the nature or title of each lesson without attempting to describe it. Since even this would consume several hours and it appeared to me to be a waste of time, I decided to take a chance and enter only a couple of weeks of advanced planning. I followed this procedure throughout the year. My hunch was correct. The record book was never checked; fortunately I did not have to be absent during the year. The following year no mention was made of the six-month policy.

► *Questions and Discussion*

1. *How far in advance should a teacher plan?*

   The teacher should plan far enough in advance so that when emergencies arise he can meet them without their disrupting the continuity of his classes. This will help prevent him and others from having to face the dreadful experience of meeting his classes poorly prepared. By planning a few weeks in advance, the teacher can arrange logical continuity in class experiences.

2. *List some reasons why a teacher should not be required to plan for months in advance.*

   If the teacher is forced to plan for months in advance, he is encouraged to plan for the purpose of satisfying his administrators. This can result in plans that look impressive on paper but are not at all helpful in the classroom.

   Moreover, because each class is unique and because student interests change from time to time, the director of the class should be flexible enough to challenge the new interests of the students as they emerge. A set of lesson plans extending throughout the year probably would not provide such flexibility. Can you think of other disadvantages of requiring teachers to plan their lessons months in advance?

3. *Why did my principal "misuse" lesson plans?*

   I believe the answer is that he saw lesson planning from an administrator's point of view rather than from a learner's. He saw the lesson plan as an instrument to force the teacher to upgrade his teaching. Some administrators tend to view everything in terms of ease of provision, expense, and other administrative terms. It is the teacher's responsibility to see everything in terms of the effect that it has on students. He should try to find a way to satisfy the administrator and the needs of the students.

4. *Was my decision to disregard the rules justifiable?*
Probably not. Although I was determined to refrain from doing what I thought would be detrimental to my teaching, I should have found a way to do this and, at the same time, satisfy the demands of my administrator. How would you respond to such a requirement?

ACTIVITIES

At the beginning of this chapter, the Objectives promised you that you would learn how to develop a complete learning unit. If you are ready for this challenge, select a topic in one of your teaching fields and apply your skills.

1. First, write a brief statement of your philosophy of education. Include your beliefs about the general purposes of secondary schools, the nature of adolescence, and the nature of learning.
2. Write at least three or four broad goals for a unit of three–six weeks.
3. For each goal write a few behavioral objectives.
4. Outline the major content generalizations for the unit.
5. Select some teacher activities and student activities to facilitate the attainment of these objectives.
6. Design a grading system and a system for evaluating the effectiveness of this unit.

SUGGESTED READINGS

BEAUCHAMP, GEORGE A. *Curriculum Theory,* 3d ed. Wilmette, Ill.: The Kagg Press, 1975.

CASCIANO-SAVIGNANO, C. JENNIE. *Systems Approach to Curriculum and Instructional Improvement.* Columbus, Ohio: Charles E. Merrill, 1978.

CURTIS, THOMAS E., and BIDWELL, WILMA W. *Curriculum and Instruction for Emerging Adolescents.* Reading, Mass.: Addison-Wesley, 1977.

DOLL, RONALD C. *Curriculum Improvement: Decision Making and Process,* 4th ed. Boston: Allyn and Bacon, 1978.

FIRTH, GERALD R., and KIMPSTON, RICHARD D. *The Curriculum Continuum in Perspective.* Itasca, Ill.: F. E. Peacock, 1973.

HASS, GLEN. *Curriculum Planning: A New Approach,* 2d ed. Boston: Allyn and Bacon, 1977.

OLLIVER, ALBERT I. *Curriculum Improvement: A Guide to Problems, Principles and Procedures.* New York: Dodd, Mead, 1974.

ORLICH, DONALD C., et al. *Teaching Strategies: A Guide to Better Instruction.* Lexington, Mass.: D. C. Heath and Company, 1980.

ORLOSKY, DONALD E., and SMITH, B. OTHANEL. *Curriculum Development: Issues and Insights.* Chicago: Rand McNally College Publishing, 1978.

RUBIN, LOUIS. *Curriculum Handbook.* Boston: Allyn and Bacon, 1977.

STEEVES, FRANK L., and ENGLISH, FENWICK W. *Secondary Curriculum for a Changing World.* Columbus, Ohio: Charles E. Merrill, 1978.

TABA, HILDA. *Curriculum Development: Theory and Practice.* New York: Harcourt Brace Jovanovich, 1962.

TRUMP, J. LLOYD, and MILLER, DELMAS F. *Secondary School Curriculum Improvement: Meeting Challenges of the Times,* 3d ed. Boston: Allyn and Bacon, 1979.

ZAIS, ROBERT S. *Curriculum: Principles and Foundations.* New York: Thomas Y. Crowell, 1976.

Teaching Strategies

OBJECTIVES

Upon completion of this chapter you should be able to:
1. Differentiate between the terms *questioning* and *Socratic method*.
2. List three unique strengths "potentials" of simulation gaming.
3. Describe a group of students for which the lecture is an appropriate teaching strategy.
4. List two teaching strategies that are good motivators.
5. Name the one most common mistake that teachers make with simulation games.
6. List two guidelines to direct teachers in using questions in classroom instruction.
7. Give three suggestions to help teachers improve their lectures.
8. Define inquiry learning.
9. Name one major advantage and one major limitation of inquiry learning.
10. List three advantages of the lecture.

Only a few years ago teachers in American schools could be described according to their particular teaching styles. Prospective teachers spent many hours wondering what their own teaching styles would be. Would they use mainly expository teaching, something like the many lectures they had listened to in college? Or would they use an entirely different approach that would lead the students themselves to discover the important truths of a subject field.

Today's education majors ask different questions, for they recognize that there are many teaching/learning styles, such as expository, inquiry, questioning, discovery, and simulation gaming. The old question, "Which style should I use?" has given way to a new one, "Which *styles* should I use? And for what purposes?" Today's education students, exposed to a number of teaching/learning styles, are aware that certain ones work best with certain objectives.

This chapter will examine several teaching/learning styles to help you, the prospective teacher, select and use a style to achieve *particular* goals. "Particular" is emphasized because if the stated goals are too broad, then there is no advantage in choosing any one particular style. For example, suppose your goal is to select and use the style that will produce maximum learning or understanding: "Of eighty-eight comparisons between traditional lecture and traditional discussion methods, as reported in thirty-six experimental studies, 51 percent favored the lecture method and 49 percent favored the discussion method."[1] In other words, 51 percent of the studies reviewed found the lecture method superior to the discussion method for effective learner attainment; 49 percent found the discussion method superior to the lecture. This does not imply that there is no difference between these two teaching methods. Nor do these studies conclude that there is no difference in the outcomes produced by various teaching/learning styles. For, on the contrary, hundreds of studies show that, when correctly used, each style is superior in the ability to produce certain, specific results. As you study each style, keep certain questions in mind: What are the unique potentials of this style? How can this style best be implemented? If I decide to experiment using this style, what precautions should I take? Finally, can I learn to implement this style effectively along with other approaches to develop an overall strategy that will lead to the achievement of my course objectives?

EXPOSITORY TEACHING

Throughout the years the lecture has been the teaching/learning style used most frequently in American classrooms and in most other countries. Though much criticized by current educators, its ability to survive through the years is evidence that the lecture possesses some unique strengths.

When Should the Lecture Be Used?

In your decision whether or not to use the lecture, keep in mind the type of students that you are teaching. Are your classes college preparatory, elective, or remedial? If they are composed of students whose potential is limited, the lecture would be a poor choice, for use of the lecture requires students to take notes, and most students are not good note takers. In fact, even college students at all levels are not able to capture most of the important ideas heard in a lecture. Even under the best conditions only 52 percent of the important ideas in a lecture get into student notes (Maddox, 1975).

A second requirement that the lecture makes of students is that they be somewhat self-motivated, for the lecture itself is a poor motivator. So, before you decide *for* or *against* using the lecture, you should consider the interest level of the particular group of students. The research suggests that the main reason for students preferring the lecture is that it demands little direct participation and involvement. Less capable students tend to favor the lecture

---

[1] David C. Berliner and N. L. Gage, "The Psychology of Teaching Methods," in *The Psychology of Teaching Methods* (Chicago: National Society for the Study of Education, 1975), Chapter 1.

over other modes of instruction that place more responsibility on them (Couch, 1973). To be sure, this would be a poor reason to use lectures with a group of low performers.

Weaknesses of the Lecture

Only well-planned and well-executed lectures are either very successful or well liked by the students. Students often offer the following criticism of lectures: They are boring, do not involve the learner, are poorly organized, focus on the lowest level of cognition, and do not recognize individual differences. Lectures also produce excessive anxiety among students, more than is produced by other modes of teaching (Ellis, 1974). Many teachers choose lecturing as an opportunity to show off their knowledge. Feeding their egos, these teachers tend to be overly formal, overly authoritative, and overly structured. They often stress technical points instead of interpreting or relating information, and they may not be receptive to student comments that question their knowledge. Such domination of students is an example of gross misuse of the lecture.

It has already been suggested that, when properly planned and executed, the lecture works best for those students who are capable and motivated. But best for teaching what? Any subjects? Best for communicating in general? No. In fact, a review of ninety-one surveys covering four decades of research on comparative teaching methods found no difference in the effectiveness of lecture and other methods of teaching (Voth, 1975). The lecture is superior only for some particular objectives, and it is inferior for others. For example, the lecture is generally *not* an effective method for stimulating interest, for promoting creativity, or for helping students develop responsibility or imagination. It has other weaknesses. The lecture is not a good approach for helping students develop skills in synthesizing, internalizing, or expressing themselves. Compared to educational games, the lecture is only equally as effective for immediate cognitive gain and is significantly less effective for retention over a period of three weeks or longer (Lucas, 1975).

Strengths of the Lecture

On the other hand, the lecture has several unique potentials. It is an extremely effective way to introduce a unit or to build a frame of reference (Kyle, 1972). The lecture is also a superior technique for demonstrating models and clarifying matters confusing to students (Thompson, 1974). It is significantly superior in its ability to set the atmosphere or focus for student activities (Haley, 1972). A short lecture can effectively introduce and summarize the major concepts presented in a lesson. It affords the teacher an opportunity to collect related information and to assemble it into a meaningful and intellectually manageable framework.

How Should the Lecture Be Implemented?

Why are some lectures good, some bad? Why are some teachers stimulating when they are dispensing information while others are so boring? If not all lectures are the same, exactly how do they differ and how can the teacher make them both interesting and informative?

Most successful lectures are relatively short. Only a few individuals have the ability to concentrate for extended periods of time. Therefore, even the best lecturers should limit their lectures to short time periods, occasionally changing to other activities (preferably to those that actively involve students). The research efforts mentioned in the next section suggest effective ways for improving the lecture through correct planning and delivery and by mixing the lecture with other instructional approaches.

Improving the Lecture

OBJECTIVES. Much attention has been given recently to instructional objectives, but does their presentation really affect learning, and, if so, how? Should they be introduced before or after the lesson?

Actually, when used either before or following a lecture, instructional objectives do affect the students' reactions to the lecture. When introduced at the beginning of the lecture, instructional objectives tend to increase intentional learning (that is, learning that the teacher seeks to stimulate); used after the lesson, instructional objectives affect the incidental learning by those students. To ensure that students will learn the most important concepts in a lesson, the teacher should always introduce the objectives prior to the beginning of a lecture. Thus they become advance organizers giving learners a basis to which they can relate the new concepts.

TEMPO. One of the most important variables in any lecture is its tempo or pace. When the pace of a lecture is too slow, students become bored; when it is too fast, they become discouraged with their inability to keep up and understand the lesson. The Pall Level — a state of physical, program-related fatigue — is reached when students lose interest because the concept is too simple or too difficult, or when the steps in its presentation are too short or too long. In both cases students tend to respond by generating their own discussions. Lectures that move at a moderate pace produce less noise than those that move at a slow or fast pace (Grobe, 1973). Research studies have found that most studio-recorded presentations are too slow. They will produce more learning if the lecturer increases the speed up to three times the normal speed. However, if the speed is too great, the students will feel rushed and begin to reject the speech compressor (Rippey, 1975).

STIMULUS VARIATION. Certain actions during a lecture help to prevent student boredom, especially among secondary students. Stimulus variation, such as teacher movement through the class, gesturing, and pausing, has a positive correlation with student recall of lectures (Wyckoff, 1973). Interestingly enough, at the elementary level such stimulus variation actually lowers student performance on lecture tests. Excessive teacher movement distracts them from lecture content.

STRUCTURE. Most lectures can be vastly improved and simplified by (1) organizing the content into only a few major concepts (three to five), (2) ordering the concepts in a logical or natural sequence, (3) limiting the lecture to ten–fifteen minutes, (4) providing tasks that require all students to use the concepts, and (5) summarizing the major concepts. English teachers often outline the major concepts in a story and order them into a definite sequence, whereas history teachers may use events and dates. Such identification and ordering of concepts is equally important in math, science, social studies, and other classes. Titus (1974) presents the following list of steps for preparing a good lecture:

1. Organization is vital
2. Stick to a limited number of concepts
3. Limit time
4. Use humor
5. Avoid tangents
6. Watch your language
7. Listen to yourself

VOCABULARY. Two comments should be made regarding the Titus list. His concern for language is especially warranted. Too many lectures are loaded with jargon, technical vocabulary, or other unfamiliar language that confuses learners. Titus's concern for self-evaluation by lecturers is reflected by many other educators, such as Whooley (1974) and Frazier (1972). Frazier suggests that video-tape recording should be used for this purpose.

AUDIO-VISUAL AIDS.   Commonwealth (1974) expresses the attitude of many educators that visual aids should accompany all lectures. The overhead projector seems to have replaced the chalkboard as the most popular visual aid in today's classroom. The most effective use of either is when the lesson is not predeveloped but is built up in front of the students. They assist in the development of the concepts either by working problems or by responding to the teacher's questions as the lesson develops. In other words, the most effective delivery depends upon student participation in developing the ideas set out by the lesson plan.

HISTRIONICS.   The common high-anxiety level during lectures can be reduced if the teacher tells jokes (Ellis, 1974). Interestingly enough, those students for whom the use of a lecture is appropriate (the high-ability, low-anxiety students) also benefit most from humor; whereas their counterparts, the slow, anxious students, retain less from humorous lectures (Weinberg, 1975). In some instances humor does not affect the immediate cognitive gains, but several weeks later students retain significantly more concepts from lectures containing humor (Kaplan, 1977).

ALTERING THE LECTURE.   Research shows that lectures are vastly improved when they are mixed with tutorials and student discussions. For example, a ten-minute lecture could be followed by a twenty-minute discussion, which could be followed by a ten-minute work period with tutorial help given. When tutorials were added to lectures in an eleventh-grade class, the combination increased immediate cognitive gains and retention measured over an eleven-week interval (Rowsey, 1975). The lower-ability and lower-achieving students especially benefited from the individual attention. The higher-ability and higher-achieving students, though, benefited most from recitation and problem solving (Ott, 1975). Adding modeling demonstrations to the lecture also tends to increase both immediate and long-term learning and improves student attitude toward the lesson. These studies suggest, then, that the pure lecture method can be improved by adding either tutorials or modeling.

But for lecture blending to be effective, students must be exposed to non-lecture teaching styles at early ages. By seventh grade many students are already conditioned to the lecture method, and alternatives should be used earlier (Starr, 1974). For those students who are accustomed to the straight lecture, the combining of lectures with student discussion produces little difference in cognitive gain among seventh graders, and may actually damage their attitude toward the lesson. To prevent students from depending too much on lectures, all teachers should balance their selection of learning methods to improve achievement and attitude.

While didactic teaching styles are severely criticized in the literature and in the educational realm, the lecture is still, after centuries, the most extensively used teaching style. The lecture has possibly also done more damage than any other teaching style; yet, when properly planned and executed, it is the most effective method for achieving some instructional objectives for some students. A poorly planned and/or executed lecture is probably the most confusing and most boring of all teaching approaches. Because the lecture has important potential, all teachers should be able to plan and deliver lectures and to select lectures for their best-suited objectives. Perhaps most important of all, teachers should use self-discipline, resisting the temptation to overuse or misuse the lecture. As new techniques of instruction continuously emerge, we need further discoveries of ways to mix the lecture with these other delivery systems for still more effective learning in the classroom.

INQUIRY LEARNING

Inquiry learning is a familiar and popular concept at all levels and in all subjects today. Yet, with all the popularity and prestige of inquiry learning, much confusion exists over what it actually is. This is not surprising, since inquiry is itself a most complicated style of learning. Furthermore, inquiry is closely related to other similar learning approaches that are often confused with inquiry.

Basic to the complexity of inquiry learning is its dichotomous nature. Although inquiry learning is concerned with solving problems, it does not require solutions to these problems. Its approach toward solutions is flexible yet systematic: systematic in that a set of activities is used, yet highly flexible in that the sequence of the activities can be changed and other activities can be substituted at any time. The success of inquiry learning is not necessarily de-

pendent on solving the problems at hand. A further dichotomy adds to its complexity: even when inquiry is approached by a group, it continues to be a highly personal experience for each individual involved.

Inquiry learning is a dual learning process. The pursuer learning about the topic being investigated is simultaneously learning about the process of inquiry. Students of inquiry learning must apply themselves totally, using their talents, ideas, and judgments to solve a problem. Even *attitude* is of utmost importance, for the investigator must be self-motivated enough to continue searching for numerous solutions without the comfort and assurance that accompany "correct" answers found in more traditional learning settings.

Advantages

A very obvious advantage of inquiry learning is the high degree of *involvement* of all who participate in the process. This is, of course, not unique to inquiry learning; many other teaching/learning styles, such as simulation gaming, individualized instruction, discovery learning, and problem solving, offer the participant a fair amount of involvement. But inquiry offers even more involvement and is thus even more meaningful. Inquiry learning is characterized by early and continuous involvement. In true inquiry learning the student must be involved from the very beginning, even in setting up the problems (Tathart, 1973).

Another major advantage of inquiry learning is its *flexibility*. In their attempt to understand their environment, human beings have fallen into a trap of trying to systematize everything within their awareness. For years our schools required students to learn a rigid set of behaviors as the "method" used by scientists to discover, to invent, and to find solutions to all problems. Yet studies have failed to show any specific pattern of thought in problem solving. Inquiry is somewhat systematic without being as rigid as the "scientific method." Instead of just answering questions, students also *ask* questions. Instead of just verifying the truth, students are actually seeking the truth.

The absence of a single, predetermined correct answer in inquiry learning is another advantage, since it frees the investigator to explore diverse, multiple possibilities and frees the psyche from fear of failing to meet another's expectations. The inquiry learner has the strongest type of motivation — internal — and is learning to work for the joy of learning. Inquiry learning improves students' attitudes toward the subject and, more important, toward school in general (Jaus, 1977). Often students in inquiry learning become so aroused that they return to class on other days eager to continue pursuing the concepts (Bills, 1971).

The nature of inquiry enhances the development of creative potentials. True inquiry learning encourages the free use of the imagination, and the learner is responsible for determining what information to gather, then for determining its importance. These are essential conditions for creative thinking.

The teacher-student relationship in inquiry classes must remain positive. Teachers must provide the students freedom to develop their hypotheses or hunches, but the teacher's role is nevertheless very important. Previous research has concluded that learners are not capable of developing critical thoughts by themselves (Brown, 1971), but they can be taught in a manner that develops critical and inquiry-oriented thinking. Something interesting happens to the whole perspective and behavior pattern of teachers who use the inquiry approach in their classes: they become student-oriented rather than subject-oriented (Lazarowitz, 1976). Students also become more cooperative, whereas students in textbook-oriented classes tend to be more competitive (Johnson, 1976).

Most important to those who are primarily concerned with cognitive gains is that the relative retention rate of inquiry learning (as opposed to lecture, for example) is extremely high. The highly personal experience involved in inquiry adds meaning to the learning. As Abraham Maslow explains, true learning is very personal; the most valuable learnings always involves our emotions.[2]

Disadvantages

Like all other teaching/learning styles, though, inquiry has its share of disadvantages. It is a slow process for exposing students to material. Teachers who feel obligated to cover certain amounts of content (for example, to complete a textbook) may find the process very inefficient for their goal. A more critical disadvantage of inquiry learning is that it requires a unique type of expertise that most teachers do not have. Today's teachers need more training in inquiry activity.

The Teacher's Role

Since inquiry learning is by nature a flexible process, the teacher may wish to set the stage in different ways. Taxey (1975) suggests that heterogeneous subgroups within a classroom be used to capitalize on the unique personalities, interests, and skills so as to use each individual's potential in contributing to the task at hand. In inquiry learning lessons, the major role of the teacher is that of a catalyst. Teachers must give students the freedom to investigate in their own ways. Students must be allowed to develop their own, individual ideas and to discover ways of explaining what they observe. Even the questions and problems that are formed are those of the students, not of the teacher. The teacher passively provides direction through helping students as they begin their selection of objects, activities, events, problems, or questions. The teacher can provide closer direction, if approached, by giving cues and supportive feedback (Wendel, 1973). Nevertheless, it should be remembered that teachers are often tempted to give information before it is necessary. They must resist this temptation and avoid making nonverbal communications such as grimacing (Balzer, 1970). Students of inquiry should not have to worry about pleasing the teachers; in fact, they must not be dominated by others.

---

[2] Abraham Maslow, "What Is a Taoistic Teacher," in *Facts and Feelings in the Classroom,* ed. Louis Rubin (New York: Viking Press, 1973).

Undoubtedly the most impressive precondition for inquiry is the autonomy of the learner. It is important that students be encouraged to form hypotheses and test them on their own initiative (Traugh, 1974). The teacher should encourage students to move toward the recognition of the variety of aspects and solutions that a problem can have (Tjosvold, 1977). Students who participate in inquiry must not be afraid to make mistakes. The teacher must encourage each student to make bold conjectures and then test them. Any hypotheses that seem at all probable to the student should be pursued.

Inquiry learning is the following of a set of activities in a purposeful pursuit toward the solving of a number of problems. It requires no solution to the problems, and its approach is student-oriented and highly flexible.

Participants in inquiry learning are self-motivated. They must learn to work for the joy of learning, even in the absence of feedback, which students in traditional classes get from test scores and grades. Inquiry is a cooperative process, not a competitive one. Even the teacher who becomes involved with inquiry soon becomes student-oriented rather than subject-oriented. The independence and separate responsibility of the student, coupled with the opportunity to pursue learning for the joy of it, produce a high level of motivation. The retention rate of inquiry learning is thus superior to most other teaching-learning styles, offsetting the disadvantages of being slow in content coverage. Effective inquiry learning does, though, require certain special skills that some teachers simply do not have. Teachers need to learn to match personalities, interest, and skills in order to get the most out of each student. Perhaps most of all, teachers need to learn to give students enough freedom to investigate in their own ways. Teachers must learn to act as a catalyst and to provide direction in a passive manner. Above all, they must learn to resist the temptation to give information before it is necessary. Diversity must be treasured by the student of inquiry, and the teacher must learn to encourage and reinforce students who take risks necessary to make bold conjectures and then explore a variety of aspects and solutions.

QUESTIONING

In Chapter 6 we examined the role that questioning plays in motivation. Now let's examine questioning in a much broader context, that is, in the many ways that teachers can use questions in various phases of their teaching methods.

When we think of using questions to teach, Socrates usually comes to mind. One of the greatest teachers of all times, Socrates used a variety of instructional techniques. He was indeed a master of the art of questioning, using them to lead his students down a treacherous path of contradiction. Tricky? Of course, but his students respected and admired him. Socrates knew the importance of self-analysis and of discovering one's own errors.

The Socratic method, that is, teaching by asking questions and thus leading the audience into a logical contradiction, is but one style of questioning. There are any number of alterations of questioning strategy in use today. While, as a teaching style, questioning is second in popularity and in common use only to lecturing, the art of questioning is grossly misused. It would seem helpful to identify several purposes for which questioning is most valid and to pursue several avenues that teachers can use to improve questioning skills.

How Should Teachers Use Questions?

In 1959–61, the Wisconsin School Improvement Program found that 90 percent of all textbooks are written at the knowledge (recall and memory) level. Therefore, if student thinking is to climb to higher cognitive levels, the teacher must find other means of stimulating it. Studies using interaction analysis have repeatedly shown that most teachers never achieve this goal; that is, most thinking in the classroom remains at the recall level (Chaudhari, 1975). Of course, some knowledge-level questions can be desirable so long as they are complemented with higher-level questions. Chaudhari suggests to teachers the following three-step model:

Phase 1: Encourage students to ask questions.

Phase 2: Emphasize questions requiring convergent thinking (application and analysis).

Phase 3: Emphasize questions requiring divergent thinking (synthesis and evaluation).

Miller (1973) provides the teacher with the following suggestions for moving up the taxonomy to higher levels of thinking. Miller suggests that the teacher move from such recall-level words as *state, name, identify, list, describe, relate, tell, call, give,* and *locate* to include evaluation-producing words such as *judge, compare, analyze, contrast, measure, appraise, estimate,* and *differentiate;* and then move on to creative, stimulating words such as *make, design, create, construct, speculate, invent, devise, predict,* and *hypothesize.*

Henson, in 1974, discusses the use of questioning based on earlier work by Dwight Allen et al. at the University of Massachusetts, suggesting that the teacher use student names to increase student response, and pause following each question, giving time for students to think about the question. Subsequent studies — Sabol (1975), Rothkopf (1974), Sund (1974), and Santieslebau (1975) — and a study conducted by Mary Budd Rowe (1974), reinforced the need for these practices. These studies show that, by waiting at least three seconds after each question is asked, several advantages are realized. Sund (1974) lists twelve of these:

1. The length of children's response increases.
2. The number of unsolicited but appropriate responses increases.
3. Failure to respond decreases.
4. Confidence of children increases.
5. The incidence of speculative creative thinking increases.
6. Teacher-centered teaching decreases.
7. Pupils give more evidence before and after inference statements.
8. The number of questions asked by pupils increases.
9. Number of activities proposed by the children increases.

10. Slow pupils contribute more.
11. The variety of types of responses increases.
12. There is more reacting to each other.

Santieslebau (1976) found that, as wait time increased to at least three seconds, the confidence of the slow students increased; speculative thinking increased; the number of experiments by the students increased; and observation and classification skills improved. It seems that the price for these advantages is cheap; just by pausing and doing nothing, the teacher can stimulate these results. A recent study, however (Rowe, 1974), found that the average wait time in the public school classroom is only one second.

Another common mistake that teachers make is the overuse of questions. Many lessons begin with a series of cognitive questions, but, as research shows, it is much more effective to wait until a knowledge base has been established and then to initiate the questioning. A short lecture, for example, is far more efficient for building this necessary framework. Furthermore, when too many questions are asked, the students' attitudes are damaged as their attention turns from the subject to other areas (Santieslebau, 1976).

Classroom questions that seek cognitive feedback often lack specificity. For example, the question "What was the cause of the Civil War?" is impossible. Often posing such questions just to create an entry into the lesson, the teacher rejects some correct responses (and there are many for this question) in hopes that a student will finally guess the particular desired response. The session proceeds as follows:

Q. What was the cause of the Civil War?
A. Slavery.
Q. O.K., but that's not what I'm looking for.
A. Economics? (*This time the student is less certain.*)
Q. What about economics? (*Another broad question.*)
A. The North's economics.
Q. What about it?
A. It was different from the South's.
Q. But what about the North's economy? etc., etc.

Besides increasing the efficiency of the lesson and preventing embarrassment, the teacher's specificity will enhance the recall of other material related to the topic (Rothkopf, 1974). Shiman (1974) suggests that, rather than limiting the questions to a series of fact-seeking questions, the teacher should move back and forth among the factual, conceptual, and contextual modes. Factual questions only elicit knowledgeable information; conceptual questions probe, analyze, compare, and generalize; and contextual questions promote judgment. To help increase the number and quality of responses to each question in these categories, teachers should first tape or write their questions, testing themselves for the answers. Such practice will result in questions that are more precise and specific.

Some experts believe that students are becoming less curious and inquisitive, less eager to ask questions. Sutton (1977), describing this as a decay of students' minds, suggests that teachers work together to produce a reversal in this trend. Far too often a student attempts to answer a question only to hear the response "Yes, but" or a murmured "uh huh" as the teacher looks quickly to another student for the "correct" answer. To improve student attitude toward answering questions, the teacher should help the faltering student with an "Oh, that's interesting. I hadn't thought of it that way," or "Oh yes, I see what you mean," or "Are you saying . . . ?" Further reinforcement can be provided by returning later to quote the student. For example, "John, what you're saying now seems to agree (or disagree) with Debbie's earlier comment that. . . ." This tells John, Debbie, and everyone else in the class that you do listen to other people's comments.

This does not suggest that all teacher questions should seek to provoke student responses. Rhetorical questions increase motivation and enhance the learning and recall of factual material among low-motivated audiences. Yet teachers must resist the temptation of answering all their questions and should let students know, by calling on an individual by name, when they expect an answer.

Questions can also be used effectively before and after a lesson. Bull (1973) found that the arousal of *incompatible* questions prior to a reading assignment was an important factor in the retention of relevant information. In a similar study Sanders (1973) found that questions given following the reading of the paragraph resulted in increased retention of both relevant and irrelevant material, while questions raised before the reading increased retention of only the relevant material. Teachers can apply this knowledge about questioning to reading assignments, field trips, laboratory exercises, and audio-visual materials such as the tape recorder, filmstrips, and films.

The previous discussion, dwelling on the teacher's use of questions, does not preclude the student's right to question. Students, too, need to learn to ask productive questions; as Alfke (1974) explains, such questions develop skills in learning how to learn, to inquire, and to conceptualize. Teachers can achieve this by providing fewer but better questions of their own and by requiring students to pose more productive questions.

The research studies suggest that all teachers should:

1. Avoid using questions to introduce lessons.
2. Delay questions about content until a knowledge base has been established.
3. Use a combination of levels of questions, extending from recall to evaluation.
4. Pause for at least three seconds following each question.
5. Not expect students to be able to guess the teacher's meaning.
6. Address questions to individual students, using students' names.
7. Keep content-oriented questions specific.
8. Help students by modifying their inaccurate answers until they become acceptable.
9. Encourage students to ask questions.
10. Help students develop skills in asking questions.
11. Listen carefully to student questions and respond, using their content.

12. Prior to making a reading assignment, showing a film, or taking a field trip, pose questions relative to the major concepts or objectives of that experience.

DISCOVERY LEARNING

Perhaps as you read the heading, your initial thought was — exactly what is discovery learning? And maybe this discussion will be somewhat different from most and will clarify what is meant by discovery learning. Or your initial thought might have been — oh no, not another writing on discovery learning. But, even so, chances are that you have some understanding of, and faith in, the discovery process; most contemporary students have experienced this approach. The following paragraphs will define discovery learning and, by summarizing numerous studies, will list its advantages and disadvantages. There are also suggestions for teachers who wish to try discovery learning for the first time or to improve their skills with planning and implementing discovery learning.

Definition

Most of the literature on discovery learning does not define it at all, leaving the reader feeling somewhat embarrassed for not knowing exactly what it is and probably ashamed to ask anyone else. But the authors probably avoid definitions because discovery learning is not at all easy to define. There is no single clear-cut definition just as there is no single process of discovery learning; in fact, there are many. Each is unique, ranging from guided discovery to open discovery. Furthermore, each type of discovery has its own advantages, and the management of each is unique. Weimer (1975) lists the following six types of discovery learning: (1) discovery, (2) discovery teaching, (3) inductive discovery, (4) semi-inductive discovery, (5) unguided or pure discovery, and (6) guided discovery. Notice that these six types are actually degrees in which discovery is controlled.

The term *discovery learning* is frequently but erroneously used simultaneously with two other terms: inquiry and problem solving. Actually, each is or can be a specific type of discovery learning. The educational process called inquiry is more accurately defined as guided discovery; that is, during an inquiry lesson the teacher is carefully guiding the student(s) toward a specific discovery or generalization. Discovery learning and problem solving are synonymous when a solution to the problem is discovered. In other words, by definition, discovery learning must involve the solving of problems. A good working definition of discovery learning is intentional learning through problem solving and under teacher supervision. In other words, individuals can sometimes solve problems without any leadership, guidance, or supervision; they can also make discoveries quite accidentally. Neither of these activities is discovery learning, for it must be intentional and supervised. At one extreme, it may be carefully guided (inquiry learning); at the other, it is very casually

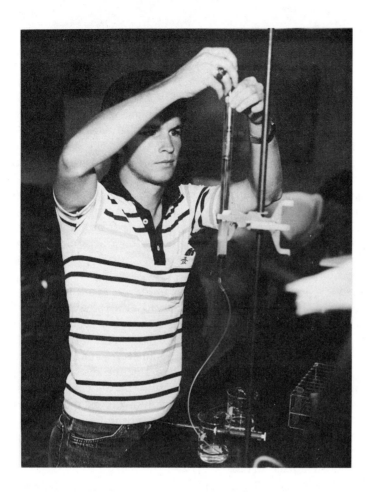

supervised (free discovery). In fact, as Jones (1970) explains, the teacher's main function may be that of supplying a stimulus. Or the teacher's job may be to organize or arrange tasks (or problems) to make the result obvious (Sickling, 1975). In inquiry learning the students themselves are involved in setting up the problem as well as in seeking its solution (Baikov, 1976).

Advantages

The advantages of discovery learning are numerous. Many of its advantages are not unique to discovery learning but are shared by other instructional approaches; for example, the high degree of student involvement is a strong motivator for most students, especially those who find it difficult to remain quiet and passive. There is little evidence to refute the assumption that discovery learning is appropriate for almost all students. Only about one-third of today's college students are able to reason in an abstract, logical way (Mitzman, 1978). An even smaller percentage of high school students is able to profit from abstractions. Do most students, then, have the ability needed to benefit from discovery learning? Yes. The Contemporary Cambridge Conference states that anyone can do and create experiences in generalizing, testing conjectures, discarding or modifying false hypotheses, and forming rules or theorems (Jones, 1970). A study involving junior high math students (Vance, 1974) found the discovery approach a superior motivator to the traditional math classes and inferior only to an experimental laboratory setting.

With increased motivation students' learning and retention, it is assumed, will also increase; but the greatest advantage of discovery learning surpasses learning and remembering. Actually, the correlation between a student's knowledge and later success in life is constantly diminishing; far more important are one's understanding of broad concepts and principles and one's ability to get along with other people. In fact, the Manpower Development Act of 1960 found that as early as then, of all people in America who lost their jobs, less than 15 percent were lost from inability to perform adequately; over 85 percent were lost from inability to get along with superordinates and coworkers (Henson, 1974). Obviously when discovery learning involves group work, the socialization is, itself, a worthy goal.

The discovery process is superior to lecture-type lessons in offering students an opportunity to focus on major concepts and principles and to develop positive social skills. Discovery learning is a cooperative process. Vance (1974) found no significant difference in the ability of junior high math students in discovery, laboratory, and traditional lessons to score on an exam administered just after the learning; however, the students in the discovery classes scored highest on a special exam designed to measure high-level thinking and problem solving. Another test designed to measure divergent thinking showed that the students in the discovery classes were superior in their ability to relate the new set of materials to the study of mathematics. Students also preferred a learning style permitting them to work at their own rates and without a teacher always telling them what to do.

Disadvantages

It may be difficult to believe that a learning system with so many advantages also has several inherent disadvantages; but it does. First of all, unlike the lecture (which requires little more of the student than his attention and an ability to take notes), the discovery method makes more demands of students and teachers. Probably its greatest demand is that both teacher and students understand and adjust to the nature of discovery. At the beginning, teachers and students are uncomfortable because the discovery approach has no constant feedback to show them how well they are progressing. The lack of competition also upsets students. Discovery learning is ideally a cooperative process, not a competitive one; the competition is between the student and the task.

At its best, discovery learning is an inefficient system in its poor ability to cover large amounts of material (Moulton, 1973). Students and teachers are usually highly concerned about completing the amount of material that they are expected to cover in a particular course. College preparatory classes are especially concerned with this limitation of the discovery learning approach.

As with any instructional approach, the degree of success of discovery learning is determined by the ability of the teacher to effectively plan and execute, that is, to manage and supervise the lesson. A review of the literature suggests the following approaches to discovery learning.

Sickling (1975) has already suggested that the teacher's task is to organize or arrange tasks (or problems). Rebrova (1976) explains the problem situation as a dilemma, deliberately created by the teacher, which forces students to think, analyze, draw conclusions, and make generalizations. In other words, the teacher's role is to provide a situation that lets students see a contradiction between what they already know and newly discovered knowledge.

Sobel (1975) suggests the following guidelines:

1. Make use of contemporary materials (daily newspaper, comic strips, and the like).
2. Use topics from the history (of the subject).
3. Introduce applications (of the subject).
4. Provide opportunity for guessing.
5. Provide for laboratory experiences.
6. Introduce new topics with innovative teaching strategy.
7. Make frequent use of visual aids.
8. Set the stage for student discovery.
9. Use motivation.
10. Teach with enthusiasm.

Bittinger (1978) makes two suggestions for the teacher of discovery learning. First, the teacher and the textbooks must use unambiguous terms. Second, the student must be allowed to discover generalizations. This seems to suggest that teachers should learn to place more trust in their students and refrain from interfering with students' work.

Like all teaching-learning approaches, the discovery method has advantages and disadvantages. While discovery learning seems equal to traditional lessons for attaining knowledge, it is superior in motivating students, in the learning of broad concepts and principles, and in developing social skills. Its main disadvantages are its inability to cover large amounts of material and its failure to provide constant feedback. Discovery learning is most effective when students are involved in planning the lesson and in making their own discoveries, conclusions, and generalizations; and when teachers blend it with the use of visual aids and contemporary, easy-to-read materials.

SIMULATIONS AND GAMES

Games have always seemed to play a significant role in children's learning. No one knows exactly when games were first used to help children learn — probably since the beginning of children. For children are quick to mimic adults and to invent games that allow them to assume adultlike roles. As recorded in *The Saber-Tooth Curriculum* (Benjamin, 1939), the first serious usage of games to learn occurred during the Great Ice Age. But for those who prefer fact over fiction, the records credit a twentieth-century schoolteacher, Maria Montesorri, as probably the first person to realize the potential of games for purposeful use in the school curriculum. By watching children play, Montesorri learned to devise games based on the natural behavior of children. Such natural curricula fits the philosophy of John Locke, Jean Jacques Rousseau, and John Dewey, who believed that children should be actively involved in the curriculum.

Today games and simulations are used extensively in industry and in schools to train and educate. The use of games in schools is actually worldwide. For example, over one-third of all schools in England and Wales now include games in their syllabi (Walford, 1975). The most popular type of game used in educational settings is the *simulation-type* game, which offers its players the opportunity to experience a variety of roles that are common in life. By definition, a simulation game must imitate some reality and afford opportunity to the players to compete in a real-life role, yet it is important that the emphasis on competition be kept in perspective. The object of a simulation game is not to win. According to Rogers (1973), games offer great socializing potential and should be used to help students learn to gain empathy for other individuals. Nesvold (1973) agrees with this goal but says that it is important that every player has a chance to win; above all, the game should be fun. Hostrop (1972) warns teachers that games using machines have a tendency to become dehumanizing and require special effort by the teacher to counterbalance this with a high level of personal contact with students.

But this does not imply that games are effective only to develop social skills. On the contrary, a good simulation-type game can provide a sound and interesting learning experience Gillespie (1972). Maxson (1973) offers the following list of their advantages. Simulation-type games:

1. Involve the student actively.
2. Create a high degree of interest and enthusiasm.
3. Make abstract concepts meaningful for students.
4. Provide immediate feedback to students.
5. Allow students to experiment with concepts and new skills without feeling the need to be correct at all times.
6. Give students the opportunity to evaluate their mistakes.
7. Allow students to practice communication skills.

Basic to the learning potential for any strategy is motivation. Watman (1973) — when using a simulation based on the stock market — found that, by having students work together in small groups and allowing them to discover strategies for playing the game, motivation was increased for low achievers and students with discipline problems. Shy students became involved, and all students felt the activity relevant. As to their academic achievement, the students quickly mastered the new math concepts, and their work improved in accuracy and neatness.

Simulation-type games offer several special opportunities to learners. Hostrop (1972) found that American history students who used a simulation on the impeachment proceedings of Andrew Johnson learned in a way far more effective than a lecture. Simulations enable students to interact at their own levels (Lewis, 1972) and to learn how to compete and cooperate with others. But exactly how effective are they as compared to more traditional modes of instruction? Wylie (1974) reports on a study in which a simulation is compared to a programmed text in social studies. After the introduction of the material by these two methods, a test showed no significant difference between the learning of the two groups. Two weeks later, however, a retake of the test by the same two groups showed that the students who played the game scored higher than the control group did. It seems, then, that simulation gaming is equal in its ability to produce learning and is superior in its ability to produce retention. Lucas (1975) found that, compared to lecture, simulation games used to teach mathematics, had similar learning and retention results for up to five weeks, but after ten weeks students using the simulation had a significantly higher retention rate. Other studies show that games are especially effective for use with slow learners (Maxson, 1974; Kelly, 1970). Learning itself can be increased during simulations when students work in small groups (Kelly, 1970), when they are permitted to evaluate their own mistakes, and when the vocabulary level is kept simple (Maxson, 1974).

But the question, "Is simulation gaming more effective than a textbook?" may not be an appropriate question, since simulation games can be used to supplement the text. Maxson (1974) found that simulations can make the abstract material in a textbook more real and vivid. Taylor (1976) gives the following advantages of developing your own simulation.

1. You are able to pick the precise subject matter.
2. You know best the ability level of your students.
3. Time constraints are not a problem.
4. You are there to change or alter it if necessary as the game proceeds.

Of course, the success of any simulation depends upon its design and implementation. To help teachers design their own simulation games, Taylor (1976) gives the following suggestions:

1. Identify your objectives.
2. Decide on a problem or simulation.
3. Define the scope of the simulation.
4. Construct the rules.
5. Identify the participants' goals.
6. Write rules and teacher instructions.
7. Design any additional parts.
8. Develop a debriefing.

The designer of simulation games should consider the management requirements of the teaching situation and the ability of the students. Simulation games are valid only if they teach the desired ideas, values, and facts. Shelly (1973) and Kerr (1974) report that the best game developed involves students; when they help to develop the game, their level of involvement in playing the game and their attitude toward the game are improved.

Success with the simulation also depends upon how the game is used. In fact, many teachers shun simulations because they are afraid of their possible failure. Heyman (1976) gives the following four rules for directing a simulation game:

1. Say no more than the few words necessary.
2. Run the simulation, not the students.
3. Run the game; don't teach.
4. Do not tell the students how to behave.

Suhor (1977) adds to this list one final suggestion: Remember that good classroom management and rapport with students are necessary for good gaming. Finally, Nesvold (1973) suggests that anyone who is adapting a game for classroom use should keep the rules simple, keep the game shorter than one class period, and attain a balance between risk, chance, skill, and knowledge in the determination of victory.

When correctly designed and implemented, simulation games are an effective mode of instruction. Besides being a sound method for learning, simulation gaming is a good motivator and can therefore increase retention. Games also promote the development of social skills. Some of the best simulation games are those designed by teachers who themselves select, relate, and adjust the game to their own students. When using a simulation game, the teacher should assure its enjoyment by involving all class members and by resisting the temptation to interfere with the students.

A DIRECTORY OF SELECTED SIMULATION MATERIALS

Blue Wodjet Company. A business simulation concerning the problems of pollution for industry.

Requirements	Designers/Suppliers
25–30 players	Interact
4–6 hours	P.O. Box 1023
	Lakeside, California 92040

Clug (Community Land Use Game). A simulation of urban land-use interactions which has been compared with combinations of chess and Monopoly and is capable of considerable elaboration.

Requirements	Designers/Suppliers
9 players (min.)	Systems Gaming Associates
3 hours (min.)	Triphammer Road
Packaged materials and kit	Ithaca, New York 14850

Community Disaster. A simulation of a community hit by a localized natural disaster.

Requirements	Designers/Suppliers
6–16 players	Western Publishing Co. Inc.
2–6 hours	School and Library Department
Packaged materials	850 Third Avenue
	New York, N.Y. 10022

Conflict (Preliminary edition). The simulation is centered on a crisis that erupts in 1999 in a world disarmed by universal agreement and policed by three international councils (based on Waskow's Peace Keeping model described in *Keeping the World Disarmed* and published by the Centre for the Study of Democratic Institutions).

Requirements	*Designers/Suppliers*
24–36 players	World Law Fund
2–3 hours	11 West 42nd Street
Packaged materials	New York, N.Y. 10036

Farming. A simulation of farm management in western Kansas at three different time periods. Part of Unit 2 High School Geography Project produced by the Association of American Geographers.

Requirements	*Designers/Suppliers*
15–30 players	The Macmillan Company
40–50 hours	866 Third Avenue
Packaged materials	New York, N.Y. 10022

Galapagos (Evolution). A simulation of the evolution of Darwin's finches in which players fill a scientific role and are required to predict the evolution rate.

Requirements	*Designers/Suppliers*
6–50 players	Abt Associates Inc.
1–2 hours	14 Concord Lane
Mimeographed materials	Cambridge, Massachusetts 02138

Inner City Planning. A role-playing simulation of urban renewal processes in the USA involving various community interest groups.

Requirements	*Designers/Suppliers*
12–40 players	The Macmillan Company
1½–3 hours	866 Third Avenue
Published materials	New York, N.Y. 10022

Panatina. A simulation of an imaginary South American nation in which players face such problems as land reform, revolution, and a Common Market proposal.

Requirements	*Designers/Suppliers*
18–35 players	Project Simile
5–6 hours	P.O. Box 1023
Kit of printed materials	La Jolla, California 92037

Location of the Metfab Company. A simulation designed as an integral part of Unit 2 of the High School Geography Project for the Association of American Geographers. The central feature of the simulation is a hypothetical metal-fabricating company facing the problem of determining a new site for a company branch.

Requirements	*Designers/Suppliers*
5–10 players per group	The Macmillan Company
4–6 hours (40-minute minimum periods)	866 Third Avenue
Packaged materials	New York, N.Y. 10022

Low Bidder. A packaged simulation of contract bidding in the construction industry.

Requirements	*Designers/Suppliers*
2–25 players with 3–8 preferable	Entelek Inc.
30 minutes (min.)	42 Pleasant Street
Packaged materials	Newburyport, Massachusetts 01950

Manchester. A simulation of the impact on the agricultural population of some of the major historical and social issues surrounding the advent of the Industrial Revolution in England.

Requirements	*Designers/Suppliers*
8–40 players	Abt Associates Inc. (for Educational
1–2 hours	Services Inc.)
Instructional manual	14 Concord Lane
	Cambridge, Massachusetts 02138

Marketplace. A simulation of the American economic system at work in a medium-size, urban manufacturing community.

Requirements	*Designers/Suppliers*
30–50 players	Joint Council on Economic Education
3–4 hours (min.)	1212 Avenue of the Americas
Packaged materials	New York, N.Y. 10036

Point Roberts. A simulation of international boundary arbitration procedures produced as part of Unit 4 of the High School Geography Project organized by the Association of American Geographers.

Requirements	*Designers/Suppliers*
30 players	The Macmillan Company
30–50 hours	866 Third Avenue
Packaged materials	New York, N.Y. 10022

Politica. A political crisis simulation set in Latin America and involving major internation conflicts.

Requirements	*Designers/Suppliers*
40–80 players	Abt Associates Inc.
2–4 hours	14 Concord Lane
Mimeographed materials	Cambridge, Massachusetts 02138

Portsville. An interactive game produced by the Association of American Geographers as part of Unit 1 of the High School Geography Project and designed to simulate the growth of the City of Portsville in three different time periods.

Requirements	*Designers/Suppliers*
6 players per map board	The Macmillan Company
8–10 hours (40-minute minimum	866 Third Avenue
periods)	New York, N.Y. 10022
Packaged materials	

Rutile and the Beach. A simulation of Australian mining, conservation and recreation groups in competition for land. Part of Unit 5 of the High School Geography Project, produced by the Association of American Geographers.

Requirements	*Designers/Suppliers*
27 player roles	The Macmillan Company
50–60 hours (40-minute minimum	866 Third Avenue
periods)	New York, N.Y. 10022

Section. A simulation designed to provide students with an understanding of conflicts of interest among the sections of a political territory as they are expressed in the political process. Used in Unit 4 of the American High School Geography Project produced by the Association of American Geographers.

Requirements	Designers/Suppliers
Over 30 players	The Macmillan Company
5–6 hours	866 Third Avenue
Packaged materials	New York, N.Y. 10022

Simulation of American Government. A simulation of certain hypothetical roles and relationships analogous to those found in various branches of American government.

Requirements	Designers/Suppliers
9 players and above	Dale M. Garvey
2–4 hours	Division of Social Sciences
Mimeographed materials	Kansas State Teachers College
	Emporia, Kansas 66801

Solution for Acme Metal. A simulation of flood prevention planning designed as an integral part of Unit 5 of the High School Geography Project, produced by the Association of American Geographers.

Requirements	Designers/Suppliers
7–28 players	The Macmillan Company
30–40 hours (40-minute minimum	866 Third Avenue
periods)	New York, N.Y. 10022
Packaged materials	

Steam. A simulation of some of the economic aspects of steam-engine development relevant to coal mining in England at the commencement of the nineteenth century.

Requirements	Designers/Suppliers
6–15 players	Abt Associates Inc.
1–2 hours	14 Concord Lane
Mimeographed materials	Cambridge, Massachusetts 02138

Venture. A school business game that is a total enterprise simulation covering many of the major decision-making areas of business and management.

Requirements	Designers/Suppliers
20–35 players	Public Relations Department
4–5 hours	(Education Services)
Complete kit available without charge	The Procter & Gamble Co.
in the USA	P.O. Box 599
	Cincinnati, Ohio 45201

Yes, But Not Here. A role-playing simulation of an urban locational conflict involving a housing project for the elderly.

Requirements	Designers/Suppliers
32 roles	The Macmillan Company
2–3 hours	866 Third Avenue
Published materials	New York, N.Y. 10022

REFERENCES

Expository Teaching

COMMONWEALTH, V., and GOOTNICK, D. M. "Electrifying the Classroom with the Overhead Projector." *Business Education Forum* 28 (February 1974): 3–4.

COUCH, RICHARD. "Is Lecturing Really Necessary?" *American Biology Teacher* 35 (October 1973): 391–95.

ELLIS, H. P., and JONES, A. D. "Anxiety About Lecturing." *Universities Quarterly* 29 (Spring 1974): 91–95.

FRAZIER, D. T., and HOLCOMB, J. D. "Improving Lectures by Videotape Self-confrontation." *Improving College and University Teaching* 20 (Autumn 1972): 340–41.

GROBE, ROBERT P., et al. "Effects of Lecture Pace on Noise Level in a University Classroom." *Journal of Educational Research* 67 (October 1973): 73–75.

HALEY, J. H.; LALONDE, E.; and ROBIN, S. "An Assessment of the Lecture." *Improving College and University Teaching* 22 (Autumn 1972): 326–27.

KAPLAN, R. M., and PASCOE, G. C. "Humorous Lectures and Humorous Examples: Some Effects on Comprehension and Retention." *Journal of Educational Psychology* 69 (February 1977): 61–65.

KYLE, B. "In Defense of the Lecture." *Improving College and University Teaching* 20 (Autumn 1972): 325.

LUCAS, LAWRENCE A.; POSTMA, C. H.; and THOMPSON, S. C. "Comparative Study of Retention Used in Simulation Gaming as Opposed to Lecture-Discussion Techniques." *Peabody Journal of Education* 52 (July 1975): 261.

MADDOX, H., and HOOLE, E. "Performance Decrement in the Lecture." *Educational Review* 28 (November 1975): 17–30.

OTT, M. D., and MACKLIN, D. B. "A Trait Treatment Interaction in a College Physics Course." *Journal of Research in Science Teaching* 12 (April 1975): 111–19.

RIPPEY, R. F. "Speech Compressors for Lecture Review." *Educational Technology* 15 (November 1975): 58–59.

ROWSEY, R., and MASON, W. H. "Immediate Achievement and Retention in Audio Tutorial vs. Conventional Lecture-Laboratory Instruction." *Journal of Research in Science Teaching* 12 (October 1975): 393–97.

STARR, R. J., and SCHUERMAN, C. D. "An Experiment in Small Group Learning." *American Biology Teacher* 36 (March 1974): 173–75.

THOMPSON, R. "Legitimate Lecturing." *Improving College and University Teaching* 22 (Summer 1974): 163–64.

TITUS, C. "The Uses of the Lecture." *Clearing House* 49 (February 1974): 383–84.

VOTH, ROBERT. "On Lecturing." *Social Studies* 66 (November 1975): 247–48.

WEINBERG, M. "Humor Works in Funny Ways." *Nation's Schools and Colleges* 2 (February 1975): 21.

WHOOLEY, J. "Improving the Lecture." *Improving College and University Teaching* 22 (Summer 1974): 183 +.

WYCKOFF, W. L. "The Effect of Stimulus Variation on Learning from Lecture." *Journal of Experimental Education* 41 (Spring 1973): 85–90.

Inquiry Learning

BALZER, LEVON. "Teacher Behaviors and Student Inquiry in Biology." *American Biology Teacher* 32 (January 1970): 26–28.

BIBENS, ROBERT F. "Using Inquiry Effectively." *Theory Into Practice* 19 (Spring 1980): 87–92.

BILLS, FRANK L. "Developing Creativity Through Inquiry." *Science Education* 55 (January 1971): 417–21.

BROWN, STANLEY B., and BROWN, L. B. "Suggested Critical Thinking and Inquiry Techniques in Science for Middle School Teachers." *School Science and Mathematics* 71 (November 1971): 731–36.

JAUS, HAROLD H. "Activity-Oriented Science: Is It Really That Good?" *Science and Children* 14 (April 1977): 26–27.

JOHNSON, R. T. "The Relationship Between Cooperation and Inquiry in Science Classrooms." *Journal of Research in Science Teaching* 13 (January 1976): 55–63.

LAZAROWITZ, REUVEN. "Does Use of Curriculum Change Teachers' Attitudes Toward Inquiry?" *Journal of Research in Science Teaching* 13 (October 1971): 547–52.

LAZAROWITZ, REUVEN, and LEE, A. E. "Measuring Inquiry Attitudes of Secondary Science Teachers." *Journal of Research in Science Teaching* 13 (September 1976): 445–60.

TATHART, J. R., and BINGHAM, R. M. "LEIB-IRA: Preliminary Report." *American Biology Teacher* 35 (September 1973): 346.

TAXEY, PAUL J. "Heterogeneous Subgroups Within a Classroom." *American Biology Teacher* 37 (March 1975): 165–67.

TJOSVOLD, DEAN, and MARINO, P. M. "The Effects of Cooperation and Competition on Student Reactions to Inquiry and Didactic Science Teaching." *Journal of Research in Science Teaching* 14 (July 1977): 281–88.

TRAUGH, C. E. "Evaluating Inquiry Procedures." *Social Studies* 65 (October 1974): 201–20.

WEBB, PATRICIA K. "Piaget: Implications for Teaching." *Theory Into Practice* 19 (Spring 1980): 93–97.

WENDEL, ROBERT. "Inquiry Teaching: Dispelling the Myths." *The Clearing House* 48 (September 1973): 24–28.

Questioning

ALFKE, D. "Asking Operational Questions." *Science and Children* 11 (April 1974): 18–19.

BULL, S. G., and DIZNEY, H. F. "Epistemic-Curiosity-Arousing Pre-Questions: Their Effect on Long-Term Retention." *Journal of Educational Psychology* 65 (August 1973): 45–49.

CHAUDHARI, U. S. "Questioning and Creative Thinking: A Research Perspective." *Journal of Creative Behavior* 1 (January 1975): 30–34.

HENSON, KENNETH T. *Secondary Teaching: A Personal Approach.* Itasca, Ill.: F. E. Peacock, 1974.

HYMAN, RONALD T. "Fielding Student Questions." *Theory Into Practice* 19 (Winter 1980): 38–44.

MILLER, H. G., and VINOCUR, S. M. "How to Ask Classroom Questions." *School and Community* 59 (February 1973): 10.

ROTHKOPF, E. F., and BILLINGTON, M. J. "Indirect Review and Previewing Through Questions." *Journal of Educational Psychology* 66 (May 1974): 669–79.

ROWE, MARY BUDD. "Wait Time and Rewards as Instructional Variables: Part One." *Journal of Research in Science Teaching* 11 (1974): 81–84.

SABOL, J. E. "Do Pupils Answer, 'I Dunno'?" *The Agricultural Education Magazine* 48 (November 1975): 114.

SANDERS, J. R. "Retention Effects of Adjunct Questions in Written and Oral Discourse." *Journal of Educational Psychology* 65 (October 1973): 181–86.

SANTIESLEBAU, A. J. "Teacher Questioning Performance and Student Affective Outcomes." *Journal of Research and Science Teaching* 13 (November 1976): 553–57.

SHIMAN, D. A., and NASH, R. J. "Questioning: Another View." *Peabody Journal of Education* 51 (July 1974): 246–53.

SUND, R. B. "Growing Through Sensitive Listening and Questioning." *Childhood Education* 51 (November 1971): 68–71.

SUTTON, R. M. "On Asking and Answering Questions." *The Physics Teacher* 15 (February 1977): 94–95.

Discovery Learning

BAIKOV, F. I.; KORTISKY, V. T.; and VALSOV, M. M. "Correlating the Problem-Solving Approach and Other Approaches to the Teaching of Biology." *Soviet Education* 18 (February 1976): 18–26.

BITTINGER, M. L. "A Review of Discovery." *The Mathematics Teacher* 61 (February 1968): 140–45.

CRUICKSHANK, D. R., and TEFLER, ROSS. "Classroom Games and Simulations." *Theory Into Practice* 19 (Winter 1980): 75–80.

HENSON, KENNETH T. *Secondary Teaching: A Personal Approach.* Itasca, Ill.: F. E. Peacock, 1974.

JONES, PHILLIP. "Discovery Teaching from Socrates to Modernity." *The Mathematics Teacher* 63 (October 1970): 501–10.

MITZMAN, B. "Toward a More Reasonable Physics: The Inquiry Approach." *Change* 10 (January 1978): 52–55.

MOULTON, PAUL. "The Mathematics Teacher as a Source of Experience." *The Mathematics Teacher* 73 (March 1973): 238–43.

REBROVA, L. V., and SVETLOVA, P. R. "The Problem-Solving Approach: A Way to Insure Solid and Thorough Learning." *Soviet Education* 18 (February 1976): 75–84.

SICKLING, F. P. "Patterns in Integers." *The Mathematics Teacher* 68 (April 1975): 290–92.

SOBEL, MAX A. "Junior High School Mathematics: Motivation vs. Monotony." *The Mathematics Teacher* 68 (October 1975): 479–85.

VANCE, JAMES H. "Mathematics Laboratories: More Than Fun?" *School Science and Mathematics* 72 (October 1972): 617–23.

WEIMER, R. C. "An Analysis of Discovery." *Educational Technology* 15 (September 1975): 45–48.

Simulations and Games

BENJAMIN, HAROLD. *The Saber-Tooth Curriculum.* New York: McGraw-Hill, 1939.

GILLESPIE, JUDITH A. "Analyzing and Evaluating Classroom Games." *Social Education* 37 ((January 1973): 33.

HEYMAN, MARK. "How to Direct a Simulation." *Phi Delta Kappan* 58 (November 1976): 17–19.

HOSTROP, RICHARD W. "Simulation as Stimulus to Learning and Retention." *Improving College and University Teaching* 20 (Autumn 1972): 283.

KELLY, WILLIAM H. "Are Educational Games Effective in Teaching?" *Agricultural Education Magazine* 43 (November 1970): 117.

KERR, DONALD R., JR. "Mathematics Games in the Classroom." The *Arithmetic Teacher* 21 (March 1974): 172–75.

LEWIS, PHILLIP. "Games, Simulations Allow Pupils 'Slice of Life'." *Nation's Schools* 89 (March 1972): 80 +.

LUCAS, L. A.; POSTMA, C. H.· and THOMPSON, J. C. "Comparative Study of Cognitive

Retention Used in Simulation Gaming as Opposed to Lecture-Discussion Techniques." *Peabody Journal of Education* 52 (July 1975): 261.

MAXSON, ROBERT C. "Simulation: A Method That Can Make a Difference." *Education Digest* 18 (March 1974): 48–50.

NESVOLD, GERALD T.; GIBBONS, J.; and CAMPBELL, J. R. "The Teacher-Made Game." *The Science Teacher* 40 (May 1973): 65.

ROGERS, VIRGINIA M., and GOODLOE, A. H. "Simulation Games as Method." *Educational Leadership* 30 (May 1973): 729.

SHELLY, ANN C. "Total Class Development of Simulation Games." *Social Education* 37 (November 1973): 687–89.

SUHOR, CHARLES. "Hypothesis-Games Can Be Fun." *The English Journal* 18 (March 1977): 381–82.

TAYLOR, A. J. R. "Developing Your Own Simulation for Teaching." *The Clearing House* 50 (November 1976): 104–7.

TAYLOR, GEORGE R., and WATKINS, S. T. "Active Games: An Approach to Teaching Mathematical Skills to the Educable Mentally Retarded." *The Arithmetic Teacher* 21 (December 1974): 674–78.

WALFORD, R. "Games and Simulations." *Times Educational Supplement* 30 (May 11, 1973): 38.

WATMAN, M. X. "A Simulation Game for General Mathematics." *The Mathematics Teacher* 66 (January 1973): 23–25.

WYLIE, R. E. "Simulation Game for General Mathematics." *Childhood Education* 54 (March 1974): 307.

SUMMARY

Recognizing that some teaching approaches work best with some students, and some with others, today's teachers need to enter the profession with a portfolio of teaching methods so that they can select the best method for a particular group of students. Correct application of each style is important. Most students prefer a good lecture over a student-centered lesson that is confusing, and vice versa. To expect to be successful with any strategy, teachers must know the strengths, weaknesses, and common pitfalls of each style. With this knowledge they can design their own strategy for effectively implementing the particular teaching methods. This is very important, for a teaching approach should parallel the teacher's own unique personality and background experiences.

As a beginning teacher you will be wise to experiment with as many different approaches as possible. Expect mistakes but turn them into opportunities for growth. To expect every lesson to be an overwhelming success is to be unrealistic. Teachers should never reach the stage where they stop observing and analyzing their own lessons. Continuous alterations with any teaching strategy are essential to continuous improvement with that strategy.

EXPERIENCES

After reading this chapter, you may have already begun making some decisions about your own teaching strategies. The following experiences should give you some opportunities to refine your decisions.

Experience 1:   A Methods Course Emphasizes Strategies

Carole Harman had enjoyed her introductory course in education. She also had taken an exploratory course in education, which had provided some very interesting field experiences. These courses had made her feel more certain than ever that she should become a teacher.

The next year Carole took two courses in her major (chemistry), two in math, and a general secondary methods course. But after only two weeks, Carole was feeling very lost in the education course. Her professor had begun talking about educational research and about teaching strategies, and the relationships between the two. Carole was uncomfortable because she had never taken a course in research methodology; nor did she have any background in teaching strategies.

Almost from the first moment her education professor began making such comments as "when selecting your strategies . . ." or "You can apply your favorite strategy." Carole had never before thought about teaching strategies, which sounded like unnecessary educational jargon to her. She wondered if her classmates felt as out of place as she did until one of them near her mumbled, "How can you have a *favorite* strategy if you don't know what one *is*?"

▶ *Questions and Discussion*

1. *Why might an education professor assume that students in a general methods course have knowledge of teaching strategies?*
   Just as teachers often get so close to their subjects and expect their students to have more enthusiasm and knowledge of the subject than they have, college professors are likely to make the same mistake. After all, educational strategies are this teacher's major subject.

2. *Why is it important that teachers have knowledge of many teaching strategies?*
   Many teachers feel that a good repertoire of methods is essential for their own survival in the classroom. What works with one group of students may fail to stimulate another group. A variety of methods enables the teacher to shift quickly from one to another when the level of interest drops. (This is only one advantage of having a repertoire of methods. Perhaps you can think of others.)

3. *What should the teacher know about each teaching strategy?*
   To get the most benefit from each strategy, teachers must know the purposes for which the method works best and the age levels for

which it is most appropriate. Besides knowing how to use a strategy, they should recognize its strengths and limitations. What else will you want to know about methods that you will choose to use? (You might consider their practicality, cost, and effects on fellow teachers.)

Experience 2:   Should Teaching in Secondary Schools Be Fun?

Louie Martinez was about the most interesting math teacher ever to come to Jackson's Corner. Before he came to Jackson High three years ago, there weren't enough students interested in math to offer more than the very basic general mathematics, geometry, and first-year algebra. But when school opened this fall, he had so many students requesting Algebra II that two sections were necessary. Also, twenty-seven students had signed up for trigonometry, and fifteen others wanted a class in first-year calculus. For a school as small as Jackson's Corner, this degree of interest in any single subject was incredible. Happy to see that so many of his students were sharing his enjoyment of mathematics, Louie became even more enthusiastic; his lessons became even more exciting.

The students enjoyed his classes for many different reasons. For one, they never knew what to expect from one day to the next; they just knew that it would be different. Most of the lessons tended to involve all of them, usually in a number of ways. Moreover, Mr. Martinez had a great collection of props, audio-visual materials, and games.

Then some of the other teachers began complaining about Louie. His classes were noisier than most; and, though he had more equipment than most of his colleagues did, his students were running all over the school borrowing other paraphernalia to use in their math classes. Basically, though, their complaints about Louie stemmed from their jealousy. Although they would never admit it, they would gladly have tolerated the noise and other minor irritants if they could have their students become that enthusiastic over their classes.

Unfortunately, the complaints reached Louie only after they had been spread around the school and community. The principal called Louie in to discuss these complaints, reminding him how important it was not to alienate his fellow teachers. Louie was perplexed to learn that his successful teaching strategies had begun to cause trouble for him.

▶ *Questions and Discussion*

1. *Is it likely that having a repertoire of teaching methods will get a teacher into trouble?*
   Although this is possible, most teachers would probably prefer having jealous colleagues over having unmanageable students and unsuccessful lessons.

2. *How might Louie react to such an accusation?*
   Louie would probably profit from admitting that his classes are noisy,

but he should then ask the principal if the complaints are worth sacrificing the success that his students are experiencing. Can you think of an amicable way of convincing the principal?

3. *How should Louie deal with the complaints coming from his fellow teachers?*
   Regardless of how much the students are achieving in this room, Louie must realize that they should not disturb their neighbors. He should explain this to the students and let them know their responsibility to hold down the level of noise.

ACTIVITIES

By this point in your academic career you have experienced many excellent teachers and others who fall short. Since our perspectives on any issue represent the total combination of our experiences, the following activities are provided to help you classify your own perceptions about good and bad teachers:

1. Think of the best teachers you have ever had, that is, those from whom you feel you have learned the most. Select one of these favorite teachers and describe this teacher's:
   a. method(s) of establishing cognitive set;
   b. method(s) of involving students; and
   c. method of relating the material to your own experiences.
2. Choosing a concept from your subject area, explain how you can combine a number of methods introduced in this chapter to teach this concept. Consider using one method for the introduction, one or more methods for involving students, and yet another method for summarizing the lesson.
3. Develop a game to be used in class to teach the above concept.

SUGGESTED READINGS

BIRKEL, L. F. "The Lecture Method: Villain or Victim?" *Peabody Journal of Education* (1973): 298–301.

CALDWELL, ROBERT M. "Improving Learning Strategies with Computer-Based Education." *Theory Into Practice* 19 (Spring 1980): 141–43.

CARIN, ARTHUR, and SUND, ROBERT B. *Developing Questioning Techniques.* Columbus, Ohio: Charles E. Merrill, 1971.

GAGNÉ, ROBERT M. "Preparing the Learner for New Learning." *Theory Into Practice* 19 (Winter 1980): 5–9.

GILSTRAP, ROBERT L., and MARTIN, WILLIAM R. *Current Strategies for Teachers.* Santa Monica, Calif.: Goodyear Publishing Company, 1975.

GRAHAM, P. TONY, and CLINE, PAUL C. "The Case Method: A Basic Approach to Teaching." *Theory Into Practice* 19 (Spring 1980): 112–21.

HENSON, KENNETH T. "Teaching Methods: History and Status." *Theory Into Practice* 19 (Winter 1980): 2–5.

HEYMAN, M. "How to Direct a Simulation." *Phi Delta Kappan* (November 1976): 17–19.

HYMAN, RONALD T. *Ways of Teaching*. Rev. ed. Philadelphia: J. B. Lippincott, 1970.

JOYCE, BRUCE R. "Learning How to Learn." *Theory Into Practice* 19 (Winter 1980): 15–27.

KAHL, H. "Teachers and Kids: Partners in Game Making." *Learning*. (January 1974): 23–25.

LIVINGSTON, SAMUEL A., and STOLL, CLARICE S. *Simulation Games: An Introduction for the Social Studies Teacher*. New York: Free Press, 1973.

ROWE, MARY BUDD. "Wait-Time & Rewards as Instructional Variables, Their Influence on Language, Logic, & Fate Control: Part One." *Journal of Research in Science Teaching* 11 (1974): 81–94.

SHIRTS, G. R. "Ten Mistakes Commonly Made by Persons Designing Educational Simulations and Games." *Simulation Gaming* (September/October 1976): 19.

TAYLOR, JOHN L., and WALFORD, REX. *Simulation in the Classroom*. Baltimore, Md.: Penguin Books, 1972.

TITUS, C. "The Uses of the Lecture." *Clearing House* (February 1974): 383–84.

TORRENCE, E. PAUL. *Encouraging Creativity in the Classroom*. Dubuque, Iowa: William C. Brown, 1970.

WANG, MARGARET C. "Adaptive Instruction: Building on Diversity." *Theory Into Practice* 19 (Spring 1980): 122–33.

WEIMER, R. C. "An Analogy of Discovery." *Educational Technology* (September 1975): 45–48.

WEINBERG, M. "Humor Works in Funny Ways." *Nations Schools and Colleges* (February 1975): 21.

WEINBERGER, ROBERT A. *Perspectives in Individualized Learning*. Itasca, Ill.: F. E. Peacock, 1971.

WILLIAMS, ROBERT O. "What Teaching Methods When?" *Theory Into Practice* 19 (Spring 1980): 82–86.

Providing for Individual Differences

Chapters 1–11 focused on generalities that can be applied to many situations. The comments about adolescents were accurate descriptions of most adolescents. The techniques for communicating and interacting with them and the methods for planning lessons are appropriate for most adolescents.

Those chapters were written with the "average" student in mind, but experienced teachers are quick to say that there are few average students and even fewer average classes. Each student is different in some ways from all others. Each ethnic group, each culture, and many individual students are so different that they require special teaching techniques.

Chapters 12 and 13 will help prepare you for providing leadership and instruction for students who are not "average."

Teaching Students with Special Needs

OBJECTIVES

Upon completing this chapter you should be able to:

1. Name five major categories of handicapped students.
2. Name the three important factors that should always be considered when working with handicapped students.
3. List three minimum requirements of all Individualized Educational Programs as set forth by Public Law 94–142.
4. Give two definitions of "gifted students."
5. Explain why the length of time a specific handicap has existed is important to a teacher of students having this handicap.
6. List three characteristics of mildly retarded students that are useful in identifying these students.
7. Name at least six rights that Public Law 94–142 gives to handicapped students and their parents.
8. Define "educationally handicapped."
9. Name the four levels of mental retardation and give the intelligence test score range for each.
10. Develop an Individualized Educational Program for a hypothetical handicapped student.

This book began with the underlying premise that a secondary school should enable all students to develop to the maximum of their potential. Chapter 4, "Classroom Management," emphasized the importance of the relationship between the teacher and students; for, without a positive attitude toward self, teachers, peers, and the school itself, the student cannot reach his or her maximum potential. But some students have special needs that cannot be met unless the teacher acts in certain ways to help them realize and develop their potentials.

Special education is that part of the education process attempting to meet the needs of young people who differ in some way(s) from average children to the degree that, to develop their maximum potential, they require modification of regularly accepted school practices. The problem is not so much that the student is different, but that the educational process needs to be different. "But," you may say, "isn't this the job of specialists who are trained to work with these students?" The answer is: Yes, there are specialists whose training enables them to work with these students, but the classroom teacher is the one who helps them move into the mainstream.

Many contemporary educators believe that such a mainstreaming approach to working with handicapped children is the best approach because:

1. Every child has a right to an equal educational opportunity, even at the expense of having different education experiences.
2. For most exceptional children, integration, not segregation, is needed.
3. Labeling is an administrative crutch that says nothing about a student's assets and desires to be accepted as a normal person.

For many years our society has recognized that a free or public education is a right of all citizens. While the methods of providing such education are left up to each state, federal legislation does guarantee this right. Since some states have been very casual in providing education for handicapped youth, federal legislation now specifies exactly what type of services must be provided and provides the finances needed to run these programs. It is essential that you become familiar with some of the more important laws that guarantee quality education for your handicapped students. Professional journals can help keep you alerted to new legislation as it occurs.

Perhaps the greatest single legislative action on behalf of handicapped students was Public Law 94–142 (the Education for All Handicapped Children Act, enacted in 1977). This law requires that each state provides special education services for its handicapped students. These services will be provided at public expense under public supervision and direction, and without charge, (b) will meet state education agency standards, (c) will include an appropriate preschool, elementary or secondary school education, and (d) will be provided in conformity with the individualized education program. Specifically, the law required that by September 1, 1978, all students ages three to nineteen were to be served; and this service includes adequate classroom instruction. But the impact of this law on schools continues to grow.

Public Law 94–142 is a highly complicated law. Nowhere in its many pages does it mention the term *mainstreaming*. Instead, it uses the phrase "least restrictive environments," which does allow for special students to be removed

---

* Credit is given to Patricia Haensly and the Department of Educational Psychology at Texas A&M University for the module on preparing teachers to teach the handicapped, upon which much of this section is based.

from regular classes if those students are restricted when placed in regular classrooms. The thrust of the law seems to be in keeping the handicapped students in the classroom with nonhandicapped students as opposed to grouping handicapped students together for instruction.

The findings that led to this law may help us understand the need for this legislation. They are as follows:

1. There are over eight million handicapped children in the U.S. today.
2. Educational needs of such children are not being fully met.
3. More than half of the handicapped children do not receive appropriate educational services.
4. One million are excluded entirely from the public school system.
5. There are many in regular programs whose handicaps are undetected.
6. Because public school systems lack adequate services, families must find other services at their own expense.
7. With appropriate funding, state and local educational agencies have the knowledge and methods to provide effective special education and related services.
8. State and local educational agencies have this responsibility but inadequate financial resources.
9. It is in the national interest to assist state and local educational agencies in providing programs to meet the educational needs of handicapped children *in order to assure equal protection of the law.*

As a future teacher, you will probably become directly involved in complying with the guidelines set forth in Public Law 94–142. This includes submitting a program plan each year, showing how your school is meeting the requirements. If your school fails to meet these requirements, it will lose its federal funding. It is one of your responsibilities as a teacher to help handicapped students get the support that they are due.

One of the major provisions of this law is its guarantee that, prior to placement or denial of placement into educational programs, students and their parents be offered (1) notice of the proposed action, (2) the right to a hearing prior to final action, (3) the right to counsel at that hearing, (4) the right to present evidence, (5) the right to full access to relevant school records, (6) the right to compel attendance of, confront, and cross-examine officials or employees who might have evidence on the basis for proposed action, (7) the right to an independent evaluation, (8) the right to have the hearing open or closed to the public at the parent's option, and (9) the right to an impartial hearing officer. The hearings are to be held at a place and time convenient to the parents. In other words, students and their parents have a right to question the appropriateness of individual educational plans or programs developed for them.

Who Are the Handicapped Students?

We could categorize all handicapped students into five deviant groups — physical, mental, emotional, sensory, and neurological — but we could not assign a group of students to these subgroups without noticing much overlap. Rather, we should view the individual differences as lying on a continuum grouped around a norm. Furthermore, we should keep in mind the *degree of involvement* (mild, moderate, or severe), the *length of time* that the student has had the condition, and the *stability of the condition*.

In the following sections several types of deviations will be discussed. As you read about each, remember that the above criteria (degree of involvement, length of time, and stability of the condition) should all be considered when trying to decide what to do for these students.

Physical Deviations

Orthopedically handicapped persons have a crippling impairment that interferes with the normal function of the bones, joints, or muscles, including internal organs and systemic malfunctions. These impairments range from congenital conditions and deformities, such as dwarfism, limb absence, heart defects, hemophilia, cerebral palsy, epilepsy, and spina bifida, to traumatic conditions such as amputations or burns.

Such students may be limited in mobility and ability to utilize materials or equipment, and lack motor control. As is true of most categories of handicapped individuals, the degree of impairment among orthopedically handicapped students varies over a wide range. If the cause was congenital (a birth defect), such as with cerebral palsy, the student may have failed to be-

come involved in experiences needed for intellectual growth and may now be suffering from secondary handicaps such as mental retardation. Visual and speech defects are common. Poor facial muscle control may cause drooling, giving the false impression of mental retardation. Therefore, each individual must be viewed and treated as an individual.

The teacher should be careful to avoid the tendency that nonhandicapped people have to underestimate the abilities of orthopedically handicapped students, for they are often able to achieve at extremely complicated tasks. Their ability to conceptualize or "know how" to do things and yet not be able to do them because of physical handicaps may lead to frustration. The following list can be used to detect frustrations among orthopedically handicapped students:

1. Verbal aggressiveness.
2. Blaming other people.
3. Repressing desires.
4. Withdrawing into fantasy.
5. Degrading the original goal.
6. Acting less mature.
7. Compensation by shifting to different interests.[1]

Of course, all students may at times display these behaviors but probably to a lesser degree, since their successes may minimize their frustrations. The

---

[1] Samuel A. Kirk, *Educating Exceptional Children*, 2d ed. (Boston: Houghton Mifflin, 1971), pp. 375–76.

teacher can reduce the frustrations among orthopedically handicapped students by providing for them a climate of success and by accepting them and including them in the social activities of the school. Teacher pity, overprotection, and ignoring may perpetuate their condition, for they must become involved if they are to learn to function and become independent. Above all else, the teacher must remember that physical impairment does not automatically signal lowered mental functioning.

MENTALLY RETARDED.   Mentally retarded students are those whose learning rates and potentials are considerably lower than the average for other students. Depending on the degree of retardation, there are four classifications based on student scores on intelligence tests. (These ranges of scores may vary slightly from state to state according to the exact legal definition of each state.)

Mild   55–69

Moderate   40–54

Severe   25–39

Profound   24 and below

Mildly retarded students may appear similar to normal classmates in height and weight, but a closer observation may reveal that they are lacking in strength, speed, and coordination. They also tend to have more general health problems.

These students may experience frustration, especially when they have been expected to function at this chronological age. They often appear to have short attention spans and to lack the ability to concentrate. Frequently this is because materials and methods are geared above their ability. If they are antisocial or impersonal, these traits, too, can be attributed to the fact that teachers and other people have expected them to perform beyond their abilities.

TRAINABLE RETARDED.   Trainable retarded students respond very slowly to education and training, since their intellectual development is only 25 to 50 percent of normal. Yet many can be trained for jobs that require single skills under adequate supervision.

Retarded mental development may include slowness in maturation of specific intellectual functions needed for schoolwork. Since they may be significantly low in memory, generalizing ability, language ability, conceptual and perceptual abilities, and creative abilities, they should be given tasks that are simple, brief, relevant, sequential, and designed for success.

Emotional Deviations

The emotionally disturbed child is most simply interpreted as one who is confused or bewildered. He does not understand his own social stresses, and he feels unaccepted in his efforts to resolve them. "Ah hah," you say, "so that is the category used to describe the troublemakers." Often this is true. Emotional deviates do tend to be either hostile or apathetic. Seriously emotionally disturbed students require psychological services; less serious or socially maladjusted students often do not.

Most students who exhibit apathy and hostility are not to be classified as emotionally disturbed. The key element is the frequency with which they display such behavior. For example, the student who occasionally disrupts or hits a classmate is probably not disturbed, but the one who disrupts a lesson or bothers others several times during the hour may be emotionally disturbed. At the secondary level emotionally disturbed students often show oversensitiveness to criticism and unusual anxiety because of their weak self-concepts. Some may show extreme depression. Again it is the frequency, duration, and intensity of their behavior that indicate the seriousness of their condition.

In dealing with emotionally disturbed students, you need to arrange for successful experiences and to use considerable reinforcement. Avoid creating highly threatening climates in the classroom, such as overemphasizing the importance of examinations and other trauma-producing elements. Students who appear unusually aggressive or timid should not be forced to make public addresses to their classmates. The classroom climate should also be free of threat, ridicule, and other abuses by fellow classmates; the responsibility for this belongs to the teacher.

Sensory Deviations

The sensory deviations category includes those students who are handicapped visually and those who have hearing impairments. The visually handicapped may be either partially sighted or blind; those with hearing impairments may be deaf or merely hard of hearing.

Visually handicapped students vary tremendously in the degrees to which they are handicapped; only about 10 percent of the legally blind are actually totally blind. Therefore, our first criterion for working with visually handicapped students is very important; that is, we should first consider the degree of their handicap. Another criterion, considering the length of time of the handicap, is also very important. Those whose problems have been lifelong will need help in developing concepts of space and form, whereas those whose blindness is recent will need help adjusting to their blindness.

Students with hearing problems range from those who can hear and understand speech with difficulty, using such supports as hearing aids, to the deaf who at most are only able to distinguish amplified sounds. In considering the extent of the hearing handicap, the teacher should look for the loudness required and clarity of what is heard. The length of time that the student has had the handicap is extremely important, since it occurred either before or after their speech and language comprehension developed. The major problem of students who have been deaf since birth is not that they are deaf but that they are unable to develop speech and language comprehension through hearing.

In working with visually and hearing handicapped students, you begin by providing psychological support. You do this by accepting the students in their condition and believing in their ability to adjust to their handicap and to become productive individuals. And, indeed, sensory handicapped students can learn to perform extremely complicated tasks. The teacher's expression of confidence in the student leads to their increased self-confidence.

You are also responsible for setting this climate of acceptance among the student's peers. Since both blind and deaf students are unable to pick up all the stimuli that provide cues as to how and when people respond, their timing may be off, or they may not respond at all. Not being sensitive to these limitations, their peers may interpret their response (or absence of response) as unfriendly or antisocial. Handicapped students' limited vocabulary may further limit their response. Above all else, do not relent to showing pity. On the contrary, the teacher should provide a positive climate that focuses on the abilities and potentials of these students rather than on their limitations.

Neurological Deviations — The Learning Disabled

Students in this category have normal intelligence but are unable to process information for learning to take place. In other words, their problem concerns a dysfunction and/or emotional disturbance as opposed to mental retardation or sensory deprivation. They may be awkward, hyperkinetic, and impulsive, or a few may appear slow. Because our school programs are not usually designed to accommodate such behavior, these students are frequently viewed as behavioral problems.

While students with learning disabilities tend to be aggressive, irritable, and highly emotional, some may be even-tempered and cooperative. They may have quick changes of emotional behavior from high-tempered to remorseful. They may even panic by what others see as mildly stressful situations.

The basis of the problem can lie in the psychomotor, visual, or auditory domain. The teacher can often recognize psychomotor disabilities when students are in poor physical condition or when they frequently bump into things. Also their written assignments can give cues: the handwriting may be unusually large (or small), and the student may tend to cramp the work into one corner of the paper.

If the basis of the student's problem is visual, the teacher may notice that the student may not be able to follow visual directions, may tend to forget things seen, and may be easily distracted by surrounding activities. Furthermore, the student may tend to move his eyes excessively or inappropriately.

Teachers can recognize auditory disabilities when students fail to follow oral directions, forget directions, are easily distracted by noise, and confuse similar sounds.

Using Individualized Instruction

Earlier it was mentioned that the current mode of working with handicapped students is to move them from groups consisting of only handicapped students and to place them back into the mainstream with all other students. Of course, this alone would not assure that their special needs would be met. To make certain that the needs of each individual (and each individual's special needs are different from others who may share his general problem), Public Law 94-142 requires a specific type of individualized program be provided for each handicapped student of ages three to twenty-one. This approach, called Individualized Educational Programming, consists of a written statement for each handicapped child identifying his particular needs and describing how these needs are being met.

As was mentioned earlier, a special meeting must be held in which the program for each handicapped student will be developed. Attending this meeting will be a representative of the local education authority who will be assigned to supervise the student's program and the student's teacher(s) and parents. When appropriate, the student will attend the meeting. In effect, you the teacher will be held accountable to see that the services planned are indeed actually rendered. Furthermore, you the teacher will be required to see that constant evaluation of the program of each handicapped student in your class is being made. The law requires that at least one progress review be made each year, and the state may require more. If the parent does not request the review, you, the teacher, should.

As a teacher of a handicapped high school student, you should try to establish good communications and good working relationships with the student and parents. Since many handicapped students of this age are capable of participating heavily in the development of their own program, you should try to create a team spirit. By uniting your efforts, you, the student, and the parents can provide a program superior to one planned by only yourself.

Each Individualized Educational Program must contain, as a minimum, these statements and projections:

1. The child's present level of educational performance.
2. Annual goals and short-term instructional goals.
3. The specific educational services to be provided — by whom, when, and for how long.
4. The extent to which the child will be able to participate in regular educational programs.
5. Appropriate, objective criteria for evaluation, and schedules for determining (on at least an annual basis) whether instructional objectives are being achieved.
6. The program's beginning and ending dates.
7. A statement of the parents' role in relation to the plan.
8. Changes needed to be made in the school situation (staffing, in-service education, etc.).

The initial draft of the IEP can be made by any of the planning team members, including the student. The rest of the team can accept the plan, revise it, or develop another plan that they would feel more useful to the teachers and other school personnel.

The following is an example of an Individualized Educational Program.[2] Although, to be approved, each program must include the preceding eight features; no two programs need or should be exactly alike. Therefore, you should view this not as the ideal model of a program but rather as what one program might look like.

REQUEST FOR INDIVIDUAL EDUCATIONAL
ASSESSMENT/RE-ASSESSMENT FORM

Student's Name: *Sebastian Wynott*   Age: *10-7*   Grade: *5*

School Building: *Sleepy Hollow Elementary*

Date of Conference: *3/15/75*   Teacher/Referrer: *Ms. Portia Streight*

Parent/s Name: *Olga & Ole Wynott*   Address: *114½ Plumb Ave.*

Phone: *CU2-0000*

Rationale For Assessment: *Sebbie has significant difficulty with academics and cannot attend to a task for any length of time. He cannot read any of the classroom material. What can be expected of him and should he be in a special program?*

Pre-assessment/Re-assessment Staffing Team Members (parents, etc.): *Mr. & Mrs. Ole Wynott (parents), Mr. Dilly Dillingham (principal), Ms. Portia Streight (5th grade teacher), Ms. Aggie Knolage (SLBP teacher).*

Objectives To Be Addressed (code to assessment team members):

1. *To determine his capability to learn and the most appropriate styles and modalities to be used in learning processes for him.*

2. *To determine his levels of reading in all components: comprehension, attack skills, etc.*

3. *To determine his levels of academic success in areas other than reading: math, science, spelling, etc.*

4. *To determine his levels of functioning in all areas of perceptual development.*

Assessment Team Members (code responsibility/objectives, when, where to be accomplished: *Ms. Wilma Reedit, Remedial Reading Teacher (2,3) — Dr. Yen, Optometrist (4)*

Mr. Herkimer Humperdinck, Psychologist (1,4)

Ms. Portia Streight, 5th Grade Teacher (1,2,3)

Ms. Aggie Knolage, SLBP Teacher (1,2,3,4)

☐ Additional Data on Attached Sheet.

Assessment: Summarization/Verification Date: *3/30/75*

I (we) consent to the individual educational assessment described above, in order to determine the educational needs of my (our) child.

Signature _____ *Mr. and Mrs. Ole Wynott* _____ Date *3/15/75*

(Parent/s-student)

---

[2] Sample IEP from Maynard C. Reynolds and Jack W. Birch in *Teaching Exceptional Children in All America's Schools,* Chapter 4 (Reston, Va.: The Council for Exceptional Children, 1977), pp. 164–71.

I (we) do not consent to the individual educational assessment described above, in order to determine the educational needs of my (our) child.

Signature _____ Date _____
(Parent/s-student)

If the Parent/s-Student Reject the Assessment, State the Reasons and an Acceptable Alternative:

The following RIGHTS and procedures MUST be reviewed prior to the conducting of the individual educational assessment:

> **Parent's-Student's rights to obtain an independent educational assessment records, information, and results.**

> **Parent's-Student's rights to obtain an independent educational assessment at their own expense.**

> **That Parent's-Student may request assistance in locating the names, addresses, etc., and fee structures of resources that they may go to for an independent educational assessment.**

> **That the student's educational status will not change unless the parent/s have signed the individual educational plan.**

> **That a "conciliation conference" may be requested if the parent/s-student refuse to permit the assessment.**

> **That an "impartial hearing" may be requested if mutual agreement is not reached after the conciliation conference.**

Any Objection Should Be Sent To: _____
(Administrator)

Any Objection Must Be Received By: _____
(date)

Address Objection Is To Be Sent To: _____

_____

Date Received: _____

Report Completed By: *Miss Aggie Knolage, Case Facilitator*

Copy of Report To Parent/Student: *3/15/75*   Parent/Student: _____O.W._____
(date received)   (initialed)

Case Management Log Updated: *3/15/75*   Update By: ___Aggie Knolage___
(name)

INDIVIDUAL EDUCATION ASSESSMENT REPORT

Student's Name: *Sebastian Wynott*

Assessment By: *Miss Aggie Knolage*   *SLBP Teacher*
(name)   (position)

School: *Sleepy Hollow Elementary*   Phone: *CU4-0002*

Date/s Assessment Conducted: *3/16, 18, 20/75*

Specific Objectives Addressed By Specialist:
All (1 thru 4): 1-capability to learn and styles/modalities of learning; 2-reading levels; 3-other academic success; 4-perceptual development.

RESULTS:

a. Indicate Assessment Setting and Materials Used:
Setting: Sleepy Hollow Elem. School — SLBP room and classroom. Instruments used: Informal observations and tests in classroom and resource room; Detroit Test of Learning Aptitude; Peabody Individual Achievement Test; Key Math Diagnostic Arithmetic Test; Durrell Analysis of Reading Difficulty.

b. Specific Results (indicate by number from "Specific Objectives To Be Addressed")

1. *Sebbie will need considerable help throughout all learning, emphasis on a tactile kinesthetic approach should be utilized both in the regular classroom and the resource room. Based on informal assessment Sebbie appears to be a very bright child that certainly has the capability to learn.*
2. *Based on the PIAT, the Durrell, and informal assessment, Sebbie is functioning approximately one year below grade placement. Major areas of difficulty were in listening comprehension, work recognition and analysis, hearing sounds in words, and phonic spelling of words.*
3. *Based on the PIAT, Key Math, and informal assessment, Sebbie is functioning approximately one year below grade placement in spelling, and approximately five months below in math. No attempt was made to measure other areas of academic achievement.*
4. *Based on the Detroit and informal assessment, Sebbie is noted to be having significant difficulty in areas of auditory discrimination and closure.*

c. Additional Comments and/or Recommendations For Additional Assessment(s)/Specialist(s) (specify objectives to be addressed).
Sebbie is very interested in athletics and finds a great deal of success in it, even though he is small. He should be encouraged to participate in any extra-curricular activities of the nature as well as at recess.
Additional assessment may be needed as to physiological and neurological factors.

d. Statement of Constraints On Performance Or On Special Learning Conditions.
Sebbie has difficulty listening and needs to have concrete visual clues presented to him at the same time. He needs concrete, specific directions and repetition of instructions within short time frames. Sebbie works best through direct involvement with tactile/kinesthetic approach.

e. Recommended Application Of Results In Performance Statements.
Sebbie should receive approximately one-third of his educational program from the resource programs. Provisions need to be made between the regular classroom and the resource rooms so that when Sebbie needs a break from the classroom he can go to the resource rooms to do his work. (This should not become a daily ongoing activity.) Sebbie should receive a special reading program provided by the remedial reading teacher dealing with specific skills in phonics and other word attack skills; listening skills, etc. He should be provided services by the SLBP program dealing with math, auditory skills, and attention. Within the classroom expectations should be matched with supplementary services

provided by the resource programs. Emphasis should be placed on a tactile/kinesthetic approach to learning. Verbal instructions should be short, to the point and reinforced with visual clues. Parents should be incorporated into the educational plan to help reinforce newly learned skills. This should not be a laborious task.

☐ Additional Data On Attached Sheet.

Signature: _____Aggie Knolage_____   Date: _____3/22/75_____
                  (specialist)   (completed)

Copy of Report To Parent/Student: *3/30/75*   Parent/Student_____O.W._____
                      (date received)   (initialed)

Case Management Log Updated: *3/30/75*   Update By: Aggie Knolage
                    (date)   (name)

INDIVIDUAL EDUCATIONAL ASSESSMENT/VERIFICATION STAFFING SUMMARY REPORT

Student's Name: *Sebastian Wynott*

Assessment Team Members (name, position, phone, address):

Ms. Wilma Reedit — Remedial Reading Teacher, CU4-0002, Sleepy Hollow Elem.

Ms. Aggie Knolage — SLBP Teacher, CU4-0002, Sleepy Hollow Elem.

Mr. Herkimer Humperdinck — Psychologist, CU2-4000, Sleepy Hollow Admin. Office

Ms. Portia Streight — 5th Grade Teacher, CU4-0002, Sleepy Hollow Elem.

Dr. Yen — Optometrist — CU2-40002, Medical Center of Sleepy Hollow

Date Of Meeting: *3/30/75*

Results — Specific Objectives (INDIVIDUAL ASSESSMENT REPORTS **MUST** BE ATTACHED)

1. *Sebbie is above average in intellectual functioning and will be functioning academically at grade level within two years as measured by group standardized achievement tests. Learning modalities that are not of a tactile/kinesthetic nature are extremely difficult for him. Visual clues should be used to reinforce any verbal directions.*

2. *Sebbie will make a minimum of at least three months growth by the end of the school year (June 10) in reading. Growth shall be measured based on pre-post assessment conducted by the remedial reading teacher. A special summer program in reading shall be developed and implemented for him, at the end of which he will have made an additional three months gain based on pre-post assessment conducted by the remedial reading teacher. At the conclusion of the summer program he will no longer be in need of special instruction in phonics and other word attack skills, as measured by sampling his oral reading and other appropriate assessment.*

3. *By the end of the year Sebbie will be completing his spelling tests each week, correctly spelling at least 14 of 20 words. Special help will be provided by his 5th grade teacher and reinforced by exercises at home with*

his parents. Through an individualized math program, Sebbie will be able to demonstrate three months growth in math by the end of the school year, which will be measured by the SLBP teacher with the Key Math Test. The parents will be given supplementary math materials to work with Sebbie during the summer to insure maintenance of the skills that he has gained prior to summer break. (Practice time will not interfere with his summer recreational activities.)

4. *Sebbie will be able to demonstrate four months growth on the ITPA in auditory skill development by the end of the school year, after receiving individualized instruction from the SLBP teacher.*

5. *By the end of the school year, Sebbie will not be leaving his seat without prior permission. After that time he will be held accountable to a plan that has been agreed to by himself and his teacher/s.*

☐ Additional Summarization Data On Attached Sheet:

Report Completed By: *Aggie Knolage, Case Facilitator*

Copy Of Report To Parent/Student: *3/30/75*   Parent/Student: <u>O.W.</u>
                                   (date received)   (initialed)

Case Management Log Updated: *3/30/75*   Updated By: *Aggie Knolage*
                             (date received)   (name)

Additional Comments: *The parents are very concerned that no matter what plan is developed that it be carried out and not forgotten about. They have requested that the providers of the program meet with them on at least a monthly basis to review progress and to re-address what they can do to help. Concentration of academics shall be on reading, math, and spelling.*

INDIVIDUAL EDUCATION PLAN

Student's Name: *Sebastian Wynott*   Date Completed: *3/30/75*

Assessment Team Members (name, position, phone, address):
Ms. Wilma Reedit — Remedial Reading Teacher, CU4-0002, Sleepy Hollow Elem.
Ms. Aggie Knolage — SLBP Teacher, CU4-0002, Sleepy Hollow Elem.
Mr. Herkimer Humperdinck — Psychologist, CU2-4000, Sleepy Hollow Admin. Office
Ms. Portia Streight — 5th Grade Teacher, CU4-0002, Sleepy Hollow Elem.
Dr. Yen — Optometrist, CU2-4002, Medical Center of Sleepy Hollow

Description Of Needs: *Sebbie has a prolonged history of poor academic achievement: difficulty with auditory discrimination and closure, reading and spelling levels, year below grade placement, doesn't complete assignments, and can't seem to sit still in classroom.*

Learning Style/Modality: *Sebbie learns best with concrete materials and a tactile/kinesthetic approach. Verbal instructions should be in short time frames and reinforced with visual clues; it may be necessary to repeat several times.*

Measurable Physical Constraints: *Auditory discrimination and closure appears to be the basis of the majority of Sebbie's problems.*

Statement Of Specific Type Of Service Needed: *Sebbie will need special supplementary instruction in reading which shall be supplied by the remedial reading teacher (a summer program shall be supplied). He will receive special help from his regular teacher in the area of spelling and completion of appropriate assignments. The SLBP teacher will supply special help to Sebbie in the areas of math and auditory discrimination and closure. A joint program will be worked out by his classroom teacher, the remedial reading teacher and the SLBP teacher dealing with his staying in his seat, etc.*

Annual Goals: *Sebbie will be able to demonstrate the following gains within 12 months.*
1. *No problem with being out of his seat without prior permission.*
2. *In reading a 12 month gain in functional level.*
3. *In math to be functioning within 2 months of grade level.*
4. *In spelling to be within 4 months of grade level.*
5. *In auditory development to be within 4 months of his age level.*

Short Term Objectives With Criteria For Attainment (first 3 months):
1. *By June 10, Sebbie will not leave his seat more than twice per day without prior permission of the teacher. The teacher will keep appropriate charts of his behavior.*
2. *By June 10, after receiving remedial reading instruction, Sebbie will demonstrate at least a 3 month growth in reading level based on pre-post assessment as measured by the remedial reading teacher.*
3. *By June 10, Sebbie will be able to demonstrate at least a 3 month growth in math skills as measured by pre-post assessment on the Key Math Test. The SLBP teacher will be responsible for carrying out the supplementary services in math.*
4. *By June 10, Sebbie will consistently complete his spelling tests and spell correctly at least 14 of 20 words on each weekly test. His regular classroom teacher shall be responsible for supplying supplementary instruction in the area of spelling.*
5. *By June 10, Sebbie will demonstrate a minimum of 4 months growth based on pre-post assessment on the ITPA, after having received special help from the SLBP teacher.*

Long-Term Objectives With Criteria For Attainment (beyond 3 months for school year): *Objectives 1, 4, and 5 will be further addressed in the new educational plan that will be developed in Sept.*
2. *By Sept. 1, after receiving special reading instruction throughout the summer, Sebbie will demonstrate a 6 month gain (from this date 3/30/ 75) in reading as measured by pre-post assessment administered by the remedial reading teacher.*
3. *By Sept. 1, Sebbie will demonstrate that he has maintained the 3 months growth that he had achieved by June 1, through a maintenance program carried out by his parents during the summer. This level of achievement shall be demonstrated by pre-post assessment on the Key Math Test.*

Special Instructional Materials/Supplies/Equipment:
None —

Other Specific Modifications: *Approximately one-third of his individual educational plan shall be carried out in the resource rooms. A special program in reading will be carried out during the summer. The parents will be given special materials to use during the summer to insure that Sebbie maintains his math skills.*

Specify Means Of Coordination With Other Programs (regular classroom, etc.): *SLBP remedial reading and regular classroom teachers will meet at least weekly to review progress on the instructional objectives and to further coordinate activities. Each specialist will spend at least 20 minutes per week in the regular classroom providing assistance in Sebbie's program. Monthly meetings will be held with the parents.*

Personnel Responsible For Providing Service — Include Telephone Numbers, Addresses, etc. (regular classroom teacher, etc.):
Ms. Aggie Knolage — SLBP Teacher, CU4-0002, Sleepy Hollow Elem.
Ms. Wilma Reedit — Remedial Reading Teacher, CU4-0002, Sleepy Hollow Elem.
Ms. Portia Streight — 5th Grade Teacher, CU4-0002, Sleepy Hollow Elem.

Location Of Program To Carry Out Plan: *Sleepy Hollow Elem. School — regular classroom and resource rooms.*

Describe Transportation Plan If Needed: *None*

Program Will Begin: *4/1/75* Number Of Days Per Week/Month/Year: *5 days/week; 20 days/month; for the remainder of the year — 48 days.*
Daily Duration Of Plan: *2 hrs. 20 minutes per day*

Method And Frequency Of Initial And Periodic Reviews (dates, etc.):
Assessment Team Members — Initial Review — 6/9/75
Ongoing monitoring of program with parents and teachers — at least monthly.

Description of Integrated Educational Activities (must be included when the student's primary placement is in special education):
Not pertinent

I (we) consent to the individual educational plan described above.

Signature: __Mr. and Mrs. Ole Wynott__ Date: *3/30/75*
(Parent/s-student)

I (we) do not consent to the Individual educational plan described above.

Signature: _____ Date: _____
(Parent/s-student)

If The Parent/s-Student Reject The Individual Educational Plan, State the Reason And An Acceptable Alternative:

Report Completed By: *Aggie Knolage, Case Facilitator*

Copy Of Report To Parent/Student: *3/30/75* Parent/Student: __O.W.__
(date received)   (initialed)

Case Management Log Updated: *3/30/75* Updated By: *Aggie Knolage*
(date)   (name)

The preceding is a set of sample forms that were developed by the staff of the Wasioja Area Special Education Cooperative in Minnesota. They include forms for *requesting* an individual educational assessment, for *reporting* assessment findings, and for *recording* an individual education program. Should this responsibility seem strange or difficult to you, the beginning teacher, you may find the following ideas comforting. First, these requirements are equally strange to most experienced teachers who seldom, if ever, have been required to keep any type of individualized instruction plan for any students. Second, it may be helpful to remember that the purpose of the plan is to assure help for the student; therefore, there is a place for good, common judgment.

Since each IEP is a cooperative effort involving parents, it will be to your advantage if you take care to keep the parents informed at every stage and solicit input of parents' ideas, including their suggestions and reactions. You should assure the parents that, should part of the plan prove inoperable or ineffective, you will recommend changing it so as to serve their child better. You should also ask the parents to keep you informed as to how the plan is working at home. A "we" approach will enable you to minimize any resistance that you might get from parents and to maximize the cooperation that you can solicit. This is especially important, for this is a team-type project in which you will actually need the suggestions of the parents.

To further enhance your relationship with parents, you should remind them that they have complete access to their child's records. You should give them copies of each report, and explain exactly how the assessments are being made. Whenever possible, you should make the parents team members in the diagnosis, treatment, and education processes. Have a positive attitude: Be sure that the parents understand the abilities and assets of their child. Emphasize the things that he can do rather than those he cannot do. Furthermore, you should help the parents learn to influence their child to think positively about himself. They should also help others who might work with their child to focus on his strengths and assets.

For years we have known of the many values that come from involving parents of students at all ages in their education. In recent years we have discovered many advantages that come from drawing students into the planning of their own educational experiences. Now we have the opportunity (and responsibility) to involve both parties thoroughly and realistically in the planning, administering, and evaluation of these needed special programs. While we may find the record keeping somewhat of a hassle, there is no doubt that we shall learn a great deal about individualizing instruction as we participate in IEP's. Surely most teachers will be willing to do whatever is necessary to help handicapped students profit from their instruction.

As a beginning teacher, you will be given assistance by experienced personnel in completing your first IEP's. Your introduction to them in this book should be helpful. It will be your responsibility to learn as much as you can about P.L. 94–142 during your clinical experiences and when you begin teaching. Once employed, you will continue learning about this law as it changes and about similar laws as they emerge.

TEACHING THE GIFTED

One of the most neglected groups of students in American schools today are those students whose abilities are unusually high — the gifted students. According to the U.S. Commissioner of Education, "Gifted children are frequently overlooked in our schools. A review of current educational practices shows that the majority of public schools need to do more to meet the needs of this special group of children."[3] The average classroom of thirty-five students today has two gifted students,[4] but very little money is spent to provide programs for them. Annually $6.5 million is allotted to the gifted students as compared to $600 million to the handicapped and a staggering $2 billion to the economically disadvantaged.[5] Obviously the gifted have been ignored in recent years, and their unique needs have not been attended to by any of the many new programs that have emerged to provide for other groups of needy students.

While we would like to believe that the practice of ignoring the gifted was not intentional, there is evidence to suggest that their neglect was purposeful. Working against programs for the gifted are the following attitudes:

1. The programs are undemocratic.
2. They are unpopular with parents of those children who are not identified as being gifted, and those children always compose the majority of the school population.
3. There is fear that special provision for the gifted will hamper improvement of general education for all.
4. The gifted already have many advantages, and this will enable them to outdistance the average child further and to obtain a number of exclusive opportunities.
5. Some feel that any extra effort and money should be used for the benefit of those who are handicapped.
6. The gifted are able to take care of themselves without any extra assistance.[6]

Opposition to programs for the gifted includes other reasons:

1. Programs for the gifted and talented reinforce the segregation of students.
2. The utilization of individualized instruction abolishes the need for separate programs for the gifted and talented.
3. Overemphasizing the gifted and talented through a special program creates an elitist population.
4. What is good for the gifted and talented is good for all children.

---

[3] Ernest L. Boyer, "What's Right with Our Schools?" *Ohio Schools* 41 (September 1978): 15.

[4] James J. Alvins and Theodore Jo Gourley, "The Challenge of Our Gifted Children," *Teacher* 96 (December 1977): 45.

[5] Barbara J. Stevens, "What about That Other Special Education?" *Pennsylvania School Journal* 126 (October 1977): 32.

[6] L. L'Abate and L. T. Curtis, *Teaching the Exceptional Child* (Philadelphia: W. B. Saunders, 1975): 409.

5. If classroom teachers were doing their job, there would be no need to offer a special program for the gifted.
6. What is offered to the gifted should be commensurate with what is offered to the students in other special education programs.[7]

Some teachers and administrators think that it is undemocratic to give bright students special attention; and other teachers, resenting the bright, superior student's competency, enforce egalitarianism as a sort of equalizer.[8] Many other educators, though, have begun questioning such purposeful neglect of this group of special students. There is historical precedent, too; even Thomas Jefferson, the greatest proponent of free education for *all* students, advocated special education provisions and settings for students of more able learning capability.[9] Throughout the nineteenth century, private schools for the intellectually elite proliferated in New England and the South. The first systematic provision of special programs for the gifted in the public school setting was in the St. Louis school system in 1868.[10] The first federal legislation for the gifted student was the 1958 National Defense Education Act, which provided loans for them to pursue higher education.[11] Only two years later the United States Office of Education began operating "Project Talent" programs to stimulate discovery and development of national human resources. In 1969 Public Law 91-230 mandated a report on education of gifted and talented from the U.S. Office of Education Commissioner to Congress.

Who Are the Gifted?

In the past we tended to use I.Q. to identify the gifted; however, recent studies suggest that this method overlooks some gifted students who do not have the aspiration or motivation needed to score highly on these tests. Unfortunately there are few measuring devices other than available tests; therefore, most schools and researchers continue to use standardized intelligence tests.

Some authors insist that the term *gifted* should be reserved to indicate students who are highly motivated as well as capable. One author provides the following definition: "The gifted student is likely to have above-average language development, persistence in attacking difficult mental tasks, the ability to generalize and see relationships, unusual curiosity, and a wide variety of deep interests."[12] Other authors who accept a broad definition of the gifted still consider only the high performers on intelligence tests in their programs

---

[7] S. Kaplan, *Providing Programs for the Gifted and Talented: A Handbook* (Ventura, Calif.: Office of the Ventura County Superintendent of Schools, 1974), pp. 7–8, 93, 123.

[8] N. Cutts and N. Moseley, *Teaching the Bright and Gifted* (Englewood Cliffs, N.J.: Prentice-Hall, 1957).

[9] W. K. Durr, *The Gifted Student* (New York: Oxford University Press, 1964).

[10] P. Witty, *The Gifted Child* (Boston: D. C. Heath and Company, 1951).

[11] B. Johnson, ed., "Federal Legislative History on Gifted and Talented," *Bulletin* (1976): 2.

[12] W. K. Durr, *The Gifted Student* (New York: Oxford University Press, 1964).

for the gifted.[13] Whatever the current definition of the gifted is, the best method for identifying the gifted is, at least at this time, the individual intelligence test.[14]

Throughout the years the gifted have been victimized by such false stereotypes as the social misfit, or the weird, mad scientist. Like all other people, the gifted feel a need to utilize their talents. When the teacher does not challenge students or provide opportunity for them to use their abilities, like all other students they are apt to become frustrated.

As a teacher, you will want to find different materials and assign different tasks to challenge these students. The traditional practices of giving them the same assignments — and, perhaps even worse, assigning them more of the same problems — must be replaced by activities that will capture their interests and challenge their intellects. Many school systems have specially trained professional personnel to work with programs for the gifted. Find out if your school or school system has such a person and inquire about any testing programs for identifying gifted students. The first single responsibility that you have to these students is in identifying them. Then, of course, you must either try to provide adequate challenges or see that someone else does.

TEACHING THE UNDERACHIEVER

Underachievers are those students with high intellectual or academic potential but whose performance falls in the middle third in scholastic achievement, or worse — in the lowest third. Few educators realize the degree of seriousness of this problem. It is serious for several reasons. First, the percentage of gifted students who are achieving far below their abilities is staggering. One study found that over half of the highly gifted students work well below their abilities.[15] The tremendous waste in potential is enough to prompt serious concern.

A second reason for concern is that these gifted students who are achieving below their abilities academically are also contributing socially below their abilities.[16] Thus, there is a further waste of human resources. Still another reason for concern about underachievers is that once gifted students begin to perform below their ability, the trend is difficult to reverse. It quickly becomes accepted as "a way of life."[17]

---

[13] R. De Haan and R. Havinghurst, *Educating Gifted Children* (Chicago: University of Chicago Press, 1961), pp. 15, 18.

[14] J. J. Gallagher, *Teaching the Gifted Child* (Boston: Allyn and Bacon, 1975), pp. 20–21, 312.

[15] John B. Milner, *Intelligence in the United States* (New York: Springer Publishing Company, 1957).

[16] T. Ernest Newland, *The Gifted in Socio-Educational Perspective* (Englewood Cliffs, N.J.: Prentice-Hall, 1976).

[17] Alison Heinemann, "Module 6: Underachievers Among the Gifted/Talented," *STAR POWER: Providing for the Gifted* (Austin, Tex.: Educational Service Center, Region XIII, 1977), p. 4.

Underachievers, like all special students, must first be identified by the teacher before help can be given to them. You may find this recognition more difficult than it seems, since underachievers are frequently mistaken as low-ability students. One teacher inservice program lists the following characteristics of gifted underachievers. You may find it useful in helping you identify underachievers in your future classrooms.

1. Belligerent toward classmates and others.
2. Extremely defensive (given to rationalizing, ad-libbing, excusing failures, lying).
3. Fearful of failure and of attempting new tasks because of the likelihood of failure.
4. Resentful of criticism, yet likely to be highly critical of others.
5. Prone to habitual procrastination, dawdling, daydreaming, sulking, brooding.
6. Frequently absent.
7. Inattentive — wriggling, doodling, whispering.
8. Suspicious, distrustful of overtures of affection.
9. Rebellious.
10. Negative about own abilities.[18]

No individual displays all these characteristics simultaneously, but a student who shows several at one time should be investigated.

Some of the likely causes of underachievement are physical limitations such as poor vision or hearing, learning disabilities, and even social maladjustments. Often low performance results from low expectations at home and school; these eventually lead to low expectations by the student. But to be sure that a particular student is indeed performing well below ability, you must check previous performance records or report cards and standardized examinations. For example, a student who is making C's but has stanine scores of 8's and 9's is clearly performing far below his or her ability.

Assisting the Underachiever

Once you have identified the underachievers in your classes, you have many approaches to helping them improve their performance, academically and socially. You may wish to consider using some of the following:

1. Special guidance for underachievers to develop positive self-concepts.
2. Extensive use of films and captioned filmstrips instead of textbooks; also use of taped lessons to improve listening/thinking/reading skills.
3. First-hand experiences to stimulate and motivate (especially for students from disadvantaged background; remember that middle-class Anglo stu-

---

[18] Ibid.

dents may come from such backgrounds, as well as the poor and some minority students).

4. Adjustment of assignments and teaching methods to individual interests and abilities of pupils, relating to hoped-for or established goals, whether personal or academic.
5. Teacher-pupil planning sessions of work to be covered.
6. Tutoring by willing and able senior citizens who can provide the warmth and understanding, the kind of encouragement and praise often missing at home.
7. Special opportunity class for underachievers of mixed ages with similar problems working out of the regular class, even out of the regular school where possible, for at least part of the day.
8. Group therapy with a warm, understanding counselor or teacher to discuss freely any fears, frustrations, angers.
9. Team approach to working with underachievers who are gifted/talented, including the teacher(s), parent(s), a counselor, perhaps at times the student.
10. Use of grades and tests *only* as measures of progress and thus as indicators of areas needing additional work.
11. Instruction in how to learn (how to concentrate, how to remember, how to understand and follow directions, use keywords, etc.).
12. Instruction in problem-solving techniques and inquiry method.[19]

SUMMARY

Special education provides experiences for those students who cannot develop to their potentials without special programs. There are currently over eight million handicapped children in this country who need special help. Public Law 94–142 requires that teachers make a special individualized program for each handicapped student. Ideally, the teacher, parent, and (whenever feasible) student should work together to develop the plan and evaluate the student's progress, and revise as needed. This mainstreaming movement is based on the supposition that handicapped learners can learn best in class with non-handicapped students if provided with a special program designed to meet their particular needs.

In working with handicapped students, you should remember that three things are of utmost importance: (1) the degree of seriousness of the handicap, (2) how long the student has had the handicap, and (3) the stability of the condition. Success in any program will depend on your ability to work with the student and parents, asking for and using their suggestions in designing and revising the student's program. Besides accepting the student's disability, you should help the student, parents, and others to do so, and you should especially seek out those who are in positions to offer services to the student.

---

[19] Ibid.

Avoiding labels is a good approach to learning to accept each student as a person.

EXPERIENCES

This chapter considered your role in working with students who have special education needs. Since the types of student needs are so many, no chapter could introduce all (or even most) of the skills a teacher needs to help these students. To extend your introduction of that role, the following experiences are included.

Experience 1: An Explosive Experience

Shirley Norton was excited about her new teaching assignment. She had edged out forty other applicants for the one vacancy in the physical education department at Sherwood High. Her first day started off with a rush. By noon she was so tired that she hardly tasted the cafeteria food that she was consuming all too rapidly.

When Shirley reentered the gym, she found one of her seniors, Debbie Stratemeyer, breaking out the windows. She was running, screaming, and crying hysterically as she punched out the panes with a broom handle. Shirley recognized the girl as one of her students who was playing volleyball (when she had become very upset) just before lunch. Approaching Debbie, Shirley asked her to hand over the broom. This proved to be a big mistake, for Debbie whirled around and began hitting her, swearing with every breath. Just as Shirley thought that her time had come, Debbie dropped the broom, collapsed on the floor, and began sobbing.

As perplexed as she was shocked, Shirley was relieved to see one of the senior P.E. teachers enter the room and take over the situation as though it were just another part of her job.

▶ *Questions and Discussion*

1. *How should a teacher approach a student who is behaving frantically and irrationally?*
   Very carefully. When people are in such a state, their behavior is unpredictable. This was evidenced by Debbie's attacking a new teacher, whom she hardly knew.

2. *What should Shirley do about this incident?*
   Obviously this girl needs help. Shirley might begin by checking Debbie's cumulative record for previous similar incidents. The school (or school system) psychologist should be apprised of the incident. If no psychologist is available, the school counselor should be informed. If the school has neither a psychologist or counselor, the principal should be alerted. Otherwise, Shirley will pose a threat to herself and to her classmates and teachers.

Experience 2:   An Introduction to Mainstreaming

After teaching social studies for three years, Dave no longer thought of himself as a novice teacher; and he had had a few unusual and challenging close encounters with parents. At the beginning of Dave's fourth year, Arnold Swartz transferred to Edison High and was assigned to Dave's social studies class. Arnold was classified as mildly retarded, and from the very beginning it was obvious that he could not meet the demands that Dave made of all students. Dave asked that Arnold be removed from the class, but the principal refused to transfer him to another section. Dave then decided to ignore Arnold, for, after all, the education of the other twenty-eight students should not be sacrificed. Arnold seemed content, and everything was working well until the first report cards were sent home.

That evening Arnold's mother, very upset, telephoned Dave. Arnold had received a *D−* in social studies, and there was no explanation as to why he had done so poorly. Dave wanted to tell her that her son was incapable of doing any better, but he knew that Mrs. Swartz was already aware of her son's limitations. Before the conversation ended, Dave and Mrs. Swartz agreed to meet with the principal. Dave would then explain exactly what he was doing (or failing to do) to help Arnold. As he went to bed that evening, Dave wondered how his principal would react and what a teacher could do to help a boy like Arnold.

▶ *Questions and Discussion*

1. *Was Dave wrong in wanting to give his time and energy to those students who could benefit most?*
   Surely a teacher's desire to experience success with his students is admirable; however, each teacher is responsible for the intellectual growth of *all* of his or her students. Dave was wrong in neglecting a student who found learning more difficult.

2. *What alternative does Dave have if Mrs. Swartz insists on meeting with him periodically to discuss the progress of her son?*
   Legally Dave has no alternative to such an arrangement. Professionally he should welcome such visits.

3. *What if Mrs. Swartz demands special attention for her son? Will Dave have to make exceptions for Arnold just because he is different?*
   Since this difference threatens Arnold's learning, yes, Dave will have to make out an Individualized Education Program and he will have to implement and coordinate the design and utilization of the plan.

In recent years it has been recognized that all teachers should know more about those students who differ significantly from most of their classmates. Some of these are brighter; some are slower. Some are physically handicapped; others are emotionally handicapped. All teachers now deal with students in all these categories. Instead of ignoring them or separating them from their "normal peers," teachers will alter the classroom to accommodate these individuals. The following activities are offered to help you begin to answer this question: How will *you* provide for the special students in your classes?

1. Since most classes contain students whose IQ's range from considerably below average to well above average, how will you attempt to meet the needs of the students on both ends of this continuum? Include a few strategies for simplifying content and making it more concrete. Also include a few techniques for challenging the bright students.
2. Suppose you recognize a handicapped student in your class. Describe, step by step, how you will attain information about this student.

SUGGESTED READINGS

DE HAAN, R., and HAVINGHURST, R. *Educating Gifted Children.* Chicago: University of Chicago Press, 1961.

DURR, W. K. *The Gifted Student.* New York: Oxford University Press, 1964.

GALLAGHER, J. J. *Teaching the Gifted Child.* Boston: Allyn and Bacon, 1975.

————. "On Educating the Gifted." *Educational Forum* 44 (January 1980): 245–46.

KIRK, SAMUEL A. *Educating Exceptional Children.* Boston: Houghton Mifflin, 1972.

L'ABATE, L., and CURTIS, L. T. *Teaching the Exceptional Child.* Philadelphia: W. B. Saunders, 1975.

LOVE, HAROLD D. *Educating Exceptional Children in a Changing Society.* Springfield, Ill.: Charles C. Thomas, 1974.

NEWLAND, T. ERNEST. *The Gifted in Socio-Educational Perspective.* Englewood Cliffs, N.J.: Prentice-Hall, 1976.

Teaching in Multicultural Settings

OBJECTIVES

When you finish this chapter, you should be able to:

1. Name three characteristics of American high schools that make success especially difficult for members of other cultures.
2. Devise a grading system that will not force individuals to compete with their classmates.
3. Give two approaches for building positive self-images.
4. Devise a daily lesson plan that will identify and exalt the unique characteristics of several cultures.
5. Explain the significance of the 1975 *Lau* v. *Nichols* Supreme Court decision.
6. List ten things a teacher of a multicultural group should do to adjust to the students.
7. List ten things a teacher of a multicultural group should avoid doing.
8. Create a one-hour simulation activity that will enable all students in a classroom to experience different cultural roles.

Unfortunately many of our stereotypes of other cultures, often based on ethnic jokes, are inaccurate; nevertheless, each cultural group does have its unique characteristics. The language and customs differences often form learning barriers in the American school classroom. Yet, "despite millions of dollars spent on special programs aimed at raising the educational performance of children from minority groups, no one has really been able to effectively reverse the disappointing results." [1]

But how much can teachers do? And exactly what can they do? Hopefully a great deal; for the teacher is the only one who can bring significant improvement to the education of minorities. American schools have several unique fea-

---

[1] Ida Santos Stewart, "Cultural Differences Between Anglos and Chicanos," *Integration* 8 (November–December 1975): 21–23.

tures that make success difficult for the multiculturals.[2] First, our schools are so large that they appear impersonal to immigrants. Teachers tend to be overly obsessed with tests and grades and too concerned with competition. Furthermore, we sell minority students short and underestimate their abilities to succeed and to contribute.

A POSITIVE APPROACH

To many students and teachers the term *multicultural* has a negative connotation: it brings forth the idea of problems. This unfortunate idea may actually cause the problems. In other words if you, a teacher, interpret multicultural settings as being problem-prone, then you may approach such classes skeptically. In turn, your students will sense this and will not trust you. If, on the other hand, you view the multicultural setting as an opportunity to increase your own knowledge and to enrich your own sense of values, you will find the assignment to be a rewarding experience.

PERSONALIZING OUR TEACHING

Our population in this country has become very mobile, with one family in five moving each year; both the large and the small schools have student popu-

---

[2] Kenneth T. Henson, "American Schools vs. Cultural Pluralism," *Educational Leadership* (March 1975): 405–8.

lations from many cultural backgrounds. Even in the small school, it is important that teachers recognize and exalt cultural differences. They need to make students of all ethnic backgrounds, economic backgrounds, and educational backgrounds feel proud of their cultures and capable of applying their uniqueness to strengthen our country.

No matter where you accept a teaching position, you will find cultural differences, whether in affluent suburbs, working-class urban neighborhoods, or rural areas. In areas where most students are of a similar ethnic background or economic class, there will still be pronounced differences in religious backgrounds. As long as there is one student whose background is different, your need for skills in working with culturally mixed classrooms will always be there.

In our larger schools, where the problems are often accentuated, the students are so numerous that even getting to know all of them is difficult. But, in a sense, the challenge and need to personalize is even greater; otherwise, members of similar cultural backgrounds tend to form cliques, which can be hotbeds for prejudice. This, of course, does not refer to organized clubs, but rather to the informal cliques that gather in parking lots, hallways and cafeterias with no constructive purposes. You can contribute to the dissolving of such groups by getting to know each student in your classes on a more personal level and by volunteering to sponsor clubs for students of similar varying backgrounds. International clubs are excellent for acquainting students with other cultures.

Perhaps you have noticed that all of these recommended techniques are equally applicable in all classes, multicultural or not. This is certainly correct. Most students, irrespective of their cultural background, would profit more if

their classes were personalized, if competition among students were reduced, and if realistic demands were made of all. However, children from other cultures are different in several specific ways, and you must be aware of these differences.

A group of teachers interested in discovering the strengths of various minority ethnic students surveyed teachers throughout much of South Florida, identifying two thousand strengths.[3] An analysis of these returns showed that the children were generally:

Highly responsive to affection	Independent
Physically dextrous	Imitative
Protective of siblings	Uninhibited
Academically persevering	Emotionally cool
Musically oriented	Monetarily proficient
Artistic	Rich in humor
Authority minded	Competitive
Resourceful	Forgiving

Being aware of these qualities can be helpful to you in designing learning experiences for multicultural classes, but resist the temptation to build yet another stereotype for all multicultural children. Each student is an individual and, as such, may possess all or none of these traits. This list is included because it gives you a beginning point for analyzing your multicultural students. And this is how you should begin — by analyzing the *strengths* of each individual student.

A REASON FOR OPTIMISM

In the *Lau* v. *Nichols* case the Supreme Court mandated that all U.S. schools having twenty or more pupils who speak a common first language other than English provide systematic instruction in that language.[4] Clearly this emphasis is going to alter many schools; however, this or any other federal mandate is in itself inadequate. It must be through the concern, skills, and efforts of the teacher that the needs of minority students are met. But exactly what is the teacher's role?

THE TEACHER'S DECISION

Actually, we are fortunate to have multicultural classes. Schooling should be learning about life — it must be. And life is multicultural. While all multi-

---

[3] Arnold B. Cheyney, *Teaching Children of Different Cultures in the Classroom* (Columbus, Ohio: Charles E. Merrill, 1976), pp. 41–42.
[4] *Lau* v. *Nichols,* U.S. 563,19S. Ct. 786.

cultural classes have some unique problems, they also offer pupils the chance to learn about contemporary life. These advantages do not emerge so quickly as the problems do; but you should first commit yourself to the enjoyment of, and capitalizing upon, cultural differences in your classes.[5] It is a matter of teacher attitude.

If you stop to consider cultural differences, surely you will realize that all children are members of some group that is rich in heritage. We should not feel that only the minority pupils are culturally disadvantaged; for, if the Anglo fails to understand the richness of a minority student's background, it is the Anglo who is culturally disadvantaged. The teacher who views a multicultural classroom as a positive environment for overall pupil learning will help erase some of each pupil's cultural ignorance. All people tend to fear and distrust that which they do not understand; as a teacher, you can do much to correct this misunderstanding. In working with the multiculturals, you cannot help but know that there are differences; hopefully you will also realize that, basically, children are children.[6]

SOME DO'S AND DON'T'S

Consider each of the following recommendations as an excellent guide to your teaching in multicultural classrooms.[7]

DO'S:

1. Do use the same scientific approach to gain background information on the culture of multiethnic groups as you would to tackle a complicated course in science, mathematics, or any subject area in which you might be deficient.
2. Do engage in systematic study of the disciplines that provide insight into the cultural heritage, political struggle, contributions, and present-day problems of minority groups.
3. Do try to develop sincere personal relationships with minorities. *You can't teach strangers!* Don't give up because *one* black or other minority person rejects your efforts. All groups have sincere individuals who welcome honest, warm relationships with members of another race. Seek out those who will accept or tolerate you. This coping skill is one that minorities have always used.
4. Do recognize that there are often more differences within a group than

---

[5] Kenneth T. Henson and Marvin A. Henry, *Becoming Involved in Teaching* (Terre Haute, Ind.: Sycamore Press, 1976), p. 164.

[6] Cheyney, *Teaching Children of Different Cultures*, p. iii.

[7] Martha E. Dawson, ed., *Are There Unwelcome Guests in Your Classroom?* (Washington, D.C.: Association for Childhood Education International, 1974), pp. 53–54. Reprinted by permission of Martha E. Dawson and the Association for Childhood Education International, 3615 Wisconsin Avenue, N.W., Washington, D.C. Copyright © 1974 by the Association.

between two groups. If we recognize diversity among races, we must also recognize diversity within groups.

5. Do remember that there are many ways to gain insight into a group. Visit their churches, homes, communities; read widely and listen to various segments of the group.

6. Do remember that no one approach and no one answer will assist you in meeting the educational needs of all children in a multicultural society.

7. Do select instructional materials that are accurate and free of stereotypes.

8. Do remember that there is a positive relationship between teacher expectation and academic progress.

9. Do provide an opportunity for minority group boys and girls and students from the mainstream to interact in a positive intellectual setting on a continuous basis.

10. Do use a variety of materials and especially those that utilize positive, true-to-life experiences.

11. Do provide some structure and direction to children who have unstructured lives, primarily children of the poor.

12. Do expose all students to a wide variety of literature as a part of your cultural sensitivity program.

13. "Do remember that in spite of the fact that ethnic groups often share many common problems their specific needs are diverse." *

14. "Do utilize the rich resources within your own classroom among various cultural groups." *

15. Do remember that human understanding is a lifetime endeavor. You must continue to study and provide meaningful experiences for your pupils.

16. "Do remember to be honest with yourself. If you can't adjust to children from multicultural homes get out of the classroom." *

DON'T'S:

1. Don't rely on school textbooks, teachers' guides, and brief essays to become informed on minorities. Research and resources will be needed.

2. Don't use ignorance as an excuse for not having any insight into the problems and culture of Blacks, Chicanos, Native Americans, Puerto Ricans, Asian Americans, and other minorities.

3. Don't rely on the "expert" judgment of one minority person for the answer to all the complicated racial and social problems of his/her people. For example, Blacks, Mexicans, Indians, and Puerto Ricans hold various political views on all issues.

4. Don't be fooled by popular slogans and propaganda intended to raise the national consciousness of an oppressed people.

5. Don't get carried away with the "save the world concept." Most minorities have their own savior.

6. Don't be afraid to learn from those who are more familiar with the mores and cultures than you.

7. Don't assume that you have all the answers for solving the other man's problems. It is almost impossible for an outsider to be an expert on the culture of another group.

8. Don't assume that all minority group children are culturally deprived.

9. Don't develop a fatalistic attitude about the progress of minority group pupils.

10. Don't resegregate pupils through tracking and ability grouping gimmicks.

11. Don't give up when minority group pupils seem to hate school.

12. Don't assume that minorities are the only pupils who should have multicultural instructional materials. Children in the mainstream can be culturally deprived in terms of their knowledge and understanding of other people and their own heritage.

13. Don't go around asking parents and children personal questions in the name of research. Why must they divulge their suffering? It is obvious.

14. Don't get hung up on grade designation when sharing literature that provides insight into the cultural heritage of a people.

15. "Don't try to be cool by using the vernacular of a particular racial group." *

16. Don't make minority children feel ashamed of their language, dress, or traditions.

These suggestions are included as general guidelines to help the teacher whose class has members of one or more minority ethnic groups. Since, from time to time, you and all teachers will have some representatives of other cultures in class, these suggestions should be appropriate for all. One additional suggestion — perhaps so obvious that it may be overlooked — is to resist the temptation to make quick generalizations about any culture. Guidelines such as these are generalities based on volumes of data; but, even when you use such scientifically derived guidelines, remember that, irrespective of culture, all students are individuals and their individuality should be respected.

SELECTING ETHNIC MATERIALS

Special materials for multiethnic groups should not be difficult to find, since more than half of the states in the country require multiethnic programs and the development of multiethnic materials.[8] In selecting materials for teaching about ethnicity — and, in fact, for all materials to be used in multicultured settings — do not automatically assume that different ethnic groups need elementary or remedial materials. The following system has been designed to help teachers select multiethnic materials at the appropriate levels of complexity, depending on the objectives of the unit.[9]

---

* Helpful suggestions of "Do's and Don't's" were made by Delores Fitzgerald and Robin Kovats of St. Paul the Apostle School and Raven Oas Burvard of St. Columbia School, both in New York City.

[8] Frank Klassen and Donna Gollnick, *Pluralism and the American Teacher* (Washington, D.C.: American Association of Colleges of Teacher Education, 1977), p. 137.

[9] Special credit and thanks is given to Dr. Jesus Garcia and Dr. Ricardo Garcia for the use of this classification system, which was taken from their article "Selecting Ethnic Materials for the Elementary School," *Social Education* 44 (March 1980): 232–36.

LEVEL I MATERIALS. Low in complexity, these materials are designed to highlight the achievement of all ethnic groups. Such material includes biographies and success stories of ethnic Americans. They are usually highly complimentary; in fact, they often exaggerate. They are very attractive and conspicuously displayed in the classroom by teachers. They should be used sparingly and selectively.

LEVEL II MATERIALS. These materials depict "true/real" experiences of ethnic groups. Problems of the group are shown in such a way as to suggest that members of other groups, such as the majority ethnic, are responsible, but without specifying who the others are. The use of these materials should be limited.

LEVEL III MATERIALS. These materials show the historical experiences of more than one ethnic group. Portrayals are limited to racial groups (Blacks, Hispanics, Native Americans) or white groups (Irish Americans, Italian Americans, or Polish Americans), but not both. A common approach is to select a major theme such as "metropolitan/urban life" and present the unique experiences of each group. Such material purposefully accentuates the differences between minority groups or white ethnic groups, yet it fails to show the experiences and behaviors common to all groups. If misused, this material could further widen the existing gaps between classmates of differing ethnic groups.

LEVEL IV MATERIALS. Designed around broad content generalizations, these are the most complex materials. They chronicle experiences common to all groups and identify characteristics common among groups. They provide students a multiethnic perspective to the American experience. These materials require critical analysis and therefore should be used with groups who are capable of conducting sophisticated discussions and critical, objective analysis. The following source list shows where materials at each of these levels can be attained.

SOURCES OF MATERIALS

LEVEL I. These materials can be ordered through major and minor publishing houses and often are packaged as multimedia. Examples of such sources include:

Multicultural Multimedia Services	Social Studies School Service
P.O. Box 669	P.O. Box 802
1603 Hope Street	1000 Culver Boulevard,
South Pasadena, California 91030	Culver City, California 90230

LEVEL II. These materials chronicle the experiences of minority groups. Materials on Chicanos and Chinese Americans can be obtained from:

Handel Film Corporation
8730 Sunset Boulevard
West Hollywood, California 90060

LEVEL III. Biethnic materials can be obtained from:

Children's Book and Music Center
5373 West Pico Boulevard
Los Angeles, California 90019

LEVEL IV. Multiethnic materials can be obtained from:

Social Studies School Service   EMF
P.O. Box 802   P.O. Box 4272
1000 Culver Boulevard   Madison, Wisconsin 53711
Culver City, California 90230

Perhaps if not the best approach in selecting materials for multicultural groups, at least a sensible one is to try to achieve some balance of materials from the varying levels of complexity. But the most important criterion for selecting each material is the degree to which it is useful in attaining the objectives of the unit or lesson.

As you approach your first teaching position, you may wish to develop a portfolio of materials to use with multicultural groups. But whether or not you choose to do this, it is imperative that you view such experiences as a challenge and an opportunity. You do not want to save the minority student from his own ethnic group nor to shape him into the ideal mold; you want to help him learn to appreciate his own heritage and at the same time learn to appreciate and respect the culture of the majority group and those of other minority ethnic groups.

In the past, teachers have made some common mistakes in working with multicultural groups. Often, they have made such a fuss over the differences between and among groups that they have spread the gap that exists in the students' minds about differing characteristics among the groups. On the opposite end of the continuum, teachers have tried to blend all cultures into one, considering America as a melting pot — a concept created by a French-born writer, Crevecoeur, in 1782.[10] Since cultural diversity has given this country strength, it does not make sense to try to melt down the cultures. On the contrary, the schools should try to help preserve many of the characteristics that make each culture unique.

Do not become a teacher who accepts low performance from minority students: "That's just the way they are." This would be a cop-out on your part. If you make an exception for minority students, letting them go along without experiencing maximum success, you cheat them of their right to develop to their maximum potential — a goal to hold for *all* your students. Try to select materials that are familiar to them and that reflect their experiences; do not settle for simpler materials that do not challenge the students.

---

[10] Manuel Ramirez and Alfredo Castaneda, *Cultural Democracy, Bicognitive Development and Education* (New York: Academic Press, 1974), pp. 5–6.

Thus far we have examined the teacher's role in working with multicultural classes with respect to instruction. But, since teaching involves more than instruction, we should now examine the many other roles that teachers play in multicultural education.

A joint project between the Teacher Corps and the Association of Teacher Educators resulted in the book *In Praise of Diversity: A Resource Book for Multicultural Education.* The book concludes with an article describing the role of the teacher multicultural groups beyond the classroom.[11] It names two avenues through which teachers can praise diversity: these avenues are process and content. Since the first part of this chapter dealt with ways of using content to meet the needs of all cultures, let us now examine some ways to use process to praise diversity.

The roles of most teachers have at least the following functions:

Director of learning

Counselor and guidance worker

Mediator of culture

Link with the community

Member of the school staff

Member of the profession

DIRECTOR OF LEARNING. Much of this chapter has focused on the teacher's instructional role. Since suggestions were provided to show how teachers should "gear up" their instruction to allow for, praise, and promote the cultural differences in the classroom, we need not discuss this dimension again.

COUNSELLOR AND GUIDANCE WORKER. Since the philosophy of this book is of personalizing education, each chapter has emphasized the need for working with each student in a way that extends beyond the academics. Only one further comment seems warranted. Each teacher in the school has responsibility for vocational guidance. The best vocational guidance programs are interdisciplinary and run throughout the grades. Each teacher should help his students become aware of the possible vocational potentials in his field. Do not assume that members from all cultures feel an equal need for long-range planning; you will need to introduce some students to this concept and its advantages.

MEDIATOR OF CULTURE. Earlier in this chapter we discussed a need for stressing the contributions of all cultures represented in the classroom to "our

---

[11] Appreciation is given to Carl A. Grant and Susan L. Melnick and to the Teacher Corps and the Association of Teacher Educators for their permission to use abstracts from the last chapter of *In Praise of Diversity*, "In Praise of Diversity: Some Implications."

culture" and to humanity at large. This should not preclude emphasis on the democratic processes and the rights and responsibilities of American citizens; rather, it should complement this goal. One way to do this is to teach problem-solving skills for coping with potential conflict areas. Simulations can be used to develop these skills. (See the simulations listed in Chapter 11.)

LINK WITH THE COMMUNITY.   In the 1970s the LINKS Project was established at Indiana State University. Written by a science educator, Chris Buethe, this project helped nonscience teachers develop science materials to use in their classes. For example English teachers were able to link the high-interest areas of science to their classes by assigning students essays or other projects that would *link* the otherwise seemingly unrelated subjects. This strategy can also be used to link the multicultural class to the community. Cultural diversity shoud be exalted in the community at large. Since most teachers sooner or later accept leadership roles in the community, they can use these positions toward these ends. Perhaps most important of all, the teacher can demonstrate his own commitment by praising diversity and affirming pluralism as he works and lives in his community.

MEMBER OF THE SCHOOL STAFF.   Since the teacher's roles within the school extend beyond the classroom and involve fellow teachers, administrators, and auxiliary personnel, they can find many opportunities to influence their colleagues. In their article "Organizing for Innovation," Huckins and Bernard stress the importance of informal systems upon organizations and upon their constituents.[12] They warn that substantial parts of the informal system operate below levels of awareness. In most schools an important location for informal influence is the teacher lounge, but, of course, not all influence there is positive. In a supervision text Henry and Beasley use the phrase "lounge lizards" to caution teachers of the potential damage that can inadvertently result from careless comments in informal climates.[13] But if such informal settings do affect the behavior of their participants, it seems that the lounge would be an ideal place for teachers who are dedicated to multicultural education to demonstrate their concerns, not in negative ways but in positive, constructive behaviors.

MEMBERS OF THE PROFESSION.   As a member of a profession, teachers are expected to use their influence and skills in whatever ways possible to improve themselves and the profession. One major responsibility is to communicate the positive dimensions of education to all members of society, especially since the 1960s and 1970's brought criticism and scorn of the American school. Individual teachers can communicate the roles and achievements of their schools through oral discussions and through writing. Professional meetings offer excel-

---

12 Wesley C. Huckins and Harold W. Bernard, "Organization for Innovation," *Humanism in the Classroom* (Boston: Allyn and Bacon, 1974).
13 Marvin A. Henry and Wayne Beasley, *Supervising Student Teachers: The Professional Way*, 3d ed. (Terre Haute, Ind.: Sycamore Press, 1981).

lent opportunities for verbal communications, and professional journals offer similar opportunities through written words. Teachers who are committed to furthering multicultural education will find that many of their associations give top priority to these ends.

SUMMARY

Most classrooms in contemporary American high schools contain students from different cultures. The rate of success for many minority group members continues to remain low in spite of the many billions of dollars spent trying to reverse this trend. If, indeed, the trend is to be reversed, it seems that it will have to be done by individual teachers. This will require certain knowledge about each cultural group and knowledge of how to work with members of different cultures. Furthermore, it will require the development of certain attitudes throughout the classroom.

To be an effective teacher in a multicultural setting, you will need to recognize the many existing learning barriers and know how to plan so as to remove or adjust each so that it becomes less harmful. In addition to knowing how to plan, you must know how to relate to each of these students. You must know what to do and what not to do. Perhaps most important, you must recognize and dispel the many false stereotypes that people hold about members of other cultures.

EXPERIENCES

This chapter has reminded you of your responsibility to teach all students, irrespective of their cultural backgrounds. The following experiences are included so that you may consider how you will not only tolerate but also acknowledge your students' different backgrounds and use this diversification to your advantage — to enrich the learning in your classes.

Experience 1:   A Student Is Hooked on Drugs

When the supervisor of student teachers came to visit Debbie Wright, he found her, to his surprise, waiting for him on the school's front doorsteps. At first Debbie could not explain what was wrong because she was crying too much. Finally she explained that she had a student in one of her classes who was addicted to heroin — a mainliner. Since this school was located in one of the city's lowest socioeconomic areas, most of the students had had experience with some form of drugs and many students were undoubtedly hooked. What was so special about this student? He was a very likable guy and had shown much affection for this student teacher.

Debbie's comments were, "I feel so sorry for him that I just want to reach out and hug him. What can I do?"

▶ *Questions and Discussion*

1. *How can a teacher help a student who is on drugs?*
Teachers can and should discuss the dangers of drug use; however, this will probably not help the student who has a drug problem. Debbie must realize that although her influence is important in many students' lives, her ability to help them with psychological and emotional adjustments is very limited. People who are hooked on drugs experience psychological, emotional, and physical disorders. Debbie should refer all drug cases to the counselor or, if available, a school psychologist or psychiatrist.

2. *Why should Debbie refrain from expressing the pity that she feels for the student?*
Because this only encourages the student to feel sorry for himself and, when in this mental state, the student will do very little to improve or attempt to overcome the undesirable conditions.

    The teacher who is really concerned for a student who is underprivileged or in trouble should put her concern into action. She should be willing to give some of her time and energy in this manner instead of feeling pity for the student.

3. *How can a teacher who feels as Debbie did show concern without showing pity?*
The teacher who shows pity for a student is often overanxious to talk to the student about his problems because she wants to express her feelings to the student. But it may not be best for the student to discuss his problems; he may be ashamed of them. To push him into a discussion of them might increase the intensity of the problems. It could also produce new emotional problems.

Experience 2: A Teacher Belittles a Slow Student

In terms of performance quality, Jerry Simms was one of the poorest students Shelly ever had. At first she tried to encourage Jerry to listen; then she tried to force him to work his daily home assignments. Nothing seemed to help. Finally, becoming disgusted, Shelly made an inexcusable response to his indifferent behavior. She remarked in front of his peers, "Jerry, you don't have one iota of understanding about the subject we are studying, do you?"

Later, as she was relating the experience to some other teachers, she learned that Jerry had almost no home life. She began to regret her comments, and decided to drive by and just see where he lived. The temperature was below freezing, and cracks in the walls showed lights through them. She learned later that the building had once been a storage house for grain and had dirt floors. A student informed her that there were only two chairs and a table inside.

Shelly's experience with Jerry began to haunt her more and more. She began to ask herself. How can I help him?

▶ *Questions and Discussion*

1. *How can the teacher learn about unusual home conditions of his students?*
   An experience such as the one Shelly had with Jerry makes the teacher want to go to see the student's home and to meet his family. This, however, is not always practical and is not necessarily a wise method for learning about the student's home life. It isn't practical because there are too many students with home lives similar to Jerry's. It is not wise because the student may be embarrassed to have his family and home exposed for observation.

   As a beginning teacher, you will be amazed at how much other teachers know about the students in your class — even those teachers who have never taught these students. Do not hesitate to ask other teachers about your students. It is perfectly professional so long as the discussion is directed to better understanding the student and does not degenerate into a gossip session.

   Your school will keep a cumulative record on each student. This record will contain comments that the student's previous teachers have made about him. Here you can discover information about his general behavior as well as information about his academic potential.

2. *Why might a dedicated teacher lose her temper with a low-performing student like Jerry?*
   Most classes have some students whose performance is low because they are too lazy to improve. The teacher cannot always know which students are lazy and which are handicapped by a disadvantaged home life. Therefore, instead of becoming irritated with those students who are not attentive, the teacher should try to determine the cause of their apathy.

3. *To what ethnic group would you guess Jerry belongs? Shelly?*
   Shelly and Jerry are Anglo Americans.

Experience 3: A Poor School Has a Good Atmosphere

When Bob, a supervisor of student teachers, first saw Rio Grande, an inner-city school, his first reaction was disbelief that such a school could exist in the twentieth century; the buildings should have been condemned decades ago because they were dangerous fire traps. Placing two begin-

ning teachers in this environment really went against Bob's better judgment. He took a deep breath and went in to meet the principal.

Mr. Lopez was a delightful middle-aged man, very gregarious and very
energetic. He introduced Bob to his secretaries and to several members
of his large faculty, which was 95 percent Latin American. Each teacher
had the same spark of enthusiasm and pleasantness.

Bob was still suspicious because he had been inside many dilapidated
inner-city schools. He was keenly aware that in schools such as this one,
the students were often discourteous, rude, disrespectful and difficult to
control. Nevertheless, his role was to assign two student teachers to this
staff for the next term, so he made the assignment — promising himself
that he would visit frequently and provide as much encouragement and
reassurance as necessary to make the experience tolerable for them.

As Bob began his visits with them, both student teachers assured him
that they were getting along well. There were apparently no major discipline problems in either of their classes. Both worked hard and enjoyed
teaching in this school.

From talking with the principal, with some of the faculty members,
and with these two student teachers, Bob found three elements that
seemed to be working together to produce the wholesome, optimistic atmosphere in a physical environment that had initially seemed so depress-
ing. The principal stressed the importance of total involvement of everyone including the faculty and students on both academic and extracurricular matters. These student teachers were immediately involved in
evening and weekend school activities. The principal considered them
important members of the faculty.

Second, the principal's enthusiasm was reflected in every faculty member and was seen in the classrooms. Most of the students at this school
were very poor readers, which severely limited the rate of learning; but
the teachers were patient and continually encouraged their students.
Bob learned the third element contributing to this school's wholesome
atmosphere when he expressed his concern at the slow rate of covering
material to one of the faculty members. She responded that many of the
students were very slow academically, that many had bad home lives that
destroyed their concern and respect for others. Therefore, she said, one
of the most important objectives was to teach the students to cooperate
with others. Certainly the faculty members at Rio Grande set good
examples for their students to follow.

▶ *Questions and Discussion*

1. *Teaching respect for others is an important objective in any deprived
   community, but exactly what can the teacher do to teach students to
   respect others?*
   Before one can learn to respect others, he must learn to associate with

others. Believe it or not, many students who attend ghetto schools have a keen sense of individual pride. They often resent working with others because it seems an admission that they are incapable of doing the task alone. The teacher in a ghetto school must assign group projects in such a way that all students feel that they can contribute. The leaders should be assigned to one group, the reserved, timid students to another, the mediocre students to a third group, and the very slow students to a fourth group. This provides students with opportunity for contributing to a particular group, and having done so, for accepting the contributions of others.

A second technique for teaching students to respect each other is to assign individuals to assist a classmate who is having difficulty with the lesson. This process affords the students opportunity to learn to feel responsible for others, which is basic to learning to respect others.

2. *Some student teachers will never teach in run-down buildings located in inner-city ghettos; therefore, why should they need experience teaching in such schools?*
One does not have to go to a ghetto to find deprived students. Many teachers will never teach in ghettos; but they will have the task of teaching deprived students, for there are many ways in which students are deprived. By teaching in ghetto schools, student teachers learn to become aware of many of the barriers that must be overcome before they can work effectively with deprived students. Many of the students' psychological and social needs must be satisfied before they reach a state of readiness to learn the academic tasks demanded of them.

3. *Could the fact that this faculty was almost entirely composed of Latin Americans explain the unexpected open climate in this school?*
This probably did have some effect on the climate at Rio Grande because Latin Americans do tend to express themselves openly and enthusiastically, using a high degree of both verbal and nonverbal communications — an observation based on three years' experience living and working in a Latin community.

Experience 4: A Teacher Learns about Discipline from a Deprived School

Dr. Rentschler led an evaluation team visiting a very deprived school to examine its curriculum and to recommend whether or not the school should be accredited. At the time that school system was in debt for $27 million, and this figure was rapidly increasing each year. The school was located in one of the toughest neighborhoods of any ghetto in this country. Each day as the team members parked, a student patrolman was assigned to protect their cars.

The team arrived at the school daily before 8:00 A.M. and remained there until 4:00 P.M. During this time Dr. Rentschler moved throughout the multistoried buildings examining classes, libraries, laboratories, and other school facilities. As he walked down the long, dark hallways, he noticed that the students were well behaved. He did not witness the running and pushing that is often seen in other schools, nor did he hear the shouting and disrespectful comments that he had expected. From time to time he asked students questions about their attitudes toward the school. He found that they really liked it; they were proud of their school. When he asked for directions, the students did not merely tell him; they showed him by going with him and leading him to the room. Everything seemed strange and atypical of his stereotype of ghetto schools.

Why were the students so well disciplined? Why did they have so much pride in an old, crumbling, debt-ridden school? Why were they so helpful, and why did they show so much respect for one another and for a stranger?

The students respected Dr. Rentschler because they respected one another because they had pride in their school — not in the building but in the institution. They were even proud of their principal, who was responsible for initiating and promoting this feeling of pride.

As is typical of most schools, each day began with a series of announcements over the public-address system. The principal always made a positive comment about the good conduct of the students. Each day ended with a five-minute announcement, which always concluded with, "I know that each student will exit the building today with the well-mannered behavior that you always exhibit."

The principal of this school was aware that by allowing people dignity and respect, you can get from them respect for others. Most teachers discover this relationship either early or late in their careers.

► *Questions and Discussion*

1. *Why is respect especially essential for discipline in a deprived school?*
   As was mentioned in Chapter 3, the ultimate goal in discipline is to have each student discipline himself. Self-discipline cannot be achieved in the absence of self-respect. Often the students who attend ghetto schools do not have self-respect. They often do not have pride in their families. By getting them to respect the school and themselves, you may find an effective means for disciplining and motivating deprived students.

2. *How can you, as teacher, help a student develop self-respect?*
   For a student to respect herself at school, she must see herself as a success; she must realize that she is making progress in her schoolwork. You can help by assigning tasks in which every student can achieve. You can provide the encouragement needed to give the student the

confidence required to attack the assignments and then reinforce this behavior by recognizing her success.

To help the student realize continuing improvement, involve the student in keeping an individual record of her achievements. The record should contain more than just test scores; it should contain short-range goals that show daily improvement.

Experience 5: A Teacher Is Baffled by the Values of Migrant Students

Avory Hill was a small rural high school with an enrollment of about three hundred. Each autumn brought with it several students who traveled with their families from season to season following the vegetable and fruit crops. Miss Yates did not know about these students until after she had accepted her first teaching position there.

It was apparent to Miss Yates that there were a number of students with characteristics that did not make them ideal students. Sometimes they spoke very poor English, and their rate of attendance was far below average. Often their success in her classes was very limited. The worst trait was their obvious lack of interest in school.

When Miss Yates tried to explain why they should acquire an education, arguing that it would enable them to earn the money needed to buy a house and many other luxuries, she found that they did not want houses, boats, and many of the other things that she treasured. Upon contacting some of the parents, she found that even they did not see anything worthwhile about school or education. They earned a living, and their work afforded them the opportunity to move frequently and far.

▶ *Questions and Discussion*

1. *How could a teacher convince migrant students that school is worthwhile?*

   The teacher of migrant children should realize the difference between their value system and that of resident students. Instead of rapidly imposing her own values and the school's values on them, she should first try to learn about and accept some of their values. She should try to understand why they have strong feelings about things that have little meaning for her and are apathetic about some things that are most important to her.

   The teacher must understand that because migrant students are deprived in many special ways, their school success will often come with difficulty and very slowly. She must have unlimited patience with them and must try to put something into every lesson that will be meaning to them.

2. *List several ways in which migrant students are deprived and explain how the teacher can assist them.*

One of the greatest disadvantages that migrant students face is that their value systems often do not let them see the importance of education. The teacher can assist by changing the lessons so that each includes something that is worthwhile to them. A second handicap is that migrant students are frequently misunderstood and hence rejected by the resident students. The teacher can help by teaching the history and culture of the migrants, and by explaining their importance to our agriculture and economy.

A third way in which migrant students and many other disadvantaged students are handicapped is that they are unable to cope with the middle-class examples that are used in today's high school classes. The teacher of any deprived or disadvantaged pupils should avoid the use of middle-class examples and, whenever possible, substitute general symbols for them. She should use many models, films, and live demonstrations, and should never let an opportunity pass to involve the student in doing things that demand direct use of the five senses.

ACTIVITIES

Since at one time or another you will teach classes that represent different cultures, you will need strategies for working with cultural differences. In fact, even in a class whose ethnic composition is similar, you will often find a diversity of cultural backgrounds. The following activities are provided to help you work with multicultured groups.

1. Most (if not all) of us have prejudices toward our own ethnic group. Make a list of your prejudices that you are able to recognize.
2. All ethnic groups have some cultural qualities that can contribute to the American society. Name some ethnic groups and identify one such quality of each.
3. Describe a strategy that would be appropriate in your subject and grade level for breaking down cultural prejudices. Consider including techniques for showing the attributes of different classes and groups.

SUGGESTED READINGS

BRICKMAN, WILLIAM W., and LEHRER, STANLEY, eds. *Education and the Many Faces of the Disadvantaged.* New York: John Wiley and Sons, 1972.

CHEYNEY, ARNOLD B. *Teaching Children of Different Cultures in the Classroom,* 2d ed. Columbus, Ohio: Charles E. Merrill, 1976.

COLES, ROBERT. *Uprooted Children.* New York: Harper and Row, 1970.

DAWSON, MARTHA E., ed., *Are There Unwelcome Guests in Your Classroom?* Washington, D.C.: Association for Childhood Education International, 1974.

GARCIA, JESUS, and GARCIA, RICARDO. "Selecting Ethnic Materials for the Elementary School." *Social Education* 44 (March 1980): 232–36.

HENSON, KENNETH T., and HENRY, MARVIN A. *Becoming Involved in Teaching.* Chapter 9. Terre Haute, Ind.: Sycamore Press, 1976.

SMITH, FREDERICK R., and COX, C. B. *Secondary Schools in a Changing Society.* New York: Holt, Rinehart and Winston, 1976.

TEACHER CORPS. *In Praise of Diversity: A Resource Book for Multicultural Education.* (Edited by Milton J. Gold, Carl A. Grant, and Harry N. Rivlin. Washington, D.C.: Association of Teacher Education, 1977.

VAN TIL, WILLIAM. *Secondary Education: School and Community.* Boston: Houghton Mifflin, 1978.

Tests and Evaluation

PART SIX

Every teacher has responsibilities for testing and evaluation, terms that are frequently confused and misunderstood. This section is designed to help you understand the many uses of tests and evaluations in the classroom. Since most American secondary schools require grades, it will behoove you to learn all that you can about constructing, administering, and scoring tests, and about converting these results, along with other criteria, into grades.

Test Construction, Administration, and Scoring

OBJECTIVES

Upon completion of this chapter you should be able to:
1. List two advantages of objective tests and two advantages of subjective (discussion) type questions.
2. Develop an objective test that measures different levels of the cognitive domain.
3. Explain how easy and how difficult test questions should be.
4. List five guidelines for administering a test.
5. Construct a discussion type test that will measure the students' ability to judge or evaluate.
6. Give two practices to ensure fairness on a discussion type exam.
7. Design a system for scoring a discussion type exam and justify your assigning of more value to some questions than to others.
8. Write a general discussion type question that promotes divergent thinking. Then rewrite the same question, making it more specific.
9. Write a multiple-choice question with five choices, two of which are viable distracters.
10. Write a question for each level of the affective and cognitive domains.

TYPES OF TESTS

Since Chapter 15 discusses standardized tests, this chapter will focus on teacher-made tests. As a teacher you will have responsibility for the testing program in your classes. Even in those secondary schools that give departmentalized tests, you will have to contribute to the construction, administering, and scoring of tests. The bulk of this chapter, therefore, is reserved for helping prospective or beginning teachers improve their skills in these areas. Before you can begin constructing tests, however, you should be aware of the many varieties of tests. This first portion of the chapter will familiarize (or

more accurately, remind) you of the many options that teachers have in choosing tests.

Written or Not

For many years American educators have been predisposed toward written tests. This practice may have been so imbedded in your own teachers that, when you hear the word *test,* you think of a pencil-and-paper exercise. But, of course, there are options to the pencil-and-paper test. Teachers can choose simply to ask questions orally to solicit oral responses. Or the teacher can give a performance test that requires students to perform a skills exercise, such as role playing in a drama class, assembling an engine in an auto mechanics class, or participating in a dialogue in a foreign language class. Oral and performance options have become popular recently because of concern that pencil-and-paper tests all too frequently measure only the recall of knowledge, ignoring the student's ability to apply it. Still, though, a vast majority of teacher-made tests are of the pencil-and-paper variety. Therefore, we shall examine several types of written tests, keeping in mind their limitations and potentials for measuring different student competencies.

If preferring a written test, the teacher must then decide between an objective test or an essay-type test, or possibly a combination of the two. The two types of written tests differ drastically in many ways. First of all, the essay test can be said to measure what students know, whereas the objective test is often accused of measuring what students do not know. Indeed the essay-type test does permit students to select from their own knowledge storehouse and to use this knowledge in the response, whereas the objective question (true-false, matching, and multiple choice) does not provide this freedom. The objective test may leave students feeling that they understood the lesson pretty well but that the test questions just happened to sample some less familiar areas. But, more important, the essay test is flexible in that it affords the student opportunities to express his own views — to reach beyond the recall level into the application, analysis, synthesis and evaluation levels, as well as into the affective domain.

Essay Tests

DISCUSSION ITEMS. Of all types of essay items, the discussion is perhaps the one most misused. When questions are stated as broadly as "Discuss Shakespeare's work" or "Discuss the Industrial Revolution," the student wonders "Where should I begin? What issues am I supposed to address?" By carefully restricting the question, you can reduce the degree of ambiguity; for example, "Discuss the types of humor in Shakespeare's *Twelfth Night*," *or* "Discuss the role of Eli Whitney's cotton gin in the Industrial Revolution."

By sharpening the focus on discussion questions, you will also simplify your scoring of these questions. In other words, the more exactly you express your expectation, the more accountable your students become for including the expected content in their answers. By giving an example, you can further clarify your expectations; for example, the question "Discuss the role of Eli Whitney's cotton gin in the Industrial Revolution" could be followed by "for example, address its effect on the labor market."

EXPLANATION ITEMS. Good questions on explanation tests focus on a certain process. For example, "Explain the water cycle." Since the water cycle involves a definite sequence of activities (for example, rain → runoff → evaporation → condensation), the students can be held accountable for a specific body of knowledge plus the sequences involved in the process). When using explanation questions, you should avoid general questions such as "Explain the Civil Rights Movement of the sixties." For, stated this way, the question is at best just a discussion question and would be better written as such.

SITUATION ITEMS. Situation test items measure a student's response to a certain situation. Students are asked to apply their knowledge, values, and judgment to decide how they would respond to certain circumstances. The teacher of a first-aid course might ask, "If you were driving down the road and came upon an accident that had left a person lying in the road unconscious and breathing heavily, what would you do?"

Like other types of essay questions, situation questions are at their best when they call forth a definite body of knowledge. They have the further advantage of requiring students to apply that knowledge.

COMPARISON OR CONTRAST ITEMS. These questions are important because they force students to sharpen their understanding about similar or dissimilar concepts. In other words, they require students to differentiate between the two (or more) concepts by focusing on particular similar or dissimilar qualities. For example, "Compare and contrast World War I with World War II." You can get more specific answers if you add limits to the question: "Compare and contrast World War I with World War II according to their ground strategies, air strategies, number of casualties, and the number of countries involved."

Objective Tests

Some popular types of questions found on objective tests include true-false, multiple choice, and matching. Less common is the fill-in-the-blank type of question, which calls for a specific, preconceived answer. As mentioned earlier, they are often criticized for testing what students do not know rather than what they do know. Furthermore, they tend to encourage guessing. On the other hand, objective tests have several definite advantages over essay tests. They are more quickly scored. This is important to today's teachers who would better invest much time in preparing lessons rather than grading tests. Furthermore, objective questions are likely to be more fairly graded since the correct answers are predetermined. This, too, is an important advantage since most teachers want their students to perceive them as fair and impartial.

PURPOSES OF TESTING

As a college student in education, you probably look forward to when you will be a teacher rather than a student. This is especially true on testing days; it seems that it would be much more pleasant to administer the test than to take it. Surprisingly enough, though, once this change in roles is made, beginning teachers often withdraw their wish; for testing is not always the easiest and most pleasant of the beginning teacher's tasks. In fact, if a graph were used to represent the morale of the beginning teacher, it might appear as in Figure 14.1. Notice that in the very beginning the teachers are a bit uneasy but their outlook brightens a little each day as they gain more confidence. Then at the end of the second or third week their morale collapses. What happened? They

Figure 14.1 The Morale Level of Novice Teachers

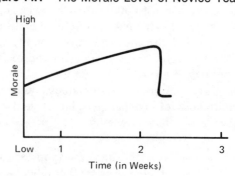

have just administered and scored their first set of test papers. Many low scores and only a few high ones resulted. Though they thought they had done an excellent job of planning and executing each lesson, these papers seem to reflect the opposite — poor teaching. But the chances are that their teaching skills were better than their testing skills. A poorly designed test can make the best of teachers look like a failure.

Now for the first time the beginning teacher begins to think deeply about testing. Several questions come up: Is testing necessary? What is the advantage of testing? Could the purpose not be achieved through some other means? How does testing assist the instructional program? and, eventually, How can I improve my testing program?

When we think of testing, we think of grades. But, if we say that the purpose of testing is to determine grades, another good question might be, Why do we need grades? Justifying tests as grade determiners is insufficient; many educators are not at all convinced that grades are necessary.

One important purpose of testing is to help your students determine their general rate of progress in a specific subject. This information is important to you and to the student. And, of course, to report a grade (which is required by most school systems and is expected, if not demanded, by most parents), you must know the student's general rate of progress. In Chapter 5 we found that, to be motivated or to be encouraged to attack further goals, students need to know their rate of achievement.

A second function of testing is to help the teacher determine the general progress in the classroom. The rate of progress in teaching is always proportional to the learning rate of the class. In other words, your teaching cannot be better than your students' learning. Test results show you where to slow down, to repeat more, or to use different methods.

Still another major function of testing is that it provides a means of diagnosing strengths and weaknesses for both student and teacher. Through testing you can help the student to spot areas in which he should spend more effort; and test results also help you identify areas where you need to improve your methodology and to clarify misunderstandings in the classroom.

Recognize the test as a tool for helping you improve your methodology and for helping your students improve their listening and study habits; then construct, administer, and evaluate it with these purposes in mind.

TEST CONSTRUCTION

If you experience mild shock on grading your first set of test papers, do not immediately begin to question your teaching abilities. Later, realizing that most of the fault lies not in the teaching but rather in the testing, you may ask, How do I make out a good test? The following suggestions should help you.

Stating the Directions

Each test should begin with a written statement directing the student how to complete the test. Like all assignments the directions should be stated in specific terms. For example:

> Each item on this test is worth one point. Select the single choice that you believe best. Do not leave questions blank and do not mark more than one choice. If you have questions, please raise your hand and I will come to your desk. When you finish, please turn your paper face down on your desk and begin working quietly on the assignment now written on the board.

Once the test is written, the teacher should check it for any possibility of its being misinterpreted, altering and clarifying it accordingly. The directions should always state the maximum time allotted for taking the test. Clear directions will prevent unnecessary interruptions during the testing period and will prevent the discomfort students feel when they are not sure what is being asked of them.

Stating the Value of Each Question

Most teachers find it convenient to specify or assign values to questions in terms of percentages. Assign relative values, asking yourself how much each question is worth in relation to the other questions. The value of each question should be proportionate to the amount of time spent on that topic in class and the amount of time required to answer the question.

Often a test will consist of several short-answer questions or short problems that carry equal value. On such tests the teacher need not specify separate values but merely state that each question has equal value. On tests that have questions of varying values, the value of each question should appear in the margin alongside the question.

Select a Variety of Questions

Students frequently ask which type of question is best, objective or subjective? As you might suppose, each type offers advantages that the other does not; therefore, most tests should contain *both* objective and subjective questions. Objective questions require more time to construct but less time to answer and to score, so many objective questions can be asked on each test. Subjective questions can measure creativity and allow the students to express their feelings and attitudes; furthermore they enable measurement of the ability to organize.

Of the types of objective questions, many testing experts believe multiple-choice to be the best; the true-and-false of merely average value; and the fill-in-the-blank the least valuable. They do agree, though, that several types of objective questions should be used. An advantage of using a variety is that students who find one type especially difficult will not be penalized by an entire test of that type. Further discussion of these and other specific types of test questions will follow later in this chapter.

Every test should have some questions that are so easy that almost every student in the class can answer them correctly. The test should begin with the less difficult questions so that each student will be encouraged to go on to the following questions. Remember that the purpose of the test is to measure ability — not tolerance. Care should be taken to avoid placing a 40-point question at the end of the test. Slower students will think it unfair if they fail the test because time ran out just as they began answering the last question.

If every question on a test were so easy that every student could correctly answer it, it would be of little use. A test should have some questions that challenge the most capable students. Each question should be a little more difficult than the preceding question, but never try to make a question difficult by wording it so that it is vague, general, or tricky. The difficult questions should be difficult because they are especially challenging and involve a complex process, and they should pertain to very important concepts.

Covering Important Material

Most teachers believe it necessary to test at least once every two weeks. From the large volume of material covered in this time span, what should be selected for inclusion on the test? A good rule is that any test should contain questions about information covered each day of the testing period. In other words, it should begin testing where the previous test stopped and should test right up through the day preceding the test date.

Ideally, the time spent studying various areas of content should be in proportion to the importance of the content. Therefore, the percentage of time studying an area should be proportional to the percentage of the test that area comprises. For example, if in a unit on astronomy a week was spent studying the sun and only one day was spent studying the moon, the total value of test questions about the sun should be about five times as great as the total value assigned to questions about the moon.

Testing the Test

Many teachers insist on taking a test themselves before administering it. Besides catching typographical errors and ambiguously worded questions, the teacher develops a master answer sheet while taking the test. This predeveloped answer sheet will be helpful in the valuation of the test and will be discussed later in this chapter.

WRITING TEST ITEMS

Upon completing a unit of study (or, as we shall soon see, even during a unit), the teacher must decide when to give an examination and then design the right type of questions or select the right type of ready-made exam. Both decisions — when to measure and what type of test to use — should be based on the purpose of the test. Discussion questions are suited to measure some skills, while objective questions are more suited to measure other skills. The following is a discussion of some of the more commonly used types of tests and some advantages and limitations of each. The suggestions given for improving the use of each type of question should be of particular interest.

Discussion Questions

While all test questions can be grouped into two categories — subjective and objective — subjective (or discussion) is a type of its own. Discussion questions have some important limitations. First of all, they are difficult to control. Actually they required the teacher to relinquish some control, for the student is free to answer (and actually *must* do so) in terms of his own perspective. This leads to another problem — the scoring. You must decide whether or not to count such variables as these:

1. Ability to focus on the teacher's perspective
2. Writing and spelling skills
3. General neatness
4. Comprehensiveness
5. Specific facts and concepts
6. Broad generalizations
7. Creativity
8. Attitudes
9. Logical reasoning
10. Other skills outside the knowledge category, such as the ability to synthesize or evaluate.

These uncertainties must be resolved before you give the test so that disagreements will not arise between you and the students. To avoid this risk, you may be ready to pass by discussion tests in favor of more specific objective type tests. But first examine some of the strengths of discussion questions.

Discussion-type questions excel in their ability to let the students express themselves. In responding to a discussion question they can be as creative, imaginative, and expressive as they wish; furthermore they can evaluate and give their own beliefs and values. This is important for two reasons: First, evaluation is the highest known level of thinking (as reflected in Bloom's taxonomy of educational objectives). Second, when responding to test questions, students often have a strong desire to express their own beliefs and to justify their responses.

A teacher who has chosen to use discussion questions will structure each question so as to emphasize the ideas that the student should address. This will minimize the degree of ambiguity in teacher and student expectations. Following are examples of good and bad discussion items.

A. Discuss the causes of the Revolutionary War.

How would *you* respond to question No. 1? What is wrong with this item? You probably would not know where to begin, as the question is far too general. Suppose it were rewritten to read:

> B. Name and discuss three main causes of the Revolutionary War.

Now the question lets you know that you are expected to cover three areas, but it is still a monumental task and time-consuming. You could not ask more than two or three questions of this type on any test. As was mentioned earlier, a test should reflect the complete range of material covered in class since the previous test. Suppose the question is altered further as seen in sample C.

> C. Name and discuss three economic factors that contributed to the development of the Revolutionary War.

Now the scope of the question has been limited drastically. The student can immediately eliminate the many political and social factors that contributed significantly to the war. By making the question more specific, you are reducing its ambiguity and thus the scope of responses the question is to elicit. But since discussion questions offer a unique opportunity to stimulate students to think independently and creatively, you probably will wish to include at least one question designed for that purpose. An example of such question is shown in sample D.

> D. Suppose that England had won the war. What changes would have occurred in the American life style?

This question does provide students the opportunity to use divergent thinking, requiring them to expand their thoughts by using their imagination. It is, therefore, of a higher order than the previous questions. Notice, though, that it requires you to give up much of your ability to regulate or restrict the area of student responses. In a class of thirty students this question would likely elicit thirty entirely different types of responses. This might create problems in scoring the answer. Therefore, before administering this question, specify your criteria for marking the papers. Since the purpose for selecting this question was to measure imagination and creativity, surely these would be two considerations that would count heavily in assessing a grade for this question.

We see, then, that both the writing and scoring of good discussion questions require much time and thought. You will find that time is well spent in very carefully wording the question so that it achieves its objectives, and you will save time in scoring discussion answers if you structure the question in an unambiguous way. To be sure, the writing and scoring of good discussion questions is not easy. The quality of the responses will likely correlate highly with the time spent in writing and rewriting the questions.

A good approach to the assignment of values to each part of a response is to take the test yourself before administering to your students. Then you can assign varying credit for each part of the expected response according to their respective values. For example, take sample question D: "Suppose that England had won the war. What changes would have occurred in the American life style?" Assume that the classroom discussion and/or authors of the texts and other materials included such concepts as (1) more rigid tariffs, (2) lower prices, and (3) worsening labor conditions. Each of these concepts could receive 2 points credit. Other reasonable responses could receive 1 point each, making the total value of the question 8 or 10 points.

Multiple-Choice Questions

The multiple-choice question is very popular in schools today, partly because of the increasing availability of machine scoring. Another reason for its popularity is that the questions themselves have merit. Like the true-false and fill-in-the-blank test, a multiple-choice test enables the teacher to ask many questions and thus cover many topics on the same test. Unlike these tests, however, the multiple-choice test restricts the amount of success derived by guessing. As one researcher has noted, "The multiple-choice item seems best suited to bring out the finer distinctions between what is good, what is best, and what represents loose thinking, if not downright error.[1] But this advantage is realized only when the teacher designs each test question appropriately. Keep in mind also that tests should be used to help students learn. When correctly worded, the multiple-choice test can become an excellent learning device.

Like the discussion question (and all other types of test questions), the multiple-choice test should be selected on its merits, that is, on its ability to achieve specific goals. It then should be designed to achieve those particular goals. If its purpose is formative (to promote learning), then it should be designed one way; if its purpose is to determine student or teacher success (summative), it should be designed differently. Specific designs for specific purposes will be discussed, but first let's take up some general questions that you might have about developing multiple-choice tests.

How many alternatives should I include? Generally, it is wise to include at least four choices. Five alternatives may be desirable if the purpose of the test is to *promote learning*.

Should I include among my alternatives "all of the above" and "none of the above"? Since "all of the above" enables one to measure knowledge about the question, it is a legitimate option. Since "none of the above" does not enable the student to relate specifically to the question, it should be avoided. The bottom space could be more wisely used to include a concept related to the material being tested.

How should I phrase the stem of a multiple-choice question? First, keep it brief. Avoid using more than one sentence, since a student may become tripped up on the question itself. Second, avoid negatives in the stem. Both of these qualities (unnecessary length and negatives) tend to confuse and interrupt the thought process. A test question should always be written so that it communicates as clearly as possible. See the following examples.

---

[1] George J. Mouly, *The Science of Educational Research*, 2d ed. (New York: Van Nostrand Reinhold, 1970), p. vi.

E. All isosceles triangles:
   a. have at least two equal sides
   b. have at least two equal angles
   c. have at least three equal sides
   d. have at least three equal angles

Item E could be simplified as follows:

E. All isosceles triangles have at least:
   a. two equal sides
   b. two equal angles
   c. three equal sides
   d. three equal angles

F. Which of the following is *not* an example of sedimentary rock?
   a. limestone
   b. sandstone
   c. chirt
   d. all of the above

Item F should be changed to read as follows:

F. An example of igneous rock is:
   a. limestone
   b. sandstone
   c. chirt
   d. all of the above

How should I select the alternatives? If you are designing the test to promote learning, you should purposefully include several alternatives that are closely related. If the purpose is grading, the number of near correct answers should be reduced to only one or two. To have all answers almost acceptable would be unduly taxing and might result in teacher preference as opposed to student preference. To write a question with only one attractive answer would be equally poor design; it would not promote learning or thinking and therefore would not discriminate between those who have mastered the material and those who have not. Examine items G, H, and I and for each question identify at least one major flaw; then rewrite each test item to eliminate those flaws.

G. Alexander Graham Bell invented the:
   a. cotton gin
   b. telegraph
   c. radio
   d. all of the above
   e. none of the above

H. Water is not an example of a:
   a. liquid
   b. solution
   c. fluid
   d. compound
   e. base

I. The Pilgrims began arriving in America in the early 1630s. Some came via Holland; others came directly from the port of Southampton in England. The real reason for the Pilgrims' coming was to:
   a. escape persecution.
   b. seek freedom of religion for all.
   c. form a new denomination.
   d. all of the above.

The obvious error in question G is the inclusion of the alternative "none of the above." The question could easily be corrected by simply eliminating the fifth choice.

The stem of question H contains a negative. The question could be corrected by deleting the *not* and changing the choices.

The stem of item I is unnecessarily long. It could be corrected by eliminating the first two sentences.

Another common error in writing multiple-choice questions is a tendency to give the student the correct answer unintentionally. Of course, this defies the purpose of tests, whether formative or summative. Items J and K contain questions making this mistake. For each question see if you can identify the part that leads the student to the correct answer; then rewrite the question to avoid this error.

J. A well-known French-Swiss psychologist:
   a. Wilburn Elrod
   b. Robert O. Williams
   c. Jean Piaget
   d. Warner Hayes
   e. Marvin Henry

K. The nickel is an example of an:
   a. alloy
   b. solution
   c. compound
   d. metal

L. The speed of light is:
   a. 100 ft/sec
   b. 100 mi/hr
   c. 120 mi/hr
   d. 186,000 mi/sec

Item J leads the student to the selection of an alternative based on grounds other than knowledge about psychologists. Of course the grammatical structure of Item K suggests the correct answer. Incidentally, the alternative being sought in this item is not the only correct alternative provided. In summative tests take care not to include more than one correct answer. The test Item L is a poor item because it fails to include a strong distracter (a near-correct choice).

Fill-in-the-Blank Questions

Although the fill-in-the-blank type question can boast of no real strengths at all, it has managed to survive throughout the history of our schools. Not only does this type question limit the teacher to measuring only knowledge (or recall) level information, but also it seldom achieves this with any degree of accuracy. The fill-in-the-blank question often places the student in the impossible position of trying to guess what the teacher wants. Mastering the material is no guarantee of success on this type of test. The fill-in-the-blank question nevertheless appeals to many teachers because this type of test can be developed quickly and effortlessly. (This does not reflect the way that it *should be* developed, but merely the way it *is often* developed.) Some teachers lift sentences right out of the text and print them verbatim on the test, substituting a blank for one or more words. Item M illustrates the all too typical fill-in-the-blank question. How would you answer it? Can you modify it to eliminate its ambiguity?

    M. The Battle of New Orleans was fought in _____.

This type of question unintentionally invites the imagination to run wild. A creative student might respond with *New Orleans; the rain; winter; anger;* or *mud, blood,* and *beer.* An infinite number of correct answers is possible and should be given full credit, but the student need not know anything about the Battle of New Orleans to respond correctly. Other students may become discouraged over the confusion and leave the space blank, therefore getting penalized for the teacher's failure to communicate clearly.

While, generally, you would be wise to choose another type of question, suppose you should wish to test for highly technical or specific factual information. When correctly written, the fill-in-the-blank test can achieve this. A teacher writing item M to test for the date of the beginning of the battle need only to insert *the year of,* that is, "The Battle of New Orleans began in the year of _____." Specificity is essential to the writing of good fill-in-the-blank items.

Another common mistake, which may be even more frustrating to students than are completion items, is that of including blanks throughout the sentence. Item N is an example of this error.

    N. _____ tests are more _____ _____ than are _____ _____ tests.

In conclusion, avoid fill-in-the-blank tests when other types of tests will achieve your objectives. If you do use them, remember that specificity is the key to the design of good questions.

Matching Tests

At some time or another, most teachers elect to use matching tests. This type of test enables the teacher to measure the students' ability to make important associations. Its value is apparent from the number of national standardized tests that test for the examinee's ability to make associations, ranging from the picture association game on Sesame Street to the Miller Analogies Test used in many college graduate programs.

Matching tests are not easy to construct. Care must be taken to avoid using a stimulus that inadvertently matches with more than one response.[2] An examiner wishing to have the students use a stimulus more than once should inform them that they may use the same number or letter in their answers repeatedly. For example, in Item O, stimulus number 1 would fit in both responses A and D.

O. Stimulus   Response
1. Noun   ___A. Water
2. Verb   ___B. Blue
3. Adjective   ___C. Fishing
4. Pronoun   ___D. Moon
5. Adverb   ___E. Slowly
    ___F. Her
    ___G. Into

Notice also that in Item O the number of responses outnumber the stimuli. This is to discourage guessing. Another important precaution in writing multiple-choice items is to avoid giving hints. Item P illustrates such carelessness in item writing.

P. Match the dates with the corresponding events.
1. 1861   A. Signing of the Magna Charta
2. 1812   B. Beginning of the Civil War
3. 1776   C. Storming of the Bastille
4. 1215   D. Signing of the Declaration of Independence
5. 1918   E. War of 1812
    F. Cardinal Principles of Secondary Education

Obviously, "War of 1812" is a dead giveaway. Such matches should be avoided on matching tests since they fail to measure any level of understanding.

HIGHER LEVEL QUESTIONS: THE COGNITIVE DOMAIN

Returning to the *Taxonomy of Educational Objectives,* we find that the major levels in the cognitive domain are these:

1. Knowledge
2. Comprehension
3. Application
4. Analysis
5. Synthesis
6. Evaluation

---

[2] Peter F. Oliva, *The Secondary School Today,* 2d ed. (San Francisco: Intext Educational Publishers, 1972), p. 523.

Most of the types of objective questions discussed so far have been limited to measuring the retention of knowledge. This does not mean, however, that such test items as multiple-choice and matching cannot be designed to test for higher levels of understanding. It is erroneous to conclude that only discussion-type questions can measure higher levels of understanding. Each type of question can be used to measure different levels of all three learning domains. The purpose for including the following examples is to show prospective teachers, student teachers, and novice teachers at least one way of designing questions to measure understanding at each level.

Level 1: Knowledge

Since we are all familiar with questions that test *only* our ability to recall facts, this first level will not be discussed.

Level 2: Comprehension

Charts, maps, graphs, and tables lend themselves well to measuring learning mastery at this level. Such questions should require the student to translate,[3] interpret,[4] or predict a continuation of trends.[5] For example, Figure 14.2 presents a graph of the general sales ratio of a book during its first three years of publication.

> If a particular book has sold 10,000 copies during its first year and a total of 30,000 copies by the end of its second year, how many copies can we estimate it should have sold by the end of its third year?

Of course, a multiple-choice question could be written to use with this graph.

> For example, the total accumulated sales projected by the end of the third year is:
> a. 10,000
> b. 20,000
> c. 30,000
> d. 40,000

Level 3: Application

Questions measuring the ability to think at the application level must require students to apply abstractions such as general ideas, rules, and methods to concrete situations. In other words, the student must use a principle or generaliza-

---

[3] Benjamin S. Bloom; J. Thomas Hastings; and George F. Madaus, *Handbook on Formative and Summative Evaluation of Student Learning* (New York: McGraw-Hill, 1971), p. 92.

[4] Lisanio R. Orland, "Evaluation of Learning in Secondary School Social Studies," in *Handbook on Formative and Summative Evaluation of Student Learning*, ed. Benjamin S. Bloom, J. Thomas Hastings, and George F. Madaus (New York: McGraw-Hill, 1971), Chapter 16.

[5] Bloom, *Handbook*, p. 96.

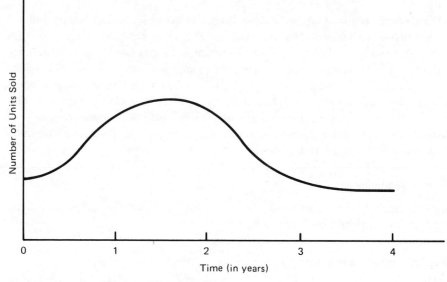

Figure 14.2 Sales Ratio of Textbooks

tion to solve a new problem. The following example is offered to clarify the process of generalizing:

> You enter the old kitchen in which there is a blazing hearthfire complete with bubbling, boiling teakettle. Oh, it's always there anyway; you've seen it before. Besides, your mind is on something else. Your quaint kitchen is pretty well turned out by you or you only perceive it at the (blob) level. Wait, something focuses your attention on the event system that is the boiling kettle. You've noticed. Now you're beginning to operate. You've noticed something and something is happening. The lid jumps up and down. You wonder why. Ah, cause, the why sets you to scrutinizing relationships. First you attend, focus, observe, isolate. Next you want the cause of something. Establishing tentative cause gets you to infer a low level generalization. "That lid will move because steam is pushing it up and down. If that particular kettle is put on that fire and it boils, then its lid will jump up and down," a relatively low level of abstraction because the particulars of the scene are still involved. The next level of abstraction, of generalization, will take you to the point of thinking, "When a kettle is placed on a fire the water will boil and cause a loose lid to move." You have gone from the particular to the general although you are still involved with the category of teakettles.[6]

Several levels of application are possible. The student can match a principle with its correct corresponding situation such as in problem Q.

---

[6] James M. Ward, "Learning to Generalize," *Science Education* 53 (December 1969): 423–24.

Q. Match each situation with the principle at play. Each stimulus can be used repeatedly.

1. Radiation   A. A sea breeze
2. Convection   B. An air conditioner
3. Conduction   C. A kite
                      D. A heater
                      E. A hot coffee cup

Another level of application requires the student to restate a problem. For example, in the story of the teakettle you might say that the problem at hand is to determine why the kettle lid is moving. Given this situation and problem, the students can be asked to state the problem without using the word *steam*.

Still another level of application would require the student to use a generalization to predict what will happen in a different situation where these principles are involved. You might ask the student a question such as: "Suppose the kettle lid were held fast and the spout were stopped up, what would happen when the kettle was placed on the stove?"

While there are other levels of application, these examples show how you can arrange experiences or tasks that force students to perform at the application stage.

Level 4: Analysis

The analysis level requires breaking down generalizations, concepts, and principles in order to better understand or clarify the ideas. A common type of test question for measuring at the analysis level is one that gives the student a passage of one or more paragraphs to read, followed by a list of questions. These questions do not ask simply for retention (knowledge level) and the ability to predict patterns or trends (comprehension level); they require the student to identify underlying assumptions of the author.

For example, the students might be asked to read the following parable on education taken from Plato's *Republic*.

> Imagine Mankind as dwelling in an underground cave with a long entrance open to the light across the whole width of the cave; in this they have been since childhood, with necks and legs fettered, so they have to stay where they are. They cannot move their heads around because of the fetters, and they can only look forward, but light comes from them from fire burning behind them higher up at a distance. Between the fire and the prisoners is a road above their level, and along it imagine a low wall has been built, as puppet showmen have screens in front of their people over which they work puppets. See then, bearers carrying along this wall all sorts of articles which they hold projecting above the wall, statues of men and other living things, made of stone or wood and all kinds of stuff, some of the bearers speaking and some silent, as you might expect.... What do you think such people would have seen of themselves and each other except their shadows, which the fire cast on the opposite wall of the cave?.... Suppose the prisoners were able to talk together, don't you think that when they named the shadows which they saw passing they would believe they were naming things?

"Now consider, what their release would be like, and their cure from fetters and their folly; let us imagine whether it might naturally be something like this. One might be released, and compelled suddenly to stand up and turn his neck around, and to walk and look towards the firelight; all this would hurt him, and he would be too much dazzled to see distinctly those things whose shadows he had seen before. What do you think he would say, if someone told him that what he saw before was foolery, but now he saw more rightly...? ...Don't you think he would be puzzled, and believe what he saw before was more true than what was shown to him now? Then suppose he were compelled to look towards the red light, it would hurt his eyes, and he would escape by turning them away to the things which he was able to look at, and these he would believe to be clearer than what was being shown to him."

Plato then has the man dragged out into the sunlight and then returned to the cave where he tells the other prisoners about his experiences, and that they are seeing only reflections. He is then ridiculed by the prisoners who find his tale unbelievable.[7]

The teacher might follow this passage with a series of questions such as the following:

1. Why does Plato select for his location for "Mankind" an underground cave?
2. Why does Plato have his released prisoner look at the blinding firelight and then the blinding sun?
3. Why did Plato choose to have the released prisoner "dragged" to the outside rather than merely led?
4. Upon his return to the cave, why was the released prisoner ridiculed for telling the truth?

Notice that each of these questions focuses on a *specific* part of the parable. This is important to the analytical process. Notice also that the student is required to *use* the particular passage to solve a problem. If this assignment seems difficult or bizarre, remember the assignments that you as a high school student had in poetry classes. You probably have had extensive contact with analysis assignments and analysis level test questions. This is but one of several types of analysis questions; it should, however, help to introduce your students to analysis tasks.

Level 5: Synthesis

In recent years students and teachers have come to hold in high esteem those types of assignments that have no single, predetermined, "correct" answer, but that require the unique talents and perceptions of each student to arrive at an acceptable answer. Unfortunately, today's teachers are feeling pressure from members of the community who want the schools to reject exercises in diver-

---

[7] From *The Greek Philosophers* by Rex Warner. Copyright © 1958 by Rex Warner. Reprinted by arrangement with The New American Library, Inc., New York, New York.

gent thinking and return to the traditional approach to teaching the "Three R's." [8] The value of synthesis tasks is summed up in the concept of Gestaltism, that is, "the whole is greater than the sum of its parts." The student is given the task of putting together a number of concepts to communicate a uniquely different idea, one that is her own. It is the essence of creativity itself, which is known by the artist, painter, song writer, movie producer, dancer, architect, and others who use their minds, bodies, and talents to express themselves. Not only rich in esthetic qualities, it also has practical value, since the synthesis process requires receiving problems from different perspectives, leading to inventions and to "building a better mousetrap."

Rather than to satisfy the current press for exercises that demand "the" correct answer, students could better spend part of their time seeking out relationships that will guide their actions. If this sounds unscientific, today's scientists would not agree that such open-ended exercises requiring divergent, creative thinking are at all unscientific. For example, if a layman were to ask a physicist for a definition of light, he would likely be told that light may be a wave phenomenon (wave theory) or it may be composed of particles (corpuscular theory). If the layman insisted on *the* correct definition of light, the physicist would probably tell him, "That isn't a useful question; physicists have stopped asking it." [9] The reason that physicists no longer are interested in a "correct" definition of light is that it is irrelevant. One definition, within a limited situation, enables scientists to account for certain phenomena; the other definition, in another set of circumstances, is more useful.[10]

We should all recognize the value of lower levels of thinking and their importance in the curriculum. Indeed, what better way is known to master the multiplication tables than via rote memory? Yet to limit classroom tasks to those that require only memorization of facts would be to limit the students in experiencing the types of problems that they must be prepared to solve in future life. Such a restriction also robs them of the ability to form new perceptions and express new conceptualizations.

In synthesis tasks the student is asked to take certain material, reorganize it, and assemble it in a new way to give it new meaning. The problem must be new to the student and, when possible, should be of special interest to him. For this reason the student should be involved in choosing the problem. This does not preclude assigning a particular problem to a group of students or to the entire class.

The teacher is responsible for either providing problems for the students or for leading them in the selection process. Since there is no single correct answer to be found, care should be taken to stipulate exactly what criteria will be used in evaluating the work. For example, consider the following problem.

---

[8] Kenneth T. Henson, "The Three R's in Futuristic Perspective," unpublished paper.
[9] James B. Conant, *Modern Science and Modern Man* (Garden City, N.Y.: Doubleday Anchor Books, 1952), p. 80.
[10] Robert S. Zais, *Curriculum Principles and Foundations* (New York: Thomas Y. Crowell, 1976), p. 14.

In many American communities the interest and participation in high school sports is so intense and the financial support is so great that there are many complaints that the school is so athletic-oriented that it neglects the academics. Suppose that you are captain of the football team at such a school. Furthermore, suppose that the classrooms have deteriorated and that the school lacks the needed money to restore the buildings. To make things even worse, suppose that your team has just ended another losing season.

Prepare a statement to justify the continuation of an interscholastic sports program in face of these critical circumstances. Devise a plan that will enable the school to finance the necessary building restorations and yet finance the team for coming years.

Or the geology teacher may present a rock for students to examine. Giving each student (or group of students) the materials needed to run tests of color, hardness and acidity, the students would tell where the rock originated and substantiate this conclusion with logic. The main objective is that the student *design a plan* for locating the derivative of particular rocks; the location itself is irrelevant.

Another example of a synthesis task would be to give each student a box of assorted materials with which to devise a container that will support the fall of an uncooked egg when dropped from a two-story window.

Studies on creativity indicate that the mind is usually more creative when the student:

1. Is encouraged to pursue a direction that seems right for her even when to others it may seem disorderly,
2. Is afforded opportunity to work alone; yet, provided (not forced) to share her work with others,
3. Works in a pressure-free environment,
4. Is protected from peer pressure to conform, and
5. Works within areas of her special interests[11]

When you develop tasks at the synthesis level, consider these conditions and try to provide an atmosphere of maximum conduciveness to creative thinking.

Level 6: Evaluation

Tasks at the evaluation level require students to make judgments based on logical accuracy, consistency, and other given criteria in addition to remembered criteria. An example of a task at this level would be to present students with a politician's election platform and ask them to examine it for accuracy, logic, and consistency. Students would also be expected to compare it with his previous political behavior or his support or rejection of bills involving similar issues. In other words, does he practice what he preaches?

Other levels of evaluation tasks require students to identify values or as-

[11] E. Paul Torrance, "Creative Teaching Makes a Difference," in *Creativity: Its Educational Implications*, ed. John C. Gowan et al. (New York: John Wiley & Sons, 1967), pp. 177–78.

sumptions on which judgments are made. For example, in your methods classes you may be asked to write a critique of your peers while they teach a mini-lesson. Suppose you were asked to respond to the following questions:

1. The critic found the lesson organized so that the concepts:
   a. flowed smoothly.
   b. were illogically presented.
   c. were arranged in chronological order.
   d. both a and b.
   e. both b and c.
2. According to the critic, the delivery of the lesson was:
   a. enhanced by the teacher's poise and self-confidence.
   b. strengthened by the use of good visual aids.
   c. augmented by the absence of unnecessary jargon and technical terms.
   d. all of the above.

Other types of evaluation questions require students to make judgments on a particular work based on similar works. The students may be afforded an opportunity to form their own list of criterion to use to evaluate.

This presentation on writing test items has related to each of the major six categories of Bloom's taxonomy of the cognitive domain, but space does not permit discussion and samples of all the sublevels. You are encouraged to explore further by examining the sources in Suggested Readings at the end of this chapter.

THE AFFECTIVE DOMAIN

The attainment of knowledge and the skills needed to apply that knowledge are in a sense what school is all about; but unless the students elect to *use* that knowledge and those skills, then a great deal has been wasted. For example, although the ability to read has some intrinsic value, suppose that a student elects not to read because he does not like to read. Suppose that another student masters just enough skills in math to pass the required courses but in the meanwhile develops such a feeling of fear or contempt toward mathematics that she refuses even to keep an accurate checkbook. In a sense the efforts of that student and her teachers have failed. For learning itself is defined as a somewhat permanent change in behavior. Then exactly what have this young man and woman failed to learn? He has failed to learn to appreciate the potential that is embodied in the ability to read. She has failed to realize her own potential in the area of mathematics.

From these two examples and from your knowing people who have chosen not to use their own knowledge and skills, you realize the significance of attitude toward knowledge. From other examples of learned people who have become destructive to society or to themselves, you can see that proper attitudes are indispensable for successful, happy living. The greatest lists of aims for American education contain entries that depend on certain attitudes; for example, reexamine the Seven Cardinal Principles of Secondary Education.

1. Health
2. Command of the fundamental processes
3. Worthy home membership
4. Vocational efficiency
5. Citizenship
6. Worthy use of leisure time
7. Ethical character

In fact, does not success in any of these aims depend on the development of certain attitudes? Even in the aim that may seem to be most separated from attitudes, that is, vocational efficiency, attitudes are necessary for success. (More than 85 percent of all jobs lost are lost because of an inability of workers to get along with their supervisors and co-workers.)

In a national poll of attitudes toward education, 44 percent of the responses listed the main purpose of American schools "to get better jobs," while 43 percent listed "to get along better with people at all levels of society." [12] It is clear that you need to lead students in the development both of certain attitudes and of necessary skills.

QUESTIONING TECHNIQUES

In the book *Taxonomy of Educational Objectives, Handbook 2: Affective Domain,* Krathwohl, Bloom, and Masia give five levels of internalization:[13]

1. Receiving — a willingness to tolerate a phenomenon.
2. Responding — voluntarily using the phenomenon.
3. Valuing — prizing and acting on the phenomenon.
4. Organization — using values to determine interrelationships between them.
5. Characterization — organization of values, beliefs, ideas, and attitudes into an internally consistent system.

As you consider your expectations of students in your future classes, take time now to list two attitudes that you wish them to have toward the subject you will teach.

Now, using the following examples as models, you should be able to write a question that will measure student attitudes at each of the first four levels: receiving, responding, valuing, and organizing.

---

[12] George H. Gallup, "Fourth Annual Gallup Poll of Public Attitudes Toward Education," *Phi Delta Kappan* (September 1972): 33–46.

[13] D. R. Krathwohl; B. S. Bloom; and B. B. Masia, *Taxonomy of Educational Objectives: The Classification of Educational Goals: Handbook 2: Affective Domain* (New York: David McKay, 1964).

Example 1: A math teacher uses the following questions to measure attitudes at each level:

1. Receiving: Would you like to join the math club?
2. Responding: When you play games that involve score keeping, do you ever volunteer to keep scores?
3. Valuing: Do you plan to take math next year when it becomes an elective?
4. Organization: Have you ever thought of math as an art?

Example 2: A history teacher teaching the Civil War asks the following questions:

1. Receiving: Would you like to have Confederate relics?
2. Responding: If your family or friends planned a vacation that had Vicksburg, Mississippi, on its route, would you suggest visiting the battlegrounds?
3. Valuing: Do you feel excited when seeing a movie on the Civil War?
4. Organization: While we have been studying this unit on the Civil War, have you ever tried to decide for yourself ways in which both governments were wrong?

Using the definition of each level of internalization and using these examples as a model, now write questions to test each level of your two statements about attitudes.

Your role in the development of attitudes will extend into yet other areas. First, you must help students learn to examine their current attitudes, particularly their values (values clarification) and to understand the basis for their values, that is, the process that they use to develop values. To achieve this, you can give students tasks requiring them to analyze their values. Second, you can help students develop their moral values by assessing their existing level of moral maturity and then giving them problem situations requiring them to perform at a level slightly above their current level of maturation.

Lawrence Kohlberg, a professor at Harvard University, has developed a hierarchy of three major stages through which each person must pass in the development of ethical awareness. These are:

1. Preconventional — behavior is determined by rewards and punishment. (What's best for me?)
2. Conventional — behavior is controlled by anticipation of praise or blame. (What will others think?)
3. Postconventional — behavior is regulated by principles embodying generality and comprehensiveness. (What's the right thing to do?) [14]

---

[14] Sidney B. Simon; Leland W. Howe; and Howard Kirschenbaum, *Values Clarification* (New York: Hart Publishing Company, 1972).

A familiar problem is a hypothetical case in which a person obeys a stop sign:

1. To avoid getting a fine. (Level 1)
2. To avoid criticism by others and to avoid breaking a law. (Level 2)
3. To avoid hurting others. (Level 3)

A different version of the same problem might be as follows:

> Recently in one of our major cities the fine for violating a stop sign was increased overnight from about $20 to $87.50. Many policemen refused to enforce the law, which they perceived unreasonable. Other policemen enforced it because they had taken an oath to enforce all laws. At what level did each group of policemen behave?

Clearly not all attitudes are limited to moral behavior. Other important behaviors that the school should foster include learning to appreciate, desire, enjoy, and empathize. Sidney Simon and his colleagues at the University of Massachusetts have developed and collected some seventy strategies for teachers to use to enable students to clarify their values. Following are two examples taken from this work.[14] In addition to affording students an opportunity to examine their values, these exercises have proven to stimulate a high level of interest among students and teachers.

*Alligator River**

PURPOSE

In this strategy, students reveal some of their values by the way they react to the characters in the story. Later on, in examining their reactions to the characters, students become more aware of their own attitudes. This strategy also illustrates how difficult it is for any one teacher to say, "I have the right values for other people's children."

PROCEDURE

The teacher tells either the X rated or G rated story of Alligator River, depending on the age of the students. Following the story, the students are asked to privately rank the five characters from the most offensive character to the least objectionable. The character whom they find most reprehensible is first on their list; then the second most reprehensible, and so on, with the fifth being the least objectionable.

After students have made their own rankings, groups of four are formed in which they share their thinking and discuss all the pros and cons with one another.

---

* Reprinted by permission of A & W Publishers, Inc. from *Values Clarification: A Handbook of Practical Strategies for Teachers and Students* by Sidney B. Simon, Leland W. Howe, and Howard Kirschenbaum. Copyright © 1972; copyright © 1978 Hart Publishing Company.

Following the discussion, the teacher might ask voting questions to find out how the class ranked each of the characters. (For example, "How many felt Abigail was the best character? How many felt she was the worst character?" Incidentally, this would also be a good way to form discussion groups, with those who ranked a given character first or last in the same group.)

The teacher can also ask some thought-provoking questions about the character they ranked as most offensive. For example: Is that the kind of person *you* least want to be like? What kind of person would be the opposite of this character? Write a description in your Values Journal. List three things you could do or are now doing to be like the opposite of the person you rated as worst. Then, the teacher might ask the students to form into groups of three to share what they have written. Or a few students could volunteer to read what they wrote to the whole class.

The Alligator River Story

RATED "X":

Once upon a time there was a woman named Abigail who was in love with a man named Gregory. Gregory lived on the shore of a river. Abigail lived on the opposite shore of the river. The river which separated the two lovers was teeming with man-eating alligators. Abigail wanted to cross the river to be with Gregory. Unfortunately, the bridge had been washed out. So she went to ask Sinbad, a river boat captain, to take her across. He said he would be glad to if she would consent to go to bed with him preceding the voyage. She promptly refused and went to a friend named Ivan to explain her plight. Ivan did not want to be involved at all in the situation. Abigail felt her only alternative was to accept Sinbad's terms. Sinbad fulfilled his promise to Abigail and delivered her into the arms of Gregory.

When she told Gregory about her amorous escapade in order to cross the river, Gregory cast her aside with disdain. Heartsick and dejected, Abigail turned to Slug with her tale of woe. Slug, feeling compassion for Abigail, sought out Gregory and beat him brutally. Abigail was overjoyed at the sight of Gregory getting his due. As the sun sets on the horizon, we hear Abigail laughing at Gregory.

RATED "G":

Once there was a girl named Abigail who was in love with a boy named Gregory. Gregory had an unfortunate mishap and broke his glasses. Abigail, being a true friend, volunteered to take them to be repaired. But the repair shop was across the river, and during a flash flood the bridge was washed away. Poor Gregory could see nothing without his glasses, so Abigail was desperate to get across the river to the repair shop. While she was standing forlornly on the bank of the river, clutching the broken glasses in her hands, a boy named Sinbad glided by in a rowboat.

She asked Sinbad if he would take her across. He agreed on the condition that while she was having the glasses repaired, she would go to a nearby store and steal a transistor radio that he had been wanting. Abigail refused to do this and went to see a friend named Ivan who had a boat.

When Abigail told Ivan her problem, he said he was too busy to help her out and didn't want to be involved. Abigail, feeling that she had no other choice, returned to Sinbad and told him she would agree to his plan.

When Abigail returned the repaired glasses to Gregory, she told him what she had had to do. Gregory was appalled at what she had done and told her he never wanted to see her again.

Abigail, upset, turned to Slug with her tale of woe. Slug was so sorry for Abigail that he promised her he would get even with Gregory. They went to the school playground where Greg was playing ball and Abigail watched happily while Slug beat Gregory up and broke his glasses again.

The Fall-Out Shelter Problem*

PURPOSE

This is a simulated problem-solving exercise. It raises a host of values issues which the student must attempt to work through in a rational manner. It is often a very dramatic example of how our values differ; how hard it is to objectively determine the "best" values; and how we often have trouble listening to people whose beliefs are different from our own.

PROCEDURE

The class is divided into groups of six or seven, who then sit together. The teacher explains the situation to the groups.

"Your group are members of a department in Washington, D.C. that is in charge of experimental stations in the far outposts of civilization. Suddenly the Third World War breaks out and bombs begin dropping. Places all across the globe are being destroyed. People are heading for whatever fallout shelters are available. You receive a desperate call from one of your experimental stations, asking for help.

"It seems there are *ten* people but there is only enough space, air, food, and water in their fall-out shelter for *six* people for a period of *three* months — which is how long they estimate they can safely stay down there. They realize that if they have to decide among themselves which six should go into the shelter, they are likely to become irrational and begin fighting. So they have decided to call your department, their superiors, and leave the decision to you. They will abide by your decision.

"But each of you has to quickly get ready to head down to your own fall-out shelter. So all you have time for is to get superficial descriptions of the ten people. You have half-an-hour to make your decision. Then you will have to go to your own shelter.

"So, as a group you now have a half-hour to decide which four of the ten will have to be eliminated from the shelter. Before you begin, I want to impress upon you two important considerations. It is entirely possible that the six people you choose to stay in the shelter might be the only six people

---

* Reprinted by permission of A & W Publishers, Inc. from *Values Clarification: A Handbook of Practical Strategies for Teachers and Students* by Sidney B. Simon, Leland W. Howe, and Howard Kirschenbaum. Copyright © 1972; copyright © 1978 Hart Publishing Company.

left to start the human race over again. This choice is, therefore, very important. Do not allow yourself to be swayed by pressures from the others in your group. Try to make the best choices possible. On the other hand, if you do not make a choice in a half-hour, then you are, in fact, choosing to let the ten people fight it out among themselves, with the possibility that more than four might perish. You have *exactly* one half-hour. Here is all you know about the ten people:

1. Bookkeeper, 31 years old
2. His wife; six months pregnant
3. Black militant; second-year medical student
4. Famous historian-author; 42 years old
5. Hollywood starlette; singer; dancer
6. Bio-chemist
7. Rabbi; 54 years old
8. Olympic athlete; all sports
9. College co-ed
10. Policeman with gun (they cannot be separated)

The teacher posts or distributes copies of this list, and the students begin. The teacher gives 15, 10, 5 and 1-minute warnings and then stops the groups exactly after a half-hour.

Each group can then share its selections with the other groups and perhaps argue a bit more, if there is time. Then the teacher asks the students to try to disregard the content of the activity and to examine the process and the values implications. He asks questions like: How well did you listen to the others in your group? Did you allow yourself to be pressured into changing your mind? Were you so stubborn that the group couldn't reach a decision? Did you feel you had the right answer? What do your own selections say to you about your values? These questions may be thought about or written about privately, or they may be discussed in the small groups or by the whole class.

VARIATIONS

1. Instead of eliminating four people from the shelter, students may be asked to rank order, the ten candidates from the most desirable to the least desirable. (There is also nothing sacred about four. It could be three or five, for example.)
2. After each member of the class has ranked the ten people, they can try to come to consensus on who is to be admitted to the shelter.
3. Instead of choosing six candidates for a remote shelter, each group may be instructed to pick four out of the ten to accompany them to their own shelter.
4. Other problem situations may be invented. For example, three (or more) people need a heart transplant and will more than likely die in three weeks if it is not performed. However, only one operation can be performed. The students are to assume the role of the doctor who will perform the operation and must make the decision of who will live.
5. The descriptions of the ten people can be changed to introduce additional values issues.

For example:

a. A 16-year-old girl of questionable IQ; a high school drop-out; pregnant.
b. The same policeman with gun; thrown off the force for police brutality (or given a community-relations award).
c. A clergyman; 75 years old.
d. A 36-year-old female physician; unable to have children (or known to be a confirmed racist).
e. A 46-year-old male violinist; served seven years for pushing narcotics; has been out of jail for six months.
f. A 20-year-old male Black militant; no special skills.
g. A 39-year-old former prostitute; "retired" for four years.
h. An architect; homosexual.
i. A 26-year-old male law student.
j. The law student's 25-year-old wife; spent the last nine months in a mental hospital; still heavily sedated. They refuse to be separated.

When using such games as these to help students understand their values, you must remember to remain objective and to resist any temptation that you may have to influence students to accept your own values. Furthermore, you should prevent ridicule among students.

As we have seen throughout this section on test construction, the writing of all tests requires time and attention. First you decide why you are giving the test; then you design it accordingly. Your best will have a variety of types of questions, reflecting both the cognitive and affective domains.

TEST ADMINISTRATION

Preliminary Adjustments

Certain preliminary arrangements are necessary if your test is to be valid. You should always see that all students are physically prepared — that they have the necessary materials, such as sharp pencils, paper, reference sources, and measuring instruments. If not, allot time before the test for each student to make these preparations.

Second, check to see that everyone is comfortable. The room should be neither hot nor cold, nor should it be noisy. The mere closing of windows facing a noisy road or the closing of a doorway to a noisy hall can help. Adjusting a room thermostat or radiator controls can help. Each student should have enough room so that he will not be cramped. Remind everyone to remove unnecessary books and papers from the desk tops; otherwise, some students will exhaust themselves by unconsciously balancing their paper on top of a stack of books or supporting books or purses in their laps.

Finally, if their test results are to reflect their true abilities, students, with your help, should be mentally relaxed. Many students become so tense on tests that they are unable to express their knowledge of the material. To relieve this tension, you can tell a joke; relate a humorous, personal experience; or simply talk for a moment about a ball game, a party, the weather, or another activity unrelated to the test.

Before the test begins, specify how the students should ask questions. Do you want them to raise their hands and direct their questions to you at once? Or do you want to go to each student to clarify questions? Usually it is better if the students do not ask questions from their seats, thus disrupting others. Also, tell them what to do when they complete the test. Should they bring it to you? Then, should they study another subject, read a library book, or just relax?

Taking the Test

Begin each test by reading the instructions aloud, with time for questions. Each student should start the test at the same time. This provides a sense of structure. Also, students should not be permitted to talk or otherwise disrupt others. Test administration should be conducted comfortably but uniformly.

Once the test has begun, do not interrupt. If questions emerge, answer the individuals who ask the questions and make a note of each necessary clarification or correction. To avoid a series of interruptions, near the end of the testing period you can inform the entire class of all these corrections at one time. Avoid making disturbing noises during the test, such as rattling papers, talking, or constantly walking through the class.

You should remain in the room at all times during the test and be available to answer student questions.

Finally, to end the test in an organized method, you should take up all remaining papers when time is called. The student who feels pressured to hand in his paper and yet sees that a few persistent students are given a few extra minutes to finish will feel cheated.

Test Scoring

Regardless of whether the test questions are objective, subjective, or both, your scoring should always be as objective as possible. Otherwise your judgment will be affected by your likes and dislikes for the students, by the general appearance of the paper, and by a force that is experienced by all teachers — a tendency to equalize the scores by subconsciously accepting poor responses from the poorer papers and being overcritical and deducting credit from respectable responses on the better papers. Because such behavior is common among beginning teachers, test scoring leaves them feeling guilty; they soon develop a real dislike for testing.

Testing is as much a part of your role and responsibility as is preparing and executing lessons. How, then, can you avoid the common distaste for testing? Learning and using the following principles should be of some help.

Specify the Answers Before the Scoring Begins

Before you begin scoring, write out the answer to each question on the test. As was mentioned in the first part of this chapter, teachers should always be the first to take their own tests. By establishing some correct responses, you will have a guideline for accepting and rejecting the students' answers. This does not mean, however, that all other answers are wrong. Inevitably you will find some student answers that are as accurate and desirable as your own predetermined ones. When this occurs, accept these answers as correct and add them to your master score sheet. This practice encourages creativity, which should be a part of all school activities — including tests.

Sometimes you will find that an unusually large portion of the class misses a relatively easy question. When this happens, you should be suspicious of the question. By examining the responses of five or six of the top scoring papers, you can check the validity of the question and determine whether you failed to cover the material in class or if the wording of the question was misleading. Whether the question was invalid or confusing, it should be eliminated.

Invariably, subjective questions will draw responses that are not exactly right and not exactly wrong. When this occurs, give partial credit, reserving full credit for those answers that reflect the major points made in class. But be sure that your test is not a measure of the student's ability to "psych out the teacher" and give the response that you want.

Conceal All Names

To protect your students from possible unfair scoring caused by your personal feelings, always conceal their names before you begin your scoring. There is no advantage in knowing whose paper you are scoring, but there are the previously mentioned disadvantages.

SUMMARY

Testing is one of your responsibilities as a teacher. It helps students know if they need to improve their study habits and to pinpoint needed areas of study. It also helps you to know if you need to change your methodology, and it pinpoints specific lessons and parts of lessons that need changing.

Most beginning teachers are discouraged when their first test is returned. Many low scores may result from a combination of unclear questions, ambiguous questions, and questions relating to material that was not covered in class. All tests should begin with written instructions. A good test has a variety of questions, some easy, some challenging; it covers the important concepts developed during the testing period.

How you administer a test is important. It should be conducted in a structured manner, and students should be made to feel comfortable. Remain in the room quietly throughout the testing period.

The evaluation of any test should be made as objective as possible. It should be anonymous. Predetermine the "correct" answer but accept other answers that are satisfactory.

Grading is a matter of private concern between the teacher and the individual student. It should, therefore, be kept confidential. Grades should reflect more than a few test scores. A term grade should represent daily assignments, weekly tests, and term projects.

EXPERIENCES

This chapter has focused on the development, administration, and scoring of teacher-made tests. These are major responsibilities of all teachers. Failure to develop expertise in any of these dimensions of testing can lead to serious problems. The following experiences show some common problem situations in which teachers find themselves.

Experience 1: A Twelfth-Grade Class Wants Information about a Forthcoming Test

Ms. Wheeler had been teaching physical education for about five years when she noticed a sudden change in student attitudes toward tests. Up until that time she had considered that discussing tests prior to their administration was unethical and absurd. If an exam was going to be a fair test of the students' knowledge about the subject, would not a previous discussion destroy the validity and purpose? The only information that she ever gave about a forthcoming test was a notification of its date. Although previous classes had teased, asking questions relative to the content on the test, Ms. Wheeler knew that they never expected her to cooperate and provide answers to their questions.

But this twelfth-grade class was different. When they asked for information about the forthcoming test, they expected her to provide it. They never asked for specific information about content, but they did ask specific questions about the test, such as "How many questions will the test have?" "How much will each question count?" "How many are true-and-false questions?" Taking these questions as good-natured jokes, Ms. Wheeler simply ignored them and went on with the lesson.

It became obvious, however, that the students were serious. They became upset when a test was administered without their previously knowing how long it would be and the type of questions it would contain. Soon after having met with this unpleasant experience, Ms. Wheeler changed her policy and began holding a discussion of each test one day prior to its administration. She found that this practice worked very successfully for two reasons. First, the students now felt that she was not trying to trick them with an unfamiliar test and that they could study in accordance with the specific type of test they were to take. Second, she felt that the practice was effective because it did not suggest what content to study as much as it did the correct method of study.

▶ *Questions and Discussion*

1. *If you reveal the number and type of questions to be included on a forthcoming test, will the test become less valid and less reliable?*

No, not if you provide this information for all the students in your class. It may help them identify the important ideas contained in the unit. It may improve the scores of those students who use the information to study for the test; but won't these students learn more in accordance with their increased scores?

If you are afraid to provide information about an objective, factual test that you are planning to administer, you can increase the length of the test. It will then be so comprehensive that the student who scores high on it will have to know a majority of the facts studied during the previous study unit.

2. *Do today's students view tests as less important than did the students of a few years ago?*

Today's students feel that tests are just as important as did their earlier counterparts. The main difference in their attitudes toward tests is that yesterday's students saw tests as important for one reason only — to determine grades. Today's students see an additional purpose in tests; they wish to score well because they know that test scores reflect the quality of their learning. It is for this purpose that they wish to know how to study for each test; they realize that a test that tricks them is not an accurate instrument for measuring their learning progress.

3. *How can you make testing more palatable?*

By removing fear from testing, you can make it less distasteful to yourself and the students. Develop a routine manner of test administration and return, and always be as pleasant as you can. Your manner will help the students to relax; and if you follow the same routine each time a test is administered, you can ease their feelings of insecurity as test takers.

When returning tests, always go over each question and explain the correct answers. Partial credit should always be given when it is earned.

Experience 2: A Typing I Class Uses Bluebirds

Mrs. Bentley's Typing I class was composed of about thirty girls and ten boys, none of whom had previously taken typing. She had a unique system for reporting the individual grades. Along one wall she posted a white sheet of paper, on which she had painted a landscape scene with a fence in the foreground and a blue sky above. Higher up, there were beautiful, fluffy cumulus clouds. On the fence sat about forty bluebirds, each with the name of one of the students, including James, who lived in one of the city's worst ghettos.

As each student developed the ability to type above fifty words per minute, the bird with his name on it would leave the fence and begin to ascend. Right away several of the birds made their departures. These represented students who owned their own typewriter and had become familiar with typing on their own prior to the beginning of the class. This frustrated James very much because he was still learning the keys when others were typing above fifty words per minute.

Each day he found himself trying a little harder and making a few more mistakes than the day before, and each mistake carried a five-word penalty. By the end of the year some of the bluebirds were flying into the clouds. James's bluebird was still sitting on the fence!

► *Questions and Discussion*

1. *Should test scores ever be made public so that a student can compare his progress with that of his classmates?*
   If Johnny outscores Bobby on a test, that is not important; it is better to have a student compete with himself. Here he always finds a challenge and yet he never faces the impossible odds of being forced to compete with students who have higher abilities.

2. *List several advantages and several disadvantages of making each individual's scores known to all students.*
   To the highly capable student, grades can be a strong motivational force. Often two friends will work hard to outperform each other in class, grades becoming a strong motivational force — provided each student has access to the knowledge of his peer's grades.

   One of the dangers in making scores public is that this can discourage the less capable student and impede progress for him. It can also harm the high performer by making him overly concerned, producing serious emotional and social problems. Another disadvantage is that publicizing the grades often causes students to focus their attention on grades and, therefore, grades become the ultimate goal. The student learns to appreciate good scores, but not to appreciate the value of learning. This may result in the student cheating to get a high score or cramming all night without really developing any degree of understanding.

Experience 3:   Faulty Test Administration Destroys Reliability

Students at our high school are required to take a series of standardized examinations often administered during the early fall. Since our air-conditioning unit stays on the blink throughout most of the hottest days, it is very uncomfortable at this time of year. On one hot test day the students had only begun taking the test when it became necessary to open all of the windows. Within minutes a man began mowing the lawns.

Throughout the morning he circled the yards. The noise from the lawn mower continuously pulsated, fading for half a round and building in intensity for the following half round. By the noon break the tension was high; everyone was a nervous wreck. The only consolation was that as they completed the first half of the examination, the yardman completed mowing the lawns.

During the afternoon session the yardman began a different task. He used a gasoline power saw to trim the trees and hedges alongside the building, just beneath the open windows. The noise produced by this machine was several times greater than that of the mower. The trimming lasted throughout the afternoon. Several students became so disturbed that they gave up and put their heads down on their tables. Others expressed their feelings that the undesirable conditions made the test unfair.

► *Questions and Discussion*

1. *How can the accuracy and reliability of a test be destroyed by an undesirable environment?*
   The purpose of any test is to determine how well each student understands certain ideas pertinent to the recent lessons. Any distracting variable that lowers the students' score makes them appear to know less about the subject.

   A second purpose of tests is to identify areas in which students are weak, so that they will know which areas to study harder and the teacher will know which areas to emphasize. Distracting forces may make students appear weak in areas that they actually know well.

2. *React to this quotation: "The testing environment does not affect the results of a test because every person is exposed to the same distractions and any ill effects will cancel themselves out."*
   This statement would be true if it were not for the fact that some students are affected much more than others by the same distractions. The scores resulting from a test administered with many distractions may really reflect each student's resistance or vulnerability to distractions.

3. *List several adjustments that you can make before the test begins, to ensure a proper environment for testing.*
   Prior to administering a test, check the temperature of the room and adjust it if necessary. Check the noise level and arrange to lower it if necessary. You are responsible for seeing that each student has adequate seating space, writing area, and lighting.

In this chapter you have read about good practices for constructing, administering, and scoring tests. You have examined questions written at all levels of the cognitive and affective domains. Now you will have an opportunity to assemble and apply your knowledge and skills on testing.

1. In your major teaching field, develop an objective test containing a combination of true-false, matching. and multiple-choice items. Include questions that measure the higher cognitive levels as well as some that measure in the affective domain.
2. Construct an essay test; then rewrite each question, making it more precise and manageable.

SUGGESTED READINGS

BLOOM, BENJAMIN S. *Taxonomy of Educational Objectives: The Classification of Educational Goals: Handbook 1: Cognitive Domain.* New York: David McKay, 1956.

BLOOM, BENJAMIN S.; HASTINGS, J. THOMAS; and MADAUS, GEORGE F. *Handbook on Formative and Summative Evaluation of Student Learning.* New York: McGraw-Hill, 1971.

GIROD, GERALD R. *Writing and Assessing Attitudinal Objectives.* Columbus, Ohio: Charles E. Merrill, 1973.

KRATHWOHL, DAVID R.; BLOOM, BENJAMIN; and MASIA, BERTRAM B. *Taxonomy of Educational Objectives: The Classification of Educational Goals: Handbook 2: Affective Domain.* New York: David McKay, 1964.

MAGER, ROBERT F. *Preparing Instructional Objectives.* Palo Alto, Calif.: Fearon Publishers, 1962.

MOSSTON, MUSKA. *Teaching: From Command to Discovery.* Belmont, Calif.: Wadsworth Publishing Company, 1972.

OLIVA, PETER F. *The Secondary School Today,* 2d ed. Chapter 18. San Francisco: Intext Educational Publishers, 1972.

RENNER, JOHN W.; BIBENS, ROBERT F.; and SHEPHERD, GENE D. *Guiding Learning in the Secondary School.* Chapter 10. New York: Harper and Row, 1972.

SIMON, SIDNEY B.; HOWE, LELAND W.; and KIRSCHENBAUM, HOWARD. *Values Clarification.* New York: Hart Publishing Company, 1972.

WILLIAMS, RICHARD H. "How to Improve Professor Made Tests." *Improving College and University Teaching Yearbook, 1975.* Corvallis: Oregon State University Press, 1974.

Evaluation

CHAPTER

15

OBJECTIVES

Upon completion of this chapter you should be able to:
1. Define *evaluation.*
2. Differentiate between testing and evaluation.
3. List three factors to be reflected in a term grade.
4. Justify the acceptance or rejection of the practice of using assignments for extra credits.
5. Describe one major limitation of the use of the bell curve in assigning high school grades.
6. Determine the stanine scores for a class of students.
7. Transfer stanines into percentages.

Evaluation differs from testing. Unlike testing, which should be conducted objectively and is independent of the teacher's own values, evaluation demands that you make a qualitative judgment or set of values upon what you are evaluating. Evaluation further differs from testing in that it is much broader. Testing encompasses such tasks as either selecting or constructing the appropriate exams, administering them, and scoring the responses; but all this is merely a prerequisite to evaluation. Once the tests are returned and the results determined, you must use these results if, indeed, the testing is to be worthwhile. The use that you make of test results is evaluation. Figure 15.1 shows the relationship between measurement and evaluation and among their parts. Notice that evaluation is divided into two main categories: formative and summative. As you read the following paragraphs, note that there is a sharp distinction between these two categories. Your effective use of evaluation depends upon your ability to separate these two basic types of evaluation.

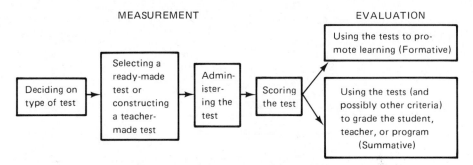

Figure 15.1   Measurement and Evaluation Relationships

FORMATIVE EVALUATION

Throughout the history of our schools little use has been made of formative evaluations. Formative evaluation can be defined as the designing and using of tests for one specific purpose: to *promote* learning. Although most teachers agree that going over test answers in class can help some students to learn a little about the material, they are aware that this will not result in total mastery of the material. A much more systematic use of evaluation to promote learning is essential.

Successful use of formative evaluation requires a change in attitude of both teachers and students, who have for too long equated tests with grades. When using tests for formative purposes, you should:

1. Avoid recording individual scores.
2. Be concerned with only whether or not the student has mastered the material at an acceptable level.
3. Involve the student in keeping a continuing record of his progress.
4. Avoid mentioning grades.
5. Assume that, when properly motivated, all students are capable of mastering the material.
6. Avoid pushing students so fast that they become confused and discouraged.
7. Reassure students that their results on these tests will not count toward their grades.

Since this is somewhat of a reversal of the way that both students and teachers have perceived evaluation, you will need to be patient and reassuring if you elect to use tests to help students learn.

SUMMATIVE EVALUATION

Since, historically, teachers have used tests almost exclusively for determining student grades, you might assume that they are systematic in converting raw scores into letter grades. In reality, though, each teacher seems to have an individual system, and many teachers use a different system each grading period. Why? Because most teachers never find a system with which they are satisfied. There is no single system that is right for all classes. When you become aware of the strengths and weaknesses of various grading systems, you will be in a better position to choose one wisely.

Should Students Compete?

All evaluation systems can be grouped into two categories: those that force a student to compete with other students (norm-referenced) and those that do not require interstudent competition, but instead are based on a set standard of mastery (criterion-referenced). Traditionally our schools have required competition among students. This practice is supported by many teachers, who believe that competition among students is necessary for motivating. (Since this issue has already been discussed in other chapters, it will not be repeated here.) Many also believe that competition is needed to prepare students for their adult life in a competitive world, especially for getting ahead in their future employment.

COMPETITIVE EVALUATION

Standardized Tests

An example of tests that force students to compete among themselves is the standardized test. There are many such tests that are very popular in our schools today. All of these have several features in common. First, they are based on a norm derived from the average scores of thousands of students who have taken the test. Usually these scores come from students throughout the country; therefore, each student's performance is compared to that of thousands of other students.

Standardized tests are usually used to measure or grade a school's curriculum. Seeking to make teachers more accountable, state officials have forced schools to use standardized tests (given to students to measure teacher success). And, yes, they are even used to measure student success. For example, the state of New York has administered its Regency Tests for many decades to determine student success. By the early 1980s, almost all of the states had legislated minimal learning standards. Tests are being developed to determine the level of attainment of each student and each school. Florida, which in July 1980 began testing its teachers for twenty-three regional competencies (Oliva, 1980), and Oklahoma, with its legislated Bill 1706, are examples of the many states that use standardized tests to make accountable their students, teachers, and colleges of education.

The Normal Curve

A second use of tests that requires students to compete with others is the normal curve, or probability curve. The curve could well be called the natural curve or chance curve because it reflects the distribution of all sorts of things in nature. This distribution is shown in Figure 15.2. The normal curve is divided into equal segments. The vertical line through the center (the mean) represents the average of a whole population. Each mark to the *right* of the mean represents one average or standard deviation above the average. Each vertical line to the *left* of the center represents one standard unit of deviation below the mean. As the diagram shows, about 34 percent of the population is within the one standard deviation unit above the mean and about 34 percent is within one standard deviation below the mean. Only about 14 percent of the population is in the second deviation range above the mean and about 14 percent is in the second deviation range below the mean. A very small portion of the population (approximately 2.3 percent) deviates enough from the mean to fall within the third unit of deviation above the mean; an equal portion deviates three standard deviations below the mean.

Another example would be the following. If the temperature is taken every day at 3:00 P.M. from June 15 until August 15 for ten years, and a mean or average were taken, the individual temperatures were listed vertically from hottest to coldest, and the line were divided into six equal parts — 34 percent of the temperatures would fall in the section just above the middle; 34 percent would fall within the section just below the middle; 14 percent would fall in the second section above the mean; and 14 percent in the second section below the mean. Only 2.3 percent of the temperature readings would fall in the third section *above* the mean, and 2.3 percent would fall in the lowest section *below* the mean.

Some of the many things that are subject to this type of distribution are the weight and height of animals and plants, the margin of error of both man and machine, and, of course, the I.Q. of human beings. Not all phenomena are dis-

Figure 15.2 Normal Probability Curve

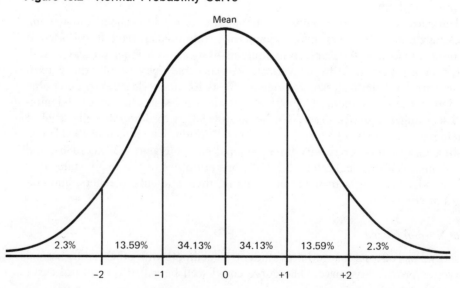

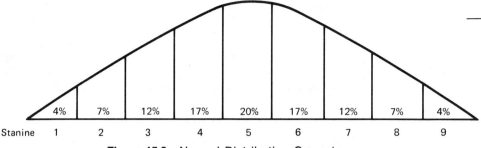

Figure 15.3 Normal Distribution Curve to Determine Stanine Scores

tributed in the ratios represented by the normal curve; for example, the chronological ages of the human population do not follow this pattern.

The normal curve, as it is often applied to the assigning of grades in a school classroom, makes several bold assumptions. First, like other evaluation schemes that are based on competition among students, it assumes that how well a particular student's performance compares to the average of a group of students (usually his classmates) is important. Second, it assumes that all students have an equal opportunity to succeed as though all have equal potential, which is extremely unlikely unless the class has been homogeneously grouped. Third, it assumes that the number of students used as a norm is large enough to reflect the characteristics of all students at the particular grade level. Unless the class size exceeds one hundred students, this is a very bold assumption indeed. The use of the normal curve assumes that 68 percent of the students will earn C's, 27 percent with earn B's, and another 27 percent D's; 2½ percent will earn A's and 2½ percent will fail.

Stanine Scores

Many schools use stanine scores to determine student performance. Meaning Standard Nine, this method uses the normal distribution curve to group test scores into nine categories. (See Figure 15.3.) This modification of the bell curve evaluation gets rid of the A's, B's, C's, D's, and F's. Many feel that the psychological advantage of escaping the letter grade stigma is important. Also, having nine categories affords the teacher more groups in which to place projects that must be evaluated arbitrarily.

Schoolwide Standards

Even more popular than the standard curve is the practice that schools have always had of setting their own standards. You are undoubtedly familiar with this system:

90 percent and above	= A	60–69 percent	= D
80–89 percent	= B	Below 60 percent	= Failure
70–79 percent	= C		

This type of evaluation plan makes an important and often false assumption: It assumes that the level of difficulty of the test is exactly fitted to the abilities of the student. Student teachers usually come to realize this error as they begin marking their first set of papers, finding that almost everyone failed the test. Although the exact percent requirements vary some from school to school, the system remains a very common method of evaluation.

NONCOMPETITIVE EVALUATION

In recent years researchers and educators have presented much evidence indicating that grading in the high school should be strictly an individual concern, involving the teacher and the student. It once was thought that competition for grades was necessary because it motivated each student to do his best. This is certainly true for those students who have the most ability. However, forcing the less capable students to compete with their classmates can discourage them and force them to concentrate on the inadequacies. Competition can also be bad for the more capable student, as was mentioned in an earlier chapter. The teacher can reduce this damage by refraining from making test scores and grades public.

Many contemporary educators feel that grades should be based on the individual's ability; that no student should receive an *A* unless he is really trying, and that no student who is exerting himself to his full potential should receive an *F*. These teachers hold that the purpose of grading is not to acknowledge high I.Q.'s and to punish those who do not possess them, but that each grade should reflect the degree of progress a student makes compared to his ability.

Students should be required to keep a record of their progress in class. Their judgment should be sought and used in determining their grades. A relevant question may be, How do you believe the quality of this work compares to your previous work? Do you believe that this is the best you can do? Of course this approach requires that the teacher know each student — not as a face, but as a developing, growing person.

Grading Involves More Than Testing

The terms *grading* and *testing* are often used synonymously; this is a mistake, for a student's grades should reflect more than his test scores. Some things other than the acquisition of knowledge are important in school. For example, as a teacher you will have responsibility for seeing that each student develops certain behavioral patterns such as honesty, promptness with assignments, the ability to work with others, and respect for others. Each of these traits should, therefore, be reflected in a student's grade. Evaluating these qualities is essentially subjective; and to avoid becoming prejudiced, you should decide at the beginning of the year just how much weight this part of the total evaluation carries, and take care not to exceed the limits.

Grades should represent all the major activities a student engages in while in your classroom. Daily work and possible term projects should perhaps carry as much weight toward the final grade for the term as the tests. If you use several tests (weekly or biweekly), daily assignments, term projects, and daily discussions, you will have enough satisfactory material on which to base the final grade.

Begin with Much Understanding

As a beginning teacher, recently exposed to college tests, you will probably grade too firmly. To avoid the risk of alienating and discouraging your students, be a little lenient at first. This does not mean that you should be quick to change a grade when you find that a student is unhappy with it, for this often results in reinforcing complaints. Being lenient at first means that you should not expect one certain answer on most types of questions and that you should not expect everyone to score 70 and above. It means that, if you believe that Jimmy is trying despite the fact that he scores 55 instead of the 60 set as passing, he may receive a *C* or *D* rather than an *F*. Discussions with Jimmy throughout the year will let you assess the degree to which he applies himself.

ASSIGNMENTS FOR EXTRA CREDIT

Some teachers include a bonus question on every major test to challenge the most capable students. This is fine if those who do not answer it correctly are not penalized. Some teachers offer extra credit to students who come to special sessions and complete extra assignments on problems with which they are having difficulties. This procedure also can be very helpful in motivating students. However, when a student asks for an assignment for extra credit at the end of the grading period, he may be less interested in learning than he is in raising his grade. Essentially the student asks, "Will you assign me some extra punishment so that my grade can be elevated?" The teacher may respond by assigning forty problems that the student already knows how to work or by assigning the task of copying two thousand words from an encyclopedia, library book, or magazine without having to learn the content. This practice is most undesirable, for it encourages some students to procrastinate until the last minute and then to subject themselves to *X* amount of punishment rather than attaining *X* amount of understanding. They also learn to dislike the subject producing the pain.

When students ask to do extra work for credit, you should base your decision about extra assignments on whether you believe that they will learn from the task. You may ask the students what type of assignment they propose to do and what they expect to learn from it. If they can convince you that they can and will learn as a result of the task, the assignment may be warranted.

Your decision on a specific grade is essentially a subjective one. Answering one question may be helpful to you each time you assign a grade: *What grade will be the best for this student?* Naturally, the answer will be determined by that student's ability and application. To assign a grade that is higher than deserved is certainly not good for the student; neither is assigning a grade lower than what is earned.

But having a philosophy alone is not enough. As a teacher you will be faced with making decisions based on the information that you have at hand. So let's begin preparing for that time by examining a typical situation at the end of a grading period. Ideally you will have a variety of feedback upon which to base each grade; for example there should be some class projects, presentations, classwork, homework, and, of course, tests. Following is what you might have for each of your students at the end of a six-weeks' grading period.

Six weekly tests

One final exam

One term paper

One oral presentation of term project

One group project

Twenty homework assignments

Twenty classroom assignments

Examine the preceding criteria, assigning relative values to each in order to arrive at a grade for the six-weeks' period. Be sure to consider the amount of time that the student has spent on each activity. You may wish to begin by rank-ordering these elements according to the time invested in each. For example:

Activity	Time Required
Homework 30 x 40 min. assign.	20 hours
Classwork 20 x 30 min. assign.	10 hours
Group project	6 hours
Six wkly tests at 50 min.	5 hours
One term paper	4 hours
Oral presentation of project (counting preparation)	3 hours
One final exam	1 hour

When totaled, these activities are found to have required forty-nine hours of student time. To simplify the process, you might simply assign an additional hour's credit to class participation. With a new total of fifty points, you may wish to assign 2 percent of the total grade to each hour spent in each activity. Thus the following system would emerge:

Homework = 40 percent

Classwork = 20 percent

Group projects = 12 percent

Weekly tests = 10 percent

Oral presentation = 6 percent

Final exam = 2 percent

Classroom participation = 10 percent

But suppose, as the teacher of this class, that you are not happy to have the final exam count only 2 percent against 10 percent for classroom participation. This is no problem, for you can now distribute 5 percent to each of them, or 7 percent and 3 percent and so on.

Naturally the distribution in your system will not be identical to this one. That does not matter so long as you assign each grade based on your chosen system. But, upon what other criteria (as opposed to the time spent on each activity) could you base your grading system? How about the degree of emphasis given each topic in class? What about the degree of cooperation with other students, and so on?

Your school may require a certain percent for an *A*, *B*, *C*, and *D*. But if you are given the freedom to design your own requirements, the answering of one question may be helpful to you each time and every time: What grade is the most appropriate and helpful to this student?

SUMMARY

Your ability to write good tests is important; however, you must know how to *use* these tests to grade your students, your program, and your own teaching. Such employment of test results is labeled summative evaluation. Generally teachers have failed to use tests to promote student learning (formative evaluation). Although most teachers use tests mainly to grade students, there is little agreement as to how this should be done.

The traditional, school-set standards such as 90–100 percent = *A*, 80–89 percent = *B*, and so on, assume that all students are capable of succeeding or that not all students should be capable of success. Use of the bell curve in secondary schools assumes that the performances of the group will fall in the same pattern (or distribute themselves) as do infinitely large numbers of student scores. Avoid using systems that are not suited to your groups of students.

Many contemporary teachers feel that students should not be forced to compete with their peers for grades; that the degree to which they master the material and the degree to which they apply themselves should determine their final grades for the course. Others feel that interstudent competition is essential to motivate students. The final decision belongs to you, the individual teacher.

EXPERIENCES

This chapter has discussed the teacher's role in evaluation. As in other aspects of teaching you will encounter new challenges daily; no list of principles, therefore, could ever be comprehensive enough to guide your behavior in all circumstances. The following experiences are included to show the complexity of such a seemingly simple task as assigning a student grade or convincing others of the limitations and functions of grades.

Experience 1: A Parent Confuses Grades with Success

Susie Bates was in the eighth grade when her schoolwork took a rapid decline. From one six-weeks' grading period to the next, her grades fell from B to F. Susie's father, a high school principal, called her principal to discuss the matter — after the report cards were passed out. The principal called Susie's homeroom teacher to the phone. Mr. Bates began with the usual question, "Can you tell me why Susie's grades have fallen so much?" The teacher responded "No" and asked if Mr. Bates knew. His response was "No," but he mentioned that Susie had started playing in a pop band one or two nights a week and had suddenly become especially interested in boys. Did the teacher think that this could have any connection with her low grades? Difficult as this may be to believe, this was the conduct of a high school principal in response to the failure of his own child.

The Bates case was typical in that the parent called after the grading period was over to ask what could be done about Susie's low grades. He was really asking, "What are you going to do about it?" The teacher can do very little after the fact, except perhaps to help Susie and her father realize that Susie's problem is not that she received an F but that she did not learn enough in a given period of time, and that very little can be done to correct the past. They can try only to avoid repeating the mistake. Teachers who are serious about helping students learn to suspect a Bates call as much as they learn to appreciate a sign of parent interest that comes early enough to help the student.

The teacher explained to Mr. Bates that he wanted to help Susie to achieve and learn, not just to get higher grades, and that perhaps together they could achieve this goal by encouraging her and then rewarding her for her achievements by letting her know of their pride in her.

▶ *Questions and Discussion*

1. *Should the teacher change a grade at the request of a parent?*

Generally no, unless there has been a mistake in the grade. To yield to the pressures of a parent will teach the student that force is a satisfactory method for achieving success.

2. *Should the teacher give an extra assignment to help the student elevate his grade?*

Only if the student can learn from the assignment; and, even then, the teacher should avoid letting this practice become too common. Extra assignments to increase a grade can teach the student to procrastinate throughout the term, as she expects to be able to increase her grade at the last moment.

Experience 2:   A Student Is Given a Break

Linda Evans, in Mrs. Rolando's ninth-grade math class, was a delightful girl, always bubbling with happiness. Perhaps her lack of seriousness explained her constant row of *D*'s and *F*'s in all of her subjects. Or, perhaps her *D*'s and *F*'s had caused her to become less serious about her schoolwork.

At the end of the second semester Linda had earned a *D+* average. The fact that she had performed higher than usual tempted Mrs. Rolando to give her a *C* rather than the earned *D+*. She decided to talk with her before assigning either grade.

Mrs. Rolando began the discussion by asking if she was aware that she was on the *C* and *D* border. She told Linda that she believed her a *C* student rather than a *D* student, and that she had a plan for finding this out. Linda eagerly listened while Mrs. Rolando explained that she would assign her a *C* for the semester if she agreed to bring her report card at the end of the first grading period of the next year. At that point they would check her math grade in her new class to see if the assumption was correct. Linda happily agreed to these terms. Mrs. Rolando thought the possibility of Linda's remembering the plan throughout the summer vacation and into another school year was remote, but no harm could come of her ploy.

When the new year began, Mrs. Rolando had a total of 180 new faces to remember and 180 new personalities to learn. At the end of the first grading period she was handing out report cards when Linda came in and handed over her new report card. Mrs. Rolando vaguely remembered her agreement. She scanned the card to find that not only did Linda have a *B−* in math but that in all her subjects the lowest grade was a *C−*. Linda explained that she was now eligible to try out as a cheerleader. This was obviously an important moment and a triumph for Linda Evans.

▶ *Questions and Discussion*

1. *Was the teacher justified in giving Linda a higher grade than she earned?*

The teacher should feel free to experiment if and when an unusual circumstance warrants it; but she should be discreet and caution the student against publicizing the event. She should always make the student understand that she is not giving the student anything except an opportunity to prove ability.

2. *What potential damage is there in telling a student that you are assigning her a grade that is above her average earned grade?*

It could encourage her to be lazy. Also, an unearned grade does not have the motivating power that an earned grade has. If you feel that a student deserves a break, you may decide to assign her a slightly higher grade without telling her, leaving her to deduce that she had scored slightly higher than she thought on the final test for the term.

Experience 3: Parents' Attempt to Motive Their Child Backfires

Dr. Bough was a very reputable M.D. whose daughter was in Mr. Hammonds's eighth-grade science class. Mr. Hammonds hardly noticed Ann for the first few weeks of the term because she was very quiet. She never volunteered to answer questions and, when asked to respond, would pause for a minute or more, hoping that he would call on another student. One day Mr. Hammonds received a note from the counselor's office to return a call to Mrs. Bough. They scheduled an appointment to discuss Ann's performance in school. When the time came, Mr. Hammonds was ready. He had studied Ann's cumulative records and her schoolwork over previous years. He found that the three I.Q. scores on file were 99, 101, and 102 — remarkably consistent and also remarkably average. Ann's grades had consistently been *B*'s, indicating that she had been performing high in relation to her ability. Currently Ann was taking five academic subjects and band — no study period. Her test scores in Mr. Hammonds's room had steadily declined from *B* to *D−*.

Both parents came to the session. As a matter of routine, Mr. Hammonds began the discussion by letting the parents talk while he listened. Right away he saw that they had two things to say. They said them politely but firmly: Ann was capable of making top grades and she was doing her best. In fact, often after she had scored a *D* or an *F* on Mr. Hammonds's test, her mother would quiz her orally and she would score 100 percent.

Following the next test, Mr. Hammonds gave Ann an oral exam, asking the same questions. She had failed the written test, but scored 90 percent on the oral repeat. Ann studied hard, learned the material, then failed the tests. Why?

Ann's parents saw themselves in her. Both of them had been *A* students, so why shouldn't Ann make *A*'s? They had considered each of Ann's *B*'s a failure. By pressuring her to raise her grades to *A*'s, Ann's parents had turned each test into a trauma that produced mental barriers.

The problem carried over into each daily lesson: when a teacher looked toward Ann, she froze stiff. Ann had developed real emotional problems. No parents were more interested than the Boughs in their child's success in school, and no parents were more willing to express their concern to the teacher; however, the Boughs were not trying to help Ann. They were trying to get her to make higher grades not because they wanted to help her, but because they saw themselves in Ann. By making straight *A*'s she would reflect the "Bough" image to her teacher and classmates.

Mr. Hammonds suggested to Ann's parents that they not discuss Ann's grades with her until he could try out an idea that he had. He promised that he would call them when the experiment was over, and they agreed to cooperate. For the next few weeks Mr. Hammonds observed Ann, and like a detective he searched for an answer. Several times he caught himself on the verge of reminding the class that specific material would be included on the next test, but each time he refrained. He soon noticed that Ann and the rest of the class became more confident and worked harder.

► *Question and Discussion*

How could Mr. Hammonds make Ann's parents understand that learning is more important than grades?
The teacher should not stress grades in his discussion with parents or students; instead, he should talk about progress. Even when discussing the student's successes, the teacher should avoid using percentages and letter grades. Eventually the parents should learn that grades are important only when they reflect how hard the student is trying and how thoroughly she is learning.

ACTIVITIES

As you read this chapter, your mind probably flashed forward to the time when you will be teaching *and grading* your own classes. Hopefully you thought about the types of activities that would become your criteria for grading. You had an opportunity to examine a grading system for a hypothetical class, but you did not have an opportunity to design a system of your own. The following activities will provide this opportunity.

1. Suppose that you have complete autonomy for grading. (This is very rare in secondary schools.) Decide whether you would use a norm-referenced or criterion-referenced system, and defend your choice.
2. Suppose that you are forced to use the *A B C D* system with 90, 80, 70 and 60 percent intervals. List those criteria that you would use for grading, and assign a relative value (percent) to each.

Tests and Evaluation

BUTTS, R. FREEMAN; PECKENPAUGH, DONALD H.; and KIRSCHENBAUM, HOWARD, eds. *The School's Role as Moral Authority.* Washington, D.C.: Association for Supervision and Curriculum Development, 1977.

BLOCK, JAMES H. "Promoting Excellence Through Mastery Learning." *Theory Into Practice* 19 (Winter 1980): 66–74.

BLOOM, BENJAMIN S.; HASTINGS, J. THOMAS; and MADAUS, GEORGE F. *Handbook on Formative and Summative Evaluation of Student Learning.* New York: McGraw-Hill, 1971.

BRANDT, RONALD. "Curriculum Evaluation: Uses, Misuses, Nonuses." Special edition on evaluation. *Educational Leadership* (January 1978).

DENTON, JON J., and HENSON, KENNETH T. "Mastery Learning and Grade Inflation." *Educational Leadership* 37 (November 1979): 150–52.

GUSKEY, THOMAS R. "Mastery Learning: Applying the Theory." *Theory Into Practice* 19 (Winter 1980): 104–11.

KIM, EUGENE C., and KELLOUGH, RICHARD D. *A Resource Guide for Secondary School Teaching,* 2d ed. New York: Macmillan 1978.

OLIVA, PETER F., and HENSON, KENNETH T. "What Are the Essential Generic Teaching Competencies?" *Theory Into Practice* 19 (Spring 1980): 117–21.

RENNER, JOHN W.; BIBENS, ROBERT F.; and SHEPHERD, GENE D. *Guiding Learning in the Secondary School.* New York: Harper and Row, 1972.

SIMON, SIDNEY B.; HOWE, LELAND W.; and KIRSCHENBAUM, HOWARD. *Values Clarification.* New York: Hart Publishing Company, 1972.

VARGAS, JULIE S. *Writing Worthwhile Behavioral Objectives.* New York: Harper and Row, 1972.

Professional Competencies

PART SEVEN

At the beginning of this book you were encouraged to begin building on your own strengths and uniqueness. Throughout each chapter you have been provided opportunities to analyze situations and decide how you should best handle them.

This last section is different only in that it provides information to help you analyze your teaching skills, and it discusses many situations that worry the beginning teacher — situations that have not been discussed thus far.

Observing Yourself—
Improvement Begins with You

OBJECTIVES

Upon completion of this chapter you should be able to:
1. List three advantages of peer teaching that are not found in classroom teaching.
2. Give five rules for critiquing a peer lesson.
3. Using interaction analysis, record a lesson and transfer the recording to a grid.
4. Write a written analysis of a lesson, including cognitive and affective domains.
5. Provide and explain two techniques for analyzing your own self as a teacher.

"To see ourselves as others see us" is a proverb that should be adapted by teachers as "to see ourselves as our students see us."[1] Educator B. O. Smith described the importance of the perceptions of teachers and students in his three-step model. Smith explains that the student perceives, diagnoses, and responds in terms of the teacher's behavior and that, furthermore, the teacher perceives diagnoses, and responds to the students' behavior. Figure 16.1 shows the teacher-student relationship. Thus, as a teacher, if you could see yourself as your students see you, you could modify your behavior so as to solicit the type of student behavior that you desire. But, since we do not share the same experiences that our students bring to the classroom, we can never actually share their exact perceptions. The closest that we can ever come is to learn to see ourselves at all, and many teachers never achieve this. So the purpose of this

---

[1] B. Othanel Smith, "A Concept of Teaching," *Language and Concepts in Education* (Chicago: Rand McNally, 1961), Chapter 6.

chapter is to help you to learn to see yourself — you as a person and you the teacher, and to do so objectively.

PEER TEACHING

In peer teaching you teach lessons or parts of lessons to fellow students in your education courses. They, in turn, critique your teaching techniques. Although peer teaching is sometimes criticized for being unrealistic, superficial, or isolated from the real thing, when properly done, peer teaching can resemble classroom teaching enough so that you will experience many of the same difficulties and feelings felt in actual classroom teaching. In addition, peer teaching offers many advantages not available to the classroom teacher. First, as a beginning teacher, you will be faced with so many variables that analyzing your entire classroom situation, with its many interactions, would be a very complicated task; even experienced teachers find it so. Peer teaching simplifies this task by reducing the length and complexity of the lesson. The teaching of a shorter, more specific lesson, often called concept teaching, enables you to focus sharply upon a few major ideas, and upon your ability to communicate them.

A second distinct advantage that peer teaching offers you over regular classroom teaching is that you will obtain constructive feedback from those who are being taught. Unfortunately, as a classroom teacher you will seldom get analytic, objective criticism from your students; even though you may get an

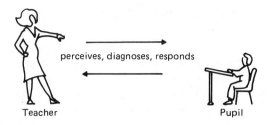

perceives, diagnoses, responds

Teacher   Pupil

Figure 16.1   Teacher-Student Relationships

abundance of feedback, you may feel successful or defeated without knowing why. Students can quickly spot a good teacher and a poor teacher; but they are not always able to pinpoint the reasons for their judgment, and their feelings often cloud their objectivity. As a peer teacher, you face an audience that shares both your interest for improving and your feelings of uncertainty. And, with proper training, your peers can critique your lesson objectively. Following are some rules for critiquing a lesson.

1. Avoid generalizations. When you catch yourself tempted to write down "This was a good or poor lesson," stop. Write down those specific behaviors that made it so.
2. Write your observations down during the lesson; it will be impossible to recall all that you noticed.
3. Focus on the exact behavior of the teacher. What the teacher does is much more important than how he or she looks.
4. Address each comment directly to the teacher (never use the third person): "Jim, you spoke so softly that I couldn't hear you. Speak up."
5. Focus on communicative skills.
6. Identify an equal number of strengths and weaknesses; for example, "These are your three greatest strengths and these are your three greatest areas of needed improvement."
7. Write all comments in a positive vein.
8. Study the peer teacher's behavioral objectives. Did your learning match these expectations? Were the objectives themselves clear? Were they too numerous?

The list may seem long, but each item is important and with a little practice will suggest itself automatically. When these guidelines are adhered to, the level of anxiety is minimal; and students quickly begin to perceive peer teaching as a cooperative, helpful exercise. The ultimate advantage is realized when peer teachers have the privilege of having their lessons video-taped. They can replay these as many times as necessary, focusing their attention on different aspects of their teaching techniques with each viewing.

Because teaching is a highly complicated activity that has numerous activities happening simultaneously, new teachers find it difficult to focus their attention on their own activities and those of all the students while they are teaching. And yet classroom management is imperative and equally as important as delivery of the lesson itself. This makes the observation period provided by most intern and student teaching programs very important. Here, for a few days, before your actual student teaching, you have an opportunity to observe interactions between teacher and students and those among students. While these models are extremely valuable for you as a prospective teacher, you will soon, as a novice teacher, need to analyze your own techniques.

OBSERVATIONAL METHODS IN THE CLASSROOM

Interaction Analysis

One system for simplifying complex classroom interactions so that they can be analyzed is called interaction analysis (I.A.). To use this system, you should familiarize (actually, memorize) the ten steps in Table 16.1. The observer who has memorized these categories can describe the behavior in the classroom at any moment by recording the appropriate number. This should be done at three-second intervals. For example, as shown in Figure 16.2, in this fifteen-second period the teacher gives direction (6), criticizes (7), lectures (5), and criticizes (7). This example is much too small to generalize sensibly; but if a significant part of the period followed in this style, we would begin to see the teacher as autocratic, aggressive, and probably defensive. On the other hand, suppose our record over several minutes contains mostly items 1, 2, and 3; then we would classify the teacher as understanding and accepting, providing a free climate in which students are willing to express themselves. It should be noted that few, if any, teachers fall into either extreme category and that either lecturing continuously or never lecturing or giving directions would probably result in little learning. Furthermore, just as generalizing from an inadequately small sample of classroom interaction is apt to lead to erroneous conclusions, an equally faulty technique is to isolate individual categories. Instead, the categories should be coupled and transferred to a grid. Figure 16.2 shows the previous recordings joined in couplets.

Each couplet can now be transferred to a grid, enabling the recorder to see many entries at once. It also gives the benefit of a visual picture of the classroom interactions. See Figure 16.3. In recording the couplets, you will note, the observer starts at the top of the upper left corner of the grid, comes down vertically to the first number in the pair and then moves horizontally to the

Table 16.1 Categories for Interaction Analysis

357

Observing Yourself

TEACHER TALK
Indirect Influence

1. ACCEPTS FEELING: Accepts and clarifies the feeling tone of the students in a nonthreatening manner.

2. PRAISES OR ENCOURAGES: Praises or encourages student action or behavior.

3. ACCEPTS OR USES IDEA OF STUDENT: Clarifies, builds, or develops students ideas or suggestions.

4. ASKS QUESTIONS: Asks a question about content or procedure with the intent that a student answers.

Direct Influence

5. LECTURES: gives facts or opinions about content or procedure.

6. GIVES DIRECTIONS: Gives instructions a student is expected to follow.

7. CRITICIZES OR JUSTIFIES AUTHORITY: Reprimands or states reason for what he or she is doing.

STUDENT TALK

8. STUDENT TALK-RESPONSE: Students talk in response to teacher.

9. STUDENT TALK-INITIATION: Students initiated talk.

10. SILENCE OR CONFUSION

Source: Condensed from Ned A. Flanders, *Teacher Influence, Pupil Attitudes, and Achievement* (Washington, D.C.: U.S. Department of Health, Education and Welfare, 1965, Catalog No. F.S. 225:25040).

right until finding the second number in the pair. For example, notice that the 6–7 pair is recorded down to 6 and across to 7, that is, on row 6 and in column 7. Using small vertical marks to record gives room for many entries in each cell and enables the recorder to cross each four entries with a diagonal that expedites the addition of entries in each cell.

Interaction analysis is one of several methods of systematically analyzing classroom interactions. By using a video-taped lesson to practice, the novice can shorten the time needed for mastering this technique. Still many teachers may feel that the system is too complicated; for those who do, a second system is offered.

Teacher Role and Dimensions in the Classroom

A very simple strategy that considers both the activities of teacher and students is a list of categories describing the teacher's role. See Table 16.2. Note

Table 16.2 Brief Descriptions of Eight Dimensions Measured in Classrooms of Elementary Student Teachers

NON-AFFECTIVE CLIMATE

A. Teacher Role
   (1) *Presence.* Teacher keep good order, is rated high on use of voice, gestures, etc.; uses clarification and neutral rejection.
   (2) *Informative.* States objectives, relates lesson to pupil needs, past learning; high on information-giving statements.
   (3) *Imaginative.* Provides for individual differences; makes use of apt, creative examples, techniques; arouses high pupil interest.

B. Pupil Role
   (4) *Activity.* High questioning behavior on part of pupils and teacher both.
   (5) *Initiative.* Variety of pupil response; sequence of lesson not rigid; teacher had difficulty getting attention at times.

AFFECTIVE CLIMATE

   (6) *Consideration.* High on affective-imaginative statements and encouraging; courteous; shows awareness of pupil needs. High pupil interest.
   (7) *Warmth.* High on support, praise; gentle reproof; more directive; reads questions from book or blackboard (!)
   (8) *Disapproval.* High on reproving and criticizing; speech pattern rated low; terminates lesson abruptly.

Source: Donald M. Medley, "Measuring the Complex Classroom of Today," in Charles W. Bugle and Richard M. Brant, eds., *Observational Methods in the Classroom* (Washington, D.C.: Association for Supervision and Curriculum Development, 1973), Chapter 5.

that this list includes suggested teacher behaviors for establishing both the affective and nonaffective or cognitive climates in the classroom. This system can be used during the observation portion of student teaching to analyze the directing teacher (with permission, of course) and to analyze your own behavior once you begin taking over classes. The benefit from this system can also be maximized by using the video tape recorder, or, if not available, the

Figure 16.2 Coupling the Recordings of
Interaction Analysis

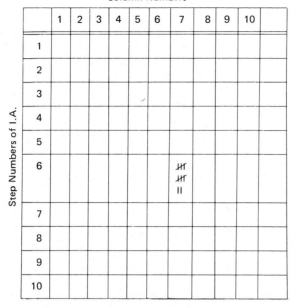

Column Numbers

Figure 16.3 Raw Data Tally Matrix

audio tape recorder. It is always more effective when you can devote 100 percent of your attention to observing your behavior and that of your students. Of course, the opportunity to stop the lesson at any point and to replay it again and again is an obvious advantage.

Self-Made Observation Systems

Some of the most useful (and therefore the best) observation instruments are made by the students themselves. These ready-made instruments are often superior for many reasons. Since you design the instrument, you understand it and can apply it correctly. Also, you are able to design each recording instrument for its particular purpose. If, for example, you wish to measure only the behavior of a few students, you can design the instrument to focus on those few students. If, on the other hand, you wish to study the teacher's behavior, you can design the instrument to focus only on the teacher's behavior. If you wish to study the interactions between teacher and students, the instrument can be designed to focus on both parties.

Following are the results of an assignment that required student teachers to choose three areas to be observed and to design an observation instrument for each problem. For each of the three observations the students were asked to: (1) present the problem, (2) design an observation instrument to use to observe the situation, (3) present the findings, (4) design a chart or graph to show these findings, and (5) discuss the implications of the findings.

Time-on-Task Observation System. The Time-on-Task Observation System is basically used to find out what students do during the time assigned for a certain task. It also helps in determining the amount of time to set aside for the task in the future. From the raw data, individual students may be observed, and in most cases learner achievement will be closely related to that student's use of class time.

Figure 16.4 is a floor plan of the classroom. At the top is the teacher's desk.

Figure 16.4 Time-on-Task Observation System

Teacher

Circled box (top right):
```
1 A 5 A
2 A 6 A
3 A 7 A
4 A
```

1 A 5 F 2 A 6 F 3 A 4 A 7 A	1 E 5 A 2 E 6 A 3 A 7 C 4 A	1 A 5 F 2 A 6 A 3 A 7 A 4 A	(circled) 1 A 5 A 2 A 6 A 3 A 4 A 7 A	1 A 5 F 2 A 6 F 3 A 7 A 4 F
1 A 5 F 2 F 6 D 3 A 4 F 7 A	1 A 5 F 2 A 6 A 3 A 7 A 4 A	1 D 5 A 2 C 6 A 3 A 7 A 4 F	1 D 5 A 2 D 6 A 3 D 4 A 7 A	1 C 5 F 2 A 6 F 3 A 7 C 4 F
1 A 5 F 2 A 6 A 3 A 7 F 4 C	1 A 5 F 2 A 6 A 3 A 7 A 4 A	⊠ (absent)	1 D 5 D 2 D 6 D 3 D 4 D 7 D	1 A 5 C 2 A 6 F 3 C 7 A 4 A
⊠ (absent)	⊠ (absent)	⊠ (absent)	⊠ (absent)	1 A 5 D 2 A 6 D 3 D 7 D 4 D
1 A 5 C 2 A 6 D 3 A 7 D 4 A	1 A 5 A 2 A 6 B 3 A 7 C 4 C	1 C 5 C 2 A 6 A 3 C 4 C 7 A	(circled) 1 A 5 A 2 A 6 A 3 A 4 A 7 A	⊠ (absent)
1 C 5 A 2 C 6 F 3 A 4 A 7 C	⊠ (absent)	1 C 5 A 2 A 6 A 3 A 4 A 7 A	⊠ (absent)	⊠ (absent)

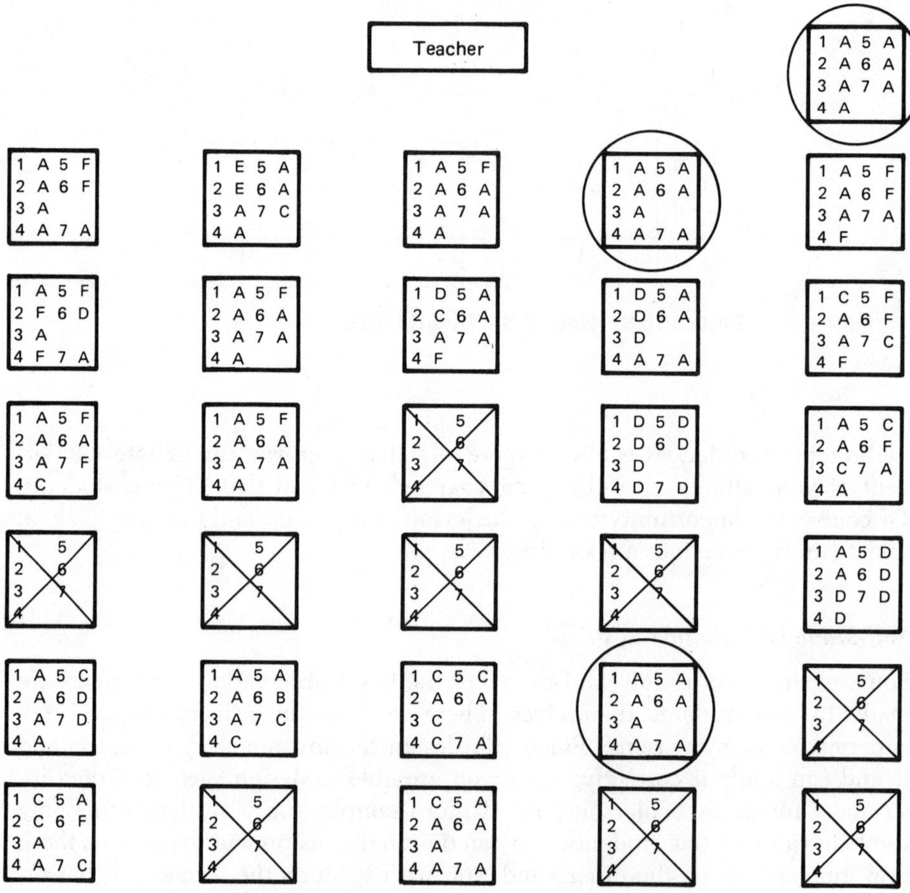

Purpose: To determine whether individual learners require as much time as provided to complete in-class assignments and to determine how individuals spend their class time.

Code: ⊠ Student absent
A. working on task   1. 9:35
B. working on another subject 2. 9:40
C. daydreaming   3. 9:45
D. out of seat   4. 9:50
E. sleeping   5. 9:55
F. talking to neighbors   6. 10:00
                             7. 10:05

Each square represents a student's desk. The squares that are crossed out indicate those students who were absent on the days of observation. The circled squares represent the only students who worked on the assignment throughout the period. These recordings were later transferred to the chart in Figure 16.5.

There are several interesting facts concerning this particular study. First, in four out of the six activities listed, the same percentage of students involved

Figure 16.5 Student Behavior at Five-Minute Intervals

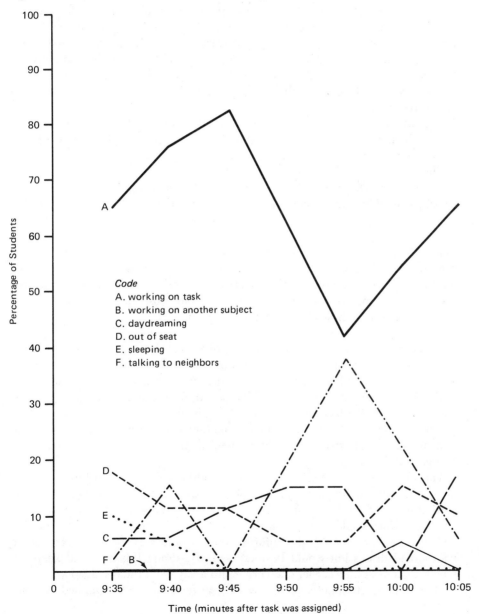

Code
A. working on task
B. working on another subject
C. daydreaming
D. out of seat
E. sleeping
F. talking to neighbors

Percentage of Students

Time (minutes after task was assigned)

five minutes after the task was assigned were also involved thirty-five minutes after (that is, 67 percent of the students were working on the task five minutes after it was given, and 67 percent were working on it when the observation ended). The only two that this does not hold true for, are those sleeping and those talking to their neighbors. This may have some significance if it is noticed that this percentage is also very close to the average percentage throughout the thirty-five minutes. This shows a consistency within the class. In other words, the number of students who wish to complete the assignment remains fairly constant throughout the period as does the number of procrastinators.

Second, in this particular case, for the first fifteen minutes the percentage of students working on the task is at its highest peak. After the first fifteen minutes the students seem to lose interest in the task and start talking, daydreaming, and running around, and so on. Toward the end of the class the students once again start working on the task. Possibly this is because they do not want to finish them at home. At this time the percentage of daydreamers also increases. These students probably forget about this class and start thinking about the rest of the day.

Individual students were not matched with certain desks but if asked to guess which students show the greatest learner achievement, it would be safe to pick the students circled on the raw data sheet.

The amount of time set aside for this task was not too much, because no one (including the three who worked on it for 100 percent of time) finished it. Considering this fact, it seemed quite fair the assignment should be due the following day.

The following implications can be made from these findings. First, much time is being wasted in classrooms across the country. Some of the waste results from necessary interruptions such as roll taking and other necessary administrative tasks. However, this investigator suspects that much of lost time may be due to poor classroom management. This observation system is an attempt to determine how classroom time is spent.

TEACHER POSITION AND VERBAL INTERACTION PATTERNS OBSERVATION SYSTEMS. The main objective of the Teacher Position Observation System is to determine teacher mobility and his attention to learners with respect to his physical location (see Figure 16.6). It is easily recognized, from the last part of this stated purpose, that this objective could not be fulfilled unless a verbal interaction patterns observation system is done simultaneously (see Figure 16.7). The Teacher Position System may help the teacher realize if he is neglecting a certain portion of the class.

The purpose of the Verbal Interaction Patterns Observation System is not only to aid in the previous system but also to determine if the entire class is getting involved in the discussion — if not, which portions are active, inactive, and why. This would be useful if the teacher could recognize who the verbally active students are. With this information he could seat them in desks where widespread discussion would be increased. By doing this he could keep the whole class alert and not let one corner slip away from the discussion.

Due to the relation between the two, the systems have been graphed together

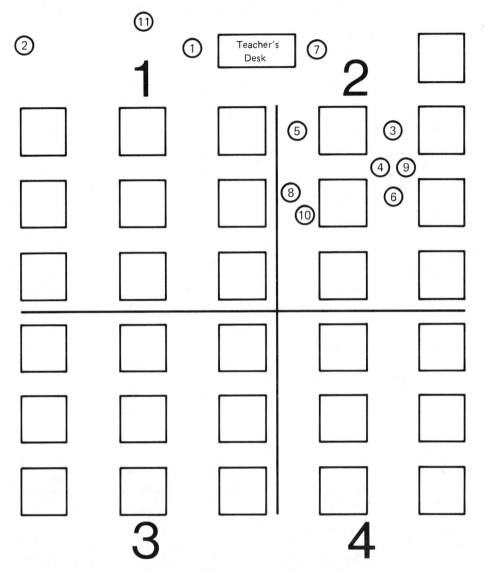

Figure 16.6 Teacher Position

Purpose: To determine teacher mobility and attention to learners with respect to physical location in the classroom.

Note: Circled number indicates sequence of teacher's position at 1-minute intervals (e.g., 1 = position at end of 1 min., 2 = position at end of 2 min., etc.)

(see Figure 16.8). During this observation, the teacher stayed in the front of the room. (It seems very seldom that any teacher will make his way to the back of the classroom, even though, it would probably increase participation.) Also, while he was talking, the teacher faced straight to the back of the room.

The question now is how is this related to the verbal activity of the class.

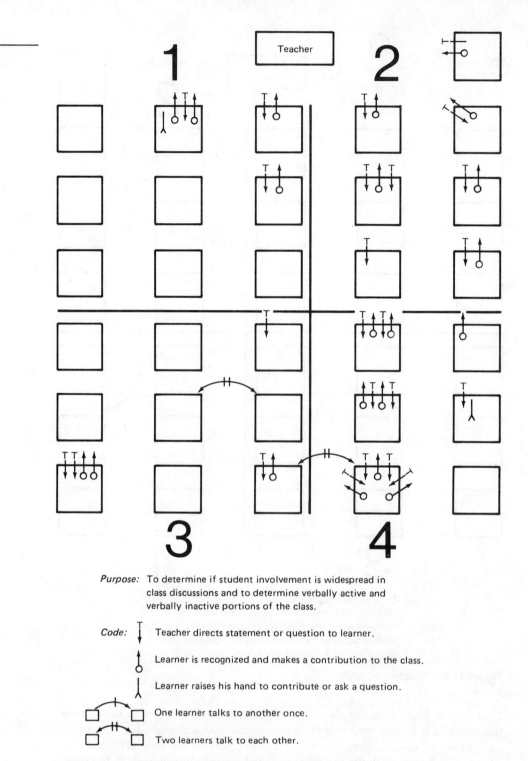

Figure 16.7 Student-Teacher Verbal Interaction Patterns

Purpose: To determine if student involvement is widespread in class discussions and to determine verbally active and verbally inactive portions of the class.

Code: Teacher directs statement or question to learner.

Learner is recognized and makes a contribution to the class.

Learner raises his hand to contribute or ask a question.

One learner talks to another once.

Two learners talk to each other.

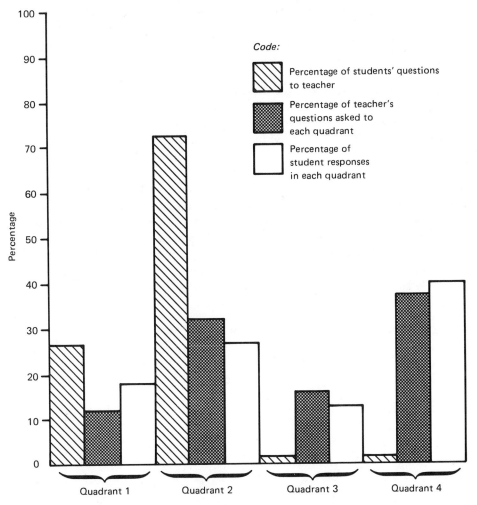

Figure 16.8 Teacher Position vs. Verbal Interaction Patterns

The relation between the two is simple. Seventy-three percent of the observation period the teacher was in Quadrant 2, facing Quadrant 4. 71 percent of the total questions were asked to students in these two quadrants; also 68 percent of the total responses came from this area. On the other hand, the teacher spent 27 percent of the period in Quadrant 1, facing Quadrant 3. 29 percent of the questions were directed to these two quadrants and 32 percent of the responses came from this area. (It is very important to note that Quadrants 2 and 4 contain *less* than one-fourth of the total number of students in the class. Thus since 1 and 3 are larger than 2 and 4, the evidence that relates Teacher Position with Verbal Activity of each quadrant of the class is even more convincing.)

Since the verbal interaction between students was so slight, it is insignificant to this case and therefore was not charted. In some cases this factor may be relevant to how much each quadrant will respond to questions asked by the teacher. The reason for this relevancy is that they may be too busy talking to each other and ignoring the teacher or a number of students may be bothered by others talking.

Throughout this discussion "quadrants" have been the main focal point, but remember that quadrants are made up of individual students. From the raw data individual learned achievement could be directly related to individual verbal activity. The circled individual probably shows good learner achievement.

NOISE LEVEL VS. LEARNING INTAKE. The following observation report is a correlation between the noise level in a classroom and the amount of subject matter being taught. In this classroom, the subject matter being taught is math. What is being considered is a relationship between the amount of math actually being discussed and the level of noise instrumented during the learning procedure. As seen in Figure 16.9, the degree of noise in the classroom adversely affects the teacher's concentration as well as his or her ability to

Figure 16.9 Noise Level vs. Percentage of Lecture Material Discussed*

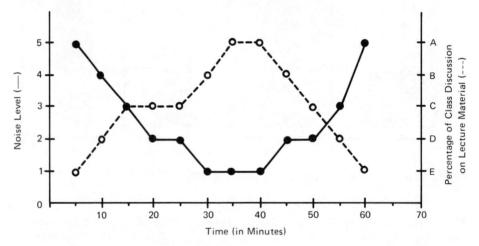

Code
1   quiet, no one talking except teacher
2   semi-quiet, no relevant talking going on
3   one student talking with teacher, an average amount of loudness
4   relatively loud, with majority talking at once
5   extremely loud, uncontrolled behavior, all talking at once
A   100% on math
B   90% on math, 10% on other matters
C   50% on math, 50% on other matters
D   90% on other matters, 10% on math
E   100% on other material besides math

* This observation system was developed by Karla Smith.

subdue the class. Hence, the amount of material being taught and learned is directly proportional to the amount of noise and confusion going on in the classroom.

ALLOTMENT OF TIME IN OBSERVED CLASSROOM:

12:30–12:35   General discussion going on
              0% of discussion about math

12:35–12:40   Discussion of yesterday's homework
              90% of discussion on matters not related to math

12:40–12:45   Boardwork going on
              50% of discussion on math

12:45–12:50   Class working homework on board
              50% of discussion on math

12:50–12:55   Class still working out homework
              60% of discussion on math

12:55–1:00   Class is now immersed in math
              90% of class doing math-oriented work

1:00–1:10   Class is at the peak of being involved
              100% of all individuals are entertaining some math aspect

1:10–1:15   The class is losing interest
              90% of discussion on math related matters

1:15–1:20   The class is fastly losing interest in math
              50% of discussion is on math

1:20–1:25   The teacher has lost all but a few of the student's attention
              90% of discussion matters not related to math

1:25–1:30   The class is not even conscious of the fact that math exists
              100% of class discussion on matters other than math

It is evident from this graph that the beginning and the end of the class period are the worst times to introduce new learning material; the best time span for a teacher to teach seems to be the first forty minutes. After that, attention to the subject dwindles. The importance of such a graph is strictly for the teacher's benefit. By knowing the best time to approach subject matter, teachers can gain a learning advantage over their students. The result of preparing lesson plans in correspondence with class attention is a more adequate learning situation in the classroom.

These are but a few of hundreds of possible ways to systematically observe classroom behavior. In selecting a problem to investigate, you should consider questions that *you* would like answered. These self-observations can help teachers recognize what is happening in their class. By isolating only one or two variables for study, teachers can gain insight into that facet of their behavior (or the behavior of their students).

In addition to learning how you perform when you teach, you also need to know how you are perceived by your students. Since it is the students' perception of you that really matters — rather than how you may think you come across — almost any meaningful self-analysis would have to represent your students' impressions, not merely yours. Therefore, think of some ways in which you can get meaningful feedback from your students to learn what they really think of you as a human being (if, indeed, they do).

One approach, though simple, has proven itself effective in secondary classrooms throughout the country. Place a notice on the bulletin board inviting students to drop a 3″ x 5″ card each day at the end of the period with one comment telling exactly how they felt about what the teacher said or did during that period. The comment can be either positive or negative, signed or anonymous, and a box for positive comments is placed adjacent to a box with negative comments.

A second means of obtaining information about students' feelings toward you is to hold "rap" sessions in which students are encouraged to express their feelings about the school in general and your class in particular. A word of caution is needed here. These sessions seem to always be interpreted by students as a field day for criticizing other teachers, students, and even administrators. Therefore, from the beginning, certain ground rules should be established; for example if other people are to be criticized in their absence, it must be done objectively and in such a manner that others will not know for sure who is being criticized. Second, there should be a systematic time set for these sessions. Students should be encouraged to plan for them, even if this means just thinking about each session before it occurs. Each session should be productive and enjoyable. Your preparation should include keeping alert to school activities including sports, extracurricular activities, and achievements of students in and outside the school. Once students learn that your interest in them extends beyond the campus, your rapport with them should improve.

SELF-ANALYSIS

Although there is no substitute for feedback that comes directly from your students, you still can benefit from a close look at yourself. Even before you begin teaching, you may benefit from examining your attitudes toward your future profession. If you are a person who simply does not like to be around other people, either your attitude must change (and it probably will not) or you should examine other possible career opportunities. This does not suggest that, just because speaking to groups makes you nervous, you don't like people. Most of us are anxious about facing new groups, some of us much more so than others. Rest assured that this is only natural; most experienced teachers share this feeling. But the big difference comes in a few days when most teachers (those who really like people) begin to relax and enjoy their students.

Actually the art of teaching is very different from that of public speaking. Teaching is relating to others and having them relate to you. By its very nature it is a highly personal role, and that is why it is essential that good teachers enjoy their students. Many people outside the teaching profession regard the teacher's role as an 8:00 to 3:00, five-day-a-week, babysitting job. Even the student teacher quickly learns the fallacy of this stereotype. During school hours teaching is a highly complex and highly demanding role. Then, when the last bell rings, there are often faculty and departmental meetings, interest-club meetings, parent-teacher meetings, and afternoon and evening sports events. Of course, many evenings must be spent marking papers, planning lessons, and collecting and preparing materials for future lessons. And, if you are to stay ahead of your students, you will need to take further courses in education and in your teaching field, as well as reading extensively in your field. You should also keep up with the news to know what is happening each day in your subject.

So teaching is a very demanding profession. Are you willing to expend the level of energy during the day that is required for being a good teacher, and are you willing to sacrifice almost every evening of the week for grading papers and planning lessons? And, are you going to really enjoy the feeling of helping an adolescent whose life is totally confused to get his head on straight? Will you feel anything special when you see a student's eyes light up when they begin for the first time to understand and enjoy the subject that you teach? These are questions that all teachers must ask. Even experienced teachers have to analyze their purposes for giving so much of their personal lives to students and to the profession. Most teachers enjoy Fridays, but the good ones also enjoy Mondays. Each day the task of all teachers is a challenge. There is nothing to equal the satisfaction of teaching an exciting lesson or the humility in teaching a boring lesson (and all of us teach some of each). Some teachers thrive on a life of challenges; others succumb to it. The only advice that is worth giving is that you should either go none of the way or all of the way; for those teachers who give everything seem to get a lot in return, and those who give only the required minimum seem to get only dissatisfaction in return. When you next get into the public schools, observe as many teachers as you can, especially one or two who have good reputations. See how much they put into their teaching and how much they derive from it.

SUMMARY

Since each student's behavior is directly affected by the teacher's behavior, it is imperative that you, the teacher, become aware of how students perceive you. To capture this insight, you must learn to employ various strategies for objectively analyzing yourself as a teacher and as a person. Some popular means for self-analysis of one's instruction include peer teaching, interaction analysis, and teacher-made observation instruments that can analyze both cognitive and affective behaviors. The benefits of these can be increased when they are complemented by visual aids. Other more subjective means can be used to measure personal behaviors. Some of the best of these include feedback from the students themselves.

EXPERIENCES

This chapter has introduced several systems that teachers can use to analyze their own behavior and the total behavior in their classrooms. As you read the following experiences, you may wish to decide which of the teachers you would most want to model, thinking of possible ways to analyze your behavior in order to know exactly the types of changes that you should make.

Experience 1: A Teacher Who Lives His Profession

At the university Mr. Carrier majored in marine biology. Since he wanted to be the best teacher possible, he earned a Ph.D. in his subject. While in high school he had developed a lust for photography and for the nearby ocean. By the time he began his high school teaching, he had taken literally thousands of photos of the ocean and of ocean life, both above and below the surface.

Since a large part of his budget went for film and developing materials, Mr. Carrier was forced to contrive his own dissolve unit for showing slides, which he synchronized to music. Needless to say, his high school students were eager to arrive at class each Monday to see what he had put together over the weekend; that is, when he hadn't spent the entire weekend with his wife and a group of his students on the Keys studying wildlife and taking photos.

Anyone who knows Dr. Carrier will quickly tell you that he really lives his profession. His enthusiasm is contagious and his energy seems endless. How he finds time and energy to teach a college class in photography and to speak to various groups about marine biology puzzles even his wife.

▶ *Questions and Discussion*

1. *Can you explain how those people who work the hardest seem to have the most energy?*

   Surely no teacher is immune to fatigue, yet a few teachers, young and old, seem to run like a spring that is wound perpetually tight. These lively, enthusiastic teachers will tell you that they don't have time to get tired. Actually, they don't have time to think about their exhausted condition. People who enjoy their activities often overlook their fatigue.

2. *Can you explain the expression "If you want to get a job done fast, give it to a busy person"?*

Very busy people have to become well organized to prevent a chaotic state. Sometimes less busy people develop a habit of procrastinating. A well-organized person can complete a whole project while the procrastinator is still thinking about the jobs that lie ahead.

Experience 2: A Teacher Resents Students' Questions

Miss Burnett, a first-year teacher in the home economics department, was very knowledgeable about her subject. Although most students realized this, some remarked that Miss Burnett thought she was the only one who knew anything about cooking, sewing, and the other topics that they were studying.

From a teacher's perspective I saw in Miss Burnett a strong personality who was self-assured and who asserted herself well. When she gave instructions, she displayed an air of authority. She would never have been criticized for failing to take a stand on any issue or "beating around the bush" when answering any question. Her response was always immediate and definite.

In the teacher's lounge Miss Burnett often expressed her resentment toward certain students for questioning her statements. At first she was appalled that a student could think of challenging a teacher's knowledge. After all, she had just spent four years studying home economics and some of the assignments that she had completed in college were so far advanced that the high school student could not begin to comprehend them.

When Miss Burnett found that students commonly question, she became more antagonized than shocked. This continued until she began to become quite furious when any question was directed to her. After one year of teaching, Miss Burnett decided to leave teaching and to enter the industrial world. Her decision was probably a very good one. At least many of the students thought so.

► *Questions and Discussion*

1. *Can a teacher have too much self-confidence?*

All teachers who want to survive in today's classrooms must believe in themselves. If and when a teacher feels insecure, the students sense it and are apt to suspect and doubt her. This, of course, assumes that her lack of self-confidence is shown repeatedly. However, as strange as it may seem, if the teacher appears overconfident, the students will suspect her for this too, because students know that the teacher is not *always* right — that even the teacher is not beyond making occasional errors. A teacher who lets her self-confidence interfere with her teaching or damage her rapport with her students does have too much self-confidence.

2. *Why do competent teachers sometimes resent questions?*
Sometimes even competent people lack self-confidence. Before a
teacher can really welcome and encourage the asking of questions, she
must possess enough self-confidence not to feel threatened by the questions. The competent teacher who resents the asking of questions in
her room either feels unsure of her ability to provide a correct response
or fails to realize the important role that questions play in classroom
learning.

More than ever before, today's students have questions for which
they expect and demand satisfactory answers. They are not at all likely
to be satisfied with an answer for which they can see no logical base.

This attitude does place a real demand on the teacher and tends to
frighten many teachers. This is why so many teachers do not welcome
the asking of questions in their classrooms.

3. *List some reasons why students should be made to feel free to question.*
It is necessary that students be made to feel free to question because:

a. Today's students have many questions for which they expect satisfactory answers.
b. Today's students ask questions that are reasonable and significant.
c. Asking questions permits students to explore more deeply the areas
where their greatest interests lie.
d. Other students are interested in hearing responses to their peers'
questions.
e. The asking of questions creates dialogue between students, and they
profit more when they can play an active part in classroom experiences.
f. Unless students are actually encouraged, many quiet and timid students will never ask a question.
g. While answering one student's question, the teacher often clarifies
uncertainties for other class members.

Of course there are many additional reasons why students should be
made to feel free to ask questions in the classroom. Have you listed
some of equal or more importance?

4. *How can a teacher create an open climate in which students will feel
free to question?*
First, the teacher must make sure that she really does believe in this
activity. She can prepare herself to openly accept questioning by admitting to herself that she probably will not know the answer to every
question asked, and by realizing that it is not essential that she does.
Her role is not just that of dispenser of knowledge: she is to stimulate
students to seek knowledge and to guide them in the search. The
teacher must realize that stimulating and guiding learning is the more
important of her two roles.

Second, once the teacher has prepared herself to accept questions, she must prepare her students to feel free to ask questions. This she can do by being honest with them and avoiding the temptation of giving a mediocre or poor response to questions for which she does not know the correct answer. She must also make sure that she never gives a sarcastic answer and that she never takes questions lightly. If a question is important enough to a student to bother asking it, it deserves a serious answer.

Finally, the teacher should always provide a satisfactory answer to a question. A common error is for the teacher to feel that the question is irrelevant and that she is responsible for getting back to the lesson. Regardless of how irrelevant the question seems, the teacher should try to relate it to the lesson.

ACTIVITIES

As you read this chapter, you probably thought of additional ways to gather information about your teaching. You may have thought of more ways of gathering such information through your students. Or you may have thought of other ways to break down the highly complicated interactions in the classroom and focus on yet a different dimension that was not discussed in the book. The following activities let you apply your own creativity in learning more about your teaching.

1. Identify one aspect of your teaching for which you wish to obtain more information. It may be your way of introducing a lesson, leading a discussion, summarizing a lesson, giving examples, asking questions, explaining a concept, establishing cognitive set, or any other area in which you would like to further perfect your skills. Design a system to record your behavior. Make a list of questions that you wish answered.
2. Design a sociogram that will show a pattern of interactions in your classroom. You might begin by drawing a picture of the seating pattern that you wish to use for your students while you observe them. Consider the type of lesson that you wish to observe, as discussion, debate, seat assignment, small-group activity, or some other type.
3. Now explain the implications that this information has for your teaching. How can you change or modify your lesson accordingly? In other words, how can you use your new knowledge to improve your classes?

SUGGESTED READINGS

ALLEN, PAUL, et al. *Teacher Self-Appraisal*. Worthington, Ohio: Charles A. Jones, 1970.

AMIDON, EDMUND, and HUNTER, ELIZABETH. *Improving Teaching*. New York: Holt, Rinehart and Winston, 1966.

AMIDON, J., and FLANDERS, NED A. *The Role of the Teacher in the Classroom.* Minneapolis: Paul S. Amidon, 1963.

BUGLE, CHARLES W., and BRANT, RICHARD M., eds. *Observational Methods in the Classroom.* Washington, D.C.: Association for Supervision and Curriculum Development, 1973.

DENTON, JON J. *Classroom and School Data Collection Procedures.* Houston: School Based Teacher Educator-Texas Teacher Center Network. Funded by the Department of Health, Education and Welfare, 1977. Obtainable from Teacher Center, 466 Farish Hall, College of Education, University of Houston, Houston, Texas 77004.

————. *Data Presentation and Analysis.* Houston: School Based Teacher Educator-Texas Teacher Center Network. Funded by the Department of Health, Education and Welfare, 1977. Obtainable from Teacher Center, 466 Farish Hall, College of Education, University of Houston, Houston, Texas 77004.

FLANDERS, NED A. *Teacher Influence, Pupil Attitudes, and Achievement.* Catalog No. F.S. 225–25040: Washington, D.C.: U.S. Department of Health, Education and Welfare, 1965.

SIMON, A., and BOYER, E., eds. *Mirror for Behavior, II: An Anthology of Observation Instruments.* Philadelphia: Classroom Interaction Newsletter, c/o Research for Better Schools, Inc., 1970.

SMITH, B. OTHANEL. "A Concept of Teaching." *Language and Concepts in Education.* Chapter 6. Chicago: Rand McNally, 1961.

WILLIAMS, S. S. "Observational System for Analysis of Classroom Communication." *Clearing House* 51 (March 1978): 346–48.

Name Index

Subject Index